Julie Emikh
Legal Department

BANKRUPTCY LAW

BANKRUPTCY LAW

MICHAEL FORDE

B.A. (Mod) and LL.B (Dublin), LL.M (Brussels), Ph.D. (Cantab.),
of King's Inns and Middle Temple Senior Counsel

and

DANIEL SIMMS

B.A. (Mod.)(Dub.), LL.M, Dr. iur. (Cologne),
of King's Inns, Barrister-at-law

ROUND HALL

THOMSON REUTERS

Published in 2009 by
Thomson Reuters (Professional) Ireland Limited
(Registered in Ireland, Company No. 80867.
Registered Office and address for service:
43 Fitzwilliam Place, Dublin 2, Ireland)
trading as Round Hall

Typeset by
Gough Typesetting Services
Dublin

Printed by
MPG Books, Bodmin, Cornwall

ISBN 978-1-85800-534-8

A catalogue record for this book
is available from the British Library

For Peter

In memoriam,
Dr. iur. Dirk Uhlenbruck
(1936–2004)

FOREWORD TO THE FIRST EDITION

The enactment of the Bankruptcy Act 1988 has made this book by Dr Forde vitally necessary for all practitioners and those interested in the law of insolvency. The changes in the law as a result of the enactment of the 1988 Act are extensive and the existing literature on the subject is now out of date. I have read this book and am satisfied that it will in the future enjoy the same reputation as has hitherto been enjoyed by the works of His Honour Judge Kisbey, Q.C., and that of Mr John Robb, Barrister-at-Law, former Registrar in Bankruptcy of Northern Ireland, in this field.

I have acted as Bankruptcy judge for the past 13 years and during that time it has become obvious that bankruptcy, as a creditors remedy, is becoming increasingly utilised. The increase is such that it behoves the ordinary practitioner, and not merely those specialising in the subject, to be fully conversant with the provisions of the Bankruptcy Act 1988, the Rules of Court and the decision of the Court. The law of Bankruptcy affects a variety of interests beyond the immediate scope of the creditor/debtor relationship, e.g. the bankrupt's spouse and family, landlords, guarantors and purchasers of property from bankrupts or insolvents. The practitioner therefore may be forced to deal with the nuances of the Bankruptcy Law in areas which extend beyond the confines of the immediate relationship between the creditor and debtor. In view of the duty of care imposed on practitioners they should be fully aware of provisions of the Bankruptcy Code.

This is a book which will be of inestimable benefit, not only to the specialist, but to the general practitioner as it deals with all these matters. It is not only a learned work but also a practical one and displays a wealth of knowledge and industry. Dr Forde and his publishers are to be congratulated once again, on producing a book which is relevant, learned and a welcome addition to Irish legal literature.

Liam Hamilton
President of the High Court

PREFACE

Except for the E.C. Regulation on Insolvency Proceedings of 2000, in the nearly 20 years since this book's first edition was published, there have been no radical changes to the bankruptcy regime under the Bankruptcy Act 1988. Those being years of unprecedented prosperity, bankruptcy questions rarely troubled the Irish courts. Notwithstanding, there has been a considerable amount of case law in Britain on these issues, much of it to be found in the Bankruptcy and Personal Insolvency Law Reports (B.P.I.R.). Last year, having finished our book (with Hugh Kennedy) on Company Insolvency, we decided that the first edition of Bankruptcy Law should be updated, that there were several aspects of the subject that required greater elaboration and that, for the foreseeable future, the economic climate would make bankruptcy very relevant for lawyers and their clients. Events since then certainly confirmed the latter point.

We express our thanks again to members of our families for their support throughout the preparation of this work, and also to the staff of Round Hall, in particular to Frieda Donoghue and Aisling Hanrahan. Regrettably, the Honourable Mr Justice Liam Hamilton died not long after he retired from the office of Chief Justice in 2000.

M.F., Ranelagh, Dublin 6
D.S., Clonskeagh, Dublin 14
Bastille Day 2009

TABLE OF CONTENTS

TABLE OF CASES

IRELAND

ENGLISH CASES

SCOTTISH CASES

NORTHERN IRISH CASES

AUSTRALIAN CASES

NEW ZEALAND CASES

CANADIAN CASES

EUROPEAN COURT OF JUSTICE CASES

EUROPEAN COURT OF HUMAN RIGHTS CASES

TABLE OF LEGISLATION

IRISH STATUTES

IRISH STATUTORY INSTRUMENTS

ENGLISH STATUTES

ENGLISH STATUTORY INSTRUMENTS

UNITED STATES OF AMERICA STATUTES

EUROPEAN UNION REGULATIONS

THE EUROPEAN CONVENTION ON HUMAN RIGHTS

CHAPTER 1

INTRODUCTION

1–01 Bankruptcy law is concerned with regulating the affairs of persons who either are unable to pay or who refuse to pay their debts. The great majority of individuals incur debts and manage to meet those liabilities, either as they fall due or in response to threats of enforcement, such as by attaching funds which are payable to them or seizure and sale of their assets by the sheriff. But a minority of persons, either as a result of misfortune or bad management, find themselves insolvent and entirely unable to pay those debts, and are forced into bankruptcy.

BANKRUPTS

1–02 There are two main categories of bankrupt. One is the business or professional person who falls on hard times; because of bad luck or incompetence, his business has failed, rendering him insolvent. Today, most industrial and commercial businesses are carried on under the aegis of registered companies so that, if the business becomes insolvent, usually the company is wound up or put in examinership[1] rather than its owners being adjudicated bankrupt. A principal object of Company Law is to provide the owners of (limited) companies with separate legal personality and limited liability, so that the failure of their incorporated enterprise will not invariably render them bankrupt. Thus in the famous *Salomon & Co* case,[2] which concerned the distribution of assets among the creditors of a boot manufacturing business that had failed during the recession of 1893, Mr Salomon, the first plaintiff, had become a pauper but was not a bankrupt. Failure of a company's business may nevertheless result in its shareholders' bankruptcy, such as where its liabilities were secured by those owners' personal guarantees. Banks which lend to private "one-person" and "family" companies often insist on guarantees from the directors-cum-shareholders as security for those loans. But many professions, such as accountants, barristers and solicitors, cannot be carried on by registered companies[3] and, accordingly, the unsuccessful professional person is very likely to be made a bankrupt.

1–03 The other main category of bankrupt is the person who borrowed too much in order to finance consumer spending. Formerly, the Bankruptcy Acts

---

[1] See generally, M. Forde et al, *The Law of Company Insolvency*, 2nd edn (Dublin: Thomson Round Hall, 2008).

[2] *Salomon v Salomon & Co* [1897] A.C. 22.

[3] E.g. Solicitors Act 1954, s.64.

applied only to traders, i.e. to indebtedness resulting from commercial or industrial activities; non-traders could not be made bankrupt. But in 1872 those Acts were extended to cover non-traders.[4] In the past, it was comparatively rare for persons who were not engaged in some business, trade or profession to be made bankrupt simply because there was little credit available for consumer spending. Granted, individuals who owned large estates, members of wealthy families and persons who were prominent in public life could obtain extensive credit in order to finance a grand lifestyle. Special provisions were made in 1872[5] for dealing with MPs who became bankrupt.[6]

1–04   Because they could not easily obtain credit from banks and other lending institutions, artisans, clerks and labourers rarely put themselves in a situation where they could even become amenable to bankruptcy. But with the great expansion of consumer credit over the last twenty-five years or so, bankruptcy is a prospect that many ordinary men and women face today.[7]

1–05   It is too early to say what impact the marked downturn in the economy in the last quarter of 2008 will have on the number of personal bankruptcies in the State. In 2008 there were in all eight adjudications. In 2009 by mid-May there were five.[8]

HISTORICAL CONTEXT

1–06   In the beginning most commercial societies developed legal collection remedies for individual creditors,[9] in part to reduce violence and other eternality-producing behaviour accompanying self help. For centuries this was done through the writ of *fieri facias*, under which the sheriff was empowered to seize the debtor's moveable assets and sell them, paying the judgment creditor from the proceeds of that sale. There was a comparable ancient procedure for obtaining satisfaction from the debtor's land, the writ of *elegit*;[10] in the middle of the 19th century it was replaced by the statutory procedure of registering a judgment mortgage.[11] In 1634 legislation was enacted against fraudulent conveyances and other devices to defeat creditors;[12] its central provisions still remain in force. With the increasing commercialisation of society, procedures were adopted whereby individual creditors could attach debts owed to their debtor or attach and obtain a charge over stocks and shares registered in his name.

---

[4]   Bankruptcy (Ireland) (Amendment) Act 1872; 35 & 36 Vic. c.57.
[5]   Bankruptcy (Ireland) (Amendment) Act 1872, ss.40–44 and cf. *Re Hazleton* [1915] 2 I.R. 425.
[6]   See para.1–17.
[7]   See para.10–73.
[8]   Inquiry with the Examiner's Office of the High Court on May 13, 2009.
[9]   Chapter 2 deals with these remedies today.
[10] Introduced in the Statute of Westminster II, 1285, 13 Edw. c.18.
[11] Judgment Mortgages (Ireland) Act 1850, 13 & 14 Vic. c.29 and see paras 2–42 et seq.
[12] Fraudulent Conveyances Act 1634, 10 Car. 1, sess. 2, c.3 and see paras 7–12 et seq.

1–07   Bankruptcy law in England can be traced to Acts of the 16th and the 17th centuries,[13] and what is commonly referred to as the Statute of 4 Anne in 1705,[14] which was amended in the following year. The 1542 statute[15] provided for the basic elements of a pro rata bankruptcy system, and that of 1571[16] empowered Chancery to appoint commissions, constituted in part of creditors, for valuing debtors' estates, approving creditors' claims, and apportioning assets. What was so novel about these Acts is that they inaugurated group collection procedures. They offered the possibility of achieving economies of scale in creditors' efforts to realise the value of their debtors' assets. These procedures also facilitated the reduction of many costs caused by the disorderly scramble of individual creditors to be first to collect, regardless of any adverse impact on other creditors or on the overall value to be realised on the debtor's assets. Rules about voidable preferences also reduced some substantial costs of uncoordinated action.

1–08   Severe limitations led to the system's infrequent use. For example, it applied only to "traders"—a classification that did not include farmers, innkeepers or shareholders of joint stock companies. Also, the commissions could not discharge a debtor's remaining unpaid obligations under distributing an estate, and thus provided little incentive to debtors to invoke them voluntarily. The system gradually improved and experienced wider use during the 17th century. Statutes enacted in 1603 and 1623[17] enhanced the power of commissions to compel testimony and avoid pre-insolvency conveyances, and Chancery became active during the latter half of the century in reviewing commission rulings. The most significant feature of the 1705 Act[18] is that it introduced the principle of discharge: that by paying a sufficient portion of the debts he incurred, the debtor could be freed from bankruptcy and was no longer legally liable for what remained unpaid on those debts. A notable protagonist for bankruptcy reform in the 17th century was the bankrupt and author, Daniel Defoe, whose *An Essay Upon Projects*,[19] published in 1679, engendered considerable debate on the topic.

1–09   The first Irish bankruptcy Act was passed in 1772,[20] the stated purpose of which was to "prevent frauds committed by bankrupts." Although it had been introduced as a temporary measure, it was continued in force by subsequent legislation, subject to various amendments. Reform of the entire system in the early 19th century was spurred by how its operation was summed up by Lord

---

[13]   The leading 19th century texts E. Christian, *The Origin, Progress and Present Practice of the Bankrupt Law Both in England and in Ireland* (London: W. Clarke & Sons, 1818) and C. Holmes, *The Law and Practice in Bankruptcy: with statutes, orders and forms: founded on Mr. Archbold's treatise*, 2 Vols (London: H. Sweet, 1869), contain accounts of the early law on the subject.

[14]   4 & 5 Anne c.17.

[15]   34 & 35 Hen. 8, c.4.

[16]   13 Eliz. c.7.

[17]   1 Jac.1 c.15 and 21 Jac. c.19.

[18]   4 & 5 Anne c.17.

[19]   See generally, Quilter, "Daniel Defoe: Bankrupt and Bankruptcy Reformer", 25 *J. Leg. Hist.* 52 (2004).

[20]   11 & 12 Geo. 2, c.8.

Chancellor Eldon in 1801: it was so often abused and facilitated fraud as to be a "disgrace to the country" and "it would be better at once to repeal all the statutes than suffer them to be applied to such purposes".[21] A notorious instance of abuse was *Re Story*,[22] involving an insolvent partnership, and where "one partner is the petitioning creditor, another an acting commissioner, another the solicitor to the commission, and the remaining one the sole assignee".[23] Reform went through three major phases, which have been described as "officialism", "retreat from officialism" and "return to officialism".[24] For Ireland these measures were the Law Relating to Bankrupts in Ireland Act 1836,[25] the Bankruptcy (Amendment) (Ireland) Act 1849,[26] the Irish Bankrupt and Insolvent Act 1857[27] and the Bankruptcy (Ireland) Amendment Act 1872.[28]

1–10   In 1962 a committee chaired by Budd J.[29] was appointed to evaluate the bankruptcy regime, and its report was published in 1973.[30] Most of their recommendations were incorporated in the present law, the Bankruptcy Act 1988 (the "1988 Act").

SOURCES OF LAW

1–11   The legal regime governing bankruptcy is based predominantly on the Bankruptcy Act 1988 and Ord.76 of the Rules of the Superior Courts (the "Bankruptcy Rules"). Where the bankruptcy involves persons or property in another EC Member State (apart from Denmark), it is subject to the European Communities (Personal Insolvency) Regulations 2002,[31] which give effect to EC Regulation 1346/2000 on Insolvency Proceedings.[32] Some special bankruptcy situations, such as partnerships, estates of deceased persons and employers, have discrete statutory provisions applicable to them. A regulation of 2001[33] altered financial limits in the 1988 Act and broadly converted them into euros.

---

[21]   See generally, V.M. Lester, *Victorian Insolvency,* (Oxford: Clarendon, 1999) Ch.1, at 25.
[22]   1 Buck. 70 (1817).
[23]   1 Buck. 70 (1817) at 74.
[24]   Lester, above fn.21, Chs 2, 4 and 5.
[25]   6 Will, 4 c.14.
[26]   12 & 13 Vic. c.107.
[27]   20 & 21 Vic. c.60.
[28]   35 & 36 Vic. c.57. The leading texts on the pre-1988 bankruptcy regime were J.H. Robb, *The Law and Practice of Bankruptcy and Arrangement in Ireland,* (Dublin: E. Ponsenby, 1907) and W.H. Kisbey, *The Law and Practice Relating to Bankruptcy in Ireland,* 4th edn (Dublin: Hodges Figgis, 1900). Other valuable texts include E.T. Baldwin, *The Law of Bankruptcy and bills of sale,* 11th edn (London: Stevens and Haynes, 1915) and M. Hunter & D. Graham eds., *The Law and Practice of Bankruptcy,* 19th edn (London: Stevens & Sons, 1979) (hereinafter *Muir Hunter & Graham*).
[29]   See short biography at Appendix 7.
[30]   Prl 2714.
[31]   S.I. No. 334 of 2002 and see paras 11–40 et seq.
[32]   [2000] OJ L160/1.
[33]   S.I. No. 595 of 2001.

1–12 This overwhelming statutory regime is operated against the backdrop of the common law and equitable principles, and is subject to the Constitution and the European Convention on Human Rights. Except where expressly so provided or very clearly implied, that regime does not alter established property or contractual rights and obligations. Unlike in Company Law, entitlements of secured creditors of the insolvent are hardly affected at all by the bankruptcy legislation.

1–13 It is possible that some of the unique pre-1988 common law doctrines or rules applied in bankruptcy were impliedly overruled by the 1988 Act, which is more favourable to creditors than were earlier regimes. As was observed of somewhat comparable legislation in Britain,

> "... the Act of 1986, although re-enacting many provisions from earlier statutes, contains a good deal of fresh material derived from the Insolvency Act 1895. In particular, the legislation now emphasises the importance of the rehabilitation of the individual insolvent, it provides for automatic discharge from bankruptcy in many cases and it abolishes mandatory public examinations as well as enabling a bankrupt to be discharged without public examination. Thus not only has the legislative approach to individual bankruptcy altered since the mid-19th century, but social views as to what conduct involves delinquency, as to punishment and as to the desirability of imprisonment have drastically changed ... In these circumstances, I feel justified in construing ... the Act of 1986 as a new piece of legislation without regard to 19th century authorities or similar provisions of repealed Bankruptcy Acts."[34]

1–14 On account of the presumption of constitutionality[35] and the similar presumption of European Convention compliance,[36] courts endeavour to construe the legislation and to apply the non-statutory rules in a manner that safeguards the rights guaranteed by the Constitution and by the Convention, respectively.[37]

1–15 To date, all constitutional challenges to the 1988 Act have failed. In *O'Donoghue v Ireland*[38] the plaintiff, who was an undischarged bankrupt, challenged s.21 of the Act, under which he could be examined in the High Court about his assets and activities. It had previously been held that this procedure did not constitute the administration of justice because it did not involve the resolution of a dispute, nor was it incidental to such a process.[39] Because, however, it was an aspect of bankruptcy proceedings already in the court and it

---

[34] *Smith v Braintree D.C.* [1990] 2 A.C. 215 at 237–238.
[35] See generally, M. Forde, *Constitutional Law*, 2nd edn (Dublin: First Law, 2004) at 43 et seq.
[36] European Convention on Human Rights Act 2003, ss.2 and 3(1).
[37] Convention issues have been raised in several English cases; see generally, D. Milman, *Personal Insolvency Law, Regulation and Policy,* (Aldershot: Ashgate, 2005), Ch.5 on fundamental rights in bankruptcy law.
[38] [2000] 2 I.R. 168.
[39] *Re Redbreast Preserving Co*, 91 I.L.T.R. 12 (1956).

was a procedure that the courts have exercised for well over a century, it was held to be sufficiently related to the administration of justice as not to contravene the separation of powers. According to Kearns J., "[t]he unbroken thread extending over centuries whereby the examination of witnesses in the context of bankruptcy is seen and perceived as forming part of the administration of justice" strongly supported this conclusion.[40] Moreover, the examination of witnesses "could be described as an administrative function or a judicial function ...".[41]

1–16   *Grace v Ireland*[42] concerned the regime by which bankrupts can obtain a discharge. It was contended that the plaintiff's bankruptcy had been allowed to continue for so excessive a duration as to contravene the guarantees of reasonably expeditious legal proceedings in art.6(1) of the Convention and an equivalent implied guarantee in the Constitution. He was adjudicated bankrupt in 1991 and the trial of the issue took place in 2006. Laffoy J. rejected the argument on the grounds that the plaintiff lacked locus standi, since there were certain options potentially open to him to obtain his discharge which he did not pursue, most notably seek a composition with his creditors. Additionally, because the successful outcome of his case would substantially interfere with his creditors' property rights, those could not be defeated by a case based simply on delay.

1–17   In 2007 a member of the Dáil mooted a challenge to the provision in the Electoral Law that disqualified undischarged bankrupts from Dáil membership but, in the event, it did not proceed.[43]

OBJECTIVES OF BANKRUPTCY LAW

1–18   Bankruptcy law seeks to achieve and reconcile several objectives. According to the Act of 1772,[44] its very purpose was to "give equal justice" to all creditors which was denied to them because of the harsh treatment meted out to bankrupts by "the obduracy of one or more creditors"; in other words, to ensure that some creditors do not secure unfair advantage over others.

1–19   When putting forward its proposals to reform bankruptcy law, the Budd report said that the main objects of bankruptcy legislation are:

  (i) "to secure equality of distribution and to prevent any one creditor obtaining an unfair advantage over the others;
  (ii) to protect bankrupts from vindictive creditors by freeing them from the balance of their debts where they are unable to pay them in full, and to help rehabilitate them;
  (iii) to protect creditors not alone from debtors who prior to bankruptcy

---

[40]   [2000] 2 I.R. at 181.
[41]   [2000] 2 I.R. at 182.
[42]   [2007] I.E.H.C. 90; cf. *Skurcak v Slovakia* [2007] B.P.I.R. 440.
[43]   Ms Cooper-Flynn, a T.D. for the Mayo constituency.
[44]   11 & 12 Geo. 2 c.8.

prefer one or more creditors to others but from the actions of fraudulent bankrupts;

(iv) to punish fraudulent debtors."[45]

Another purpose might be to facilitate debt collection in that, in order to coerce the debtor to pay what is owing, a creditor may issue a bankruptcy summons with the intention of petitioning for the debtor's bankruptcy if what is due has not been paid.

1–20 Most bankruptcies commence at the initiative of one or more creditors; usually, the debtor does not satisfy a bankruptcy summons, which leads to a petition being presented to the High Court to have him adjudicated a bankrupt. But the 1988 Act also permits the debtor to petition for his own bankruptcy, with a view to him ultimately settling with his creditors and obtaining a discharge. This Act also contains a mechanism whereby a debtor who is in serious financial difficulties can petition the court for its protection from creditors, pending coming to some arrangement with them, that renders it unnecessary to have him adjudicated a bankrupt.

1–21 While the main concern of bankruptcy legislation is to safeguard creditors' interests and also to afford debtors protection, there can be differences in degree between the amount of protection that exists, and the balance may favour creditors generally or else may favour debtors somewhat more. In the past, insolvent debtors were treated extremely unfavourably and special stigma attached to bankruptcy. That was particularly so before limited liability was introduced; the Limited Liability Act 1855[46] was severely criticised by many contemporary commentators because it enabled business people to in effect go bankrupt without having to bear the legal incidents of bankruptcy. From then on, the legislature acted on the assumption that not all bankrupts were fraudsters and rogues who in the end got their come-uppance. Several provisions of the Irish Bankrupt and Insolvent Act 1857,[47] which was the principal Irish law on the subject until 1988, sought to safeguard the insolvent debtor against his creditors. The 1988 Act is even more protective of debtors. However, this Act could not by any stretch of the imagination be regarded as a debtors' charter. The laws of some countries tilt the balance far more against creditors' interests than this Act does.

Its central themes are as follows:

1–22 *Arrangements:* In order to avoid bankruptcy, a debtor can seek the court's protection with a view to negotiating some general settlement with his creditors. If a sufficient number of them accept his proposals and they are approved by the court, then all the creditors are bound by the terms as were agreed.

---

[45] Prl 2714 at 45. For an excellent account of the various policy issues involved, see generally Milman, above fn.37 and also the *Cork Report*, i.e. *Insolvency Law and Practice*, Report of the Review Committee, Cmnd. 855 (H.M.S.O. 1981).

[46] 18 & 19 Vic. c.133.

[47] 20 & 21 Vic. c.60.

1–23   *Petition of Bankruptcy:* Where a debtor cannot pay or refuses to pay his debts, and in certain other stipulated circumstances, a creditor can petition the court to have him adjudicated a bankrupt. Where such petition is acceded to, the debtor's property becomes vested in either the Official Assignee or in the creditors' trustee in bankruptcy.

1–24   *Administration of the Estate:* The Assignee or trustee, as the case may be, then takes over the management of the debtor's assets and proceeds to realise them. In doing this, he may have to carry on the debtor's business for a short while, become involved in litigation and make compromises with certain creditors or those claiming to be creditors. Among the Assignee's or trustee's main tasks is to interrogate the bankrupt and others who have been involved in his affairs about his assets, which may lead to proceedings being brought to have set aside certain transfers of property by the debtor on the eve of adjudication, on the grounds that they were fraudulent conveyances or fraudulent preferences or were voluntary settlements or improvident dispositions.

1–25   *Proof and Distribution:* Those claiming to be owed money by the bankrupt must "prove" their debts, which is the formal procedure for establishing that such money is indeed owing and the actual amount of the debt. Following payment of the costs of the bankruptcy and satisfying certain "preferred" creditors, what remains in the estate is distributed among the general creditors on a pro rata basis. In the exceptional event of there being a surplus, that is returned to the bankrupt.

1–26   *Discharge:* If all the creditors are paid in full, the bankrupt will be discharged from bankruptcy, entitling him to conduct his business affairs unhampered by restrictions in the 1988 Act. Even after realising his entire estate, if he succeeds in paying his creditors more than 50 cent in the euro, the court may order his discharge, provided that all his preferential creditors were paid in full and, in all the circumstances, it is "reasonable and proper" that he should be discharged. The effect of discharge in such a case is that he can no longer be held liable for the debts he incurred prior to being adjudicated a bankrupt.

CHAPTER 2

CREDITORS' REMEDIES

2–01   The principal objective of bankruptcy proceedings is to make the insolvent person's assets available to his creditors. Frequently, the creditor who made the petition that results in him being adjudicated bankrupt will have obtained a judgment against him. Various methods of enforcing that judgment against the debtor's property may have been tried, with little or no success. Or it is possible that none of those methods were employed and the judgment creditor decided to seek recovery immediately through the bankruptcy machinery; he is not obliged to exhaust any non-bankruptcy processes that may be available to him. Because the procedures for recovering debts are closely connected with bankruptcy, it is instructive briefly to consider what modes of redress, other than bankruptcy, are available to creditors.

SECURED CREDITORS

2–02   Ordinarily a secured creditor will not have to resort to these remedies, as he ought to be able to recover what it owed to him from his security, which usually is a mortgage or charge or lien of some kind, or else personal security in the form of a guarantee.[1] But insofar as his security is not sufficient to discharge the debt, he may avail of the unsecured creditors' remedies, one of which is to petition for his debtor's bankruptcy.

PRE-JUDGEMENT RECOURSE

2–03   There are certain remedies that are available to unsecured creditors even before they have obtained a judgement against their debtor. Persons claiming an interest in land or in shares may register a *lis pendens* or a stop notice, respectively.[2]

Contractual Restrictions/Requirements

2–04   At times the debtor-creditor contract, the loan agreement, may contain stipulations as to what the debtor may not do or must do where full payment of the liability is being put at risk in certain specified ways. Often these requirements

---

[1]   See generally, M. Forde *Commercial Law,* 3rd edn (Haywards Heath: Tottel, 2005) Ch.7 and J. Breslin (with K. Smith), *Banking Law,* 2nd edn (Dublin: Thomson Round Hall, 2007) Chs 9 and 13, and 10–12.

[2]   Cf. *Lee v Buckle* [2004] 3 I.R. 544.

relate to security that the debtor holds. Apart from and often in addition to obtaining security, agreements with some financial institutions may contain covenants that enable the lender to have a say in managing the debtor's business and even to alter its composition. Intervention may be triggered not just when financial catastrophe is imminent but when the debtor has not met stipulated guidelines, such as goals set out in a business plan regarding, inter alia, cash flow projections, finding a specified number of customers by a particular date, and producing a working prototype. If these are not met, effective control of running the business may pass to that creditor.

Self Help

2–05   There are several modes of redress that may conveniently be described as forms of legitimate self help.

Set-Off

2–06   Where the creditor owes money to the debtor, he can set off his debt against his creditor's indebtedness, thereby reducing that debt pro tanto.[3] Entitlement to set-off requires mutuality between creditor and debtor in respect of those sums.

Detention of Chattels and Documents

2–07   Rights exist to detain a debtor's property, pending payment of a debt related to that property or some entirely separate debt. At common law, certain creditors enjoy a lien over the property of their debtors which is in their possession or control. Liens are a form of security interest, as are pledges.[4] Equivalent rights can also be conferred by contract, as in *De Lorean Motor Cars Ltd v Northern Ireland Carriers Ltd*.[5] The plaintiff car manufacturer agreed that the defendant should transport its cars from its Belfast factory to the dock side. A clause in the agreement provided that the defendant would have a general lien over the goods carried for "all moneys whatsoever due from" the plaintiff; the agreement went on to confer on the defendant a power of sale if not paid within a reasonable time, which suggests that the real intention was to create a pledge, not a lien. Several statutory provisions give creditors rights to detain their debtor's property, including at times entitlement to sell that property and reimburse themselves from its proceeds.[6]

Distress

2–08   Distress against a tenant's goods is an ancient self-help remedy available to landlords for non-payment of rent.[7] Distress may be levied without any

---

[3]   See generally, R. Derham, *The Law of Set Off*, 3rd edn (Oxford: O.U.P., 2003).
[4]   See generally, Forde, above fn.1 at 202 et seq. and Breslin, above fn.1 at 301 et seq.
[5]   [1982] N.I. 163.
[6]   E.g. in *Bristol Airport Plc v Powdrill* [1990] 1 Ch.74.
[7]   See generally P.P. Eddy, *Eddy on the Law of Distress*, 3rd edn (London: Sweet & Maxwell,

recourse to the court. Whether or to what extent this procedure is compatible with the Constitution and/or the European Convention on Human Rights is questionable. There are some statutory provisions that give certain creditors comparable rights to levy distress on their debtor's property.[8]

Freezing/"Mareva" Injunction

2–09 Unlike the position in parts of continental Europe, formerly Irish and United Kingdom law provided comparatively little assistance to unsecured creditors until they had first obtained a judgment against their debtors. Generally, the fact that the creditor was confident of winning his claim, when heard, did not entitle him to attach or otherwise hold or restrict the use of his debtor's property. Until at least a judgment was obtained against him, the debtor was free to carry on his business and deal with his assets in the normal way. A modern exception to this principle is what is popularly referred to as the "freezing" or *Mareva* injunction.[9] Before 1975 the law was that "you cannot get an injunction to restrain a man who is alleged to be a debtor from parting with his property".[10] In that year, the English Court of Appeal[11] gave a plaintiff an ex parte interlocutory injunction restraining the defendant from removing its property outside of the jurisdiction, on the grounds that there would be no assets left there against which the plaintiff could enforce its judgment if it should succeed. Doubts were cast on the correctness of this decision and especially on its applicability to assets within the court's jurisdiction, but in 1981 it was put on a statutory footing.[12]

2–10 Although it does not have an equivalent basis in Ireland, the courts here attribute their jurisdiction to make such orders to their general competence under s.28(8) of the Supreme Court of Judicature (Ireland) Act 1877,[13] to grant interlocutory orders whenever "it shall appear to the court to be just and convenient that such order should be made ...".[14] *Mareva* type orders operate in personam against the persons to whom they are addressed; they do not create any proprietary or security interest in the property in question.[15] But once a defendant or third party has been notified that an order of this nature was made, he risks being held in contempt of court if the acts in a manner inconsistent with it.

2–11 The purpose underlying these injunctions is to prevent a defendant from dissipating his assets, to the detriment of the plaintiff if his action succeeds. The following broad guidelines for obtaining such orders are that:

1961); note that abolished for residential tenancies since commencement of the Housing (Miscellaneous Provisions) Act 1992, s.19.
8   *E.g. R. v Carrick D.C., Ex p. Prankerd* [1999] Q.B. 1119.
9   See generally, B. Kirwan, *Injunctions, Law & Practice* (Dublin: Thomson Round Hall, 2008) Ch.8.
10 *Lister & Co. v Stubbs* (1890) 45 Ch. D. 1 at 13.
11 *Mareva Co. Naviera S.A. v Int'l Bulk Carriers S.A.* [1975] 2 Lloyd's Rep. 509.
12 Supreme Court Act 1981, s.37(3).
13 40 & 41 Vic. c.57.
14 Supreme Court of Judicature (Ireland) Act 1877, 40 & 41 Vic. c.57, s.28(8).
15 *Flightline Ltd. v Edwards* [2003] 1 W.L.R. 1200.

"1. The plaintiff should make a full and frank disclosure of all matters in his knowledge which are material for the judge to know.
2. The plaintiff should give particulars of his claim against the defendant, stating the grounds of his claim and the amount thereof and fairly stating the points made against it by the defendant.
3. The plaintiff should give some grounds for believing that the defendant has assets within the jurisdiction. ... The existence of a bank account is enough, whether it is in overdraft or not.
4. The plaintiff should give some grounds for believing that there is a risk of the assets being removed.
5. The plaintiff must give an undertaking in damages in case he fails."[16]

It is entirely a matter of judicial discretion whether pre-judgment relief of this nature should be given.[17] There are several statutory provisions that confer a comparable jurisdiction in particular circumstances.[18]

Detaining Absconding Debtors

2–12 Procedures exist for arresting and detaining debtors who are about to leave the country in order to avoid their creditors. One is the writ of *ne exeat regno*, with which the old Chancery Court would order the detention of absconding debtors.[19] But it has not been determined whether *ne exeat* remains part of Irish law; there is no reference to it in the Rules of the Superior Courts and, in any event, it might be unconstitutional. In proceedings in England and also in Ireland, that were not contested, comparable orders have been made, known as *Bayer* injunctions.[20] Unless there are very significant safeguards against this jurisdiction being abused, it may be unconstitutional.

2–13 An absconding debtor can be arrested under the Bankruptcy Act 1988,[21] provided that a bankruptcy summons was served on him before the petition for his bankruptcy can be presented. In that event, the High Court can order his arrest if there is reasonable cause for believing that he is about to abscond, either so as to avoid examination into his affairs or to avoid or delay the bankruptcy proceedings. The court will order discharge from custody where he offers such security or makes such payment as the court deems reasonable. It is also an offence for any debtor to leave the State taking property valued at least €634.87 (ex £500), or attempting to do so, where the purpose is to defraud the creditors.[22]

---

[16] *Third Chandris Shipping Corp. v Ultra Marine S.A.* [1979] Q.B. 645 at 668–669.
[17] See Kirwan, above fn.9 at 293 et seq.
[18] E.g. Company Law Enforcement Act 2001, s.55.
[19] *Al Nahkel for Contracting and Trading Ltd v Lowe* [1986] 1 Q.B. 235.
[20] See generally, Kirwan, above fn.9 at 335 et seq.
[21] Section 9.
[22] 1988 Act, s.124.

IMPRISONMENT

2–14   Creditors are concerned primarily with remedies against their debtors' property. But execution in a sense can also be levied against the defaulting debtor himself, by having him imprisoned. In the past debtors were frequently sent to prison for non-payment of what they owed, by way of the procedures notably of *capias ad respondendum* and *capias ad satisfactiendum*.[23] There is an extensive literature on what life was like in the Georgian and Victorian debtors' prisons.[24] But while he was in prison, the debtor's lands could not be seized from him. Occasionally, a debtor would take advantage of this by having a "friendly" creditor imprison him and thereby enable his family to continue in possession of all of his freehold estates.

2–15   Reforms were made to this system, in particular by the Debtors (Ireland) Act 1840,[25] and the Insolvent Debtors (Ireland) Act 1840.[26] Eventually imprisonment for mere non-payment of debts was prohibited by the Debtors (Ireland) Act 1872.[27] Subject to exceptions set out therein, "no person shall ... be arrested or imprisoned for making default in payment of a debt contracted ...".[28] These exceptions have been described as "all of a character which indicates that the Legislature wished merely to limit the term of imprisonment in regard to certain debts which were not simple debts, contracted in the ordinary intercourse between man and man, where credit is given by one person to another, but were debts the incurring of which was in some degree worthy of being visited with punishment."[29] What is forbidden is imprisonment for inability to pay, *not* for refusal to pay. Also, the debt in question must arise under a contractual obligation; this prohibition does not apply where the debt arises from liability in tort or from some statutory duty, or is based on a specific order of a court. It most likely would be unconstitutional if the law today permitted imprisonment of persons merely because they cannot pay their debts. Such a practice would contravene the European Convention on Human Rights, which provides inter alia that "[n]o one shall be deprived of his liberty merely on the grounds of inability to fulfil a contractual obligation."[30]

2–16   The Debtors (Ireland) Act 1872[31] empowers the superior courts, the civil bill courts and, since 1924, the District Court,[32] to order the imprisonment of a

---

[23]   See generally, W. Blackstone, *Commentaries on the Laws of England,* (1766: U. Chicago Press, 1979) Vol.3 at 414 et seq. Executors of estates and also peers and M.P.s were exempt from this.

[24]   See generally, V.M. Lester, *Victorian Insolvency,* (Oxford: Clarendon, 1999) Ch.3 and Ford, "Imprisonment for Debt", 25 *Michigan L. Rev.* 24 (1926). Of particular Irish interest is A. Trollope, *The Way We Live Now* (1875: reissued Oxford: O.U.P., 1979).

[25]   3 & 4 Vic. c.105.

[26]   3 & 4 Vic. c.107.

[27]   35 & 36 Vic. c.57.

[28]   Section 5 and also s.8.

[29]   *Middleton v Chichester* (1871) 6 Ch. App.152 at 156.

[30]   Art.1 of the Convention's 4th Protocol.

[31]   35 & 36 Vic. c.57.

[32]   Courts of Justice Act 1924, s.81.

recalcitrant judgment debtor. High Court and Supreme Court judgments can be enforced in this manner regardless of their amount; Circuit Court judgments and District Court decrees, on the other hand, must exceed €63.49 (ex £50). Before any order for imprisonment may be made, the court must be satisfied that the debtor has "the means to pay" the debt and that he "has refused or neglected, or refuses or neglects" to pay it.[33] Children's allowances, widows' and certain other pensions, and most social welfare benefits will not be taken into account when ascertaining the debtor's means.[34] In these proceedings, the court is empowered to order that the debt in question shall be payable by way of instalments. The period of imprisonment must not exceed six weeks and if, before then, the debt is discharged the prisoner must be released. But the mere fact of the debtor's imprisonment does not discharge the debt.

2–17   The Enforcement of Court Orders Act 1926,[35] as amended in 1940, gives the District Court substantially similar powers of imprisonment.[36] The debt in question must have been the subject of an instalment order made by the court. There is no monetary limit to the amount of the judgment or of the order; it can even be for payment of the entire amount in one instalment. Before ordering imprisonment, the judge must be satisfied that the debtor's failure to pay was due either to "his wilful refusal [or] to his culpable neglect". That is to say, mere inability to pay the debt cannot justify imprisonment. Even where there was a deliberate refusal to pay, the judge is not obliged to make the order; imprisonment will be ordered only where, in the circumstances, the judge "thinks proper". Detention under such an order must not exceed three months. If, before then, the amount owing is tendered to the court clerk or to the prison governor, the debtor must be released immediately. Additionally, the Minister for Justice, Equality and Law Reform is given an overriding discretion to direct that anybody being detained under these procedures be released, either forthwith or on condition of all or part of the money owing being paid. If the debtor has been adjudicated bankrupt, the court may order his release.[37]

2–18   The laws of some countries provide that the procedures for dealing with contempt of court have no application to non-payment of judgment debts, and this is also the case in Ireland. Orders of "attachment and all subsequent orders that may issue for giving effect thereto" are not included among the various methods of execution that may be ordered by the High Court for enforcing judgments for the recovery or payment of money.[38] Similarly the Circuit Court cannot order attachment or committal of the debtor for non-payment of such debts[39]

---

[33]   Considered in e.g. *Smith v Braintree D.C.* [1990] 2 A.C. 215 and *Woodley v Woodley (No. 2)* [1994] 1 W.L.R. 1167.

[34]   Social Welfare Consolidation Act 2005, s.284.

[35]   Section 18.

[36]   See generally, J.V.Woods, *District Court, Practice and Procedure*, 12th edn (Limerick: J.V. Woods, 1997). This provision was declared unconstitutional by Laffoy J. in *McCann v Judge of Monaghan District Court*, June 18, 2009.

[37]   Bankruptcy Act 1988, s.26.

[38]   R.S.C. Ord.42, r.26.

[39]   Cf. Circuit Court Rules—Ord.36, r.4 and Ord.37, r.1.

and the District Court has no such jurisdiction. Furthermore, since attachment and committal are discretionary remedies, it is only in the most exceptional circumstances that this machinery will be set in train to recover money debts. Attachment requires that the judgment debtor be brought before the court to answer allegations of contempt; committal is an order that he be kept in prison until such time as he has purged his contempt.

Execution of Judgments

2–19 The word execution is a term of art, meaning some formal process for enforcing a court or other judicial order.[40] Some methods of execution are based on common law, most notably the *fieri facias* procedure whereby the under-sheriff or county registrar can seize a debtor's goods and chattels. Other execution methods are provided for by statute, such as the system for registering judgment mortgages against the debtor's lands. Several methods are supplemented by rules of court, which stipulate the precise steps to be followed in levying execution. According to the Rules of the Superior Courts 1986, "A judgment for the recovery by or payment to any person of money may be enforced by execution order or by any other mode authorised by these Rules or by law".[41] An "execution order" is defined there as "includ[ing] orders of *fieri facias*, sequestration and attachment" against the debtor.[42] The "other modes" set out there are charging orders and stop orders, attachment of debts and appointment of a receiver by way of equitable execution. These remedies are also available in the Circuit Court,[43] except that it will never enforce money judgments by way of committal of or attachment against the debtor's person, and it does not have jurisdiction to order sequestration of a debtor's assets. The only form of execution that can be channelled through the District Court is imprisonment for refusal to pay a debt.

2–20 Many of the enforcement mechanisms described here applied originally to judgments of the High Court and of the Supreme Court, or their predecessors, the "Superior Courts" of Ireland.[44] But there are various statutory provisions placing judgments of the Circuit Court and decrees of the District Court on the same footing, for the purpose of the enforcement method in question, as those of the Superior Courts; for instance with regard to judgment mortgages, execution by the sheriff and charging orders over stocks and shares. In 1937 the procedure for registering judgments in the Central Office of the High Court was extended to Circuit Court judgments[45] and in 1981 that procedure was extended to District Court decrees.[46]

---

[40] See generally, T.K. Anderson, *The Law of Execution* (London: Butterworths, 1889).
[41] R.S.C. Ord.42, r.3.
[42] R.S.C. Ord.42, r.8.
[43] Cf. Circuit Court Rules, Ords 36 and 37. See generally K. Dowling, *Civil Procedure in the Circuit Court*, (Dublin: Thomson Reuters, 2008) at 273 et seq.
[44] Supreme Court of Judicature (Ireland) Act 1877, 40 & 41 Vic. c.57.
[45] Circuit Court (Registration of Judgments) Act 1837.
[46] Courts Act 1981, s.25.

Seizure by the Sheriff

2–21   *Fieri facias* (commonly known as "*fi. fa.*") is a method, under common law, whereby the sheriff of the county could seize the debtor's goods and chattels, and have them sold, paying the proceeds to the judgment creditor, less the expenses of the execution.[47] As described, "[t]he writ of *fieri facias* is that writ of execution by which a suitor usually puts into effect a judgment recovered either for debt, damages or costs ... . By this writ the sheriff is commanded that of the goods and chattels of the party against whom judgment is recovered, being in his bailiwick, he cause to be made the sum recovered, with interest ... immediately after the execution of the writ, to be paid to the party by whom judgment has been recovered."[48]

2–22   Execution by way of this procedure is carried out in Dublin and Cork by under-sheriffs, and elsewhere by county registrars. Money and certain securities can be taken, as well as personal chattels. The procedure applies with regard to judgments of the Supreme Court, of the High Court, of the Circuit Court and decrees of the District Court. Unpaid taxes can also be collected in this way by Revenue sheriffs without the need for judgment being given against the taxpayer.

Fieri Facias

2–23   Before filing the *praecipe* or requisition, which must be done before a *fi. fa.* is issued, the creditor is not obliged to make any formal demand for payment of what is due.[49] Nor is there need to leave a reasonable time for payment to be made before having the order issued.[50] Save in exceptional circumstances, the application for an order must be on notice. The procedure to be followed is laid down in Ord.42, rr.8–35 of the Rules of the Superior Courts 1986 and in Ord.36 of the Circuit Court Rules 2001.

2–24   Not every form of personal property can be the subject of execution in this manner.[51] At common law, the sheriff could execute only against tangible goods and chattels, severable fixtures to land, leases and growing crops. In 1840, in recognition of the greater commercialisation of society, the legislature also rendered exigible any "money or bank notes ... and any cheques, bills of exchange, promissory notes, bonds, specialities, or other securities for money belonging to" the debtors.[52] Money for these purposes does not include book debts owing to the judgment debtor. Cheques which were issued to but not

---

[47]   See generally, G. Y. Dixon & W. L. Gilliland, *The Law Relating to Sheriffs in Ireland,* (Dublin: E. Ponsonby, 1888); and C.R. Wigan and D. Meston, *Mather on Sheriff and Execution Law,* 3rd edn (London: Stevens & Sons Ltd: Sweet & Maxwell, 1935).
[48]   Dixon & Gilliland at 23.
[49]   *Kelly v O'Beirne* (1867) 1 Ir. Eq. 540 and *Land Credit Co of Ireland v Lord Fermoy* (1870) 5 Ch. App 323.
[50]   *Smith v Smith* (1874) L.R. 9 Exch 121.
[51]   *Dixon & Gilliland,* above fn.47, Ch.4.
[52]   Debtors (Ireland) Act 1840, s.20 (3 & 4 Vict. c.105).

delivered to him are not his property and, accordingly, are not exigible.[53] Securities for money, which are exigible, include fully-paid-up life insurance policies[54] but not a beneficiary's interest in an insurance policy.[55] The basis for this distinction is that the 1840 Act empowers the sheriff to hold securities for money and to sue but, since it contains no express authority to keep up payments, for instance insurance premiums, policies which have not matured are not rendered exigible. The precise scope of the term "securities for money" remains somewhat unclear. It would seem that Government securities and stocks and shares in registered companies, and in public bodies, are not encompassed by the term.

2–25 Equitable interests in land and equitable interests in personal property other than goods and chattels, such as property comprised in a debenture, cannot be taken by way of *fi. fa.*[56] Some partial legal interests in goods are exigible, like a pawnbroker's interest in redeemable pledges[57] and goods owned jointly by the judgment debtor with another,[58] but not goods which are being held by virtue of a lien for work done.[59] After 1877 even some equitable interests in goods were deemed exigible.[60]

2–26 The sheriff cannot take property belonging to third parties, such as property acquired under hire purchase and property otherwise subject to retention of title. As was observed, "the right of a judgment creditor under an execution is to take the precise interest, and no more, which the debtor possesses in the property seized, and consequently that such property must be sold by the Sheriff with all the charges and encumbrances, legal and equitable, to which it was subject in the hands of the debtor. In other words, what the debtor has power to give is the exact measure of that which the execution creditor has the right to take".[61]

2–27 Formerly any goods and chattels owned by the debtor which were in his possession when the *fi. fa.* was issued were exigible. Because of the obvious injustice that this rule caused to purchasers of goods from the debtor, who were not aware of impending execution, the Sale of Goods Act 1893[62] stipulates that delivery to the sheriff of the order shall not prejudice subsequent buyers of goods in good faith and for valuable consideration, unless they had notice of the *fi. fa.*'s existence.[63] Where a dispute arises with regard to what goods

---

53 *Courtoy v Vincent* (1852) 15 Beav. 486.
54 *Beamish v Stephenson* (1886) 18 L.R. Ir. 319.
55 *Re Sergeant's Trusts* (1879) 18 L.R. Ir. 66.
56 *Re Opera Ltd* [1891] 3 Ch. 260.
57 *Re Rollason* (1887) 34 Ch. D. 495.
58 E.g. partnership assets.
59 *Legg v Evans* (1840) 6 M & W 36.
60 *Stevens v Hince* (1914) 110 L.T. 835, at 937.
61 *Wickham v New Brunswick & New Caledonian Rly. Co* (1865) L.R. 1 P.C. 64, at 431–432.
62 56 & 57 Vic. c.71.
63 Section 26(1).

can be taken in execution there exists a procedure known as interpleader for resolving the matter.[64]

2–28 A return will be made stating the outcome of the under-sheriff's or county registrar's attempts at execution.[65] If no goods have been taken, the return will state "*nulla bona*". A sale of any goods seized will then be arranged for the best price obtainable in the circumstances.[66] Where goods have been seized but not sold, the creditor can get an order known as *venditioni exponas* directing sale of the goods.[67] After deducting fees, expenses and poundage, the balance of the proceeds of sale will be paid over to the judgment creditor, up to the amount of his debt.

The Revenue

2–29 There are various modes by which the Revenue Commissioners collect income and other taxes which have become payable. One of these is recovery by the sheriff or county registrar seizing the taxpayer's "goods, animals and other chattels", and selling them.[68] This empowers the Collector General to certify that a certain sum is owing by the taxpayer and naming the person on whom that sum is levyable. The sheriff can then seize his chattels and is given all the rights and powers of a sheriff levying execution under a *fi. fa.*

2–30 Where the debtor owes income tax, and some other party causes his goods or chattels to be seized by way of execution, that process is ineffective until such time as that creditor pays the Revenue the outstanding tax or the tax payable in the year when the seizure took place.[69] But this does not apply where a landlord takes possession in respect of outstanding rent.

Attachment of Debts

2–31 Attachment of debts, which is also referred to as garnishment, enables the judgment creditor to get money which is owing to the debtor paid instead to himself.[70] A credit balance in the debtor's bank account, as well as other sums due to him, can be attached for the benefit of the judgment creditor. This remedy is both a powerful and a harsh one, because it can greatly diminish the debtor's cash flow and it can put third parties on notice of the judgment awarded against the debtor. Attachment originated in the Common Law Procedure Act 1856,[71] and the present procedure is set out in Ord.45 of the Rules of the Superior Courts 1986 and in Ord.38 of the Circuit Court Rules 2001.

---

[64] See generally, M. Crababé, *Interpleader and Attachment of Debts,* (London: W. Maxwell, 1881).
[65] Dixon & Gilliland, above fn.47, Ch.16.
[66] Dixon & Gilliland, above fn.47, Ch.9.
[67] Dixon & Gilliland, above fn.47, Ch.11.
[68] Taxes Consolidation Act 1997, s.962.
[69] Taxes Consolidation Act 1997, s.97.
[70] See generally, Anderson, above fn.40 at 448 et seq.
[71] 19 & 20 Vic. c.105.

Garnishee Order

2–32 Before attachment will be directed, there must be a judgment or order of the Superior Courts, or of the Circuit Court or the District Court, requiring the debtor to pay money, and that money must not have been paid. In that event, the judgment creditor can then proceed ex parte to have attached funds which are payable by others to that debtor. The debtor may then apply to have the order discharged, if there are good grounds for doing so. The order will be made against "all debts owing or accruing from" the third person, known as the garnishee, to the debtor. For the garnishee's debt to be so "owing and accruing", payment by him must not be subject to any conditions or contingencies other than the effluxion of time.

2–33 An "accruing debt" for these purposes means,

"… any debt which may at any future time arise between the judgment debtor and the person sought to be made a garnishee, there being no contract at that time between the judgment debtor and such person, or anything which can make any relation of any kind, legal or equitable, between them? To state the proposition is to shew its absurdity. Then can it be this, that it may be a debt which there is some probability may in future arise? Who can say where there is nothing out of which a debt can be said in law to arise, that it is probable that a debt may arise, as for instance a probability that the parties will make a contract. If it is not a debt it will not do. It must be something which the law recognises as a debt."[72]

2–34 Instances of liabilities which have been held incapable of garnishment include a portion of the surplus due to a shareholder in the winding up of a company[73] and money in a savings bank account belonging to the judgment debtor.[74] Payments to be made under a building contract upon the issue of an architect's certificate can be attached in anticipation of the certificate being given.[75] A contrary view was taken by the English courts.[76] A joint bank account cannot be garnished by the creditors of one depositor.[77] But old cases on where a husband puts money into an account jointly owned with his wife or into her own account[78] may no longer represent goods in law.[79]

2–35 Even where the debt is capable of being attached, the courts have a discretion whether to direct this mode of execution. Garnishment will not be allowed where it would result in the judgment creditor obtaining an unfair

---

[72] *Webb v Stanton* (1883) 11 Q.B.D. 518 at 523.
[73] *Spence v Coleman* [1901] 2 K.B. 199.
[74] *Bagley v Winsome* [1952] 2 Q.B. 236 and *Re Australia & New Zealand Savings Bank* [1972] V.R. 690.
[75] *O'Leary v Buttimer* [1953–4] Ir. Jur. Rep. 15.
[76] *Dunlop & Ranken Ltd v Hendall Steel Structures Ltd* [1957] 3 All E.R. 344.
[77] *Hirschorn v Evans* [1938] 2 K.B. 801.
[78] *Harrods Ltd v Evans* [1937] 2 All E.R. 236 and *Plunkett v Barclays Bank Ltd* [1936] 2 K.B. 107.
[79] Following *Stack v Dowden* [2007] 2 A.C. 432 (a case involving an unmarried couple).

advantage over all the other creditors[80] or where the result would be most unfair to the judgment debtor[81] or, indeed, to other persons who have claims to the money it is being sought to attach.[82] The ex parte application is for an order nisi, directing the garnishee to show cause why the funds in question should not be attached and, in the meantime, attaching that debt to the amount specified. Until this order is duly served, the intended garnishee is free to deal with the debt in whatever way the judgment debtor requires. Once the order nisi is served on the garnishee, it binds the debt specified to the amount stated. But it would seem that the "binding" is far from having an absolute effect and that service of the order does not operate to transfer or assign the debt to the judgment creditor, either absolutely or by way of security.[83] The garnishee is forbidden to pay the debt either to the judgment debtor or to someone else at the latter's directions; the money or an equivalent sum must instead be paid to the judgment creditor. While the judgment creditor's rights regarding the debt attached nisi have occasionally been called a charge, the better view and the logic underlying the cases is not to regard them as a charge or a lien.[84]

2–36   Like an executing creditor, an attaching creditor can only attach such property in the debt as the debtor possesses. The garnishee order "only binds the attached debt in so far as the judgment debtor is entitled to deal with it, and does not affect the claims of creditors in whose favour he has charged it, even though they may not have given notice of their claims, and ... no charge affecting the debt when the garnishee order is made is displaced by that order".[85]

Revenue Attachments

2–37   The Revenue can attach funds owing to a taxpayer without going through the above procedure.[86] Where a person has not paid a tax which has been assessed or is otherwise due by him, the Revenue can require persons who owe money to that taxpayer or who have financial assets belonging to him to pay directly to the Collector General a sum equivalent to these outstanding taxes.

Charging and Attachment of Stocks and Shares

2–38   When the scope of *fi. fa.* was extended in 1840, not all forms of choses in action were brought within its reach. But the Debtors (Ireland) Act 1840,[87] created an alternative method of execution, by obtaining a court order in respect of the debtor's stocks and shares.[88] These are "any Government stock, funds, or annuities, or any stock or shares of or in any public company in Ireland

---

[80]   *Pritchard v Westminster Bank Ltd.* [1969] 1 All E.R. 999 and *G. Lee & Sons (Bldrs) Ltd v Blink* [1972] 1 All E.R. 359.
[81]   *Martin v Nadel* [1906] 2 K.B. 26.
[82]   *Roberts v Death* (1881)8 Q.B.D. 319.
[83]   *Norton v Yates* [1906] 1 K.B. 112.
[84]   *Norton v Yates* [1906] 1 K.B. 112.; *Robson v Smith* [1895] 2 Ch. 118.
[85]   *O'Connor v Ireland* [1897] 2 I.R. 150, at 155.
[86]   Taxes Consolidation Act 1997, s.1002.
[87]   3 & 4 Vic. c.105, ss.23 and 24.
[88]   See generally Anderson, above fn.40 at 475 et seq.

(whether incorporated or not ...)." The creditor can obtain ex parte a charging order, which is a declaration that the securities in question stand charged for his benefit. The judgment debtor may then apply to have that order discharged, if there are grounds for doing so. An argument could be made that these orders are not executions in the strict sense and that statutory provisions regarding "execution" do not apply to them; that contention has been rejected in England in respect of charging orders on land.[89]

2–39   The precise scope of the term "Government stock, funds or annuities" has never been judicially determined. It is questionable whether such securities issued by or for some foreign governmental entity cannot be charged under this procedure. It also is questionable whether securities issued by local government bodies and the like are "governmental" for this purpose. As for the term "public companies", the modern system of incorporating companies by registration was not established when this procedure was created. The courts have interpreted the term liberally, as including all kinds of entities which could be called companies and which have an element of compulsory publicity, such as the duty to maintain registers of members and to file annual returns with the companies' office. Thus the shares of private registered companies, as well as in private limited companies and other statutory corporations, can be charged under these procedures.[90] But the company must be registered in Ireland or be established by Irish legislation; it is unlikely that the shares of a foreign company which is registered under Pt XI of the Companies Act 1963 can be so charged. Debentures are not stocks or shares for these purposes.[91]

2–40   Charging orders apply to judgments of the Superior Courts and also of the Circuit Court and decrees of the District Court. When a charging order is made, the securities affected "stand charged" with payment of the judgment sum and the interest thereon. And it is provided that this order "shall entitle the judgment creditor to all such remedies as he would have been entitled to if such charge had been made in his favour by the judgment debtor." The full import of this provision has not been determined; if it is given its literal meaning, then a charging order will be treated as a consensual charge and, accordingly, as more than a method of executing judgments.

2–41   Even where such an order is not made, the Common Law Procedure Amendment Act (Ireland) 1853,[92] authorises the court to attach and to order the transfer to the sheriff of certain securities belonging to the judgment debtor. These securities are the same as those which can be the subject of a charging order.[93] As well as being a judgment creditor, the applicant for orders under this execution procedure must be in a position to issue execution and there must be in existence a *fi. fa.* which is levyable.[94]

---

[89]   *Re Overseas Aviation Engineering (G.B.) Ltd.* [1963] 1 Ch. 24.
[90]   *Honniball v Cunningham* [2006] I.E.H.C. 326.
[91]   *Sellar v Bright* [1904] 2 K.B. 446.
[92]   16 & 17 Vic. c.113, ss.132 and 133.
[93]   *Fletcher v Egan* (1858) 8 I.C.L.R. App. 5.
[94]   *Donohue v Mullarkey* (1886) 18 L.R. Ir. 425.

Judgment Mortgage

2–42   Where the judgment debtor owns land, the judgment against him can be enforced against that property by means of a judgment mortgage.[95] At common law, execution could not be levied against land or any interest in land, with the anomalous exception of leasehold interests. Consequently, for most interests in land to be exigible, there must be legislation providing for such process. The present procedure is contained in the Judgment Mortgage (Ireland) Act 1850[96] as amended in 1858.[97] It replaced a similar procedure in the Debtors (Ireland) Act 1840[98]; methods of enforcement against land provided for in this Act, of *elegit* and statutory receivership, were abolished in 1850. Thenceforth, the only means of enforcing judgments against land has been the judgment mortgage. It applies to judgments of the Supreme Court, of the High Court, of the Circuit Court and decrees of the District Court.

2–43   If the judgment is registered against the land in the appropriate registry, it almost operates as if the debtor had mortgaged that land to the judgment creditor. If payment is not duly made, the creditor can proceed to enforce sale of that land, reimbursing himself from the proceeds. As described, "[j]udgments are converted into statutory mortgages by the registration of an affidavit of ownership by the judgment creditor."[99] To register an effective judgment mortgage, the procedure laid down must be followed with precision. In particular, all the requisite details must be set down in the affidavit which will be registered either in the Registry of Deeds or the Land Registry.

2–44   The interests in land which can become the subject of a judgment mortgage are where the debtor "is seised or possessed at law or in equity of any lands, tenements or hereditaments of any nature or tenure or has any disposing power over such [property] which he may without the assent of any other person exercise for his own benefit".[100] Thus, an extensive range of legal and equitable interests are covered so long as they are in existence when the judgment is registered. Leasehold interests,[101] tenancies at will,[102] lands subject to an order for sale[103] and even other judgment mortgages[104] are all exigible in this manner. Among the matters remaining to be resolved is whether judgment mortgages can be registered against the interest of an unpaid or partly-paid vendor of land, under an agreement for sale, and also against the purchaser's interest under an agreement for the sale of land where all or part of the purchase price has not been

---

[95]   See generally, D. Madden, *Registration of Deeds, Conveyances and Judgment Mortgages*, 2nd edn (Dublin: W. McGee, 1901) and N. Madox, *Mortgage Law & Practice,* (Dublin: Thomson Round Hall, 2008) Ch.11.
[96]   13 & 14 Vic. c.29.
[97]   21 & 22 Vic. c.105.
[98]   3 & 4 Vic. c.107.
[99]   Madden, above fn.95 at 117.
[100] 1850 Act, s.6.
[101] *Tevlin v Gilsenan* [1902] 1 I.R. 514
[102] *Devlin v Kelly* 20 I.L.T.R. 76 (1886).
[103] *Re Scanlon's Trustee's Estates* [1897] 1 I.R. 462.
[104] *Rossborough v McNeill* (1889) 23 L.R. Ir. 409.

paid. Interests of an individual joint tenant and of a tenant in common in land are exigible, even where their co-tenants owe nothing to the judgment creditor. The effect of registering a judgment mortgage against property held under a joint tenancy is to convert the holding into a tenancy in common.[105]

2–45 The legal effects of registration of a judgment are defined as "operat[ing] to transfer and to vest in the creditor registering such affidavit all the lands, tenements and hereditaments mentioned therein, for all the estate and interest of which the debtor ... shall at the time of such registration be seised or possessed at law or in equity, or might at such time create by virtue of any disposing power which he might then without the assent of any other person exercise for his own benefit ...".[106] Thus, the beneficial title in the debtor's interest is transferred to the registering judgment creditor, for whom that interest in the land is thereby mortgaged. But that mortgage is subject to all equities subsisting at the time the affidavit is registered. On several occasions it has been stressed that the judgment mortgage is only "a process of execution and is not a charge created for valuable consideration."[107]

Receiver by way of Equitable Execution

2–46 There are several circumstances where the courts will appoint a receiver over all or part of another's property, such as to enforce the rights of creditors with a security interest in that property or to preserve it pending litigation. In an appropriate case, the courts will also appoint a receiver over a debtor's property in order to enforce a judgment rendered against him, by taking his property and paying the proceeds of sale over to the creditor.[108] In a suitable case, a receiver can be appointed even before judgment has been given so as to prevent property from being dissipated.[109] This method of execution was devised by the Chancery Courts in an era when the common law methods were most inadequate and before the statutory reforms of 1840. The present procedure is provided for in Ord.45, r.9 of the Rules of the Superior Courts 1986 and in Ord.39 of the Circuit Court Rules 2001.

2–47 This remedy is not available over assets against which execution could be levied by way of any of the other methods for enforcing judgments. According to Fry L.J.:

> "The idea that a receivership order is a form of execution is in my opinion erroneous. A receiver was appointed by the Court of Chancery in aid of a judgment at law when the plaintiffs shewed that he had sued out the proper writ of execution, and was met by certain difficulties arising from

---

[105] *Milroy v Edgar* (1881) 7 L.R. Ir. 521.

[106] 1850 Act, s.7.

[107] *Tempany v Hynes* [1976] I.R. 101 at 110.

[108] See generally, Anderson, above fn.40, at 489 et seq. and G. Lightman & G. Moss, *The Law of Administrators and Receivers of Companies* (London: Thomson, Sweet & Maxwell, 2007) Ch.29.

[109] *Anglo Italian Bank v Davies* (1878) 9 Ch. D. 275.

the nature of the property which prevented his obtaining possession at law, and in these circumstances only did the Court of Chancery interfere in aid of a legal judgment for a legal debt. Relief by the appointment of a receiver went on the ground that execution could not be had, and therefore it was not execution. Moreover, the appointment of a receiver was an act requiring the exercise of judicial power on the part of the court; the circumstances to which I have referred had to be proved before the court would make the order. All these considerations tend to shew that the appointment of a receiver was not execution, but was equitable relief granted under circumstances which made it right that legal difficulties should be removed out of the creditor's way. It has often been spoken of by judges as 'equitable execution', but I am afraid that this concise expression has led to the erroneous idea that the appointment of a receiver is a form of execution which can be obtained without shewing to the court the existence of the circumstances creating the equity on which alone the jurisdiction arises."[110]

2–48　On this basis, in *National Irish Bank v Graham*,[111] Keane J. refused to appoint a receiver over the defendant's milking herd, because he was their legal owner and there was nothing to prevent the sheriff seizing the herd under a *fi. fa.* Similarly, in *Honniball v Cunningham*,[112] Laffoy J. refused to appoint a receiver over the defendant's shares, which by court order had been charged in favour of the plaintiff, because the defendant was their legal owner rather than the holder of an equitable interest in them.

2–49　A restriction formerly imposed was that this remedy could not be used against an asset which was not exigible either at common law or in equity before the Judicature Acts, such as the debtor's future earnings[113] or future profits of his business,[114] or an amount to be paid when a contract to execute work is performed.[115] However, it has been held that the broad equity jurisdiction is not entirely bound by particular categories established in the 19th century and that, in an appropriate case, a receiver can be appointed to attach future assets, provided that the debtor can be adequately protected against double jeopardy. A receiver may be appointed to take payment of money that in the future would become owing to the debtor under contract, whether in the state or abroad.[116]

2–50　Appointment of a receiver by way of equitable execution over specified property does not give the judgment creditor any mortgage, charge or lien over that property.[117] And when the receiver takes possession, the property is not held

---

[110] *Re Shephard* (1889) 43 Ch. D. 131, at 138.

[111] [1994] 1 I.R. 215.

[112] [2006] I.E.H.C. 326.

[113] *Holmes v Millage* [1893] 1 Q.B. 551.

[114] *Manchester & Liverpool District Banking Co v Parkinson* (1880) 22 Q.B.D. 173.

[115] *Re Johnson* [1898] 2 I.R. 551. Cf. *McCreery v Bennett* [1904] 2 I.R. 69.

[116] *Ahern v Michael O'Brien & Co.* [1991] 1 I.R. 421, also *Masri v Consolidated Contractors International UK Ltd (No.2)* [2009] 2 W.L.R. 621.

[117] *Re Lough Neagh Ship Co Ex p. Thompson* [1896] 1 I.R. 29.

for the creditor but for the court, which will direct what shall be done with it, such as by selling it and paying the proceeds over to the creditor. As Bowen J. observed, regarding the appointment of a receiver over a fund, "[i]t does not amount to the creation of an equitable interest in the nature of a charge on the fund. It falls short of that. It is a mere direction to the receiver to receive money, and to pay it over to the creditors when he does receive it. There is nothing to create an interest in the fund ...".[118]

Examination in Aid of Execution

2–51 A problem with which judgment creditors are often faced is ascertaining what property the debtor indeed owns. For instance, the debtor may have owned or was believed to have owned certain property at one stage but, after the judgment was given, his interest in that property cannot readily be established. Or the property may have entirely disappeared and the debtor may deny all knowledge of its whereabouts or of his ownership of it. Accordingly, it was necessary to devise machinery whereby the debtor and others can be interrogated with regard to dealings in his property.

High Court

2–52 Judgment debtors and other persons who are believed to know about the debtor's property and financial transactions can be summoned before the High Court and examined.[119] This procedure is similar to that laid down in the Bankruptcy Act 1988, for enquiring into the transactions of bankrupts.[120] Persons summoned for examination who do not attend, or who do not produce whatever books and documents they were ordered to bring with them, can be committed for contempt of court. The examination is on oath and the answers given will usually be written down. Questions must relate to the discovery of assets; they must deal with "whether any and what debts are owing to the debtor, and whether the debtor has any and what other property or means of satisfying the judgment ...".[121]

2–53 As Jessel M.R. once observed, the debtor "must answer all questions fairly directed to ascertain from him what amount of debts is due, from whom due, and to give all necessary particulars to enable the plaintiffs to recover under a garnishee order."[122] There are no leading modern authorities on the test for determining, in this context, whether the answers given are satisfactory, but the test used in bankruptcy and liquidation examination cases most likely would be applied by analogy. A person can refuse to answer questions on matters covered by privilege. Should the court so direct, it would seem that these examinations may be conducted in camera.[123]

---

[118] *Re Potts* [1893] 1 Q.B. 648 at 662.
[119] R.S.C. Ord.42, r.26.
[120] See paras 6–23 et seq.
[121] R.S.C. Ord.42, r.36.
[122] *Cesta Rica Republic v Strousberg* (1880) 16 Ch. D. 8 at 12–13.
[123] Cf. *Re Redbreast Preserving Co (Ir.) Ltd* 91 I.L.T.R. 12 (1957).

District Court

2–54   The Enforcement of Court Orders Act 1926, as amended in 1986,[124] contain a similar procedure whereby judgment debtors may be examined as to their means by a District Judge. For the purpose of such examination, the debtor is required to lodge with the court clerk, at least one week in advance, a "statement of means", which must set out his assets and liabilities, his income and the means by which it is earned and its sources, and those for whose support he is "legally or morally liable". The examination is conducted on oath. Both the creditor and the debtor can adduce additional evidence as to the latter's means. If the judge concludes that the statement of means lodged is materially inaccurate, to the debtor's knowledge, he can order the latter's imprisonment. If, as a result of the examination, the judge is of the view that the debtor has the means to pay the debt, either in one sum or in instalments, he can order that the debt be paid, along with the costs of the inquiry. Unlike under the High Court procedure, persons other than the judgment debtor cannot be compelled to submit themselves for examination in the District Court.

---

[124] Courts (No.2) Act 1986, s.1.

CHAPTER 3

ARRANGEMENTS WITH CREDITORS

3–01 Instead of being put into bankruptcy, the insolvent debtor may succeed in making some arrangement or compromise with his creditors. There are several advantages in such a course. The debtor is saved the expense, publicity, embarrassment and inconvenience of being declared a bankrupt. For his creditors, they may be able to secure the prompt payment of a substantial part of their debt. Also, the major creditors may have some special interest in keeping the debtor out of bankruptcy; it may be some business or professional reason, or it may be because of family connections. But there are several disadvantages for creditors in becoming parties to out of court compromises with an insolvent debtor. They may possibly be persuaded to accept a smaller sum than they would have obtained in bankruptcy proceedings. They will not be able to avail of the statutory machinery for thoroughly investigating the debtor's financial affairs. Nor can they avail of the statutory procedures for setting aside a scheme which previously was agreed to. Conversely, out of court arrangements are far more attractive to debtors.

3–02 If the arrangement involves conveying the debtor's property to a trustee for it to be distributed among all the creditors, the Deeds of Arrangement Act 1887,[1] must be complied with. Arrangements with creditors can also be made within the framework of Pt IV (ss.87–109) of the 1988 Act, which provides for arrangements under the supervision of the High Court as an alternative to bankruptcy proceedings. Arrangements can even be made and rendered effective after bankruptcy proceedings have commenced.

DEEDS OF ARRANGEMENT

3–03 A deed of arrangement is a formal agreement with creditors whereby, in return for them releasing their claims, the debtor will give up virtually his entire assets for the benefit of those creditors. In the 19th century, before most small traders ran their businesses as limited companies, deeds of arrangements were frequently resorted to as an alternative to bankruptcy. They are rarely used these days. One reason for their relative unpopularity, the "relation back" rule, was abolished by the 1988 Act.[2] Under this rule, dispositions of a debtor's property within a specified period after he committed an act of bankruptcy could be declared void at the instigation of the trustee or assignee in bankruptcy. Because

---

[1]   50 & 51 Vic. c.57.
[2]   Section 44(2) and see para.5–51.

entering into a deed of arrangement is an act of bankruptcy,[3] dispositions of property in accordance with the deed by the debtor or his trustee, within the ensuing three months, could be struck down by the court. Thus, within that period, the trustee of the deed could not safely, without incurring personal liability, either get in or distribute any of the debtor's property. A complaint often made in the past was of unscrupulous and untrustworthy persons inducing debtors to designate them deed trustees and assigning assets to them for distribution among the creditors; such trustees would frequently make off with assigned property.

Definition and Form

3–04   A deed of arrangement includes,

> "… any of the following instruments ... made by, for or in respect of the affairs of a debtor for the benefit of his creditors generally ... that is to say:
>
> (a) An assignment of property
>
> (b) A deed of arrangement for a composition
>
> And in cases where creditors of a debtor obtain any control over his property or business:
>
> (c) A deed of inspectorship entered into for the purpose of carrying on or winding up a business;
>
> (d) A letter of licence authorising the debtor or any other person to manage, carry on, realise or dispose of a business, with a view to the payment of debts; and
>
> (e) Any agreement or instrument entered into for the purpose of carrying on or winding up the debtor's business, or authorising the debtor or any other person to manage, carry on, realise or dispose of the debtor's business, with a view to payment of his debts."[4]

3–05   Thus, the arrangement must be for the benefit of the creditors generally; this definition does not include, for example, an arrangement for the benefit of specified creditors with no option for the others to come in if they choose.[5] It has been said that a deed is for the benefit of the creditors generally if it "is one by which the debtor offers to make a settlement with the general body of his creditors and invites all to come in and to share the benefits of the deed. In such a case all creditors may assent or take the benefit of the deed, that is, are in a position to become beneficiaries under the deed, whether they actually do so or not".[6] It, therefore, is not necessary for the creditors to have agreed in advance to its terms. In applying the above definition, the courts strive for consistency with s.7(1)(a) of the 1988 Act.[7]

---

[3]   See paras 4–05 et seq.

[4]   1887 Act, s.4(2).

[5]   *Re Saumarez* [1907] 2 K.B. 170.

[6]   *Re Saumarez* [1907] 2 K.B. 170 at 178. See too *Re Lee* [1920] 2 K.B. 200.

[7]   *Lipton Ltd v Bell* [1924] 1 K.B. 701.

3–06 What happens in practice is that the debtor and his creditors meet to consider proposals for composition and, when agreement is reached on those terms, a contract or a deed is executed by the debtor and, where applicable, by a trustee. Unlike the position in England,[8] a majority of creditors cannot bind the others in respect of such arrangements; there must be unanimity.

3–07 There are two major types of deed. Under one, the terms on which the debts are to be discharged are set out and the parties agree that payments shall be made in accordance with those terms. Under the other, property is assigned to a trustee for those purposes; usually the debtor will assign most of his property to a trustee so that the latter can then make payment along the lines as agreed. Trustees appointed under deeds of arrangement do not possess the powers of a trustee in bankruptcy, but the terms of a particular deed may seek to confer comparable powers on the arrangement trustee. Where the terms of the arrangement provide for the creditors getting control of the debtor's business or property, they may be authorised to carry on the business or to wind it up. But "deeds of inspectorship" and "letters of licence", as such arrangements are called, are most exceptional these days.

3–08 There is no statutory form for deeds of arrangement, although certain standard forms tend to be used. A special form was prescribed by the Stock Exchange Rules for whenever a stock broker was "hammered".[9] New provisions were adopted following the Insolvency Act in Britain[10] but special provision has yet to be made for comparable circumstances in Ireland.

Registration

3–09 Unless it is duly registered, a deed of arrangement is void.[11] Registration must take place within seven days of the instrument being executed, but it is possible to get an extension of time.[12] The instrument must be duly stamped.[13] The registrar for bills of sale must be provided with the following.[14] He must get a copy of the instrument and of every schedule and inventory annexed to it. He should be given an affidavit verifying when this instrument was executed and describing the debtor's occupation, residence and place or places of business. There must be an affidavit by the debtor stating the estimated total amount of property and liabilities included in the deed, the total amount of the composition payable under it, if any, and the names and addresses of his creditors.

3–10 On application to the court, permission may be given to register the instrument after the seven days has expired if "the omission to register ... within

---

[8] Deeds of Arrangement Act 1914, s.3; now, Insolvency Act 1986, ss.4 and 5.
[9] Cf. *Tomkins v Saffery,* (1877) 3 App. Cas. 213. The last deed of arrangement registered in Ireland was by a stockbroker who was "hammered".
[10] Rules 960–985.
[11] 1887 Act, s.5 and e.g. *Re Lee* [1920] 2 K.B. 200.
[12] 1887 Act, ss.5 and 9.
[13] 1887 Act, s.6(2); stamp duty is as for conveyance.
[14] 1887 Act, s.6(1) and R.S.C. Ord. 82.

the time required ... was accidental or due to inadvertence, or to some cause beyond the control of the debtor and not imputable to any negligence on his part ...".[15] An application can be made to rectify some omission or misstatement on the register of deeds, on the same grounds. Any interested party can apply for an extension of time or for rectification. Where the court accedes to such application, it will impose "such terms or conditions as are just and expedient".[16]

COURT-SUPERVISED ARRANGEMENTS

3–11   Part IV (ss.87–109) of the 1988 Act provides for debtors reaching arrangements with their creditors and which are supervised by the High Court. The main advantages this mechanism has over that under the Deeds of Arrangement Act 1887 is that the mere commencement of Pt IV proceedings prevents execution from being levied against the debtor's property. Also such Pt IV schemes as a specified majority of the creditors agree on, and which secure the Court's approval, become binding on the remainder of the creditors. The 1887 Act does not apply to Pt IV schemes.[17] This mechanism resembles that under ss.201–203 of the Companies Act 1963 for reorganising companies.[18]

Petition for Protection

3–12   An insolvent debtor who is anxious to conclude some compromise with his creditors can apply to the court for its protection which, if acceded to, will prevent enforcement of several creditors' remedies against his property.[19] This application takes the form of a petition, setting out the "reasons for" the applicant's insolvency, and asking that he and his property be protected from the creditors.[20] The petition must be verified by an affidavit[21] and be supported by a further affidavit of the debtor,[22] giving particulars of and descriptions of his assets, an estimate of their value, an estimate of his liabilities, details of any proceedings that may have been taken by creditors to recover their debts, whether the debtor's solicitor has been paid any sums on account of the costs of the proceedings and, if so, the amount paid. If the proposed arrangement is to involve vesting property in the Official Assignee, €650 (ex £500) must be lodged with the Assignee along with such further sums as the court shall from time to time direct[23]; otherwise, €130 (ex £100)

---

[15]   1887 Act, s.9.
[16]   1887 Act, s.9.
[17]   1988 Act, s.109.
[18]   See generally, M. Forde & H. Kennedy, *Company Law in Ireland,* 4th edn (Dublin: Thomson Round Hall, 2008) at 406 et seq. For the comparable regime in the U.K. see generally S. Lawson et al., *Individual Voluntary Arrangements,* (Bristol: Jordons, 2007).
[19]   See paras 5–67 et seq.
[20]   Form No.26. Cf. *Re A.D.,* 63 I.L.T.R. 50 (1929).
[21]   RSC Ord.76, r.90(1).
[22]   RSC Ord.76, r.90(2).
[23]   RSC Ord.76, r.90(3); sums amended by S.I. No. 595 of 2001.

must be lodged and any such further sum as the court may direct. If two or more partners are seeking protection under these procedures, their affidavit must disclose their separate assets and liabilities, and these must be distinguished from partnership assets and liabilities.[24]

3–13 The 1988 Act does not indicate what criteria should be applied by the court when dealing with such applications other than, if the applicant is a member of a partnership, protection may be made conditional on all the other partners joining in the petition.[25] Protection usually will be given if the petition and supporting affidavit are in order, and there would appear to be assets which require protection or there are other grounds for making such an order.

3–14 Once an order for protection is made, the debtor must send to the Official Assignee a memorandum setting out his name and address, the date of the order for protection, the amount of his assets and of his liabilities, secured, partly secured and unsecured.[26] A duplicate of this memorandum must be filed with the Central Office of the High Court.

Scope of Protection

3–15 An order for protection from "any action or further process" has the following advantages for the intending arranging debtor. If at the time he is in prison for non-payment of debts, the court may order his release.[27] A bankruptcy summons cannot be served on him.[28] It is not clear whether protection extends to a petition being presented on a bankruptcy summons which has already been served on him, but it would seem that there is no protection in such a case. That was the position under the previous legislation; in *Re McVeigh*[29] it was held that the term "process" in this context means "a process in a suit for the creditor's exclusive benefit, and does not extend to a proceeding like a petition for adjudication in bankruptcy for the benefit of creditors in general, and under which the property is affected by the operation of the law, not by the act of the party".[30] What the arrangement machinery protects a debtor against is "every proceeding which may have the effect of preventing an equal distribution of his assets among his creditors".[31]

3–16 A judgment mortgage cannot be registered against the intending arranging debtor's property.[32] Nor can execution be levied by the sheriff against it,[33] except that, where the sheriff has already seized goods or has gone into possession of

---

[24] RSC Ord.76, r.90(4).
[25] 1988 Act, s.87(3). Cf. *Re Lore* (1889) 23 L.R. Ir. 365 and *Re Parrott* (1859) 8 Ir. Ch.391.
[26] 1988 Act, s.90(c).
[27] Section 87(6).
[28] Sections 87(1) and (4); compare *Re Dobson* (1859) 8 Ir. Ch. R. 391.
[29] (1880) 5 L.R. Ir. 183.
[30] (1880) 5 L.R. Ir. 183 at 187.
[31] (1880) 5 L.R. Ir. 183 at 188.
[32] 1988 Act, ss.87(4) and (5); compare *Re Lambe's Estate* (1869) Ir. R. 3 Eq. 305.
[33] 1988 Act, s.89; compare *Re R. C.* (1888) 21 L.R. Ir. 546 and *Re P.J.W.* [1896] 1 I.R. 44.

property, the execution creditor is entitled to be paid whatever sum the fruits of execution would have realized.[34] It is not clear whether granting protection invariably operates to put a stay on all proceedings being brought against the debtor; it would seem that, in order to block proceedings, the court should make a stay part of its order. In *Re Vahy*[35] it was held that the creditors must not resort to forms of self-help in order to safeguard the debtor's assets, and to do so is a contempt of court. When the petitioning debtor failed to attend a private sitting of the court, where his affairs were to be considered, his creditors appointed an accountant to take possession of his property. It was held that such action contravened the court's order because "protection against 'process' by creditors is at least equally inconsistent with their arbitrarily taking possession of the property for the purpose of administering it for their own benefit".[36]

3–17   A protection order also places restrictions on the debtor. Except for transactions in the ordinary course of his trade or business, or unless he gets the court's prior approval, he is prohibited from disposing of, parting with or pledging any of his property.[37] If he gets goods on credit, within fourteen days of the protection order being made, knowing at the time that he would not be able to pay for them, he may be obliged to return those goods or to pay for them in full;[38] the person who supplied those goods on credit can apply to the court for such an order.

3–18   It has never been established whether appointing a receiver and/or manager over the debtor's property, under a provision in a debenture or charge, constitutes "action" or a "process", for these purposes. The restricted interpretation given to the term "process" suggests that the answer is no, as does the fact that the 1988 Act's provisions in no place seek to override the interests of secured creditors. Whenever an order for protection has been granted, any creditor can apply to the court to appoint a receiver or manager over the debtor's business or property.[39]

Preliminary Meeting

3–19   Frequently the general outlines of a proposed compromise will be negotiated at informal meetings between the debtor and representatives of his creditors, before the requisite preliminary meeting and private sitting of the court take place. If it agrees to grant protection, the court will direct the debtor to call a preliminary meeting of his creditors to consider his circumstances. The object of such meetings has been described as "the investigation as to the representation of the trader as to his affairs, and the reasonableness of the composition offered upon the basis of such representations".[40]

---

[34]   1988 Act, s.89(2).
[35]   [1894] I.R. 335.
[36]   [1894] I.R. 335 at 346.
[37]   1988 Act, s.88.
[38]   1988 Act, s.103.
[39]   1988 Act, s.73 and RSC Ord.76, r.96.
[40]   *Re An Arranging Trader,* 2 I.L.T.R. 446 (1868).

3–20   Usually the preliminary meeting will take place at the offices of the debtor's solicitor or such other place as the court directs.[41] Sufficient time will be given to enable the Official Assignee to fix a time for submitting proofs and for ascertaining the debtor's liabilities.[42] Creditors must be given at least four days' notice, in the prescribed form,[43] of when the meeting is to take place, and the notices must state that the debtor will attend the meeting so that he can be fully examined regarding his circumstances and his proposals for arrangement.[44] To that end, he must present the meeting with a preliminary statement of his affairs, i.e. of his assets and liabilities.[45] Valuations of these should be realistic; for instance goods and chattels, such as stock in trade, should usually be valued on the basis of a forced sale, and care should be taken with the values to be placed on book debts. The debtor is required to take a minute of the proceedings at the meeting.[46]

3–21   Following this meeting and at least two days before the court sits to consider the compromise proposals, as described below, the debtor must provide the Official Assignee with the following[47]: a copy of the statement of affairs which was given to the creditors at that meeting, a copy of the minutes of the meeting's deliberations, including any proposals which were made at it, and a statement of affairs, in the prescribed form,[48] which must incorporate the debtor's proposals for settlement.

Statement of Affairs and Debtor's Proposals

3–22   The format for the statement of affairs is the same as that for bankruptcy proceedings.[49] There is a balance sheet, setting out the aggregate values of the debtor's various assets and liabilities, and there are also lists giving details of the following: unsecured creditors; creditors for rent, rates, taxes, salaries and wages; debts which are fully secured; debts which are partly secured; liabilities for which the debtor has not obtained any consideration; liabilities on bills discounted by the debtor; movable chattels; debts due to the debtor; freehold and leasehold property, whether or not mortgaged; annuities, government and other securities, stocks and shares in companies, fees, pensions and allowances and other like property; property in expectancy; books, papers, deeds, writing and other documents relating to the debtor's estate and effects or dealings. The statement of affairs must be sworn by the debtor and be signed by his solicitor.[50] There must be endorsed on the statement of affairs the debtor's proposals for an arrangement.[51]

---

[41]   Rule 92(1).
[42]   Rule 92(1).
[43]   Form No.27.
[44]   Rule 92(2) and (3).
[45]   1988 Act, s.90(a) and r.95(1).
[46]   1988 Act, s.90(a).
[47]   1988 Act, s.91.
[48]   Rule 95(3), Form No. 23.
[49]   Bankruptcy Rules, rr. 82 and 83, and Form No.23.
[50]   Bankruptcy Rules, rr. 82 and 83, and Form No.23.
[51]   1988 Act, s.91(a).

3–23   Precisely what kind of proposed arrangement will be agreed on depends on all the circumstances of each case. The scheme may involve payment of a single composition of a specified amount in the euro or the composition may be made payable in instalments; and one or more persons may be required to secure such payments.[52] Different percentages in the euro may be payable to different categories of creditors. According to the Bankruptcy Rules, the proposals may be in "such ... form as may be acceptable to his creditors".[53] These then set out the forms such proposals "may" take[54]; it remains to be seen whether the "may" here will be interpreted as an imperative or whether proposals can take a form other than one of those enumerated. If the "may" here permits other forms, then a scheme can provide for stocks, shares, bonds and other securities, and also real and personal property, being distributed in composition. In the past, schemes invariably involved payments of cash, or of bills of exchange or promissory notes, or partly in cash and partly in such bills or notes, and it is such schemes which are contemplated by r.91(2)(a).

3–24   Where the scheme involves bills of exchange or promissory notes, they must be secured to the creditors' satisfaction. Such instruments or any other security must not be signed by or enforceable against the debtor alone.[55] Completed bills of exchange and promissory notes must be lodged with the Official Assignee[56] and, to the extent that the composition is payable in cash, the requisite sums must be lodged with the Official Assignee.[57]

3–25   The proposed scheme may be for a "vesting" arrangement, meaning all or some of the debtor's assets being transferred to the Official Assignee,[58] so that they can be realised and the proceeds paid to the creditors. Proposals of this kind cannot be put before the court until the Assignee has consented to them; he can give or refuse such consent as he "thinks proper".[59]

Private Court Sittings

3–26   The next and critical stage in the entire proceedings is the "private sitting" of the High Court, where the proposals for the arrangement will be considered by the creditors and the Court. Provision is made for proving debts there.[60] Every creditor is entitled to attend or to be represented at this sitting.

Procedure

3–27   Notices of the sitting must be posted to all the creditors and must set

---

[52]   Cf. *Re An Arranging Debtor* [1935] I.R.733.
[53]   Rule 91(1).
[54]   Rule 91(2)(a).
[55]   Rule 91(2)(b).
[56]   Rule 91(2)(c).
[57]   Rule 91(2)(d).
[58]   Rule 91(3).
[59]   Rule 91(3).
[60]   1988 Act, s.92(5).

out the proposed composition.[61] Service of notices must be duly vouched at least two days before the sitting takes place.[62] Almost invariably, the debtor will be examined by the court, and he may be required to sign a transcript of the evidence.[63] Any witness produced by him may be examined, as may any creditor or person claiming to be a creditor; they too may be required to sign a transcript of their evidence.[64] The same procedure for summoning witnesses and enforcing their attendance applies in such proceedings as obtain in bankruptcy hearings.[65] Except for publication in a bona fide trade journal of particulars of such documents as are filed at the Central Office, information regarding the debtor's affairs or of the proceedings before the Court must not be published, without the sanction of the court.[66] Two requirements must be satisfied before any proposed compromise can be made binding on every creditor who got notice of the sitting.

Requisite Majority

3–28 The proposal must have obtained the support of the specified majority of the creditors who voted, in person or by proxy; this majority is three-fifths in number *and* in value of the creditors.[67] Creditors whose debts are less than €130 (ex £100) are not permitted to vote for this purpose.[68]

3–29 Votes of creditors who were offered a special advantage over the others for supporting the proposal do not count in its favour. In *Re C., An Arranging Debtor*,[69] where the majority in favour of the arrangement was extremely close, it was said that where a debtor "continued to purchase goods on credit at a time when he knew that he was quite insolvent, and that he would be unable to pay for these goods, ... it would not be proper that creditors, who had not suffered in this particular way, should, by a majority vote, carry a proposed arrangement".[70] Where the decisive votes for a proposed scheme are those of the debtor's spouse, absent specific evidence of improper motive, those votes count. In *Re. H., An Arranging Debtor*[71] where, but for his wife's support, the debtor would have failed by a considerable margin to secure a majority in value of the creditors, Maguire C.J. observed that "[s]he is entitled to vote and I cannot see why her vote should in effect be taken away by treating it as given for a wrong motive because of her position as the wife of the debtor".[72]

---

[61] Rule 93 and Form No. 28.
[62] Rule 93 and Form No. 28.
[63] Sections 92(3) and (4).
[64] Sections 92(3) and (4).
[65] Section 107.
[66] Section 99.
[67] Section 92(1)(a).
[68] Section 92(2).
[69] [1925] I.R. 14.
[70] [1925] I.R. 14 at 28.
[71] [1962] I.R. 232.
[72] [1962] I.R. 232 at 243.

Discretion to Refuse

3–30 Secondly, the proposal accepted by the requisite majority of creditors must get the court's approval. Unlike the position under the 1857 Act,[73] the 1988 Act does not set out the criteria which should guide the court in evaluating proposals the creditors have adopted. But it is most likely that the court will follow similar criteria, one of which is wide enough to cover practically every reasonable grounds for objection. This is that the proposal is not "reasonable and proper to be executed under the direction of the Court".[74] An extensive body of case law exists on what kinds of proposals have been regarded either as unreasonable or improper.[75] But the focus is on the terms of the scheme itself, not on the quality of the claims held by the creditors who voted for it.[76]

3–31 In *Re C., An Arranging Debtor*[77] the Supreme Court laid down the approach to be taken in ascertaining if proposals are "reasonable and proper" to be sanctioned. According to Kennedy C.J.,

> "… there must be some specific ground for rejecting an arrangement accepted by a majority of creditors, and … suspicion of impropriety is not enough … . [S]uch specific ground must be either that the arrangement would work a gross injustice upon the opposing creditors … or that it offends against the public policy to which the Court should look in exercising discretion in its bankruptcy jurisdiction, that is to say, that the Court should not lend its countenance to a transaction shown to be actually characterised by commercial immorality or dishonesty."[78]

3–32 It depends on all the circumstances whether proposals are oppressive to the opposing minority. In the *Re C.* case, that minority were the two largest creditors, who supplied the petitioner with tobacco for his retail tobacconist business in the years before the scheme was broached. Although he continued to trade after it became apparent that he was insolvent, those creditors did not extend any further credit from that time. Accordingly, they could not complain that he had engaged in reckless trading thereafter. There is no statutory minimum sum that must be paid by way of composition, although it has been held that "[t]he smaller the composition offered, the greater the onus of proving reasonableness".[79] There must be full disclosure to the court of all the significant features of the scheme. Consent was refused where a debtor first settled with a number of creditors and then went to court with proposals to settle with the remainder in respect of the balance owing. It was held that a scheme "which is intended to settle with the debtor's creditors ought to be brought before the Court as a whole and considered by the Court as a whole".[80] In one instance,

---

73 i.e. the Irish Bankrupt and Insolvent Act.
74 The Irish Bankrupt and Insolvent Act, s.353.
75 Many of these cases are analysed in *Re C.* [1925] I.R. 14 and *Re J.H.* [1962] I.R. 232.
76 *Re A Debtor (No. 259 of 1990)* [1992] 1 W.L.R. 226.
77 [1925] I.R. 14.
78 [1925] I.R. 14 at 18.
79 *Re Harris* [1918] 2 I.R. 570.
80 *Re Pilling* [1903] 2 K.B. 50.

where the debtor would not permit some creditors to verify the valuation that he placed on certain of his assets, the court withheld its approval because the case was "one which calls for the fullest investigation and inquiry".[81] Schemes have been rejected in England where they would leave creditors worse off than if the debtor were adjudicated a bankrupt.[82] But in one instance it was observed that there is no Irish authority to this effect.[83] There used to be a practice of rejecting schemes where the period for payment of the composition extended beyond one year.[84] Also, proposed compositions which were wholly unsecured used to be rejected.[85]

3–33 A proposed scheme will be rejected where the debtor's conduct seriously transgressed commercial morality. Thus, where two auctioneers, who had converted several of their clients' money for their own purposes, sought approval for a scheme, it was rejected by Hanna J. because their "business was carried on fraudulently, contrary to the principles of commercial morality, and ... their liabilities were not due to such misfortune or imprudence as an ordinary case the Court will overlook".[86] In *Re C.*,[87] by contrast, the debtor's acute insolvency resulted mainly from adverse trading conditions. It was held that his failure to keep proper accounts can cause the scheme to be rejected where the absence of accounts indicates dishonesty; but the scheme may be upheld where nevertheless the trader "made a full and honest disclosure so far as it is possible for him to do so."[88] A scheme will not invariably be rejected where the debtor's insolvency was due to "rash and hazardous speculations".[89]

Adjudicating the Debtor Bankrupt

3–34 If it does not approve of the proposals as agreed by the requisite majority of the creditors, the court has the option, "if it thinks fit", instead to adjudicate the debtor a bankrupt there and then in specified circumstances.[90] Under the 1857 Act, the court's discretion in this regard was not phrased as broadly; in the specified circumstances it was "lawful for" the court so to adjudicate. The more discretionary current phraseology suggests that adjudication should not almost invariably follow the court's rejection of proposals. But if the court decides to make the adjudication, it must cause a notice to that effect to be published in the *Iris Oifigiúil* and in one daily newspaper.[91]

3–35 One of the grounds for adjudication—where the proposed scheme "is not reasonable and proper to be executed" under the court's direction—has

---

[81] *Re Garton* [1922] 2 I.R. 179.
[82] Ex p. *Bischoffsheim*,(1887) 19 Q.B. 33.
[83] *Re J.H.* [1962] I.R. 232 at 241.
[84] *Re Maclure* (1873) I.R. 7 Eq. 176 and *Re M'.K & Co* [1930] I.R. 619.
[85] *Re Maclure* (1873) I.R. 7 Eq. 176.
[86] *Re McKeown* [1934] 1.R. 219, at 230–231.
[87] [1925] I.R. 14.
[88] [1925] I.R. 14 at 23.
[89] *Re E.A.B.* [1902] 1 K.B. 457, at 466–467; contrast Ex p. *Rogers* (1884) 13 Q.B.D. 438.
[90] 1988 Act, s.105.
[91] 1988 Act, ss.105(2) and 106(2).

been considered above.[92] The remaining grounds are as follows: where the prescribed documents have not been duly filed with the Official Assignee; where the affidavit grounding the petition for protection is "wilfully untrue" or the debtor did not make full disclosure of his affairs; where it appears that the debtor does not wish to make a bona fide arrangement with his creditors; where the debtor disobeys a court order against him in connection with the arrangement[93]; where the debtor was party to some "corrupt agreement" with his creditors to secure that the proposals would be accepted; where the debtor does not attend a private sitting of the court or any adjourned sitting; where at any such sitting the debtor's proposal, or modification of it, is not accepted or not approved, or is annulled by the court.[94] Where the proposed arrangement is being made by two or more members of a partnership in respect of their joint and several liabilities, the court must adjudicate both of them bankrupt if their proposals are not accepted.[95] It has been the practice, where an arrangement hearing has been adjourned into bankruptcy, to allow the petitioning debtor the costs of the proceeding; the costs are allowed to the extent that the work done was beneficial in the bankruptcy and, in exceptional instances, the debtor's general costs are allowed.[96] But the court has a discretion in appropriate circumstances to disallow all such costs.

3–36   Where the debtor is adjudicated bankrupt in these circumstances, all debts and claims already proved and entered shall be deemed to have been proved or entered in bankruptcy. But the court can order that the proofs shall be expunged wholly or in part.[97] On such adjudication, the Official Assignee is permitted to appoint a solicitor to have carriage of the proceedings and to advise him.[98]

Effects of Approval for Proposals

3–37   Once the proposed arrangement secures the court's approval, its terms are rendered "binding on the arranging debtor and on all persons who were creditors" at the date of the petition for protection and who had notice of the private sitting.[99] The arrangement does not legally affect creditors who had no notice of the court sitting[100] or post-petition creditors. Where the creditor has more than one category of claim, notice to him that refers to that category only was held in *Re Bradley-Hole*[101] to be sufficient notice, to render the scheme binding in respect of all categories of claim.

3–38   Formerly, dissenting creditors could levy execution against the arranging

---

[92]   See paras 3–30 et seq.
[93]   E.g. *Re Birt* [1906] 2 I.R. 452.
[94]   Cf. *Re C. & L.* [1937] I.R. 521.
[95]   1988 Act, s.106.
[96]   *Re McKeown* [1934] I.R. 219.
[97]   Rule 99.
[98]   Rule 100.
[99]   1988 Act, s.92(1)(b).
[100] *Re A Debtor (No. 64 of 1992)* [1994] 1 W.L.R. 264.
[101] [1995] 1 W.L.R. 1097.

debtor's property up to the time he got his certificate of discharge,[102] but that power would now seem to be precluded by the arrangement being "binding" on all.[103]

3–39 The scheme as adopted binds the preferential creditors who took part in the voting. It is possible that a preferential creditor might be permitted to vote against a proposed scheme while reserving his right to assert his preference should the scheme be adopted.[104]

3–40 Except to such extent as they participated in it, the scheme does not affect the rights of secured creditors vis-à-vis their security, and the debtor's property available for the scheme creditors is subject to all pre-existing rights and interests of third parties.[105] In contrast with the position in a bankruptcy, the 1988 Act does not stipulate the extent to which secured creditors who came into a scheme of arrangement lose their right to stand on their security. But it has been held that, where a scheme eventually is not carried out, any secured creditors who were parties to it become again entitled to enforce their security.[106]

3–41 Nor does the 1988 Act deal with the effect of approval of the scheme on third parties, such as co-debtors and sureties. Unless the scheme purports to do so, it was held in *Johnson v Davies*[107] that a term will not be implied into it to that effect as, albeit perhaps desirable, such a term is not necessary to give the scheme efficacy. But the question arises of whether a scheme is capable of having that effect at all. The earlier Bankruptcy Acts addressed this question in the case of discharge from bankruptcy, as does now the Companies (Amendment) Act 1990.[108] Even before then, in several Company Law cases involving schemes of arrangements approved by the court, it was held that the effect of such approval was not equivalent to the consensual compromise of a liability,[109] which does release co-debtors and sureties. Because the scheme under the legislation considered in *Johnson* was stated to be binding on every creditor "as if he were a party to the arrangement", it was held that this put it on the same footing as a consensual release.

3–42 Unless the terms of the scheme stipulate otherwise, the arranging debtor can continue to trade. Any debts incurred by him during that period are not payable out of the assets vested in the Assignee, which is one of the reasons why the court does not encourage lengthy periods for paying compositions.

---

[102] *Moran v Reynolds* (1868) I.R. 3 C.L. 353.

[103] 1988 Act, s.92(1)(b).

[104] *Re D.* [1927] I.R. 220 at 228, 234 and 239.

[105] *Hylands v McClintock* [1999] N.I. 28.

[106] *Re Campion* [1899] 2 I.R. 112.

[107] [1999] Ch. 117.

[108] See M. Forde et al., *The Law of Company Insolvency* (Dublin: Thomson Round Hall, 2008) at para.6–81.

[109] E.g. *Re London Chartered Bank of Australia* [1893] 3 Ch. 540.

Further Private Sittings

3–43   Provision is made for convening subsequent court sittings to consider adjustments to whatever arrangements as were adopted.[110] The same procedural rules apply to these sittings.[111] On the application of the debtor and where the court considers it "necessary and desirable to do so", it may convene a special sitting.[112] At that meeting, the scheme may be confirmed, altered or annulled. The majority required for such a decision is lower than that needed to adopt the scheme at the outset: it is a bare majority in value and number of creditors who have proved debts of a €130 (ex £100) or more.[113] Provision, however, is made for where comparatively few creditors attended the sitting. If less than one-third in number and value did attend, any decision taken by the bare majority regarding the scheme is not valid until it has been approved by the court.[114]

3–44   Additionally, at any time, on the application of the Official Assignee or any "person interested" in the matter, the court may hold a private sitting to investigate any question which it "considers relevant to" the arrangement.[115] The court can summon anyone and examine them about the matter.

Implementing the Scheme

3–45   Arrangements adopted under Pt IV of the 1988 Act can take a great variety of forms. Sometimes the Official Assignee will have no direct part in implementing whatever scheme was adopted. Even then the debtor is required to lodge with the Assignee, for the purpose of having it distributed, the funds necessary to pay expenses, fees, costs and preferential payments.[116] Also, if the proposal provides for any cash, bills or promissory notes, the cash and the completed bills and notes, and also the necessary funds to cover them, must be lodged with the Assignee.[117] At any time application may be made to the court for a direction that the Assignee shall possess and receive all or any part of the debtor's property.[118]

3–46   At times, the scheme will be a "vesting arrangement", in that all or part of the debtor's property is to vest in the Assignee with a view to it being realised and distributed to the creditors in accordance with the agreed terms.[119] Before such vesting can take place, the Assignee must have agreed to accept the debtor's property on those terms.[120] The court will then issue a certificate

---

[110] 1988 Act, s.95.
[111] See para.3–27.
[112] 1988 Act, s.95(1), r.94 and Form No.29.
[113] 1988 Act, s.95(2).
[114] 1988 Act, s.95(3).
[115] 1988 Act, s.104.
[116] 1988 Act, s.97.
[117] 1988 Act, s.97.
[118] 1988 Act, s.100.
[119] 1988 Act, s.93(1).
[120] 1988 Act, s.93(1) and r.91(3).

to the effect that the property has vested in the Assignee;[121] he then has all the powers in respect of such property as if it had vested in him following the debtor being adjudicated a bankrupt.[122] Such vesting entirely divests the debtor of any proprietary interest in those assets, even if it is clear that there will be a surplus on realisation which must be returned to him. In *Harrison v Ancketell*,[123] where it was held that the arranging debtor could not bring proceedings touching his assets which had vested in the Assignee, Porter M.R. observed that:

> "In the case of a mortgage, the mortgagor retains in equity all his property, subject only to the rights of the mortgagee. In the case of an arranging debtor, the debtor (by the vesting) parts with all he has, and retains and has nothing, till his debts are paid; that is, till a surplus is ascertained and paid, or reconveyed to him, or at least till he is in a position to call for such payment or conveyance. Till then, the assignees, and not he, are the owners; and their duties are precisely the same as in bankruptcy when once they have been ordered to realise. ... [Accordingly,] the possibility, or probability, of there being a surplus available for the debtor personally, after payment of all his debts, does not, till the surplus has been actually established, by full conformity, and by payment of all creditors, confer on the debtor any right whatever to maintain an action in respect of the estate vested in the assignees."[124]

3–47 Sometimes the Assignee's role in the scheme is to hold all or part of the debtor's assets as security for an offer which has been made.[125] In that case, the Assignee must have consented to being so involved in the scheme.

3–48 In a vesting arrangement, when the debtor's property is realised and the Assignee has sufficient funds to implement the scheme, the following must be presented to the court for its approval[126]: a report on the realisation of the estate, a list of the creditors admitted or to be admitted to proof, a copy of the debtor's relevant accounts and particulars of the expenses, fees, costs, preferential payments and dividends payable to the creditors. The court will then make "such order as it deems fit" for the distribution of the estate, defraying the various costs of the entire proceedings and paying off the creditors, taking account of the statutory priorities and the terms contained in the scheme of arrangement.[127] Where there are insufficient funds or indeed no funds to pay the creditors, the court will direct how the proceeds of realisation are to be distributed.[128]

---

[121] 1988 Act, s.93(3).
[122] Section 93(2).
[123] [1905] 1 I.R. 25.
[124] [1905] 1 I.R. 25 at 31 and 42.
[125] 1988 Act, s.93(1)
[126] 1988 Act, s.94(1).
[127] 1988 Act, s.94(2).
[128] 1988 Act, s.94(5).

Variation

3–49 Apart from its provisions on further private sittings, Pt IV of the 1988 Act makes no provision for varying the compromise, once it has been approved. Where the scheme contains a mechanism for its variation, it then can be varied in compliance with those procedures. Where there is no such mechanism, ordinarily a power to vary will not be implied into it. Notwithstanding, it was held in *Raja v Rubin*[129] that, as a matter of contract, all the creditors can agree between themselves to vary their entitlements. Further, even if there is not unanimity, where a particular variation would not prejudice the rights of some of the creditors, the other creditors may agree between themselves to vary their own rights. A partner of an insolvent solicitor agreed to waive the £60,000 owing to him if the other creditors would agree to an arrangement, which they did. When the insolvent acquired certain pension rights which appeared to be outside the scope of the arrangement, he proposed to vary it by making available those sums. All his creditors, other than his former partner, agreed to that, which it was held they could, as he wasn't prejudiced in the scheme by this change.

Default and Setting Aside the Scheme

3–50   Occasionally, the debtor will default in honouring his side of what was agreed. In that event, the court is not entitled, there and then, to adjudicate him a bankrupt; adjudication can only follow breach of some specific order of the court. In *Re Birt*,[130] where the debtor failed to pay instalments, due to inability to collect money owing to him, he was ordered to sign and lodge composition notes but refused to do so. It was held that little point would be served by attaching him for contempt; that instead "the right thing for the creditors is to turn the case into bankruptcy and realise the assets".[131] Breach of the agreed terms may cause the court simply to dismiss that petition for protection. That, in turn, could lead to an adjudication, because an assignment of a debtor's property to a trustee for the benefit of his creditors is an act of bankruptcy.

3–51   Breach of the arrangement's terms remits the creditors to their original rights. Where an instalment falling due has not been paid, the creditor is entitled to sue for the original debt.[132] However, the court may not permit a creditor to withdraw his proof and sue for his debt where that creditor supported the original scheme but then by his conduct compromised it.[133] Furthermore, where the creditor sues for his unpaid instalment, he is deemed to have elected his remedy and cannot then sue on the original debt.[134] Where there has been default in payment of any instalment, a secured creditor, similarly, is remitted to his original rights. A secured creditor's proof, which is filed for the purposes of the arrangement, is entirely contingent on the arrangement becoming effective.[135]

---

[129] [2000] Ch. 274.
[130] [1906] 2 I.R. 452.
[131] [1906] 2 I.R. 452 at 456.
[132] *Re D.* (1888) 21 L.R. Ir. Ch.281.
[133] *Re Barrington* (1878) 50 L.R. Ir. Ch.130.
[134] *Re Butler* (1878) 50 L.R. Ir. Ch.225.
[135] *Re Campion* [1899] 2 I.R. 112.

Where an arrangement has broken down and the debtor then petitions for another arrangement, a creditor can prove for the original debt in the second arrangement; but if he does so, he must give up all rights and securities he acquired in the first arrangement.[136] In an appropriate case, the court will relieve an arranging debtor's surety from liability to the creditors. But it is only in the most exceptional circumstances that a surety will be so relieved.[137]

3–52   Where the creditors' agreement to the scheme was procured by fraud, it will be set aside by the court, such as where one or more creditors were bribed to vote for the proposals[138] or some secret deal was done whereby one or some of them were to be paid more than the other creditors.[139] It was emphasised in *Cadbury Schweppes Plc v Somji*,[140] which concerned a statutory scheme where the procedures are somewhat different, that there is a strict requirement of good faith as between the competing unsecured creditors. Accordingly, where one or more creditors offered an inducement to one or more others to support a proposed compromise, that should be disclosed to all the creditors voting on the proposals. Because this had not been done, the court declared the settlement void. Apart from this type of consideration, it has been held that, once a scheme was confirmed by the court, it will not be set aside, "no matter how unjust it may appear to have been in the light of subsequent events".[141]

3–53   Nor does the debtor's subsequent bankruptcy upset the arrangement. As explained in *Re Bradley-Hole*,[142] once the scheme is adopted, the bankrupt's then assets are held in trust for the scheme creditors and no longer vest in him. Consequently, his then creditors' entitlement to be paid from the proceeds of these assets cannot be defeated by him subsequently becoming bankrupt.

Discharge

3–54   In the case of a vesting arrangement, the scheme is deemed to have been carried into effect when the court approved the scheme.[143] Any other type of scheme is carried into effect in the following manner.[144] In the case of a cash composition, the scheme takes effect as soon as the debtor has paid the Assignee the full amount of the composition, together with any expenses, fees and costs. In the case of a composition payable by bills and/or notes, it takes effect as soon as the debtor has lodged with the Assignee the completed bills, notes or other securities, together with any expenses, fees and costs. Where the composition is partly in cash and partly by way of bills or notes, the arrangement is complete

---

[136] *Re R.* (1888) 23 L.R. Ir. Ch.19; *Green & Sons Ltd v Gogarty* (1926) 60 I.L.T.R. 151.
[137] *Re An Arranging Debtor* [1935] I.R. 733.
[138] Ex p *Baum* (1878) 7 Ch. D. 719.
[139] Ex p *Milner* (1885) 15 Q.B.D. 605.
[140] [2001] 1 W.L.R. 615. See too, *Monecor (London) Ltd v Armed* [2008] B.P.I.R. 458.
[141] *Re Q.* [1923] 2 I.R. 89 at 91.
[142] [1995] 1 W.L.R. 1097.
[143] 1988 Act, s.96(a).
[144] 1988 Act, s.96(b) and r.97.

as soon as the cash, bills and notes are lodged, along with the expenses, fees and the completed costs and such further sums as the court may allow.

3–55   Exceptionally, a protection order will be discharged before the scheme is fully implemented. The debtor, with the consent of every creditor who had notice of the private sitting where the scheme was adopted, can apply to the court for an order discharging its protection.[145]

3–56   When a scheme of arrangement has been carried out, the debtor will want a certificate of discharge, which operates to extinguish his debts to every creditor who had notice of the scheme, in much the same way as the discharge of a bankrupt.[146] But the discharge of an arranging debtor has been held not to apply extra-territorially, in the sense of providing a good defence to a claim being brought in a foreign court by a creditor in respect of a debt which was incurred and made payable outside of Ireland.[147] In order to obtain the certificate of discharge, the scheme must have been fully implemented and the Official Assignee must have reported to the court to that effect.[148] But no such certificate will be issued if there was fraud.

3–57   In the event of there being a surplus in the Assignee's hands, the court will order that it be revested in or returned to the debtor, as the case may be.[149]

ARRANGEMENTS WITHIN BANKRUPTCY

3–58   Even where the debtor has been adjudicated bankrupt, a mechanism exists whereby he may make a binding arrangement to pay his creditors an agreed sum and thereby have the bankruptcy proceedings terminated. The 1988 Act describes this as a "composition after bankruptcy".[150] In order to have such a scheme rendered effective, it must obtain the support of three-fifths in number *and* in value of the creditors, and secure the court's approval. Making the payments in accordance with the agreed terms will result in discharging the debtor from bankruptcy.

3–59   This procedure commences with the bankrupt applying to the court for a stay on the realisation of his estate, pending consideration of his proposals for composition.[151] The court has a discretion as to whether a stay should be granted. If there is no reason for believing that the application is not a genuine attempt to reach a settlement with the creditors, then further distribution of the bankrupt's estate will be stayed for such period as the court deems appropriate.

---

[145] 1988 Act, s.101.
[146] 1988 Act, s.98; cf. *Carry v Harper* [1897] 2 I.R. 92.
[147] *Re Nelson* [1918] 1 K.B. 459.
[148] Rule 98 and Form No.30.
[149] 1988 Act, s.102.
[150] 1988 Act, s.38–41.
[151] 1988 Act, s.38.

3–60 A meeting of the creditors before the court must then be convened to consider the proposed composition.[152] The date of this meeting will be fixed by the Examiner, who will ensure that the Official Assignee is given sufficient time to deal with proofs of debt and to ascertain the bankrupt's liabilities.[153] At least ten days before it takes place, the bankrupt must have published a notice of the meeting in the specified form, in the *Iris Oifigiúil* and must post a copy of the notice to every creditor's last known address.[154] The Examiner may also direct that a copy of the notice be published in a newspaper or newspapers.[155] These notices must contain the details of what settlement is being proposed, and must state that a copy of the statement of affairs can be obtained from the bankrupt free of charge and that the bankrupt will be attending the creditors' meeting.[156] Copies of the statement of affairs which are sent to the creditors should have endorsed on them the terms of the offer of composition.[157]

3–61 The requisite majority for securing approval of the proposals is three-fifths in number *and* in value of the creditors, excluding all creditors with debts of less than €130 (ex £100).[158] Creditors may vote either in person or by an agent duly authorised in writing. They may accept either the original proposals or a modification of them. There are no hard and fast rules regarding the general terms of such composition, although the less in the euro being offered the less likely it will obtain the court's approval. But payment must be in money and not *in specie*. It may be in cash, payable either within one month or in such further time as the court permits, by instalment or partly in cash and partly by instalments.[159] No instalment shall be secured against the bankrupt alone.[160] The instalments can extend beyond two years, but the court is given an express discretion to refuse its consent for that reason.[161]

3–62 As is the case with arrangements under Pt IV of the 1988 Act, the Act does not set down the criteria against which the court should evaluate compositions assented to by the creditors, other than that schemes for payment which last longer than two years may be refused.[162] Presumably, the court will be guided by the same matters as arise in Pt IV cases. In *Re Harris*, Moloney L.J. observed that "there could be no hard and fast rule as to the amount of composition which might be accepted in a particular case, except that the sum should not be so small that no reasonable person would in the circumstances accept it".[163] A proposal for payment of one shilling in the pound was rejected, primarily because no statement of affairs was filed until five years after the

---

[152] 1988 Act, s.39(1).
[153] Rule 87.
[154] Section 39(2).
[155] Rule 85.
[156] Rule 85.
[157] Rule 86.
[158] 1988 Act, s.39(3).
[159] 1988 Act, s.40(1).
[160] 1988 Act, s.40(2).
[161] 1988 Act, s.40(3).
[162] 1988 Act, s.40(3) Cf. *Re Maclure* (1873) 7 Eq. 176.
[163] [1918] 2 I.R. 570 at 575.

debtor's petition for bankruptcy and the statement was inadequate. Having a statement of affairs filed is now required by the Act.[164]

3–63   Approval by the court of the proposed composition does not operate to discharge the bankrupt. Instead, the bankrupt or his personal representative must apply to the court for a discharge. The court will then consider a report made by the Official Assignee,[165] which should show that all costs of the bankruptcy proceedings and all preferential creditors have been paid, and that the agreed composition either has been paid to the creditors or was lodged with the Official Assignee. A discharge will be given if the requisite sums and securities were lodged with the Official Assignee.[166] But no discharge will be directed if there was fraud.

---

[164] Section 39(5).
[165] Rule 88.
[166] Section 41.

CHAPTER 4

THE BANKRUPTCY PETITION

4–01　The procedure for seeking to have a person declared bankrupt commences with presenting a petition to the High Court, which must point to an act of bankruptcy committed by the debtor within the preceding three months. The vast majority of petitioners are unsatisfied creditors. But an insolvent person himself can also petition to be declared bankrupt.

ACTS OF BANKRUPTCY

4–02　One of the principal differences between the law of personal insolvency and that of company insolvency is the concept of the "act of bankruptcy". Before a person can be adjudicated bankrupt he must have committed what is termed an act of bankruptcy. Unless the petitioner can point to such an act, which must have occurred during the three months before presenting the petition, adjudication will be refused.[1] These acts are all strong indicia of insolvency when they occurred; the one which is most frequently invoked is non-payment of a debt following presentation of a formal demand for payment. But it is not necessary for the debtor actually to be insolvent in order to have committed an act of bankruptcy. Conversely, the mere fact of being insolvent is not itself an act of bankruptcy.

4–03　Some of these acts require culpable action on the debtor's part. Because of the very serious consequences that result from adjudication as a bankrupt, the court requires strict compliance with whatever "act" the debtor is alleged to have committed. The only instance where a person can be made bankrupt without having committed one of those acts is where the court rejects proposals for an arrangement and proceeds to adjudication.[2]

Declaration of Insolvency

4–04　When a person petitions to be made a bankrupt himself,[3] his property secures the protection of the court, so that it can be equitably shared among all his creditors. On presenting such a petition, he is deemed to have made a declaration of insolvency[4]. Filing a declaration of insolvency in court is an

---

[1]　1988 Act, s.11(1)(c).
[2]　1988 Act, s.105 and see paras 3–34 et seq.
[3]　1988 Act s.11(3).
[4]　Rule 18.

act of bankruptcy,[5] even if the debtor does not intend to proceed with his own petition. The declaration, in the prescribed form,[6] must be signed by the debtor in the presence of a solicitor, who must explain to him its nature and effect.[7] That solicitor is required to witness execution of the declaration and to file an affidavit, in the prescribed form, verifying it.[8]

Assignment of Assets for Benefit of Creditors Generally

4–05   It is an act of bankruptcy where a person "makes a conveyance or assignment of all or substantially all of his property to a trustee or trustees for the benefit of his creditors generally".[9] In other words, where he transfers all or most of his assets to somebody with a view to having them distributed among all of his creditors, he is party to a deed of arrangement and thereby commits an act of bankruptcy. The objection to such arrangements is that, even if not so intended, their effect would be a division of his assets other than in accordance with the scheme for distribution laid down in bankruptcy law and under the court's supervision.

4–06   For a transfer to fall within this heading, it must be of "all or substantially all" of the debtor's property; it depends on the circumstances what constitutes "substantially all" for these purposes. Moreover, the beneficiaries of the arrangement must be his "creditors generally" i.e. all of the creditors or a class of creditors. But a transfer of assets for the benefit of just one or for some creditors may be what is termed a "fraudulent preference" or a "fraudulent conveyance", and would constitute an act of bankruptcy for that reason.[10] It is essential that an actual "conveyance or assignment" of the assets has taken place. Thus, the mere declaration of a trust or of some other form of arrangement for disposing of property is not sufficient.[11] Nor is an escrow sufficient, i.e. a deed of assignment which is to have postponed effect. But there is an effective transfer of property for these purposes once the escrow is ready to take effect.[12] It is not essential that the deed of assignment has been acted upon; it suffices once the deed is capable of being given effect, notwithstanding that it has not been stamped or has not been registered.[13]

4–07   While rendering a transfer of assets for the benefit of all creditors an act of bankruptcy would seem to discourage concluding a composition or a scheme of arrangement without resorting to the court, there is no such disincentive because of the estoppel principle. For any creditor who agreed to or who was a party to such an arrangement will not, for so long as the arrangement remains

---

5   1988 Act, s.7(1)(e).
6   Form No. 9.
7   Rule 17.
8   Rule 17 and Form No. 10.
9   1988 Act, s.7(1)(a).
10   See paras 4–08 et seq.
11   *Re Sparkman* (1890) 24 Q.B.D. 728.
12   *Turner v Hardcastle* (1862), 11 C.B. (N.S.) 683.
13   *Re Hollinshead* (1889) 58 L.J.Q.B. 297.

in force, be permitted to petition for bankruptcy on those very grounds.[14] Any creditor who acquiesced in the arrangement is so estopped. What constitutes acquiescence depends on the circumstances: for instance, being present at the meeting which adopted the arrangement and not voicing any dissent[15]; also, knowingly accepting any benefit or advantage from the scheme.[16] But assent or acquiescence which was secured through fraud or misrepresentation does not operate as an estoppel. The fact that a creditor acquiesced in such an arrangement does not preclude him from petitioning for bankruptcy on some other grounds. Actual parties to the arrangement, on the other hand, cannot so petition for as long as the scheme remains operative.

Fraudulent Conveyance

4–08　It is also an act of bankruptcy where a person "makes a fraudulent conveyance, gift, delivery or transfer of his property or any part thereof".[17] By "fraudulent" in this context is meant, not fraud at common law, but the intention to defeat or delay his creditors by attempting to put the property in question beyond their reach.[18] This particular "act" encompasses two categories of transaction. One is a fraudulent conveyance of property as contemplated by s.10 of the Act of 1634, entitled "an Act against convenous and fraudulent conveyances",[19] which prohibits various forms of transfers of land and of chattels which are designed to delay, hinder or defraud creditors.[20] This Act renders such transfers of property invalid, and such conveyances are often impeached at the behest of the transferor's creditors.[21] That the transferee paid consideration does not necessarily prevent a transfer of property from being fraudulent for these purposes.

4–09　This act of bankruptcy includes a transfer of any kind of property where the debtor intended to defeat or delay all of his creditors by preventing a distribution of his assets in accordance with the bankruptcy procedures.[22] The transfer can be of any part of the debtor's property, and it can be in favour of one or more persons. It depends on all the circumstances whether the requisite "fraudulent" intent, which does not even necessarily import moral blameworthiness, was present.

4–10　Regardless of the debtor's motives, a transfer by him of all of his property in consideration of an existing debt will be deemed fraudulent for these purposes, because no valuable consideration would have been provided and the effect would be to prevent the creditors generally from sharing in the proceeds of that

---

14　*Re S.* (1873) I.R. 8 Eq. 51 and *Re A Debtor* [1936] Ch. 728.
15　*Re A Debtor* [1939] Ch. 145.
16　*Re Brinkley* [1906] I K.B. 377.
17　1988 Act, s.7(1)(b).
18　*Re Sparkman* (1890) 24 Q.B.D. 728 and *Re David and Adlard* [1914] 2 K.B. 694.
19　10 Car. 1, sess. 2, c.3.
20　E.g. *Re Moroney* (1887) 21 L.R. Ir. Ch. 27.
21　See paras 7–12 et seq.
22　E.g. *Tomkins v Saffrey* (1877) 3 App. Cas. 213.

property. For instance, in *James v Moriarty*,[23] the defendant had lent the debtor money and later sought security for the loan. When the debtor agreed to give a bill of sale over virtually all his goods and chattels, and to assign all of his land as security, a further small sum was advanced; when these assignments were executed, a further, small sum was advanced. It was held that those transactions were fraudulent conveyances and constituted an act of bankruptcy. According to Fitzgerald J., "an assignment by a [person] in embarrassed circumstances of all his effects, or of all save a colourable part, to a creditor, in consideration of a pre-existing debt, is in itself an act of bankruptcy and void against the assignees in bankruptcy".[24] In the circumstances, the very small additional advances made to the debtor did not save these transactions from invalidity.[25]

Fraudulent Preference

4–11   Another act of bankruptcy is where a person "makes any conveyance or transfer of his property or any part thereof, or creates any charge thereon, which would under this or any other act be void" as a fraudulent preference if he were adjudicated bankrupt.[26] Certain dispositions of property are characterised as "fraudulent preferences". These are, making payments to or transferring property to one or to several creditors with the primary intention that their debt or debts shall be settled in preference to the claims of the other creditors.[27] Such transactions contravene one of the fundamental principles of insolvency law, which is that all general creditors should be treated equally. Again, it will depend on the circumstances whether the debtor's objective was improperly to prefer a particular creditor or creditors, although certain kinds of transactions carry a strong presumption of such intent. As is the case with fraudulent conveyances, not alone are fraudulent preferences acts of bankruptcy but, if they took place within a specified period before the debtor was made a bankrupt, the court will declare the transaction in question invalid and will order the creditor who was preferred to reimburse the insolvent estate.

Avoiding Creditors

4–12   A person who is avoiding his creditors in any of the following ways commits an act of bankruptcy, viz. "with intent to defeat or delay his creditors he leaves the State or being out of the State remains out of the State or departs from his dwelling house or otherwise absents himself or evades his creditors".[28] The debtor must have been deliberately evading the creditor or creditors so as to delay or to avoid paying them. The court will not readily presume such intent merely because the debtor left his home or went abroad. For instance in *Re Radcliffe*,[29] when the debtor's retail business failed and her health broke down,

---

23   (1874) 8 I.R.C.L.R. 454.
24   (1874) 8 I.R.C.L.R. 454 at 473.
25   Compare Ex p. *Izard* (1874) 9 Ch. App. 271.
26   1988 Act, s.7(1)(c).
27   See paras 7–29 et seq.
28   1988 Act, s.7(1)(d).
29   [1912] 2 I.R. 534.

she sold her stock and fixtures, paid most of the proceeds to a firm of solicitors so that it could be rateably divided among her creditors, then closed her shop and went to England where she got a job in a hotel. It was held that she had not the requisite improper motive. O'Brien L.C. observed that "[i]t would be a strange thing if, on these facts, the Court was bound to hold as an irrebuttable presumption of law, that when she left Ireland for the purpose of taking up a new situation, she left with the intention of defeating or delaying her creditors".[30] The question is one of fact, which is whether, in leaving, the debtor "had an intention of depriving her creditors of any remedy which they would have had if she had remained".[31] The answer depends on the entire circumstances of the case.[32] There is no authority on the meaning of "otherwise evades" his creditors, a concept adopted in 1988, although one which is implicit in the previous version of this act of bankruptcy.

Execution Levied or Attempted

4–13 Somewhat like for a petition to wind up a company on the grounds of insolvency,[33] it is an act of bankruptcy by a person where "execution against him has been levied by the seizure of his goods under an order of any court or if a return of no goods has been made by the sheriff or county registrar whether by endorsement on the order or otherwise...".[34] Where, under an order of a court or a *fi. fa.*, the sheriff seizes a debtor's goods, or attempts to seize them but there are no goods, an act of bankruptcy takes place. Where the basis for the petition is a return of *nulla bona*, the question arises whether that return can be impeached on the grounds that the debtor did indeed possess sufficient goods to satisfy the execution. Interpreting a slightly different formulation in the equivalent provision in Northern Ireland, it was held in *Re Alexander*[35] that the sheriff must at least have attempted to levy execution; that "for a return of no goods to be an act of bankruptcy [there] the return must be made after a genuine attempt to execute the writ".[36] McVeigh J. observed that "[i]f a bailiff by means of an execution which was a sham and a pretence brought about a false return of no goods it would be a startling and disturbing situation if the court were powerless to examine into its own processes and rectify the position of the parties concerned in accordance with the true facts".[37]

4–14 Since the sheriff is not the debtor's agent, payment of money to the sheriff does not satisfy the execution creditor's claim. That claim is only satisfied when the judgment creditor is in a position to maintain an action against the sheriff for money had and received in respect of the sum in question.[38]

---

[30] [1912] 2 I.R. 534 at 543.
[31] [1912] 2 I.R. 534 at 549.
[32] See *Re McClement* [1960] I.R. 141 at 150.
[33] Companies Act 1963, s.214(b).
[34] 1988 Act, s.7(1)(f).
[35] [1966] N.I. 128.
[36] [1966] N.I. 128 at 141. Cf. *Re Crossey* [1974] N.I. 1.
[37] [1966] N.I. 128 at 145.
[38] *Re A Debtor* [1979] 1 W.L.R. 956.

Bankruptcy Summons

4–15 The final act of bankruptcy, and the one most frequently relied upon, is similar to the statutory demand procedure prior to a creditor petitioning to have a company wound up.[39] This is where a bankruptcy summons, formerly known as a debtor's summons,[40] has not been satisfactorily answered: where "[t]he creditor ... has served upon the debtor in the prescribed manner a bankruptcy summons, and he does not within fourteen days after service of the summons pay the sum referred to in the summons or secure or compound for it to the satisfaction of the creditor".[41] Before it can be served, the creditor must apply to the court for the summons, which may be issued if he can satisfy the court on the following matters[42]: that a notice in the prescribed form[43] has been served on the debtor who presently owes at least €1,900 (ex £1,500),[44] that debt being a liquidated sum. Several features of these requirements are considered in detail below when discussing the creditor's petition for adjudication as a bankrupt.[45]

4–16 Although the bankruptcy summons and the former debtor's summons are not a process, in the sense of an action or a mode of enforcing judgments,[46] the summons is treated as a process for the purpose of an arrangement with creditors under Pt IV of the 1988 Act.[47] Formerly, the court's protection in such arrangements did not extend to a debtor's summons which was served prior to the protection order.[48]

Liquidated Sum Presently Owing

4–17 The petitioning creditor must be owed at least €1,900 (ex £1,500) by the debtor.[49] But two or more creditors who are owed less than this amount can apply for a summons, which may be granted if the aggregate sum they are owed

---

[39] Companies Act 1963, s.214(a).

[40] For an account of the history of this proceeding, see Moloney J. in *Re Murray* [1916] 2 I.R. 554 at 559.

[41] 1988 Act, s.7(1)(g). The comparable former English procedure, under the 1914 Act, is dealt with in M. Hunter and D. Graham, eds. *The Law and Practice of Bankruptcy* 19th edn (London: Stevens & Sons, 1979) at 29–40. But the two procedures are not identical. Chancellor O'Brien once warned, "[o]ne has to be cautious in applying an English authority upon a judgment summons to proceedings in Ireland on a debtor's summons": *Re A Debtor's Summons* [1917] 2 I.R. 417 at 420.

[42] 1988 Act, s.8(1).

[43] Form No. 4.

[44] Subsitution of € for £ sum by S.I. No. 595 of 2001.

[45] See paras 4–31 et seq. Note that a previous High Court blanket practice to require a return of "no goods"/ "*nulla bona*" for the issue of a summons has now been overruled ex tempore on appeal by the Supreme Court: *Gerald Harrahill v E.C.* [2008] I.E.H.C. 250, Dunne J.; and Supreme Court decision of February 20, 2009.

[46] *Re A Debtor's Summons* [1917] 2 I.R. 417 and *Re A Debtor* [1984] 1 W.L.R. 1143 at 1153.

[47] 1988 Act, s.87(4).

[48] *Re Kerr* (1877) 1 L.R. Ir. 67 and *Re McVeigh* (1880) 5 L.R. Ir. 183.

[49] 1988 Act, s.8(1)(a) and see paras 4–33 et seq. on aspects of the debt and the creditor. Subsitution of euro for pound figure by S.I. No. 595 of 2001.

exceeds €1,300 (ex £1,000).[50] The debt in question may have been acquired by way of subrogation or have been duly assigned to the petitioner. This debt must be "due to" the creditor, i.e. be presently owing as contrasted with being a future or a mere contingent liability. And it must be a liquidated sum, i.e. the amount owing must be readily ascertainable and its quantification must not be dependant, for example, on proceedings being brought in order to have the quantum owing determined. Thus, liability in tort cannot form the basis for a bankruptcy summons whereas liability under a contract generally suffices. The fact that a receiver by way of equitable execution was appointed over a part of the debt owing to the creditor does not render defective a summons claiming payment of the entire amount of that debt.[51]

Procedure

4–18   The procedure for issuing and serving a bankruptcy summons, set out in rr.10–15 of the Bankruptcy Rules, must be strictly followed. In *Re Moore*,[52] Walker L.C. observed that "[h]aving regard to the effect of a debtor's summons, it is right that the procedure prescribed for obtaining it should be strictly followed. A creditor passes by the ordinary procedure of bringing an action, and adopts this summary process, fraught with great consequences to the debtor, and also involving important consequences to all creditors or debtors of the debtor".[53] There a debtor's summons was dismissed because the creditor did not, as was required, state in his affidavit the particulars of the debt and the fact that payment had been demanded. In *O'Maoileóin v Official Assignee*,[54] following an exhaustive review of the authorities, Hamilton P. concluded that,

> "... the bankruptcy code, having regard to the consequences which flow from an adjudication of bankruptcy, is penal in nature and the requirements of the statute must be complied with strictly; that the debtor's summons ... must be served in the prescribed manner and the amount due in accordance with a judgment, when a judgment is relied on, must be accurate and a claim for an amount in excess of the amount due in accordance with such judgment would render the notice defective and a subsequent adjudication void."[55]

But not every deviation from the prescribed forms will invalidate a summons. In *Re Shiel*,[56] Walker L.C. held that "it is not necessary to follow literally the prescribed forms. It is enough if they have been complied with in substance and the debtor has not been misled".[57] There the debtor had been sent monthly

---

50   1988 Act, s.8(2).
51   *O'Maoileoin v Official Assignee* [1989] 1 I.R. 647.
52   [1907] 2 I.R. 151.
53   [1907] 2 I.R. 151 at 156, Cf. *Kleinwort Benson Australia Ltd v Crowl*, 62 A.L.J.R. 383 (1988).
54   [1989] 1 I.R. 647.
55   [1989] 1 I.R. 647 at 654.
56   [1910] 2 I.R. 399.
57   [1910] 2 I.R. 399 at 402.

statements of account from which, it was held, he should have easily been able to ascertain the nature of the debt.[58]

4–19   *Demand Notice:* The first step is serving on the debtor a notice, in the prescribed form, demanding immediate payment of the debt within four days.[59] Detailed particulars of the debt must be set out in this notice. It was emphasised in *Re Sherlock*[60] that a degree precision is required in the documentation grounding bankruptcy proceedings and that over-stating the sum owed was a substantial defect, as the debtor could not be expected to pay the sum demanded of him. In contrast, in England it has been held that the debtor should tender payment of the sum that it is actually owed and then apply to have the demand set aside because the remaining amount is disputed.[61] That was because the purpose of these demands is to activate the presumption of insolvency, and the best way to rebut it is to tender the sum which is actually owed. Where the debt is in a foreign currency, the demand may be made in that currency.[62]

4–20   No special mode of service is prescribed. Once four clear days have elapsed from when it was served, a copy of the summons should be filed with the Examiner.[63] Along with that copy, there should be filed an affidavit, in the prescribed form,[64] as to the truth of the debt, stating that no execution has issued and remains unsatisfied in respect of that debt; and all contracts, bills, notes, guarantees, judgments and orders referred to should be exhibited. Where the debt is in respect of costs owed to a solicitor, he is not required to wait for at least a month after delivering his bill of costs before serving the demand, nor is he required to have his bill first taxed.[65]

4–21   *Granting and Serving the Summons:* Application is then made ex parte to the court for a bankruptcy summons.[66] A summons in the prescribed form[67] will be issued to a partnership, a company, two or more creditors who are not partners, as well as to individual creditors.[68] Usually, the summons will be issued to the creditor's solicitor. The following information should be stated on it.[69] Detailed particulars of the debt must be endorsed on or annexed to it. But objection will not be allowed to those particulars unless the court considers that the debtor was misled by them. The summons must state the bankruptcy consequences of not paying the debt. And the debtor must be informed that, if he wishes to dispute the debt and to have the summons dismissed, he has fourteen days from the date of service to file an affidavit stating either that he is not duly

---

[58]   See too *Re Coyne* [1948] Ir. Jr. Rep. 27 and *Re a Debtor's Summons* [1936] I.R. 355.
[59]   1988 Act, s.8(3) and Form No. 4.
[60]   [1995] 2 I.L.R.M. 493.
[61]   *Re A Debtor (No. 490/SD/91)* [1992] 1 W.L.R. 507.
[62]   *Re A Debtor (No. 51/SD/91)* [1992] 1 W.L.R. 1294.
[63]   Rule 11(1).
[64]   Rule 11(1) and Form No. 5.
[65]   *Re A Debtor (No. 88 of 1991)* [1993] Ch. 286.
[66]   Rule 11(3).
[67]   Form No. 1.
[68]   Rule 12.
[69]   Rules 12(4) and 13.

indebted to the creditor or, alternatively, that before the summons was served he obtained the court's protection under Pt IV of the 1988 Act. The name and place of business of the solicitor issuing the summons should be endorsed on it; if a solicitor is not employed for the purpose, the summons should say that it was granted to the creditor in person, whose address in the State should be stated as well as an address where any notice the debtor might wish to give can be delivered. Where the creditor is based outside the jurisdiction, an address within the State at which payment can be made should be given. At the time of issue, a sealed original and copies of the summons, and particulars, must be filed with the Examiner.[70]

4–22 Even though all the formalities were complied with, the court is not obliged to issue the summons; a summons "may be granted" to a person who complies with the statutory requirements.

4–23 The summons must be served on the debtor within 28 days of its being issued.[71] Service must be personal, by delivering a sealed copy of it together with the particulars of demand. An extension of time may be granted if personal service cannot be effected within those days.[72] Where prompt personal service cannot be effected, the creditor may apply to the court for an order to serve some other way; for instance, by delivery to the debtor's spouse, to an adult member of his family or to an employee or partner. Application may be made for substituted or other service, such as by letter, advertisement or otherwise.[73] Every summons must be endorsed with the day and date of service, and every affidavit of service shall be in the prescribed form and state when this endorsement was made.[74]

4–24 *Dismissing the Summons:* The debtor may seek to have the summons set aside;[75] for instance, because he has duly tendered the amount owing or that no money is owed, or that there is a dispute about whether any money is indeed owing. The notice of application for a dismissal and grounding affidavit to be filed, in the prescribed forms, shall be served on the creditor not less than four days before the time fixed for the registrar to hear the matter.[76] If the creditor employed a solicitor then service on the solicitor suffices.

4–25 The court is given a general discretion to dismiss the summons and must do so "if satisfied that an issue would arise for trial".[77] Formerly the court could put a stay on the summons procedure, usually on the provision of suitable security, pending the trial of the validity of the debt claimed. But this option no longer seems to be available. It is likely that the court would let the summons

---

[70] Rule 12(4).
[71] Rule 14(1).
[72] Rule 14(1); *Re A Debtor* [1984] 1 W.L.R 353.
[73] Rule 14(1); cf. *Re Murray* [1916] 2 I.R. 554.
[74] Rule 14(2) and Form No. 3.
[75] 1988 Act, s.8(5).
[76] Rule 15 and Form Nos. 7 and 6.
[77] 1988 Act, s.8(5) and (6) and cf. Note in 123 *Cam. L.J.* 42 (2007) on where the debt is disputed.

stand where the dispute is only about the amount owed, provided it is clear that at least €1,900 (ex £1,500) is owing. What the court usually would do in such a case is to declare the amount which it found was due and then stay proceedings on the summons for a reasonable time so that the debtor has sufficient opportunity to pay what it was found was owing.[78] A summons will be set aside where there was a material irregularity in the form of the demand notice or in its service. But it will not be set aside merely because the debtor offers his creditor some security which it is contended was unreasonably refused.[79]

4–26   Because bankruptcy summonses are obtained by way of an ex parte procedure, the debtor not being present or represented, the applicant is obliged to inform the court of any facts in his knowledge which might tell in the debtor's favour. In *Ryley v Taaffe*[80] the Supreme Court emphasised the need for the creditor to disclose all material information. The affidavit, on which the summons was obtained, omitted to state that the creditor had secured the appointment of a receiver by way of equitable execution over the debtor's property. Kennedy C.J. found that this appointment and "the fact that sufficient time had not elapsed to permit effective action by the receiver, were matters which should have appeared in the affidavit ...".[81] Fitzgibbon J. came to the contrary conclusion, principally because a receivership is not a security within the terms of bankruptcy law.

4–27   In *Re D.*[82] the Supreme Court dismissed a bankruptcy summons because it found that the debtor had in fact tendered payment of the debt. The circumstances there were somewhat equivocal but Lavery J. expressed doubts as to "the necessity of a formal and complete tender to avoid an act of bankruptcy."[83]

4–28   Where the summons is based on a judgment, it was held in *Re P.*[84] that the bankruptcy court will even go behind the judgment, where there is evidence that it was obtained by fraud, collusion or a miscarriage of justice. According to Johnston J.,

> "... the Court ... can, in a case of this kind, proceed to investigate the circumstances under which the judgment was obtained for the purpose of discovering whether it was collusive or fraudulent or whether there had been a miscarriage of justice. This power [is] primarily as a protection for the other creditors of a debtor. Such persons might be seriously prejudiced by the debtor allowing a collusive judgment to be marked against him at the suit of a relative or a favoured creditor. The power may secondarily be resorted to by a debtor himself who is entitled to bring the matter before the Court for the purpose of showing that there was something in the nature of fraud on the part of the judgment creditor, or that there had

---

[78]   *Re Moore* [1907] 2 I.R. 151 at 158.
[79]   *Re A Debtor (No. 415/SD/93)* [1994] 1 W.L.R. 917.
[80]   [1932] I.R. 194.
[81]   [1932] I.R. 194 at 198.
[82]   [1962] I.R. 253.
[83]   [1962] I.R. 253 at 260.
[84]   66 I.L.T.R. 194 (1932).

been a miscarriage of justice, or that there was some equity in the debtor enabling him to raise a defence that he had not raised or that having raised, he had withdrawn."[85]

4–29 Even if all the requirements and procedures were strictly complied with, the court will dismiss the summons if it concludes that the bankruptcy mechanism is being used for an improper purpose: where the real objective is not to secure payment of a debt. An excellent example is *McGinn v Beagan*,[86] which concerned a situation that could have come out of *Faustus Kelly*.[87] Both parties had been involved in local government in Castleblaney; the plaintiff for many years as town clerk in the U.D.C., the defendant as a member of and also as chairman of the council's estimates committee. The defendant had run a garage and he also owned a farm but, when his garage business failed, he moved to an adjoining town, where he secured employment. For over three years he had owed a debt of £165 to a local firm, until they assigned it to the plaintiff for £100, who then took out a debtor's summons. A motion was brought to have the summons dismissed on the grounds that the plaintiff was motivated entirely by vindictiveness and was simply attempting to use the bankruptcy machinery in order to settle old scores. It transpired that there had been considerable friction between the two parties when they were involved in the U.D.C. For instance, on occasions, the plaintiff had obstructed the defendant from obtaining access to the town council's books and, at another time, had refused to give such access. On two occasions the plaintiff omitted the defendant's name from the list of local electors which, if that omission had not been rectified by the defendant, would have disqualified him from being re-elected to the council. Another time the plaintiff attacked the defendant publicly and eventually was forced by the County Manager to apologise. According to the defendant, the only reason why the plaintiff was seeking the summons was to have him adjudicated bankrupt, the consequence of which would be to disqualify him from re-election to the council. In the light of these circumstances, it was held that the debtor's summons was issued not in order to recover money and was an abuse of the legal process. According to Budd J., "[t]he proper purpose of bankruptcy proceedings is to make assets available to creditors" and he would "not allow the Court's processes to be used for an ulterior and collateral purpose ...". The proceedings had been brought for "improper reasons", which was not to recover the debt or part of it but to "make Mr Beagan a bankrupt and unseat him".[88]

4–30 Bankruptcy legislation is somewhat exceptional in that it authorises departure from the usual res judicata principle, by conferring a jurisdiction on the court to revisit its previous decision on any matter.[89] But this jurisdiction will not readily be exercised and, where an application to dismiss a summons has already been rejected, cogent new evidence is required to have the matter again

---

[85] 66 I.L.T.R. 194 at 194–195 and *Eberhardt & Co v Mair* [1995] 1 W.L.R. 1180.
[86] [1962] I.R. 364.
[87] *Faustus Kelly*, play by Brian O'Nolan (Flann O'Brien), 1942.
[88] [1962] I.R. 364 at 369.
[89] 1988 Act, s.135.

considered by the court.[90] The same constraints on admitting fresh evidence on an appeal do not apply; it is entirely at the court's discretion.[91]

Debt Not Satisfied

4–31   At least 14 days must elapse from the date of the bankruptcy summons being served, to provide the debtor with a last opportunity to come to terms with his creditor. If by then the debt has not been paid or, alternatively, if it has not been satisfactorily secured or compounded, then the debtor is deemed to have committed an act of bankruptcy.[92]

CREDITOR'S PETITION

4–32   For a creditor's petition to adjudicate a bankrupt to be entertained, the following must be satisfied.[93] The debtor must have the necessary contacts with the State for the court to exercise its jurisdiction. He must owe the petitioning creditor a liquidated sum amounting to at least €1,900 (ex £1,500). The act of bankruptcy, on which the petition is based, must have occurred within three months of the petition having been presented; for instance, within three months prior to that time the debtor must have failed to pay the debt referred to in a bankruptcy summons. On being satisfied that these requirements have been complied with, the court will adjudicate the debtor bankrupt.[94] However, he then has a brief period within which he may contest the validity of that adjudication.[95] Unless its order has been set aside, the court will set a date for the "statutory sitting" and will cause notices to be published of that hearing.[96]

The Debtor

4–33   Not every kind of debtor comes within the bankruptcy jurisdiction, although many categories who were once excluded are no longer so. Aliens as well as citizens can be adjudicated bankrupt, provided that they possess the requisite contacts with the State. These contacts are that the debtor is domiciled in or is ordinarily resident in the State, or that he carries on a business in the State either personally or through an agent or in partnership, or else that he possesses a dwelling, home or a place of business there.[97] Since 1872, non-traders came within the bankruptcy jurisdiction[98] as, since 1957, did married women who were not traders.[99] Infants can be made bankrupt but only in respect of debts which they

---

90   *Re A Debtor (No. 32/SD/91)* [1993] 2 All E.R. 991.
91   *Re A Debtor (No. 32/SD/91)* [1993] 2 All E.R. 991.
92   1988 Act, s.7(1)(g).
93   1988 Act, s.11(1).
94   1988 Act, s.14(1).
95   1988 Act, s.16.
96   1988 Act, s.17.
97   1988 Act, s.11(1)(d), and see paras 11–04 et seq.
98   Bankruptcy (Ireland) (Amendment) Act 1872 (12 & 13 Vic. c.107), s.17.
99   Cf. Married Women's Status Act 1957, s.17(2); *Re Long* [1905] 2 I.R. 343 and *Re Somers* [1930] I.R. 1.

are legally obliged to pay, such as for necessaries and unpaid taxes.[100] There are special provisions for the estates of persons dying insolvent.[101] Members of the Oireachtas are not immune from the bankruptcy jurisdiction[102] and, waiver aside, the immunity of diplomatic agents is not complete.[103]

The Creditor

Several aspects of the creditor also call for attention.

Assignee

4–34 A person can become a creditor for these purposes by taking an assignment of another's debt.[104] Since 1877, absolute assignments can be made of debts by the assignor executing a written instrument of assignment and notifying the debtor of that fact. Where the assignor is a registered company, the instrument must either be under the company's common seal or else be by an attorney appointed for this purpose under the seal.[105] An assignment in writing of part of a debt was not rendered fully effective in 1877, so that an equitable assignee cannot enforce the debt or petition for the debtor's bankruptcy without joining the assignor as a party. This somewhat anomalous rule has survived the fusion of law and equity, although it has been held not to apply to a petition to wind up a company.[106] In *Coulter v Chief Constable*[107] it was held that a sufficient equitable assignment occurred, where a debt was owed to the Chief Constable of a county, who then retired, and the statutory demand was made on the instructions of his successor. The retired officeholder did not hold the benefit of the judgment debt personally for himself but held it in trust either for his successor or for those who funded the police service.

Subrogation

4–35 A person also can become a creditor by way of being subrogated for another creditor.[108] While there does not appear to be any reported authority on the matter, it would seem that creditors by subrogation are entitled to petition for their debtor's bankruptcy. At least, the courts have permitted such creditors to petition to have companies wound up.[109]

---

[100] *Re Mead* [1916] 2 I.R. 285 and *Re A Debtor* [1950] 1 Ch. 282.
[101] See paras 10–31 et seq.
[102] Cf. 1872 Act, s. 40 and *Re Hazleton* [1915] 2 I.R. 425.
[103] Vienna Convention on Diplomatic Relations, art.31(1)(c).
[104] See generally M. Smith, *The Law of Assignment,* (Oxford: O.U.P., 2007).
[105] *Re A Debtor's Summons* [1929] I.R. 139.
[106] *Perak Pioneer Ltd v Petroliam Bhd.* [1986] A.C. 849.
[107] [2004] 1 W.L.R. 1425.
[108] See generally C. Mitchell and S. Watterson, *Subrogation, Law and Practice,* (Oxford: O.U.P., 2007).
[109] *Re Healing Research Trustee Co Ltd* [1991] B.C.L.C. 716.

Receiver

4–36   Whether a receiver appointed over the creditor's assets can petition to have that creditor's debtor adjudicated bankrupt depends on the receiver's very terms of appointment: whether he was actually conferred with authority to sue for the debt. A receiver appointed by the court to wind up a partnership has been held to be a good petitioning bankruptcy creditor.[110]

Secured Creditor

4–37   For the purposes of the 1988 Act, a secured creditor is "any creditor holding any mortgage, charge or lien on the debtor's estate or any part thereof as security for a debt due to him".[111] Getting an order appointing a receiver by way of equitable execution over the debtor's assets does not render one a secured creditor.[112] That the debt is fully secured is not a bar to an adjudication being made[113] but, depending on the circumstances, may justify putting a stay on proceedings.[114] The particulars of the security must be set out in the secured creditor's bankruptcy petition and two options are given.[115] One is for the petitioner to state that he is willing to give up his security in the event of an adjudication being made. Alternatively, he may give an estimate of the value of his security; provided it is genuine and not an entire sham, his estimate will not be impeached by the court. His debt then for the purposes of the petition will be the difference between this estimate and the amount owing to him. Following the adjudication, the Official Assignee is entitled to call on him to give up his security on payment to him of the amount estimated.[116]

4–38   A secured creditor who does not disclose his security will have his petition dismissed or, where granted, subsequently annulled. However, the court may permit the petition or adjudication to stand, for instance, if the security is virtually worthless or if the omission to disclose it was due to inadvertence.[117] Here, the court has a wide discretion but it will not condone what the petitioner has done if the debtor or other creditors stand to suffer any injustice. In one instance where, acting on legal advice that he was not a secured creditor, which in the event was wrong, the petitioner did not make formal disclosure of a valuation, the court declined to set aside the bankruptcy proceedings. In the circumstances, it was held that there was "nothing unfair in the petitioning creditor's attitude, no attempt to get paid twice, no withholding of assets from other creditors, no concealment of facts from the debtor or from the Court".[118]

---

[110] *Re Macoun* [1904] 2 K.B. 700.
[111] Section 3(1).
[112] *Ryley v Taaffe* [1932] I.R. 194.
[113] *Zandfarid v Bank of Credit & Commerce Int'l SA* [1996] 1 W.L.R. 1420.
[114] Cf. *Re Bula Ltd* [1990] 1 I.R. 440.
[115] 1988 Act, s.11(2).
[116] 1988 Act, s.11(2).
[117] *Re Small* [1934] Ch. 541.
[118] *Re A Debtor* [1977] 3 All E.R. at 496.

The Revenue

4–39   The Collector General is authorised by s.999 of the Taxes Consolidation Act 1997 to sue out a debtors' summons and to present a bankruptcy petition in respect of any tax or duty he is empowered to collect or levy. Revenue debts from other EC Member States are now recoverable, and the question arises whether the authority in s.999 of that Act extends to those debtors.

The Debt

4–40   To obtain a bankruptcy summons or an adjudication of bankruptcy, the applicant or petitioner, as the case maybe, must be owed an enforceable debt. Usually the debt will be based on contract but it also can derive from statute, such as liquidated sums due under employment legislation and unpaid taxes, rates and other levies due under fiscal legislation.[119] Some features of the debt call for attention at this stage. Other aspects are dealt with when considering what debts can be "proved" in bankruptcy,[120] but not every debt which can be so proved can form the basis for a bankruptcy summons or petition.

Liquidated Sum

4–41   A bankruptcy summons will be issued and a bankruptcy petition will be granted only where the debt in question is a liquidated sum. That is to say, it must be possible at the time to ascertain the full amount which is owed; it should not be necessary to await judgment by the court to determine the quantum payable. Accordingly, a claim in tort does not give rise to a debt for these purposes nor, it has been held, are claims under a contract which embody a penal element.[121]

€1,900 (ex £1,500) Threshold

4–42   For 116 years all that needed to be owed to the applicant for a bankruptcy summons and to a petitioning creditor was £40; in 1988 this was increased to £1,500,[122] and with effect from January 1, 2002 altered to €1,900. [123] If the proceedings are being brought by two or more creditors jointly, the threshold for the bankruptcy summons is that their aggregate debts amount to at least €1,300 (ex £1,000);[124] but for the bankruptcy petition that aggregate must amount to at least €1,900 (ex £1,500).[125] The 1988 Act does not say whether the value of any right the debtor has to counter-claim or to set off against the creditor must be deducted from the debt for the purpose of reckoning this threshold.[126]

---

119   *Re McGreavey* [1950] 1 Ch. 269.
120   See paras 8–02 et seq.
121   *Re A Debtor* (1962) 106 Solicitors' Journal and Reporter 468.
122   1988 Act, s.11(1)(a).
123   Bankruptcy Act 1988 (Alteration of Monetary Limits) Order 2001 (S.I. No. 595 of 2001).
124   Bankruptcy Act 1988, s.8(2).
125   Bankruptcy Act 1988, s.11(1)(a).
126   Cf. s.1(1) of the English 1914 Act and *Re A Debtor* [1984] 1 W.L.R. 353.

Legally Enforceable Debt

4–43   The sum owing to the petitioner must be a legally enforceable debt. Liabilities which contravene statutory provisions or public policy, such as commitments in breach of exchange control and claims by revenue authorities in countries outside the E.C.,[127] are not debts for these purposes. A liability incurred by an infant, accordingly, is not such a debt unless it was in respect of necessaries. In *Re Mead*,[128] where the applicant had previously obtained judgment against the respondent for money owed for the sale of a horse, the court dismissed a debtor's summons in respect of that sum because, on the evidence, the horse was not a necessity and the debt was unenforceable under the Infants Relief Act.[129] Ronan J.L. observed that, "[i]f a judgment is produced in bankruptcy proceedings, the Court of Bankruptcy has no power to set it aside, but it may look into the circumstances to see whether or not there is any real debt behind it, and if there is not, the Court will not adjudicate in respect of it".[130] The question of the debt being for necessaries had not been determined by the court of trial.

4–44   The application also can be resisted where the debt is statute barred. Where costs to be taxed were awarded in legal proceedings, which are statute barred once six years expired after the order (a judgment) "became enforceable"; in *Chohan v Times Newspapers Ltd*[131] it was held that this means six years from the date of their certification. This was because the word "enforceable" here means enforceable in a particular manner. It is only at the time that the costs are certified that they become enforceable in law: "the order becomes enforceable ... only when the costs are quantified".[132]

Debt "Due" or "Owing"

4–45   The debt in question must be "due" to the applicant before a bankruptcy summons will be issued[133] and, while there does not seem to be any authority on the matter, it would appear that the debt has to be payable there and then. To present a bankruptcy petition, the debt must be "owing" to the petitioner.[134] Under the 1872 Act, that debt need not have been "payable at a certain time".[135] The 1988 Act contains no comparable provision and the better view would seem to be that the debt must be payable at the very time payment was demanded and not at some time in the future. In contrast with the position since 1908 for winding-up companies,[136] a bankruptcy petition cannot be based on a contingent

---

[127] *Re Gibbons* [1960] Ir. Jur. Rep. 60 and *Government of India v Taylor* [1955] A.C. 491. Intra-EC revenue debts are now legally enforcible.
[128] [1916] 2 I.R. 285.
[129] 37 & 38 Vict. c.62.
[130] [1916] 2 I.R. at 295.
[131] [2001] 1 W.L.R. 184.
[132] [2001] 1 W.L.R. 184 at 189.
[133] 1988 Act, s.8(1)(a).
[134] 1988 Act, s.11(1)(a).
[135] 1872 Act, s.21 (final paragraph).
[136] Now Companies Act 1963, s.215.

debt or liability.[137] As in applications to wind up companies, if there is a dispute about whether the debt is owing, or if the debtor has a cross-claim or a claim to a set-off, this requirement is not satisfied.[138] However, there must be some real basis for his dispute or claim; it should not be fanciful.

4–46 Where the petitioner or applicant for a bankruptcy summons is the Revenue, the tax debt is not due and owing until the assessment for the taxpayer has become final and conclusive and the requisite demand has been made.[139] Ordinarily, the adequacy or accuracy of assessments may not be challenged in the bankruptcy court but must be pursued through the normal appeal system.[140] In a recent instance however,[141] a petition based on V.A.T. liability was not the respondent's personal debt but the indebtedness of a company he owned and controlled. Rather than adjourn the petition until the dispute about whose liability it was could be resolved, the court deemed it preferable not to make the adjudication.

4–47 Notwithstanding principles of res judicata and issue estoppel, even where the debt is founded on a judgment, the bankruptcy court has jurisdiction to go behind that judgment and ascertain whether there really was the indebtedness.[142] As was stated in *Eberhardt & Co v Mair*, "[i]t has long been established that the bankruptcy court has a power and indeed a duty to ensure that a bankruptcy is not instituted in circumstances which amount to injustice and has exercised the power to enquire into the consideration for a petitioning debt even to the extent of going behind judgments".[143]

Act of Bankruptcy

4–48 The petition must be founded on one or other of the acts of bankruptcy which were considered above. The act being relied on must have occurred within the three months preceding presentation of the petition.[144] Where that act is non-payment on a bankruptcy summons, the petitioner does not have to be the same person as the one in whose favour that summons was issued although, generally, he would be the same person.

Abusing Right to Petition

4–49 While generally it is not an actionable wrong to institute legal proceedings without reasonable or probable cause, one of the exceptions to this is to present

---

[137] Cf. *Glenister v Rowe* [1999] 3 W.L.R. 716.
[138] E.g. *Ashworth v Newnote Ltd* [2007] B.P.I.R. 102 and *Chan Sui v Appasamy* [2008] B.P.I.R. 18.
[139] *Criminal Assets Bureau v Hunt* [2003] 2 I.R. 168.
[140] *Owen v H.M.Revenue* [2008] B.P.I.R. 164.
[141] *H.M.Revenue v Potter* [2008] B.P.I.R. 1033.
[142] *Re P.*, 66 I.L.T.R. 194 (1932) and see para.4–28.
[143] [1995] 1 W.L.R. 1180 at 1186.
[144] 1988 Act, s.11(1)(c).

a bankruptcy petition against a trader who is solvent. The position has been explained by Bowen L.J. as follows:

> "... [A]lthough [bringing] an action does not give rise to an action for malicious prosecution, inasmuch as it does not necessarily or naturally involve damage, there are legal proceedings which do necessarily and naturally involve that damage; and when proceedings of that kind have been taken falsely and maliciously, and without reasonable or probable cause, then, inasmuch as an injury has been done, the law gives a remedy. Such proceedings [include] a bankruptcy petition against a trader. In the past when a trader's property was touched by making him a bankrupt in the first instance, and he was left to get rid of the misfortune as best he could, of course he suffered a direct injury as to his property. But a trader's credit seems ... to be as valuable as his property, and the present proceedings in bankruptcy, although they are dissimilar to proceedings in bankruptcy under former Acts, resemble them in this, that they strike home at a man's credit and therefore ... the false and malicious presentation, without reasonable and probable cause, of a bankruptcy petition against a trader ... gave rise to an action for malicious prosecution."[145]

It remains to be seen whether this principle applies where the debtor was insolvent and, also, whether it will be extended to bankruptcy proceedings that were instituted against non-traders.[146]

Procedure

4–50   The procedures to be followed when seeking to have one adjudicated bankrupt are set out in rr.19–32 of the Bankruptcy Rules.

Filing Petition and Affidavit

4–51   The originating document is a petition grounded by an affidavit, along with an affidavit proving the bankruptcy summons if that was the relevant act of bankruptcy. These will be retained by the Examiner, who will endorse on them the time of filing and the date appointed for the court hearing.

4–52   The petition, in the prescribed form,[147] must state[148] "the nature and amount of the debt", and it must show that the debt has not been paid, secured or compounded; in other words, that the debt is still outstanding. It must recite the particular act of bankruptcy by the debtor which is being relied upon. It must state that the debtor has the requisite connection with the State, which gives the court its jurisdiction. It must state that the petitioner, at his expense, undertakes to advertise notices of the adjudication and the statutory sitting as directed by the court. Finally, it must state that the petitioner indemnifies

---

[145] *Quartz Hill Consolidated Gold Mining Co v Eyre* (1883) 11 Q.B.D. 674 at 691.
[146] Cf. *Doreen Ltd v Suedes (Ireland) Ltd* [1982] I.L.R.M. 126.
[147] Form No.11.
[148] Rule 19.

the Official Assignee with regard to such costs, fees and expenses as are allowed by the court.[149] A notice of the date fixed by the Examiner for the hearing will be endorsed on the petition.[150] The petition must be signed by the petitioning creditor or creditors if there are more than one. Where they are partners, the signature of one partner suffices.[151] Where the petitioner is a limited company or other body corporate, the petition must bear the company seal and be signed by either two directors or by one director and the secretary; and the seal and signatures must be attested.[152] Special provisions in the petitioner's articles of association regarding affixing the seal must also have been complied with.[153] Usually, the petition will also be signed by the creditor's solicitor. If it is not co-signed by a solicitor, it cannot be filed until the petitioner identifies himself sufficiently to the Examiner.[154] The petition must be verified by an affidavit.

4–53 This affidavit, in the prescribed form,[155] must prove the debt owing to the petitioner and also the debtor's act of bankruptcy.[156] Where that act was non-compliance with a bankruptcy summons, the affidavit must state that the debt has not been secured or compounded. Where the debt giving rise to the petition is for money lent by or interest owing to a money-lender, the affidavit must state the particulars set out in s.16(2) of the Moneylenders Act 1933.[157] The petitioner must swear that, to the best of his knowledge and belief, the allegations contained in the petition are true.[158]

4–54 On presenting a bankruptcy petition, the creditor must lodge €650 (ex £500) with the Official Assignee to cover the latter's costs, fees and expenses; and the Assignee's receipt for the deposit must be given to the Examiner.[159] Directions may be given by the court for additional sums to be lodged with the Assignee.

Serving the Petition

4–55 A copy of the petition, containing a notice of the date fixed for the hearing, must be served on the debtor not less than seven days before the date appointed for the bankruptcy hearing.[160] Service must be personal, by showing the debtor the sealed original and giving him a copy. However, the court is given a broad discretion to direct some substituted manner of service.[161] At least two clear days before the hearing, an affidavit of service must be lodged with the Examiner.

---

[149] Cf. r.23.
[150] Rule 32.
[151] Rule 20(1).
[152] Rule 20(2).
[153] *Re Hussey* (Hamilton P., September 23, 1987).
[154] Rule 22.
[155] Form No. 12.
[156] Rule 21.
[157] *Re McNeela and Kilkenny,* (Hamilton P., September 23, 1987).
[158] Rule 28.
[159] Rule 29; S.I. No. 595 of 2001.
[160] Rule 25.
[161] *Bank of Ireland v D.H.* [2000] 2 I.L.R.M. 408.

Adjudication

4–56 The Examiner determines when the petition will be heard.[162] At that time the court will determine whether, in the circumstances, the debtor should be adjudicated bankrupt. It may adjourn the hearing, for instance, to hear objections regarding the claimed indebtedness, or to give the debtor a final opportunity to pay off or come to terms with his creditors. If he pays off the petitioning creditor, one or more of his other creditors may wish to take over the petition.

4–57 On being adjudicated, a copy of the order must be served on the bankrupt.[163] Service of this copy order is done by the Bankruptcy Inspector or by one of his assistants, who must then swear an affidavit of service and file it with the Examiner.

Appointing Receiver and Manager

4–58 One consequence of adjudication is that almost all of the bankrupt's property thereupon becomes vested in the Official Assignee.[164] However, the Assignee or the petitioning creditor may be concerned about the immediate possession and management of that property; it may, for instance, be some wasting asset or the bankrupt's business. At any time after adjudication, the court may appoint a receiver or manager of all or part of the bankrupt's property, who can then take immediate possession of it and, if it is a business, manage it for the time being. An application for such appointment must be supported by an affidavit.[165] The court will fix the receiver's or manager's remuneration, in respect of which he cannot exercise a lien; and he must submit his accounts for examination to the Official Assignee.[166]

Showing Cause

4–59 Following adjudication, an opportunity is given to the bankrupt to come to court to show cause why his adjudication should be annulled.[167] In order to show cause, between three and fourteen days of being served with the order of adjudication, as the court directs, the bankrupt must lodge with the Examiner a notice of his intention to make such application, together with an affidavit.[168] The notice, in the prescribed form,[169] must stipulate that the alleged grounds for adjudication did not in fact obtain. The affidavit must set out in detail the grounds on which it is said that the adjudication is invalid. When these are filed, the Examiner will fix a time for hearing the application. The bankrupt must then serve on the petitioning creditor or his solicitor and also on the Official Assignee copies of the notice, with the date for hearing endorsed on it, and also of the

---

[162] Rules 24 and 32.
[163] Rule 38 and Form No. 15.
[164] 1988 Act, s.44.
[165] Rule 36.
[166] Rule 37.
[167] 1988 Act, s.16.
[168] Rule 39.
[169] Form No. 16.

affidavit. On paying an appropriate charge, the bankrupt will be furnished with copies of the papers on which his adjudication was founded.[170]

4–60 "Cause" in this context may be, for example, that the requisite procedures were not complied with, that the debt is not owing to the petitioner, that the alleged act of bankruptcy never occurred or that the petitioner has improperly abused the bankruptcy mechanism.

4–61 Where the bankrupt succeeds in showing cause, his adjudication will be annulled.[171] In that event the petitioning creditor is made responsible for the costs, fees and expenses of any receiver or manager who may have been appointed.[172]

4–62 Even where cause is not shown, the court has a discretion to adjourn the application on such conditions as it sees fit.[173] Further adjournments may be ordered, for instance, where there is new evidence to be given or where a witness about any of the relevant matters is not present for cross-examination.[174] Where in the event cause is not shown the court must dismiss the bankrupt's application.[175] If, within the allotted time, cause was not shown, the court will direct that a notice of adjudication be placed in the *Iris Oifigiúil* and in at least one daily newspaper that circulates in the area where the bankrupt resides.[176] If the application to show cause was adjourned, the court may stay publication of those notices.[177]

Statutory Sitting

4–63 The next stage is a statutory sitting of the court.[178] A notice of this sitting, in the prescribed form, must be advertised by the petitioner, at least ten days previously, in the *Iris Oifigiúil* and in such newspaper or newspapers as the court directs.[179] Where cause for an annulment is not shown or where the time for showing cause has expired, the bankrupt will be summoned to attend this sitting.[180] The summons, in the specified form, must be served by the petitioner's solicitor on the bankrupt personally; but the court is empowered to direct some other mode of service. An affidavit of service should then be promptly filed with the Examiner. At least two clear days before the sitting is due to take place, the bankrupt must lodge a statement of affairs, in the prescribed form,[181] with the

---

[170] Rule 40.
[171] 1988 Act, s.16(2).
[172] Rule 36(2).
[173] 1988 Act, s.16(2).
[174] Rule 41.
[175] Rule 41.
[176] 1988 Act, s.17(2).
[177] 1988 Act, s.17(4).
[178] 1988 Act, s.17(3).
[179] Rule 64(1) and Form No. 19.
[180] Rule 42.
[181] Form No. 23.

Official Assignee.[182] The statement must be verified by him on oath and signed by him on every page with all columns and blanks accurately filled up. Before a copy of this statement can be filed with the Examiner, the Assignee must be satisfied that it is complete and stamped.[183]

4–64   Several important functions are carried out at the statutory sitting. It is there that the creditors can decide to appoint their own assignee to represent them in administering the bankrupt's estate.[184] All creditors, either in person or by proxy, are entitled to vote on this matter and the appointment is made by a bare majority in value of the creditors. Indeed, the creditors may go even further and decide that the bankrupt's estate should not be administered by the Official Assignee but instead should be wound up by a trustee of their own choosing, much like a liquidator winds up a company. Such a decision requires a majority of at least three-fifths of those creditors in number *and* value who vote either personally or by proxy.[185] Creditors may also prove their debts there; the procedure and requirements regarding proofs is dealt with separately below.[186]

4–65   Most importantly of all, perhaps, the bankrupt is required to attend the sitting and to "make full disclosure of his property" to the court.[187] To that end, he is obliged to deliver up to the Official Assignee, when requested, such accounts and papers he has regarding his estate, to disclose to the Assignee who else has such papers and to give the Assignee every reasonable assistance in administering the estate.[188] To that end as well, the court may examine the bankrupt on oath, either orally or on written interrogatories. The powers and procedures under this section are also considered in detail below.[189]

DEBTOR'S OWN PETITION

4–66   Occasionally, the debtor himself will petition to be adjudicated a bankrupt. One of the objectives of bankruptcy law is to protect debtors against their creditors, and being made a bankrupt in circumstances can be a form of protection. The debtor's assets are placed beyond the reach of one or several creditors and, being vested in the Official Assignee, will be distributed equitably among the creditors generally, subject to the statutory requirements regarding preferential debts. By being made a bankrupt, the debtor may be able to bring a prolonged and unsatisfactory state of affairs to a head, in the expectation of obtaining an eventual discharge and making a fresh start. On the other hand, some

---

[182] 1988 Act, s.19(c) and r.82.
[183] Rule 83.
[184] 1988 Act, s.18.
[185] 1988 Act, s.110.
[186] See paras 6–05 et seq.
[187] 1988 Act, s.17(3).
[188] 1988 Act, s.19(a) and (d).
[189] See paras 6–23 et seq.

debtors may seek to abuse this facility, as a method of thwarting the legitimate claims of one or several creditors.

4–67 It is an act of bankruptcy for a debtor to make a formal declaration of his insolvency.[190] When petitioning for his own bankruptcy he is deemed to have made such a declaration[191] and, accordingly, does not have to go through the formality. The debtor's petition, in the prescribed form,[192] must contain undertakings that he will advertise notice of his adjudication and the statutory sitting, will attend that sitting in person and will lodge such sums as may be directed to cover costs, fees and the Official Assignee's expenses.[193] There must be an accompanying affidavit of the debtor, setting forth particulars regarding his assets, so that the court can be satisfied that they are worth at least €1,904.61 (ex £1,500).[194]

4–68 Once it is satisfied that the debtor is insolvent and that he has assets worth at least €1,904.61 (ex £1,500), the court may adjudicate him a bankrupt, which will cause his assets to vest in the Official Assignee, the convening of a statutory sitting and all the other usual bankruptcy procedures. Although it is provided that the court "shall" so adjudicate in such circumstances, it would seem that the court has a residuary discretion to refuse to make such order if it believes that the petition is an abuse of the statutory procedure. What constitutes an abuse depends entirely on the circumstances of the case. It has been held that a petition is not an abuse where the objective is simply to save the debtor's own hide in contrast to wanting an equitable distribution among the creditors. As Lord Evershed M.R. remarked, "[t]here is nothing ... in the policy of the Act which disentitles a debtor to say: 'I will go bankrupt and protect myself ... and get rid, whether or not they are provable debts, of any claims which are made against me'".[195]

---

[190] 1988 Acts, s.7(1)(e) and Rule 17.
[191] Rule 18.
[192] Form No. 13.
[193] Rule 26.
[194] Rule 27; S.I. No. 595 of 2001.
[195] *Re Dunn* [1949] 1 Ch. 640 at 647.

CHAPTER 5

EFFECTS OF ADJUDICATION

5–01 The principal consequence of a person being adjudicated bankrupt is that, subject to certain exceptions, his property vests in the Official Assignee. Moreover, any property he acquires in the future may often be claimed by the Assignee. Bankruptcy also brings certain political and professional disabilities, and the Assignee can apply to the court to stay proceedings being brought against the bankrupt.

PERSONAL EFFECTS

5–02 In the past going into bankruptcy had profound personal effects on an individual's status and entitlements, but the trend in the law since the early nineteenth century has been to diminish those impacts. At present, a person who is adjudicated bankrupt suffers some political incapacities and also is subject to certain disabilities in commercial life. Additionally, the 1988 Act places several restrictions on what he can do.

Political Incapacities

5–03 Electoral law prevents a bankrupt who has not been discharged from being elected to or from sitting as a member of the Dáil, the Seanad or the European Parliament.[1] A sitting Dáil member who is adjudicated a bankrupt thereupon ceases to be a member.[2] Any member of a nomination committee for a panel of Seanad candidates ceases to hold that office on becoming a bankrupt.[3] But undischarged bankrupts are no longer disqualified from becoming or remaining a member of a local authority.[4] Whether imposing such political disabilities is consistent with the Constitution is a highly debatable matter.[5]

Business and Professional Disabilities

5–04 Becoming a bankrupt operates to prevent persons from exercising certain occupations and professions. It is an offence for an undischarged bankrupt to act as a company director or indirectly to take part in or to be concerned in the

---

[1] Electoral Act 1992, s.41(k) and European Parliament Elections Act 1997, s.11(2)(a).
[2] Electoral Act, 1992, s.42(3).
[3] Seanad Electoral Panel Members Act 1947, s.23.
[4] Local Government Act 2001, s.13.
[5] Cf. *Campagnano v Italy*, 48 E.H.R.R. 997 (2009).

management of a company.[6] For these purposes, a company includes not alone one registered in the State but also an unregistered company and a company incorporated abroad which has a place of business in the State. But the court, on application, may permit a bankrupt to become involved in a company's management on such terms as the court deems appropriate.

5–05   Adjudication as a bankrupt operates to suspend immediately a solicitor's practicing certificate[7] and, where the applicant for such a certificate is a bankrupt, the Law Society may refuse to issue the certificate or may issue it subject to terms and conditions as the Society thinks fit.[8] A special compensation fund is established under the Solicitors (Amendment) Act 1961, to ensure that clients who suffer loss because of their solicitor's bankruptcy are compensated.

5–06   Adjudication disqualifies persons from holding many senior positions in the public sector.[9] A bankrupt is not allowed to act as an insurance intermediary or to be a director of or be concerned in the management of a building society, an industrial or provident society or a credit union.[10] The Stock Exchange's Rules effectively prevents bankrupts from acting as stockbrokers.[11]

5–07   An undischarged bankrupt is disqualified from obtaining a certificate of qualification which is necessary to act as an auctioneer.[12] Where an auctioneer becomes bankrupt the funds in his clients' account vest in the Official Assignee.[13] To the extent that bankruptcy indicates that a person does not possess the "financial ... resources ... adequate for discharging his actual and potential obligations in respect of the business", he will be refused a tour operator's or a travel agent's licence[14] or, if he has such licence, it may be revoked.[15]

Restrictions under the 1988 Act

5–08   Part VII (ss.123–132) of the 1988 Act established a variety of bankruptcy offences, which can still be prosecuted notwithstanding the process having been annulled. Undischarged bankrupts are not allowed, either jointly or severally, to obtain credit for €634.87 (ex £500) or more without disclosing to the other party that they are bankrupt and have not been discharged.[16] They are not prevented

---

[6]   Companies Act 1963, ss.183 and 183A, and see M. Forde & H. Kennedy, *Company Law*, 4th edn (Dublin: Thomson Round Hall, 2008) at 152–153.
[7]   Solicitors Act 1954, s.50.
[8]   Solicitors Act 1954, ss.49(1)(j) and (2)(b).
[9]   E.g. membership of an Bord Pleanála: Planning and Development Act 2000, s.106(13)(d)(i).
[10] Insurance Act 1989, s.55(a); Building Societies Act 1989, s.64(1); Industrial and Provident Societies (Amendment) Act 1978, s.31; Credit Union Act 1966, s.26(1).
[11] Rules of the Irish Stock Exchange Limited, Release 13, February 2, 2009. Rule 2.8 describes bankruptcy as a matter that would "call into question a member firm's suitability for membership of the Exchange".
[12] Auctioneers and House Agents Act 1947, s.13(b).
[13] Auctioneers and House Agents Act 1967, s.7.
[14] Transport (Tour Operators and Travel Agents) Act 1982, s.6(3)(a).
[15] Transport (Tour Operators and Travel Agents) Act 1982, s.8(1)(a).
[16] 1988 Act, s.129(a).

from trading but, when they engage in trade or do business under any other name, they must disclose to the other party to a commercial transaction that they are bankrupt.[17] Where they get "after-acquired property" they must disclose that fact to the Official Assignee or to the creditors' trustee.[18] On an application by the Assignee or trustee, the court may direct that letters, telegrams and postal packets addressed to the bankrupt at a specified place be re-directed to the Assignee or trustee.[19] Any such order must not exceed three months.

PROPERTY

5–09   On being adjudicated a bankrupt and as from that date, all the debtor's property vests in the Official Assignee, subject to certain exceptions and qualifications.[20] In the event of the creditors choosing to have the bankrupt's estate administered by a trustee, the Assignee is divested of this property and it vests in the trustee.[21]

5–10   Vesting under these provisions is by operation of law, i.e. without the need for the bankrupt to execute any conveyance or do any act. In those circumstances where the law requires conveyances of property to be registered, a certificate may to be issued under the seal of the court.[22] This certificate is deemed to be evidence that the property has vested in the Assignee, who must have it registered promptly. Its registration has the same effects as if an actual conveyance had been registered. If more than two months elapse from the date of adjudication before this certificate is registered, the Assignee runs a risk of losing title to the property. That would occur where a purchaser of the land for valuable consideration, in good faith and without notice of the adjudication, registered his conveyance before the certificate was registered.

"Property" Vesting

5–11   For the purposes of the 1988 Act, property is defined extensively, as "includ[ing] money, goods, things in action, land and every description of property, whether real or personal and whether situated in the State or elsewhere; also, obligations, easements and every description of estate, interest and profit, present or future, vested or contingent, arising out of or incident to property as above defined".[23] Thus, there vests in the Assignee or trustee, as the case may be, all land, chattels, choses in action and money that belong to the debtor, together with various interests in such property.[24] The bankrupt is completely

---

[17]   1988 Act, s.129(b).
[18]   1988 Act, s.127.
[19]   1988 Act, s.72.
[20]   1988 Act, s.44.
[21]   1988 Act, s.111.
[22]   1988 Act, s.46.
[23]   1988 Act, s.3.
[24]   1988 Act, s.44(1).

divested of his property and he ceases to have any interest in it, other than to such surplus as may exist on his discharge.

5–12 What constitutes property in this context is most extensive. Dealing with an equivalent definition, the Canadian Supreme Court observed that the legislature's intention to include assets not normally considered as "property" at common law should be respected, to achieve the statutory purpose, concluding that a fishing licence came within the net.[25] Property here includes money in a trustee saving bank or in the Post Office Savings Bank to which the bankrupt is entitled, and also securities to which he is entitled and which are issued through An Post.[26] Rights of action in "proprietary", as contrasted with "personal", torts vest in the Assignee, as do most contractual rights or claims. An interest of a residuary legatee in a deceased bankrupt's estate is property here and, consequently, where the estate was discharged from bankruptcy before it was fully administered, that interest was held to have vested in the trustee.[27] In this context, property is defined to include all powers which the bankrupt could exercise with regard to the property, such as powers of appointment under a trust.[28] It also includes property which the debtor disposed of in a transaction which the court later declared invalid as a voluntary settlement, a fraudulent transfer or an improvident disposition, under ss.57–59 of the 1988 Act.[29]

Insurance and Pensions

5–13 Property here includes the proceeds of insurance policies and pension entitlements, although some pension schemes can provide otherwise. In *Cork v Rawlins*,[30] the debtor had been a self-employed gardener who took out two whole life insurance policies, each of which provided for a benefit if he became permanently disabled. Following an injury he was unable to work and, three years later, he was adjudicated a bankrupt. It was held that the sums due to him under the policies were property that vested in the bankruptcy trustee; they were contractual claims to be paid money that had existed at the time he was adjudicated. Even if the injury had occurred after his adjudication, the outcome would have been the same because the contingency that would trigger payments had existed before then. Because damages he would recover in legal proceedings for pain and suffering caused by his injury are not deemed to be property here,[31] he contended that the same principle should apply to his disability entitlements. But that was rejected, on the grounds that the money was paid under the policy, not for his pain and suffering, but because of his unemployability.

5–14 Beginning with the Naval and Marine Pay and Pensions Act 1865,[32]

---

[25]   *Saulnier v Royal Bank of Canada*, 298 D.L.R. (4th) 193 (2008).
[26]   1988 Act, s.47(b).
[27]   *Re Hemming* [2009] 2 W.L.R. 1257.
[28]   1988 Act, s.44(3)(a).
[29]   1988 Act, s.44(3)(b).
[30]   [2001] Ch. 729.
[31]   See paras 5–18 and 5–19.
[32]   28 & 29 Vict. c.73

statutory pension provisions in much of the public sector expressly provide that pensions under them shall not form part of the estate that vests in the Assignee or in bankruptcy trustees. The rules of many occupational pension schemes stipulate that, on a member's bankruptcy, his right to benefit is forfeited on his membership ceasing. But this is often supplemented by a provision that the fund's trustees shall have a discretion to pay the equivalent of a pension to any of those who are in need. In the case of occupational pension schemes, this position has been put on a statutory footing.[33]

5–15   Insofar as personal pension schemes based on the annuity principle are concerned, it was held in *Krasner v Dennison*[34] that entitlements under these form part of the bankrupt's estate that vests in his trustee, because they are based on a right to obtain payment of money that existed prior to the adjudication. Both pension schemes there provided that the individual's right to a lump sum retirement benefit "may not be assigned or surrendered". But they did not prevent the money vesting in the bankruptcy trustee because, first, what was envisaged there was a contractual assignment and not a statutory vesting.[35] Secondly, even if this purported to defeat the trustee's entitlement, it could not succeed because it would offend against the general rule of public policy that prevents parties from contracting out the bankruptcy code.[36] In other words, a person may not contract that he shall be divested of all or some of his property in the event of him becoming a bankrupt, and such a provision in a pension contract did not fall within the recognised exceptions. Although income within these schemes also fits the definition of pre-adjudication property, the 1988 Act makes an exception for it, whether the bankrupt is an employee or is self-employed.[37] Apart from statutory provision,[38] forfeiture clauses in many occupational pension schemes are not caught by the public policy against bankrupts contracting to divest their property where payments are entirely discretionary.

5–16   In *Re Malcolm*[39] the different treatment of pension entitlements of employed and self-employed bankrupts was unsuccessfully challenged, as being contrary to art.14 of the European Convention on Human Rights, because it was not differentiation based on status or any of the other basis stipulated there. A challenge to this disparity, based on art.1 of the Convention's first protocol, has also been rejected.[40]

Intellectual Property

5–17   Rights of authors, performers and others to payment by collecting societies, in the form of royalties and the like, were held in *Performing Rights*

---

[33]   Pensions Act 1990, s.36(2).
[34]   [2001] Ch. 76.
[35]   *Re Landau* [1988] Ch. 223.
[36]   Ex p. *Mackay* (1873) L.R. 8 Ch. App. 643.
[37]   Section 65.
[38]   Pensions Act 1990, s.36(2).
[39]   [2005] 1 W.L.R. 1238.
[40]   *Krasner v Dennison* [2001] Ch. 76.

Soc. v Rowland[41] to be property that vests in the bankruptcy trustee. This is because these rights relate to work completed prior to adjudication and are not a mere expectancy or possibility; they do not depend on the society member performing any further obligations in connection with the copyright material. This conclusion was reinforced by the rules of the society in that case, which permitted performance members to assign their right to distributions from the society.

Legal Proceedings

5–18 Subject to exceptions, his claim for damages in legal proceedings that relate to events that preceded the adjudication form part of the bankrupt's estate for these purposes. For property is defined to include "things in action", which encompasses legal claims. An exception is for claims of a uniquely personal nature, for instance for assault and for defamation, and also for the pain and suffering component of personal injury claims. As formulated in *Heath v Tang*,[42] the exception is "certain causes of action personal to be bankrupt [which] include cases where 'the damages are to be estimated in respect of his body, mind or character, and without immediate reference to his rights of property'".[43] Claims for unfair dismissal have been held to be personal rather than proprietary.[44] It has been suggested that a claim against an insolvency practitioner for negligence in the handling of a client's case, which resulted in her being made bankrupt, falls within this category; that it may not vest in the bankruptcy trustees because then "[t]hey would be claiming damages for the making of the very bankruptcy order under which their claim arose".[45]

5–19 At times, the claim is hybrid: in part personal and the remainder proprietary. In *Ord v Upton*,[46] a medical negligence claim against the debtor's doctor seeking damages for pain and suffering, and for loss of earnings, it was held that the latter part of the claim was proprietary and, accordingly, vested in his trustee. As explained as far back as 1844, "[t]he skill and labour of an industrious man are in the nature of his stock in trade: they would be foreseen, and might be prudently relied on as a ground for giving credit, and the creditors therefore have reason for saying that the benefit of all contracts relating to that source of value, on which they may have relied on when they gave credit, ought to pass to them".[47] Earning capacity is treated as a capital asset. A claim for damages for race discrimination has been categorised as a hybrid.[48] A hybrid claim vests in the Assignee or trustee, who must hold what is recovered for the

---

[41] [1997] 3 All E.R. 336.
[42] [1993] 1 W.L.R. 1421.
[43] [1993] 1 W.L.R. 1421 at 1424.
[44] *Grady v Prison Service* [2003] I.C.R. 753.
[45] *Mulkerrins v Pricewaterhouse Coopers* [2003] 1 W.L.R. 1937 at 1942.
[46] [2000] Ch. 352.
[47] *Beckham v Drake* (1849) 2 H.L. Cas. 579 at 608.
[48] *Khan v Trident Safeguards Ltd* [2004] 1 C.R. 1591.

personal part of the claim in trust for the bankrupt.[49] In the *Ord* case, there was a single cause of action, negligence.

Pre-Emption

5–20   In *Dear v Reeves*,[50] it was held that the bankrupt was divested of his right of pre-emption over land. Authority that a right of that nature does not create an interest in property[51] was distinguished and was suggested to be wrong. A pre-emption entitlement is a "thing in action" because it comprises a negative obligation; it is binding on the grantor who is not legally free to sell the property to a third party; proceedings can be brought to prevent any such sale taking place; and the right can be assigned.

Property Not Vesting

5–21   Various categories of property do not vest in the Assignee or trustee, as the case may be. The mere possibility of the debtor acquiring property is neither property, a "thing in action" nor an "interest ... contingent ... to property."[52] Accordingly, where the debtor suffered serious injuries in a criminal assault, and after being made bankrupt was awarded a substantial sum by the Criminal Injuries Compensation Board, it was held that he was not divested of that sum. For his application to the Board for compensation was not a cause of action and did not otherwise come within the statutory definition.

5–22   Except for uniquely personal items, once what is in dispute fits the definition of property, the bankrupt is divested of it unless it falls within a statutory exception.[53] This is so even if the item is of no value to the bankrupt. But there are several provisions which stipulate that certain assets shall not comprise part of a person's estate for these purposes.

Property Not Acquired and Property Disposed of

5–23   The Assignee or trustee does not acquire title to property which belongs to some third party, such as goods held under a hire purchase agreement or a retention of title clause. If the debtor has mortgaged the property, the same principle applies, subject to the bankrupt's equity of redemption re-vesting. It was held in *Re Lind*[54] that this even applies to an agreement to assign property by way of a mortgage, because "an agreement to charge future property creates an immediate equitable charge upon the property coming into existence, independently of the contract to execute some further charge ...".[55] On the grounds that equity regards that as done which the parties agreed to be done,

---

[49]   *Khan v Trident Safeguards Ltd* [2004] 1 C.R. 1591.
[50]   [2001] 3 W.L.R. 662.
[51]   *Pritchard v Biggs* [1980] Ch. 338.
[52]   *Re Campbell* [1997] Ch. 14.
[53]   *De Rothschild v Bell* [2000] Q.B. 33.
[54]   [1915] 2 Ch. 345.
[55]   [1915] 2 Ch. 345 at 358; also *Cotton v Heyl* [1930] 1 Ch. 510.

once it is clear that the intention is to give a charge the courts will give effect to that intention.

5–24   Under the 1857 Act, there was the "reputed ownership" rule whereby if goods or chattels belonging to another were being held by the debtor in circumstances that suggested it was he who owned them, the court could order that they should vest in the trustee in bankruptcy.[56] This rule, which never applied to company insolvencies, was one of the reasons why it was not practicable for individuals to give floating charges over their assets. It was repealed by the 1988 Act.

5–25   At the time he was adjudicated bankrupt the debtor may have been a party to a sales transaction. In that event, it is important to know whether the property in what was being sold vested in him at the very moment of adjudication because, if it did, then it will vest in the Assignee or the trustee, as the case may be. If the property did not vest in him at that time then, generally, all that the Assignee or trustee may be entitled to is a proportion of the price the buyer agreed to pay for it, or of the money he paid for it. An exception to this principle is the agreed sale of land and of certain other unique property; equity will intervene, by way of ordering specific performance, to compel completion of contracts to sell them.[57] Thus, if the debtor had agreed to sell land, the purchaser on paying the price (to the Assignee or trustee) can compel transfer of it. On tendering the price, the Assignee can compel completion of the sale where the debtor is the purchaser. But for the vast majority of sales of goods and chattels, and choses in action that are traded on markets, equity will not compel performance of a sales agreement.

5–26   For sales of goods, the critical time is when property in them actually passed, which may be when the sale agreement was made, when the goods were delivered or when they were paid for, depending on the terms of the agreement and the nature of the transaction.[58] It was said in *Re Wait*[59] that the Sale of Goods Act 1893, contains an exhaustive statement of the various rules regarding the transfer of property in goods and this Act, by implication, excludes any equitable rights which might otherwise arise in such transactions. According to Atkin L.J.:

> "The rules [in the 1893 Act] for transfer of property as between seller and buyer, performance of the contract [and the like] appear to be complete and exclusive statements of the legal relations both in law and equity. They have, of course, no relevance when one is considering rights, legal or equitable, which may come into existence dehors the contract for sale. A seller or purchaser may, of course, create any equity he pleases by way

---

[56]   Irish Bankrupt and Insolvent Act 1857, s.313, 20 & 21 Vic. c.60.
[57]   See generally, H. Delany, *Equity and the Law of Trusts*, 4th edn (Dublin: Thomson Round Hall, 2007), Ch.14 and paras 5–56 and 5–57.
[58]   See generally, M. Forde, *Commercial Law*, 3rd edn (Haywards Heath: Tottel, 2005) at 55 et seq.
[59]   [1927] 1 Ch. 606.

of charge, equitable assignment or any other dealing with or disposition of goods, the subject matter of sale; and he may of course create such an equity as one of the terms expressed in the contract of sale. But the mere sale or agreement to sell or the acts in pursuance of such a contract mentioned in the [1893] Code will only produce the legal effects which the Code states."[60]

Co-Owned Property

5–27   Perhaps the most common type of co-owned property is the family home[61] and joint bank accounts. Co-owned property is held under joint tenancies and under tenancies in common. What principally distinguishes these is that, on the death of one or more joint tenants, the property vests in the remaining one(s), whereas under the latter, the interest of a tenant in common who dies vests in his estate. The bankruptcy of a tenant in common does not legally affect the rights of his co-tenants to their share of the property, which continues to vest in them. But adjudicating a joint tenant bankrupt has the effect of severing the co-ownership and converting it into a tenancy in common.[62] Formerly, when the "relation back" rule applied, the joint tenancy was deemed to have been severed once the act of bankruptcy took place.

Trust Property

5–28   Property held in trust by the bankrupt does not vest in the Assignee or trustee.[63] This includes not only where he is constituted an express trustee of the property but also where, by operation of law, he is rendered a trustee; such as profits made in breach of fiduciary duty, money payable to him as vendor under a specifically enforceable contract, or property held by him as a stranger who received or dealt with trust property. Where property was transferred to the bankrupt expressly to hold in trust, then even the bare legal title does not vest in the Assignee.[64] That also is the case where the bankrupt holds the property by virtue of his office, such as an executor or an administrator of an estate, or qua creditors' trustee in bankruptcy. However, if the bankrupt has a beneficial interest in the trust property it is not then being held for an "other person" and, consequently, is not excluded from vesting in the Assignee; although this is without prejudice to the rights of the cestui. As is explained later, certain voluntary settlements made by the bankrupt in the period leading up to his adjudication may be avoided.[65] Also the act of constituting himself a trustee of certain assets for the benefit of particular creditors may amount to a fraudulent preference.[66]

---

[60]   [1927] 1 Ch. 606 at 636.
[61]   See para.6–46.
[62]   *Morgan v Marquis* (1853) 9 Ex. 145.
[63]   1988 Act, s.44(4)(a).
[64]   *St. Thomas' Hospital v Richardson* [1910] 1 K.B. 271.
[65]   See paras 7–49 et seq.
[66]   See paras 7–29 et seq.

5–29   For an express trust to be created, the "three certainties" must have been complied with, i.e., the subject matter of the trust must be certain, its objects or the persons to benefit from it must be certain, and the words used must be such as they ought to be construed as imperative.[67] Trusts of land or of any interest in land must be evidenced in writing. An example of an express trust of money paid is *Re McKeown*,[68] where the debtor, who was a building contractor, borrowed money from the applicant in order to pay the costs and fees of an arbitration and thereby take up the arbitrator's award. They agreed that this loan should be repaid from money paid to the debtor under the award. He was then adjudicated bankrupt and the question arose whether all of the money payable under that award must be distributed among his general creditors or whether a portion of it, equivalent to the loan, should be held in trust for the lender. It was held that the amount of the original loan was impressed with a trust. As Lowry L.C.J. put it, the debtor's agreement to repay the loan from the proceeds of the award "raises as clear an equity as would have been attracted by a breach of the (undertaking) to use the loan to obtain the award. What the bankrupt was in effect saying was that having used the loan to obtain the award he would hold an equal part thereof in trust for the applicant".[69] Furthermore, had the bankrupt not used the loan for the agreed purpose and the funds remained in his bank account, they would still be affected by the trust.[70] The proceeds of an insurance policy taken out by the bankrupt but for the benefit of another person belong to that person.[71]

5–30   A solicitor's client account is held in trust for the clients and, accordingly, will not vest in the Assignee or trustee. In *Re Hughes*,[72] Kenny J. held that the Assignee does "not get any valid claim to the moneys standing to the credit of a client account until all the claims of the clients in respect of their moneys which have been lodged to the account have been satisfied".[73]

5–31   Trusts can also arise by operation of law; in particular, what are known as "resulting trusts" and "constructive trusts". Under the former, the beneficial interest in the trust property reverts to the settlor who previously transferred it to the trustee.[74] Generally, where the ownership of property is transferred to a person who gives no consideration for it, the inference is that he holds it by way of a resulting trust for the transferor. But this presumption can be rebutted by evidence of a contrary intention or by what is known as the presumption of advancement, i.e. the presumption that the transfer was intended to be by way of gift outright. Many of the circumstances where these questions arise involve

---

[67]   See generally, H. Delany, *Equity and the Law of Trusts*, 4th edn (Dublin: Thomson Round Hall, 2007) Ch.4.
[68]   [1974] N.I. 226.
[69]   [1974] N.I. 226 at 231.
[70]   *Barclays Bank Ltd v Quistclose Investments Ltd* [1970] A.C. 567.
[71]   *Re O'Dowd* [1968] N.I. 52.
[72]   [1970] I.R. 237.
[73]   [1970] I.R. 237 at 242.
[74]   See generally, Delany, above fn.67, Ch.7.

transactions in family property, such as joint bank accounts held by a husband and wife and the family home.[75]

5–32   A constructive trust is imposed on property to satisfy the demands of justice and conscience, and may be imposed contrary to the very intentions of the persons concerned.[76] This type of trust is regarded as constituting a residual category, and is adaptable to meet the justice of particular circumstances.

5–33   The court will readily "trace" trust funds, i.e. where money which is held in trust, or the proceeds from the sale of property which is held in trust, is improperly converted to the trustee's personal benefit (if that money can be identified) the court will compel the trustee to give it up to the beneficiary.[77] Thus the court will trace trust money which was improperly paid into the trustee's bank account and, if the trustee is bankrupt, that money will not vest in the Assignee or trustee.[78] Where a debtor paid some of his own money into a trust account and also made drawings from that account, he is deemed to have taken out his own money first before any trust money is withdrawn.[79] Any balance remaining in the account will be attributed to the beneficiaries of the trust. In *Re Hughes*,[80] where a bankrupt solicitor had drawn amounts from his client account, it was held that the balance in the account went to those clients in respect of which the most recent lodgements were made. If the account contains funds attributable to several trusts then the rule in *Clayton's* case[81] determines how much is attributable to each trust; under this rule, the sums first paid in are deemed to be the amounts withdrawn first.[82]

Vesting Subject to Equities

5–34   On it vesting, the Assignee or creditors' trustee, as the case may be, acquires no better tide to the property than the bankrupt himself had. If the property was subject to some security arrangement, such as a mortgage, it continues to be subject to it[83]; similarly, if it is subject to any lien or a right of set-off. This statutory vesting is subject to equities in the sense that, if a third party has any right in or claim against the property, the change of ownership does not adversely affect his entitlement. Because the statutory assignee is not an incumbrancer for value, the property is acquired subject to all equities as existed on the date of adjudication.[84] A spouse's equitable interest in the family home is such an equity.[85] Where the debtor gave a mortgage on property, which

---

[75]   See para.10–51.
[76]   See generally, Delany, above fn.67, Ch.8.
[77]   See generally, Delany, above fn.67, Ch.18.
[78]   *Sinclair v Brougham* [1914] A.C. 398, *Re Diplock* [1948] Ch. 465 and *Re Calvert* [1961] N.I. 58.
[79]   *Re Hallett's Estate* (1879) 13 Ch. D. 696.
[80]   [1970] I.R. 237.
[81]   (1816) 1 Mer. 572.
[82]   *Re Stenning* [1895] 2 Ch. 433.
[83]   1988 Act, s.136(2).
[84]   *Re Wallis* [1902] 1 K.B. 719 and *Re Nolan and Stanley* [1949] I.R. 197.
[85]   See para.10–49.

was not registered until after he was adjudicated a bankrupt, the mortgagee does not lose the benefit of his security merely because it was not duly registered at the time of the adjudication.[86]

5–35 In *Re McCafferty*[87] it was held that not alone can the Statute of Limitations run against the Assignee, and thereby defeat a title he has acquired under these provisions, but that even the bankrupt himself can set up adverse possession for these purposes. For almost 45 years since he was adjudicated a bankrupt, the debtor continued in possession of his lands, which had vested in the Assignee by virtue of the statutory provisions. When eventually the Assignee sought to be put on the title, the debtor, who had never been discharged from bankruptcy, claimed adverse possession. Kenny J. held that "the possession by a bankrupt of freehold land which belonged to him at the date of the bankruptcy or which he subsequently acquired is adverse to the Official Assignee".[88]

Uniquely Personal Rights

5–36 There are certain forms of property that represent uniquely personal rights that, in consequence, have been held not to vest in the Assignee or trustee. One, already referred to, in rights of action of a purely personal nature. This is because "the creditors cannot legitimately have looked to the pain of a bankrupt from a broken limb, or wounded affection, or blasted character, as a source of profit, they being in their nature causal and unforeseen, and unconnected immediately with property".[89] But where the cause of action is a hybrid, it vests in the Assignee, who holds the personal element of it in trust for the bankrupt.[90] Certain non-assignable statutory tenancies of residential property also come within that category.[91]

5–37 In *Haig v Aitken*,[92] which concerned the disgraced former British M.P. and cabinet minister, it was held that personal correspondence between him and former parliamentary and ministerial colleagues, and with current and former heads of state, also come within this category. It was said to be "inconceivable that Parliament envisaged by passing the Act that the effect of bankruptcy should be that a bankrupt's personal correspondence should be available for publication to the world at large at the behest of the trustee in bankruptcy". That would be a "gross invasion of privacy" and possibility unconstitutional.

Bare Necessities

5–38 Certain essentials for the bankrupt and his family to live do not vest in

---

[86] *Re Collins* (Hamilton J., June 27, 1980).
[87] [1974] I.R. 471.
[88] [1974] I.R. 471 at 478.
[89] *Beckham v Drake* (1849) 2 H.L. Cas. 579 at 609.
[90] *Ord v Upton* [2000] Ch. 352.
[91] *London City Corp v Bown*, 60 P. & C.R. 42 (1989); contrast *de Rothschild v Bell* [2000] Q.B. 33.
[92] [2001] Ch. 110.

the Assignee or trustee. These are "such articles of clothing, household furniture, bedding, tools or equipment of his trade or occupation or other like necessaries for him, his wife, children or dependant relatives residing with him ...".[93] The bankrupt is entitled to select which of these items he wants but he cannot retain more than €3,100 (ex £2,500) worth of them unless, on application, the court permits him to keep more. Formerly, books and the like of professional people were held not to be excluded from vesting but, as "equipment of [their] occupation", they are now so excluded. As for necessities in excess of the €3,100 (ex £2,500) limit of which he is divested, the bankrupt may call on the Assignee or trustee not to dispose of them until the court orders that he should do so.[94] An application may also be made to the court for an order postponing removal or the sale of such goods and to permit the bankrupt to use them.[95]

Social Welfare Benefits

5–39 Social welfare benefits do not vest in the Assignee or trustee. On the bankruptcy of a person entitled to a social welfare benefit, assistance or allowance, they shall "not pass to any trustee or other person acting on behalf of the creditors".[96]

Future Income

5–40 Being after-acquired property, the bankrupt's future earnings do not automatically vest in the Assignee or trustee.[97] It used to be that the bankrupt could retain out of his earnings sufficient to maintain himself and his family in reasonable comfort[98] and, it appears that this practice continues under the present legislation. But the Assignee or trustee may to apply to the court for directions regarding the bankrupt's earnings, which are defined as "any salary, income, emolument or pension" he is in receipt of or is entitled to receive, whether as an employee or as a self-employed person.[99] The court may direct the bankrupt or whoever is making the payment to him that all or part of those earnings be paid to the Assignee or trustee on such terms as the court stipulates. In so ordering, the court will have regard to the bankrupt's "family responsibilities and personal situation". Any such order can be varied by the court in the light of those considerations. The 1988 Act does not define what is a "salary, income, emolument or pension" for these purposes; presumably these terms will be interpreted in the same way as they are under the Income Tax Acts.[100]

---

93 1988 Act, s.45(1).
94 1988 Act, s.45(2).
95 1988 Act, s.45(3).
96 Social Welfare Consolidation Act 2005, s.283 and cf. *Re P.F. and M.I.F.* [1952] N.I. 172.
97 1988 Act, s.44(5).
98 *Re Walter* [1929] 1 Ch. 649.
99 1988 Act, s.65.
100 Cf. *Re Rogers* [1894] 1 Q.B. 425 and *Re DeMarney* [1948] 1 Ch. 126.

Compensation for Personal Injury

5–41   There is an exception for compensation which the bankrupt may receive for personal injury or loss he has suffered. The rule entitling the Assignee or trustee to claim after-acquired property is "[w]ithout prejudice to any existing principle or rule of law or equity, established practice or procedure in relation to damages or compensation recovered or recoverable by a bankrupt for personal injury or loss suffered by him...".[101]

Third Party Insurance

5–42   Formerly, a most unjust situation could arise where the debtor was legally responsible for injury to somebody's person or property and was insured for the loss thereby caused. Apart from where the injured party may have had a direct right of action against the insurers, the proceeds of the policy was not payable to that party but to the debtor—the tortfeasor. Once the tortfeasor became bankrupt, those proceeds would vest in the Assignee or trustee to be distributed pro rata among all the general creditors, including the injured party.[102] If the debtor was heavily insolvent, the injured party would recover comparatively little of the insurance, most of which would go to the preferred creditors.

5–43   That situation was rectified by s.62 of the Civil Liability Act 1961, which provides that the money paid under the insurance must be used to discharge the injured party's claim, and none of that money shall form part of the bankrupt's assets for the purpose of distribution among his general creditors.

Copyright

5–44   The interests of authors are protected where the author holding copyright in his work, or of any interest in such copyright, becomes bankrupt. Formerly, the effect of the copyright vesting in the Assignee or trustee, and it then being sold, was to deny the author any further right to royalties.[103] Although he would be entitled to claim damages for breach of copyright, the amount recovered in the circumstances might be very little. The copyright was regarded as no different from a chattel.

5–45   Now, no more copies of the work can be sold nor performances made unless the author is paid his royalty or share of the profits in accordance with the copyright agreement.[104] If the Assignee or trustee wishes to transfer the copyright or grant a licence under it, he must first obtain the author's consent, or that of the court, on terms that the author will be paid no less than the copyright owner was obliged to pay in such circumstances.

---

[101] 1988, s.44(5).
[102] *Hood's Trustees v Southern Union* [1928] Ch. 793.
[103] *Re Grant Richards* [1907] 2 K.B. 33.
[104] 1988 Act, s.48.

Leases and Hire Purchase Agreements

5–46 Contracts sometime stipulate that the obligations under them shall terminate should either party become bankrupt. Such clauses are common in leases and in hire purchase agreements, and go on to provide that, in the event of bankruptcy, the rights of the lessee or of the hirer, as the case may be, shall be forfeited or terminated.[105] Such provisions in leases and in hire purchase agreements are rendered void, as against the Assignee or trustee.[106] Accordingly, they acquire all the rights of the lessee or the hirer, but also the latter's liabilities as well, such as to pay rent or the hiring charges. To an extent, however, such liabilities can be shed by the Assignee or trustee applying to the court under the procedure for disclaiming onerous obligations.[107]

Shares in Companies

5–47 Where the bankrupt owns shares in a company, although they vest in the Assignee or trustee, that vesting is far from conferring on him all rights and powers as a shareholder. Until he is registered as a member, he cannot exercise the rights of shareholders, such as to vote in general meetings or to petition to have the company wound up.[108] However, proceedings can be brought against the bankrupt to compel him to cast his votes in a particular manner and, it would seem, even to petition to have the company wound up.[109] In a winding up, the Official Assignee represents him as contributory and any calls on the shares can be proved by the liquidator in the bankruptcy.[110]

Voluntary Settlements

5–48 If shortly before the bankruptcy, the debtor made certain gifts of his property, which accordingly do not vest in the Assignee or trustee, there is a jurisdiction to set aside those transactions and revest the property in them.[111] In this regard, there are distinct rules for marriage settlements.

After-Acquired Property

5–49 Unlike property held by a bankrupt at the date of the adjudication, his "after-acquired" property does not vest until the Assignee or trustee claims it.[112] Under the 1857 Act, which did not in its terms provide for making a claim to the property before the bankrupt was divested of it, the position was as follows. Until the trustee in bankruptcy "intervene[d] all transactions by a bankrupt after

---

[105] Cf. *Smith v Gronow* [1891] 2 Q.B. 394. In some circumstances the bankrupt tenant used to be entitled to relief from forfeiture under the Conveyancing Acts: cf. *Re Drew* [1929] I.R. 504 and *Monument Creameries Ltd v Carysfort Estates Ltd* [1967] I.R. 462.

[106] 1988 Act, s.49(1).

[107] See paras 7–02 et seq.

[108] *Morgan v Gray* [1953] 1 Ch. 83 and *Re H.L. Bolton Engineering Co* [1956] 1 Ch. 577.

[109] *Morgan v Gray* [1953] 1 Ch. 83 and *Re H.L. Bolton Engineering Co* [1956] 1 Ch. 577.

[110] Companies Act, 1963, s.211.

[111] See paras 7–49 et seq.

[112] 1988 Act, s.44(5).

his bankruptcy with any person dealing with him *bona fide* and for value, in respect of his after-acquired property, whether with or without knowledge of the bankruptcy, are valid against the trustee".[113] It was felt necessary to place this qualification on ss.267 and 268 of the 1857 Act because, if those provisions were strictly applied, persons dealing bona fide with a bankrupt but who had no knowledge of his legal status would be deprived of all title to acquisitions from him and for which value was paid.

5–50 The requirement that the Assignee or trustee must lay claim to the property applies only to property that strictly fits the description of "after-acquired". Transactions in property following the date of adjudication but which are based on a commitment made before that date may not be a transaction in after-acquired property.

"Relation Back" Rule Repealed

5–51 Formerly, there was the "relation back" rule, whereby this statutory vesting operated retroactively in respect of all property held by the debtor since he committed an act of bankruptcy within the three months prior to the petition being presented.[114] Accordingly, dispositions of such property in the period between the act of bankruptcy occurring and the date of adjudication could be impeached by the trustee in bankruptcy. Because this rule was seldom invoked in recent years and it gave rise to considerable uncertainty, and at times operated harshly,[115] it was discontinued in 1988.[116] It was replaced by empowering the court to invalidate certain improvident dispositions of property made within three months prior to the adjudication.[117]

Disclaiming Onerous Property

5–52 Where property vesting in the Assignee or trustee involves commitments that tend to significantly deplete the estate, the Assignee or trustee is empowered to apply to the court for permission to disclaim that property.[118] This can be an extremely valuable power because it can put a stop to a virtual haemorrhage of resources which is diminishing the assets available for division among the creditors.

---

[113] *Cohen v Mitchell* (1890) 25 Q.B.D. 262. See e.g. *Re Ball* [1899] 2 I.R. 313, *Re Doyle* [1906] 2 I.R. 538, Ex p *X.Y.* [1938] I.R. 821, *Re Ryan* [1939] I.R. 284, *Re Fox* [1940] N.I. 42, *Re Keaney* [1977] N.I. 67, *Rimar Pty. Ltd v Pappas* (1986) 160 C.L.R. 133.

[114] Cf. *Re Dennis* [1996] Ch. 80; this common law rule was given statutory basis in England but not in Ireland.

[115] E.g. *Jones & Sons (Trustee) v Jones* [1997] Ch. 159.

[116] 1988 Act, s.44(2).

[117] 1988 Act, s.58 and see paras 7–60 et seq.

[118] 1988 Act, s.56 and see paras 7–02 et seq.

CONTRACTS

5–53 It depends entirely on the terms of a contract with a debtor how the contract will be legally affected by his bankruptcy.[119] Express and implied terms and special circumstances aside, an act of bankruptcy or adjudication as a bankrupt does not automatically discharge such contracts to which the debtor is a party. Sometimes bankruptcy may operate as a breach of the contract entitling the other party to rescind[120]; occasionally bankruptcy may terminate the contract by way of frustration.[121] The contract may even expressly provide for how it shall be affected by bankruptcy, such as forfeiture clauses in leases and equivalent clauses in hire purchase agreements.[122] However, such clauses in leases and in hire purchase agreements are void against the Assignee or trustee.[123]

Vesting as Property

5–54 The benefit of many contacts will vest in them, as part of the bankrupt's property, as for instance in *Re Casey*.[124] Prior to adjudication, a farmer contracted with a sugar manufacturer to grow beet and sell it to the company. Additionally, the company agreed to supply him with goods and services in connection with his farming activities, and provision was made for the deduction and set-off of the price of those supplies from what he would be paid for the beet. It was held by the Supreme Court that, on adjudication, the contract was novated by operation of law, and the Assignee became entitled to enforce it and also was subject to its obligations, unless it was duly disclaimed.

5–55 But there is no such vesting and novation in the case of contracts that require the bankrupt's personal services, such as employment contracts.[125] Very specific statutory provisions are required in order to assign an obligation of personal service.[126]

Specific Performance

5–56 Specific performance may be ordered of a contract to which a bankrupt is a party, such as an agreement to buy or sell land or other unique items of property.[127] Where the vendor becomes bankrupt, the Assignee or trustee can be compelled to complete the sale. For he takes "the legal estate in the property,

---

[119] See generally, H. Beale et al., *Chitty on Contracts*, 28th edn (London: Sweet & Maxwell, 1999) at 1074 et seq. and Wee, "Insolvency and the Survival of Contracts", [2005] *J.Bus. L.* 494.

[120] E.g. Ex p. *Stapleton* (1879) 10 Ch. D. 586.

[121] E.g. Ex p. *Garners* (1873) L.R. 8 Ch. App. 289. Cf. *Re Casey* (Hamilton P., July 21, 1986).

[122] E.g. *Re A.D.*, 63 I.L.T.R. 50 (1929).

[123] 1988 Act, s.49.

[124] [1991] I.L.R.M. 385.

[125] *Knight v Burgess* (1864) 33 U. Ch. 727.

[126] *Noakes v Doncaster Amalg. Collieries Ltd* [1940] A.C. 1014.

[127] See generally, H. Delany, *Equity and the Law of Trusts*, 4th edn (Dublin: Thomson Round Hall, 2007) Ch.14.

subject to the equity of the purchaser under the contract, which gave the purchaser the right to say, convey me the estate on my paying you the purchase money".[128]

5–57 Where the purchaser becomes bankrupt before completion, in the past he could not insist on specific performance because he was no longer in a position to perform. Because of the former "relation back" rule, he did not own the wherewithal with which his side of the bargain could be honoured. In *Jennings' Trustee v King*[129] it was conceded that the act of bankruptcy operated as a repudiation, disentitling the insolvent purchaser to insist on having the agreement performed. Now that "relation back" had been repealed, it would seem that if the bankrupt tendered the price, he could insist on the land being conveyed, unless the agreement was a prohibited improvident transaction. If this is so, then the Assignee or trustee can also insist on specific performance. In any event, in the *Jennings'* case it was held that, even though the pre-1988 insolvent purchaser lost the right to specific performance, the trustee in bankruptcy could hold the vendor to the agreement by tendering the purchase money. The court would not agree that a vendor ought to be allowed to treat an act of bankruptcy before the date of completion as an anticipatory breach entitling him immediately to repudiate, or to wait for the day fixed for completion and then treat the contract as though time were of the essence, failure to complete on that day entitling the vendor immediately to rescind. In that case, damages were awarded against the vendor for wrongfully repudiating the contract on learning of the purchaser's act of bankruptcy. Since in the meantime the vendor resold the property, the equitable remedy was not sought.

Disclaiming Onerous Contracts

5–58 If the contract imposes particularly burdensome obligations on the bankrupt's estate, a disclaimer application may be made to have that contract rescinded on such terms as the court deems fit.[130]

LITIGATION

5–59 Occurrence of an act of bankruptcy or adjudication affects litigation being brought by and against the debtor in several ways. The courts distinguish between essentially personal actions and actions involving property rights, property in this context being extensively defined.

Bankrupt Plaintiff

5–60 The right to bring or to continue claims of an essential personal nature being brought by a bankrupt remains in him. But if the claim relates to an injury

---

[128] Ex parte *Rabbidge* (1878) 8 Ch. D. 367 at 370, and *Pearce v Bastable's Trustee* [1901] 2 Ch. 122.

[129] [1952] Ch. 899.

[130] 1988 Act, s.56 and see paras 7–02 et seq.

primarily to his estate, it constitutes property that vests in the Assignee or the trustee.[131] For instance in *Siroko v Murphy*,[132] an action for breach of warranty in a contract to supply the plaintiff with goods was held to vest in the Assignee because it was not for "a mere personal wrong". Accordingly, the plaintiff was no longer entitled to continue the action and, it was held, the proper course for a defendant in such circumstances is to apply to the court to stay or dismiss the action. But in an anomalous instance,[133] where a district judge's order that a claim did not vest in the bankruptcy trustee was never appealed, it was held that the bankrupt was entitled to sue her former insolvency advisors for damages, on account of their alleged negligence causing her to lose her nursing home business. Because the earlier court order had not been appealed, the defendants could not assert that she lacked authority to sue them.

5–61 The Assignee or trustee can take over the action or appeal and continue it, having applied to the court for liberty to do so. Alternatively, he is entitled to compromise such proceedings on such terms as he deems reasonable.[134] Since a legal claim is a chose in action, it can be assigned.[135] In light of the statutory duty to realise the assets, assigning a claim does not offend against the law on maintenance and champerty.[136] It may even be re-assigned back to the bankrupt[137] and, it has been held, such assignment can even be on terms that the bankrupt will pay the Assignee a proportion of such damages as he may recover.[138] If the Assignee declines to pursue a claim and permits the bankrupt to commence or to continue proceedings in his own right, the other party to the action may be entitled to an order for security for costs. Where the bankrupt is dissatisfied with the Assignee's refusal to prosecute the claim, he can apply the directions that the action or appeal may proceed, either by the Assignee or by the bankrupt.

Bankrupt Defendant

5–62 Insolvency law encourages the resolution of essentially financial claims against bankrupts through the machinery for proving debts rather than immediately in the courts. It is likely that the Assignee or trustee will reach a satisfactory accommodation with the claimant but, if a compromise cannot be reached, the matter can then be submitted to the court. Allowing the matter be dealt with in this way conserves the estate's resources, to the benefit of all the creditors.

5–63 Where the plaintiff can be characterised as a "creditor" and is claiming in respect of any debt which can be proved in the bankruptcy, those proceedings

---

[131] See para.5–18.
[132] [1955] I.R. 77.
[133] *Mulkerrins v PricewaterhouseCoopers* [2003] 1 W.L.R. 1937.
[134] *Re Gibbons* [1958] I.R. 98.
[135] E.g. *Stein v Blake* [1996] A.C. 243.
[136] *Grovewood Holdings Plc v James Capel & Co Ltd* [1995] Ch.90.
[137] *Wedell v Pearce & Major* [1987] 3 All E.R. 625.
[138] *Ramsey v Hartley* [1977] 1 W.L.R. 686.

cannot be commenced without first getting leave of the court.[139] But because proceedings to recover possession following forfeiture of a lease are not a "remedy against the property or person" of the bankrupt in respect of the rent, leave is not required.[140] When granting leave, the court can allow the case to proceed on such terms as it sees fit. Because this leave requirement is not procedural but is a condition precedent to the court's jurisdiction to hear the claim, leave cannot be given for proceedings that, through oversight, were already commenced. Such proceedings are a nullity and will not be retrospectively validated.[141]

5–64 It was held in *Heath v Tang*[142] that the principle here applies even to appealing the judgment that established the indebtedness that resulted in the bankruptcy. The debtor's right of appeal was part of the estate that he had been divested of and, accordingly, he could no longer prosecute that appeal.[143] The possible injustice that may result from this state of affairs is usually remedied by the court staying the hearing of the petition, pending the outcome of the appeal, where it appears to be bona fide.[144] In any proceedings concerning property, or a claim for debt or damages against a debtor who becomes bankrupt, where the only asset that could satisfy the claim vests in the Assignee, it has been held that the bankrupt has no locus standi to defend them or to appeal any order made in them against him.[145] Whether this would be followed in Ireland, in light of the constitutional position, is questionable. It has been accepted in those decisions that, in exceptional circumstances, the bankrupt should be entitled to take steps in the proceedings where urgent action is needed.[146] In proceedings where there are concurrent wrongdoers, one of whom becomes or is likely to become bankrupt, the court is required to ensure that any damages awarded to him are not recovered by him for so long as his liability to others who suffered loss in the circumstances exceeds what they owe him.[147]

5–65 Actions being brought by a secured creditor to realise his security or to otherwise deal with it are not automatically stayed,[148] such as applications to appoint a receiver by way of equitable execution, for sequestration and for an order for sale of the charged property. Nor are purely personal actions against the bankrupt stayed. In one instance a bankrupt was permitted to appeal an injunction obtained against him, restraining passing off, as it was "a personal order against him".[149]

5–66 The Assignee or trustee may apply to have any existing proceedings being

---

[139] 1988 Act, s.136(1).
[140] *Harlow D.C. v Hall* [2006] 1 W.L.R. 2116.
[141] *Re Taylor* [2007] 2 W.L.R. 148.
[142] [1993] 1 W.L.R. 1421.
[143] Applying *Rochfort v Battersy* (1849) 2 H.L. Cas. 388.
[144] E.g. *Re Noble* [1965] Ch. 129.
[145] *James v Rutherford-Hodge* [2006] B.P.I.R. 973.
[146] *Dadourian Group Int'l Inc v Simms* [2008] B.P.I.R. 508
[147] Civil Liability Act 1961, s.39
[148] 1988 Act, s.136(2).
[149] *Dence v Mason*, 41 L.T. 573 (1879).

brought against the bankrupt stayed or restrained.[150] "Proceedings" for these purposes are interpreted extensively to include any process that a creditor may deploy to secure payment, including an application to have a person committed to prison for failure to make a required payment.[151] Where the proceedings may prejudice the general interests of the creditors and, in particular, where some bankruptcy point is being raised that can better be dealt with in the Bankruptcy Court, the action will usually be stayed, on such terms as the court dealing with the matter sees fit. Otherwise, the action usually will be permitted to proceed.[152] Where the court does not permit proceedings against the bankrupt to proceed or continue, the plaintiff is not liable for any costs incurred in the action by the bankrupt.[153] Where he was being sued as a co-defendant the court's order does not prevent proceedings from being brought against the other party or parties.[154]

CREDITORS' REMEDIES

5–67   Once the debtor becomes a bankrupt, unsecured creditors' remedies may not be deployed against him or his property. Following adjudication, "a creditor ... for any debt provable in bankruptcy shall not have any remedy against the property or person of the bankrupt in respect of his debt apart from his rights under this Act ... shall not commence any proceedings in respect of such debt unless with the leave of the Court ...".[155] Thus, a creditor cannot enforce any of the remedies, such as *fieri facias*, attachment and the like. His redress is against the entire estate on the same basis as the other unsecured creditors; it would be unfair if one or some creditors could recover proportionately more than the others by levying execution or whatever on the bankrupt's estate or property. This principle is subject to qualifications and exceptions.

Secured Creditors

5–68   The restriction on resort to creditors' remedies does not apply to secured creditors: it does "not affect the power of a secured creditor to realise or otherwise deal with his security in the same manner as he would have been entitled to realise or deal with it if [s.136(1)] had not been enacted".[156] Thus, secured creditors remain free to enforce and to realise their security. A secured creditor, for these purposes, is "any creditor holding any mortgage, charge or lien on the debtor's estate or any part thereof as security for a debt due to him".[157] The terms "mortgage", "charge" and "lien" have specific meanings but have been held not to extend, for example, to issuing a writ of sequestration against

---

[150]   1988 Act, s.137(1).
[151]   *Smith v Braintree D.C.* [1990] 2 A.C. 215.
[152]   E.g. *Re Hutton* [1969] 2 Ch. 201.
[153]   1988 Act, s.137(2)(a).
[154]   1988 Act, s.137(2)(b).
[155]   1988 Act, s.136(1).
[156]   1988 Act, s.136(2).
[157]   1988 Act, s.3(1).

a debtor[158] or having a receiver by way of equitable execution appointed over his property.[159] While registering a judgment mortgage would seem to render the judgment mortgagee a secured creditor, it is provided that such mortgagee shall not be entitled to any priority or preference over the general creditors unless the affidavit was registered at least three months prior to the date of the adjudication.[160] In so far as a charge applies to post-adjudication receipts, a charge on future income or on book debts does not render the chargee a secured creditor for these purposes.

Set-Off

5–69 Where there are "mutual credits and debts", set-off is required in bankruptcy,[161] although there may be circumstances where this right may be waived.

Distress

5–70 Formerly, landlords enjoyed a somewhat privileged position as creditors in a bankruptcy in that, subject to certain qualifications, after adjudication, they could distrain on the bankrupt's goods or effects for unpaid rent which was due. This is no longer the case: "[n]o distress shall be levied" following adjudication.[162]

Uncompleted Execution

5–71 Neither the 1857–1872 Acts nor the 1988 Act contain provisions similar to those in s.40 of the former English 1914 Act, which specifies when execution against a debtor's property shall be deemed to be completed, thereby taking that property out of his estate and rendering it no longer available for the Assignee or trustee in bankruptcy. Under that Act, if execution or attachment was "completed" before a specified date, then the enforcing creditor was entitled to the "benefit" of the process; if there was no such completion, he could not benefit from the process. Completion was defined, as in the case of execution against goods, seizure and sale; in the case of attachment of a debt, receipt of the debt; in the case of execution against land, seizure or, if it is an equitable interest, the appointment of a receiver. Equivalent provisions are contained in s.291 of the Companies Act 1963.

5–72 The following, therefore, would seem to be the position under the 1988 Act. Provided that the affidavit for the judgment mortgage was registered at least three months prior to the date of adjudication,[163] the judgment mortgagee has all the rights of a secured creditor. Presumably a charging order over

---

[158] *Re Hoare* (1880) 14 Ch. D. 41.
[159] *Re Lough Neagh Ship Co., Ex p. Thompson* [1896] 1 I.R. 29.
[160] 1988 Act, s.51(1) and cf. *Re Murphy* [1895] 1 I.R. 339.
[161] See paras. 8–28 et seq.
[162] 1988 Act, s.139.
[163] 1988 Act, s.51.

stocks and shares is completed once the court has declared that the securities in question stand well charged. A receivership by way of equitable execution is completed once the receiver enters into possession. As for seizure by the sheriff and attachment of debts, what constitutes "completion" for these purposes is not entirely clear, which is why the legislature in 1963 adopted a statutory definition for the concept in the context of liquidations.[164] It remains to be seen whether the court will apply the same criteria as set down in s.291 of the Companies Act 1963 when dealing with this matter or whether it will look exclusively to the case law for guidance. Reasons of convenience would favour following the definition there but, against that, if the legislature had intended that this definition of "completion" should apply in bankruptcy cases, surely provision to that effect would have been made.

5–73   For practical purposes it will rarely be necessary to determine whether execution by the sheriff has been completed. Even though goods have been seized or sold, or money has been paid over in full satisfaction of the debt in question to avoid seizure and sale, that money or the proceeds from the sale must be held for 21 days. If during that period the sheriff, the county registrar or the execution creditor is notified that the debtor has been adjudicated bankrupt, the property seized or the money must be delivered or paid over to the Official Assignee.[165] The execution creditor is thereby deprived of the benefit of the process, but will have a first charge over the goods or the money in respect of the costs he incurred in levying execution. Where during this twenty-one days period a person purchases the goods seized and sold by the sheriff or the county registrar, he obtains a good tide as against the Assignee if the purchase was in good faith.[166]

---

[164] Companies Act 1963, s.291(5).
[165] 1988 Act, s.50(2).
[166] 1988 Act, s.50(3).

CHAPTER 6

ADMINISTERING THE ESTATE

6–01 Ordinarily, the administration of the bankrupt's estate is the responsibility of the Official Assignee; occasionally the creditors will opt to have the estate administered instead by a trustee of their own choosing.

OFFICIAL ASSIGNEE

6–02 Unless the creditors appoint their own trustee, the bankrupt's estate and affairs will be administered by the Official Assignee (hereinafter referred to as the Assignee).[1] He is a corporation sole and an officer of the High Court under the Courts (Supplemental Provisions) Act 1961.[2] Since 1849 the affairs of bankrupts have been administered in his office. Provision is made for him to employ a bankruptcy inspector and assistants in order to carry out various functions under the 1988 Act.[3] These persons must follow his instructions and be subject to the directions of the court.[4] Once the statutory sitting takes place, he can appoint a solicitor to give advice and to have carriage of the proceedings on his behalf.[5]

6–03 The Assignee is a full time officer of the court; he may not directly carry on any trade or business or be engaged in any other office or employment.[6] His status was considered in *Re McGovern*,[7] which concerned the question of re-vesting the bankrupt's estate following an order annulling his bankruptcy. It was held that, because the Assignee is a corporation sole, under the 1857–1872 Acts the property had to be reassigned to the bankrupt and that the conveyance must be made by the Assignee under his own name and title.[8] In the circumstances, the re-vesting could not be done by the Assignee's deputy. It was held in *Re Fitzpatrick*[9] that, where an Assignee resigns or dies, or is replaced, the bankrupt's property will vest in the successor, without the need for a re-conveyance.

6–04 At the date of the adjudication all of the bankrupt's property vests in

---

1   1988 Act, s.60(1).
2   Schedule 8, para. 9. Cf. Court Officers Act 1926, s.12.
3   1988 Act, ss. 60(2) and 62.
4   1988 Act, s.62(2)(d).
5   Rule 43.
6   Rule 145.
7   [1971] I.R. 149.
8   No longer the case under s.85(6) of the 1988 Act.
9   [1939] I.R. 252.

the Assignee, with certain exceptions.[10] His duties in general are "to get in and realise the property, to ascertain the debts and liabilities and to distribute the assets in accordance with ... this Act".[11] To this end, the 1988 Act confers on him various specific powers and duties.[12] As well as being authorised to bring, continue and defend proceedings relating to the bankrupt's property,[13] he is authorised, in any "case of doubt or difficulty", to seek the directions of the court regarding the matter.[14] The Assignee is personally liable for all the costs incurred in the course of litigation by or against him. But he is entitled to be indemnified from the assets of the estate, in respect of any damages, costs or expenses he incurred, provided he acted bona fide.[15]

CREDITORS' TRUSTEE

6–05   Instead of the Official Assignee, the bankrupt's estate and affairs may be administered by a trustee chosen by his creditors (hereinafter referred to as the trustee), in very much the same way as creditors can choose a liquidator for the voluntary winding up of a company.

Appointment

6–06   In order to have the administration conducted in this manner, the trustee must be appointed at the "statutory sitting" which is held after the petition was presented, or at any adjournment of the sitting.[16] He may be proposed either by the Official Assignee or by any creditor; such proposal must be grounded on an affidavit, setting out the reasons therefor and the particulars of the nominee, along with an exhibit of his consent to act as trustee.[17] There are no stipulated qualifications or disqualifications for this office. In the past, as a general rule, only a creditor would be appointed[18] but, in special circumstances, the court would appoint someone else who was particularly appropriate to do the job. Where a proposal has been made to appoint a trustee, the court will adjourn the statutory sitting so that the Assignee can fix a time for sending in proofs of debt and to ascertain the bankrupt's liabilities.[19] In the case of filling a vacancy, the court must convene a creditors' meeting to decide the matter.[20]

6–07   Selection of the trustee requires a substantial majority of the creditors: three-fifths in number *and* value of the creditors voting at a meeting, either

---

[10]   See paras 5–09 et seq.
[11]   1988 Act, s.61(2).
[12]   1988 Act, s.61(3).
[13]   1988 Act, s.61(3)(d).
[14]   1988 Act, s.61(6).
[15]   1988 Act, s.84(5).
[16]   1988 Act, s.110.
[17]   Rule 103.
[18]   *Re Bany & Rumley* (1867) I.R. 1 Eq. 48.
[19]   Rule 104.
[20]   Rule 115.

in person or by proxy.[21] Notice of the appointment must be advertised, in the prescribed form,[22] in the *Iris Oifigiúil* and in at least one daily newspaper circulating in the area where the bankrupt resides.[23]

6–08 At the same time, the creditors are required to appoint a committee of inspection, comprising not more than five of them, to supervise the trustee's activities.[24] Once a trustee and a committee of inspection are chosen, an application must then be made to the court to have the bankrupt's property vested in the trustee.[25]

6–09 When a trustee is appointed, provision must be made at the statutory sitting for several matters: notably, making regular reports to subsequent sittings, lodging money received and auditing accounts.[26] Another matter to be dealt with then is his remuneration.[27] Neither the 1988 Act nor the rules make any express reference to an indemnity.

Functions

6–10 All the bankrupt's non-exempted property will become vested in the trustee subject to certain exceptions.[28] He is given all the powers and is authorised to perform the same functions as are conferred on the Assignee,[29] those primary functions being "to get in and realise the property, to ascertain the debts and liabilities and to distribute the assets in accordance with ... this Act".[30] In carrying out this task, he is subject to the control of the court[31] and also must "have regard to" any directions given by the committee of inspection or any resolutions passed by a properly constituted meeting of the creditors.[32] In performing his tasks, the trustee is subject to the same duty of care and general fiduciary duties as other trustees.[33] One particular conflict of interest is prohibited by the rules: unless the committee of inspection decides otherwise, a trustee who is an auctioneer is not permitted, by himself or any partner, to act in the sale of a bankrupt's property.[34]

Termination of Appointment

6–11 For a trustee in bankruptcy to resign effectively from the office, he must

---

[21] 1988 Act, s.110.
[22] Form No. 32.
[23] Rule 107.
[24] 1988 Act, s.110.
[25] 1988 Act, s.111.
[26] 1988 Act, s.112(3).
[27] 1988 Act, s.112(3)(a).
[28] 1988 Act, s.111 and see paras 5–09 et seq.
[29] 1988 Act, s.112(2) and r.102.
[30] 1988 Act, s.61(2).
[31] 1988 Act, s.112(1).
[32] 1988 Act, s.112(1).
[33] Cf. *Smedley v Brittain* [2008] B.P.I.R. 219.
[34] Rule 109.

first obtain the release of the court.[35] Before the court decides the matter, he must summon a meeting of the creditors and inform them of the details of his application for release. The bankrupt must also be notified of this meeting. Any creditor or the Assignee may appear in court to oppose the trustee's application for release.

6–12   Upon "cause shown", the court is empowered to remove a trustee.[36] It would seem that "cause" here connotes "some unfitness of the person—it may be from personal character, or from his connection with other parties, or from circumstances in which he is mixed up—some unfitness in a wide sense of the term".[37]

6–13   On ceasing to be a trustee, he must file with the Assignee an account, verified on oath, of his activities while he held the office and accounting for all the bankrupt's property and money.[38] All books, documents, papers and accounts in the former trustee's possession, relating to the office, must be delivered on oath to the Assignee or the new trustee if there is one.[39]

Supervising the Trustee

6–14   A Committee elected by the creditors will supervise the trustee's activities, and the Examiner is given a supervisory role.

The Committee of Inspection

6–15   Where the creditors decide to appoint their own trustee to administer the bankrupt's estate they must also appoint a committee of inspection to act along with and to supervise him.[40] This committee must consist of not more than five creditors, all of whom are qualified to vote at a creditors' meeting.[41] The quorum for meetings of the committee is three and decisions can be made by a majority resolution of the members present at a meeting.[42] Either the trustee or any member of the committee can summon meetings.[43] Notices of meetings, stating the time, place and purpose of the meeting, must be sent by post to each of the members at least seven days before the meeting is due to take place. A notice must also be sent to the trustee. The trustee is obliged to "have regard to" any directions the committee may give him.[44] Any member of the committee may resign.[45] A vacancy can be filled by convening a creditors' meeting and by

---

[35]   1988 Act, s.113.
[36]   Rule 114.
[37]   *Re Sir John Moore Gold Mining Ltd,* (1879) 12 Ch. D. 326 at 331, regarding the grounds for removing company liquidators.
[38]   Rule 117.
[39]   Rule 118.
[40]   1988 Act, s.110.
[41]   1988 Act, s.110.
[42]   Rule 122.
[43]   Rule 123.
[44]   1988 Act, s.112(1).
[45]   Rule 124.

resolving, by a majority of three-fifths in number and value of the creditors, to appoint a replacement.[46]

6–16　Where any creditor wishes to remove a member,[47] he should apply to some member of the committee to convene a special meeting of the creditors for that purpose. If that member does not convene the meeting, the creditor should apply to the court, stating on affidavit the reasons which would justify such removal and the court may direct a meeting to be held before the Official Assignee. Alternatively, the court may notify the member in question to show cause why he should not be removed by the court.

6–17　The committee is obliged to monitor closely the trustee's activities. As was explained above, the various records kept by the trustee must be submitted for the committee's inspection[48] and they must audit his estate book every three months.[49]

The Examiner

6–18　The Examiner has some supervisory functions over the creditors' trustee and their committee of inspection. A certified copy of the quarterly audit of the estate book must be forwarded to the Examiner who, in an appropriate case, may refer a matter arising from the audit to the court.[50] There also is a general obligation on the Examiner to "take cognisance of the conduct of the trustee".[51] Where any creditor or the bankrupt makes a complaint about the trustee or where the trustee is "not faithfully performing his duties" or is not "duly observing" what he is required to do, the Examiner must inquire into the matter.[52] If he is not satisfied with any explanation which is given, a report must be made to the court. A copy of this report and a notice of the court hearing must be sent to the trustee. After hearing the matter, the court may remove the trustee or make such other order as it deems fit.[53]

POWERS AND DUTIES

6–19　Many powers and duties of the Assignee or creditors' trustee are set out in the 1988 Act[54] and in the Bankruptcy Rules, and certain obligations arise by virtue of the trustee's fiduciary position. Company liquidators are given equivalent powers by the Companies Acts and are subject to similar obligations. Unlike liquidators, however, the consent of the court is not required before exercising

---

[46]　Rule 126.
[47]　Rule 125.
[48]　Rule 112.
[49]　Rule 113(1).
[50]　Rule 113(2).
[51]　Rule 120.
[52]　Rule 120.
[53]　Rule 121.
[54]　Especially s.61(3).

several of these powers, although the court may stipulate that its consent must be obtained before some powers can be exercised. Also, the creditors or the committee of inspection may require the trustee to get their approval before exercising certain powers.

Get in the Assets and Protect them

6–20   Perhaps the first major task is to get in all of the bankrupt's property, other than the excepted assets. To that end, the 1988 Act gives the Assignee several powers; it also contains provisions for invalidating various improper dispositions of the bankrupt's property which occurred prior to the date of adjudication. It is more convenient to deal with some of these provisions in the next chapter, such as contesting fraudulent preferences and voluntary settlements.

6–21   On being requested to do so, every person who possesses money and securities which have vested in the Assignee must deliver them up.[55] Among the Bankruptcy Inspector's duties is to take an inventory of the bankrupt's assets and, undoubtedly, the trustee has a similar obligation.[56] A warrant can be issued by the court directing the Bankruptcy Inspector or any of his assistants to seize the property.[57] To that end, where necessary, the person seeking to seize the property is empowered to break into any house or other place belonging to the bankrupt where it is believed part of his property is kept. Where the court has reason to believe that some of that property is concealed in another person's house or place, the court may issue a search warrant authorising the Inspector or an assistant to look for that property.[58] But the Act does not confer an express power to enter forcibly that other person's property. Persons who are duly authorised to seize property or to conduct searches are protected from liability with regard to anything done bona fide pursuant to their warrants.[59]

6–22   It is provided that "the property of every bankrupt, and the income and proceeds thereof, shall be possessed and received" by the Assignee.[60] Thus the Assignee or trustee, as the case maybe, is given all the powers of a receiver to get in the bankrupt's property, unless the court directs otherwise. All money or securities they receive must be lodged forthwith in the Assignee's account at the Central Bank.[61] The court may give permission to invest that money from time to time.[62]

Examination

6–23   One of the most effective instruments in the Assignee's or trustee's

---

[55]   1988 Act, s.66 and cf. ss. 22, 54 and 68.
[56]   1988 Act, s.62(2)(b) and (c).
[57]   1988 Act, s.27.
[58]   1988 Act, s.28.
[59]   1988 Act, s.29.
[60]   1988 Act, s.69(2).
[61]   Rule 150.
[62]   Rule 149.

armoury is the examination under oath in court of a wide category of people who had dealings with the bankrupt.[63] Company liquidators possess similar powers.[64] The purpose underlying this examination has been described as "for the sole purpose of enabling a thorough and searching examination to be conducted to ascertain the truth as to the property of the bankrupt".[65]

Summoning Witnesses and Documents

6–24 Those who can be summoned for examination and compelled to produce documents, are "any person who is known or suspected to have in his possession or control any property of the bankrupt or to have disposed of any property of the bankrupt or who is supposed to be indebted to the bankrupt, or any person whom the Court deems capable of giving information relating to the trade, dealings, affairs or property of the bankrupt".[66]

6–25 As well as the Assignee or trustee, any creditor and even the bankrupt himself may apply to the court to have someone examined.

6–26 Exceptionally these applications may be made ex parte, and the evidence used to ground such applications exceptionally may be withheld from the bankrupt and the intended witness.[67] This is because the investigative power is a special procedure designed to facilitate enquiries into the bankrupt's affairs, and advance notice and disclosure may frustrate the entire exercise. But there must be a real likelihood of the investigation being obstructed before the normal rule of prior notice and full disclosure of all the evidence may be dispensed with. Where the justification being offered is urgency, that must not be of the applicant's own making. That the evidence supporting the application is overwhelming or that the application may be fiercely resisted is no justification for proceeding ex parte.[68]

6–27 The court has a wide discretion who it will summon for these purposes. It may require the applicant to make out a prima facie case that the person being sought can supply information that would be useful for getting in the bankrupt's assets or otherwise helpful to the administration of the estate.[69] Even the Assignee or trustee himself can be called.[70] Since they are not parties to the proceedings, witnesses cannot be ordered to pay the costs of an examination.[71]

6–28 Witnesses can be required to produce in court any books or papers concerning the bankrupt's property or affairs which are in their possession or

---

[63] 1988 Act, s.21.
[64] Companies Act 1963, ss. 245 and 280.
[65] *Hollingshead v M'Loughlin* [1917] 2 I.R. 28 at 34; see too *Re Poulson* [1976] 1 W.L.R. 1023 at 1033.
[66] 1988 Act, s.21(1).
[67] *Re Murjani* [1996] 1 W.L.R. 1498.
[68] *Re Murjani* [1996] 1 W.L.R. 1498.
[69] Ex parte *Nicholson* (1880) 14 Ch. D. 243.
[70] Ex parte *Crossley* (1872) L.R. 13 Eq. 409.
[71] *Re Cooper,* 80 I.L.T.R. 70 (1946).

control.[72] They cannot refuse to produce those merely because they have a lien on them.[73] It would seem that a registered company can be called to produce documents but not to give evidence.[74]

6–29   Where the bankrupt is summoned but does not appear at the appointed time, the court can have him arrested and brought to be examined.[75] The same applies for others who are summoned, provided that they were offered a reasonable sum to cover their expenses.[76] However, the court will not order such arrest if, at the time fixed for the hearing, a reasonable excuse was given and which was acceptable to the court. This power to order arrest is without prejudice to the ordinary powers of the court regarding contempt or enforcing the attendance of witnesses.[77]

Conduct of the Examination

6–30   The court has a discretion whether the examination should be conducted in private. In *Re Redbreast Preserving Co Ltd*[78] the Supreme Court rejected the contention that, under the Constitution, equivalent proceedings under the Companies Acts must be held in public. This was because such examinations do not constitute administration of justice in the strict sense; they are more in the nature of "the collection and preparation of the material upon which a judge pronounced his decision ...".[79]

6–31   Although the examination can be conducted by the judge or by the Master, usually the questions are put by the applicant for the examination, through his solicitor or counsel. The person being examined is entitled to be legally represented, and be questioned by his solicitor and counsel in order more fully to explain his position. Questions may be put in the form of interrogatories. What the Assignee or trustee will be seeking to ascertain, principally, are the reasons for the bankruptcy, whether the statement of affairs is indeed a complete account of the bankrupt's financial situation, whether claims can be brought against third parties to recover property which was improperly transferred, such as fraudulent preferences and voidable settlements. Another matter is whether any of the criminal laws relating to insolvency have been contravened. It has been said that the object of these examinations is "not merely for the purpose of collecting the debts on behalf of the creditors or of ascertaining simply what sum can be made available for the creditors who are entitled to it, but also for the purpose of the protection of the public in the cases in which the bankruptcy proceedings apply ...".[80] To concentrate attention on the mere

---

[72]   1988 Act, s.21(3); cf. *Re Joseph Hargreaves Ltd* [1900] 1 Ch. 347.
[73]   1988 Act, s.21(3).
[74]   *Penn Texas Corp v Murat Anstalt* [1964] 1 Q.B. 40.
[75]   1988 Act, s.23(2).
[76]   1988 Act, s.23(3).
[77]   1988 Act, s.23(4).
[78]   91 I.L.T.R. 12 (1957).
[79]   91 I.L.T.R. 12 (1957) at 23.
[80]   *Re Paget* [1927] 2 Ch. 85 at 87.

debt collecting and distributing assets aspects is to fail to appreciate one very important side of bankruptcy proceedings and law. Many of the authorities on examinations in the context of company liquidations are apposite to the bankruptcy examination.[81]

6–32 The actual tenor of questioning the bankrupt has been described in *Hollingshead v M'Loughlin* as follows: "that examination ... ought to be conducted in such a way as to avoid any kind of concussion upon the bankrupt to make him give evidence in one direction rather than another. A bankruptcy examination ought not to be converted into a torture chamber. The sanctions of the law behind the evasions or concealments or untruths of bankrupts are strong enough without concussions in the course of the examination being practiced".[82] Ronan L.J. observed that "[t]he object of such examinations is to get at the truth, and the judge must be guided in the exercise of his discretion as to the mode of examination by this. He has a perfect right to form his own opinion as to whether a witness is telling the truth or not, and to put such questions himself, and to allow counsel to pursue such method of examination as the judge thinks necessary for the purpose of ascertaining the truth".[83] In that case the House of Lords rejected the contention that, in conducting the examination, the judge adopted an unduly partisan approach. It was held that, in the circumstances, he acted properly in committing the bankrupt and his spouse to jail because their answers were so unsatisfactory that it was not possible to believe they were making a candid disclosure.

6–33 In *Re Poulson*,[84] the inquisitorial nature of the proceedings was emphasised: "although doubtless the procedure can be used in an accusatorial manner if that is what will best serve the trustee's overriding purpose, it is also capable of being used, and frequently is used most fruitfully, in an inquisitorial manner. And when so used, many answers given by a witness who is prepared to be co-operative and prepared to volunteer information may be of the utmost assistance to the trustee although they might well not be proper answers, or even admissible answers, in the more normal proceedings".[85]

6–34 Questions cannot be put simply in order to build up a case or with a view to probing defences in a case which is already in train. Where an action is pending between the Assignee and the witness, while the Assignee is entitled to "reasonable information", the court will not permit "anything like a dress rehearsal of the cross examination in the action".[86] Questions which are mere "fishing" exercises also will be disallowed.[87]

---

[81] See generally M. Forde et al., *The Law of Company Insolvency,* 2nd edn (Dublin: Round Hall, 2008) at 209.

[82] [1917] 2 I.R. 28 at 36.

[83] [1916] 2 I.R. 583 at 605.

[84] [1976] 1 W.L.R. 1023.

[85] [1976] 1 W.L.R. 1023 at 1032.

[86] *Re Franks* [1892] 1 Q.B. 646, at 647–648; also *Re Castle New Home Ltd* [1979] 1 W.L.R. 1075.

[87] *Re Gregory* [1935] 1 Ch. 65.

6–35   Witnesses may be entitled to refuse to answer particular questions on the grounds that the information is privileged. The privilege against self-incrimination is protected: an answer cannot be refused on the grounds that it might incriminate the witness; but any answers that he gives cannot be admitted as evidence against him in any other proceedings, be they criminal or civil.[88] An exception is perjury: the witness can be prosecuted for that offence if he gave false evidence at the examination. Any answers given can be used as evidence against third parties, including a company of which the person being examined is an officer.[89] Other privileges that can be claimed in such proceedings include the legal professional privilege, which covers all communications between the witness and his legal advisors which are directly referable to litigation. A lawyer who is a witness can equally claim this privilege.[90] However, where the witness is the bankrupt's own solicitor and the questions are being put on behalf of the Assignee or trustee, this privilege has a far narrower compass.[91]

Committal for Non-Co-operation

6–36   The court is empowered to commit to prison persons who will not co-operate in the examination by either refusing to be sworn, by refusing to answer or by failing to answer any question properly put, or not fully answering such questions or not complying with any order of the court under the Act.[92] One such order is to sign and subscribe to a written record of one's examination. Committal shall last until such further order of the court. And the court can direct a person whom it has committed to appear before it to be examined and, if he complies with the court's requirements, to order his release. It is only in the most exceptional circumstances that an application for a committal order may be made ex parte. If the order is made in those circumstances, it should stipulate that, once the person in question has been arrested, he should be brought before the court at an early opportunity. It also should stipulate the grounds on which it was made.

6–37   In *Re Carroll*,[93] Johnston J. cautioned against too readily resorting to committal, remarking that "power of committal for unsatisfactory answering must be exercised with the utmost caution and only in the rarest cases ... I have never committed a witness for mere untruthfulness. There must be something more, some probability that the making of such an order will have practical results in the ascertainment and the realisation of the bankrupt's assets. If no practical purpose is to be served by committal, no such order ought to be made, even in the case of a bankrupt who is not telling the truth".[94]

6–38   Because a committal hearing is not a trial on a criminal charge but is

---

[88]   1988 Act, s.21(4) and cf. *Re McAllister* [1973] I.R. 238.
[89]   *Irish Commercial Soc v Plunkett* [1986] I.L.R.M. 624.
[90]   Ex parte *Campbell* (1870) L.R. 5 Ch. 703.
[91]   *Re Wells* (1892) 9 Mor. 116.
[92]   1988 Act, s.24, and cf. *Hickling v Baker* [2007] 1 W.L.R. 2386.
[93]   71 I.L.T.R. 119 (1937).
[94]   71 I.L.T.R. 119 (1937).

designed simply to elucidate satisfactory answers to pertinent questions, it was held in *Re McAllister*[95] that there is no constitutional right to trial by jury before the imprisonment order is made. But a person who has been so committed is entitled to apply for bail.[96] The court may issue a warrant to have the detainee brought before it.

Carry on the Business

6–39   The list of powers do not include carrying on the bankrupt's business.[97] But the court can appoint somebody as a receiver and manager of the property, thereby authorising carrying on the business, subject to such terms as the court may lay down.[98] It would seem that even the bankrupt himself could be appointed receiver and manager of the estate or part of the estate.

Give Charges

6–40   If money has to be raised, power is given to mortgage or pledge the bankrupt's assets in order to obtain the necessary funds.[99]

Compromises and Arrangements

6–41   Authority is given to make compromises with creditors and with classes of creditors, including persons claiming to be creditors or who claim that the bankrupt is liable to them in damages in one way or another.[100] The power to compromise includes taking security for discharging the settlement. Schemes of arrangement can be entered into with classes of creditors or with persons claiming damages from the bankrupt.

Litigation and Arbitration

6–42   Administering the bankrupt's affairs may require the Assignee or the trustee to resort to litigation or arbitration, either as plaintiff/claimant or as defendant/respondent. There is specific statutory power to do any of these things.[101] Also, there is a power to apply to the court to stay any proceedings being brought against the bankrupt[102] and, in "a case of doubt or difficulty", the Assignee or trustee can apply for the directions of the court in connection with the estate or the bankrupt's affairs.[103] In *Tormey v E.S.R.I.*,[104] it was held that the fact that the plaintiff is a bankrupt is not of itself a good ground for ordering security for costs. The Assignee was joined by order of the court as a second

---

[95]   [1973] I.R. 238.

[96]   [1973] I.R. 238.

[97]   Cf. Ex p. *Emmanuel* (1881) 17 Ch. D. 35 and *Re Walsh* (1859) 9 Ir. Ch. 6.

[98]   1988 Act, s.73.

[99]   1988 Act, s.61(3)(f).

[100]   1988 Act, s.61(3)(b) and (c) and cf. *Re Gibbons* [1958] I.R. 98.

[101]   1988 Act, s.61(3)(d) and (e) and s.30.

[102]   1988 Act, s.137.

[103]   1988 Act, s.61(6).

[104]   [1986] I.R. 615.

plaintiff in an action by the bankrupt for damages for his wrongful dismissal. Hamilton P. expressed agreement with the statement that "[t]he plaintiff will not be compelled to give security for costs merely because he is a pauper, or bankrupt, or insolvent, and this is even in a qui tam action; and this rule applies where the plaintiff is a trustee of a bankrupt and is suing for the benefit of the estate".[105] An Assignee or trustee who loses an action or an arbitration, where costs are awarded against him, is personally liable for the costs.[106] Usually, however, he will be indemnified those costs from the estate.[107]

Realise the Assets

6–43   The power to realise the bankrupt's assets is formulated as "to sell the property by public auction or private contract, with power to transfer the whole thereof to any person or to sell the same in lots and for the purpose of selling land to carry out such sale by fee farm grant, sub fee farm grant, lease, sub-lease or otherwise and to sell any rent reserved on any such grant or any reversion expectant upon the determination of any such lease".[108] In the case of stocks and shares, the Assignee or trustee has the same rights to transfer them as the bankrupt had hitherto.[109] As is the case with company liquidators, there is a duty to obtain the best price as could reasonably be obtained in the circumstances.[110] If the bankrupt is beneficially entitled to land as a tenant in tail, the entail may be barred with the consent of the court.[111]

Sale of Property

6–44   Subject to directions to the contrary from the court or the committee of inspection, it is for the Assignee or the trustee to determine the particular mode of sale, whether it be by public auction or by private contract, and whether it be in one part or in lots.[112] Except where the committee consents, a trustee who is an auctioneer must not sell the property by himself or by any of his partners.[113] And it would be a breach of fiduciary duty for the trustee to acquire that property for himself.[114]

6–45   Before the sale an auctioneer retained should give the Assignee or trustee an opinion as to what price the property should fetch. Another auctioneer or valuer may even be retained to advise about the value for the purpose of fixing a reserve price.[115] Whether there should be such a reserve is at the discretion of the Assignee or trustee. Any such reserve must not be disclosed until the bidding

---

[105] [1986] I.R. 615 at 619.
[106] Cf. *Re Wilson Lovett & Sons Ltd* [1977] 1 All E.R. 274.
[107] Cf. 1988 Act, s.84(5).
[108] 1988 Act, s.61(3)(a).
[109] 1988 Act, s.67.
[110] E.g. *Re Brook Cottage Ltd* [1976] N.I. 78.
[111] 1988 Act, s.64.
[112] 1988 Act, s.61(3)(a).
[113] Rule 109.
[114] *Smith v Kay* (1859) 7 H.L.C. 750.
[115] Rule 59.

is completed, unless the Assignee otherwise consents or the court so directs. Where property has been sold by auction, as soon as is possible thereafter the auctioneer should certify to the Assignee the result of the auction. Where an order for sale was made or where the Assignee otherwise requires, a statement of title and conditions of sale must be prepared by the solicitor having carriage of the sale.[116] The Assignee may direct searches to be made, that specified persons be notified and advertisements placed in newspapers, and may settle a statement of title or conditions or have them settled by Counsel.

6–46 *Family Home:* Special provision is made for realising the "family home" as defined in the Family Home Protection Act 1976. In order to dispose of it, prior sanction of the court must be obtained;[117] any purported disposition without such sanction is void. Where such an application is being made, the court can order postponement of the sale. The criteria relevant to such a decision are "the interests of the creditors and of the spouse and dependants of the bankrupt as well as ... all the circumstances of the case". The court therefore has a wide discretion to determine whether the home should be sold.

6–47 *Charged Property:* Where it is sought to sell property which is subject to a mortgage, charge or lien, an application can be made by way of a notice of motion, grounded on an affidavit setting forth the particulars of the amounts due to the chargee and the details of any other security for that amount held by the applicant.[118] The court must be satisfied that the property is not subject to any other charge or incumbrance and, if it is so incumbered, that the incumbrancer has got notice of the application to sell. If the court is satisfied that the applicant is duly charged for the sum in question, it may declare his claim to be proved, subject to taking accounts and making enquiries as the court may direct, and it may give directions as to the manner of and conditions for selling the property. In the event of property being charged but no application is made to have it sold, the court may direct that it be sold subject to such mortgage, charge or lien. Provided that he got the leave of the court, the mortgagee of the bankrupt's property may bid for it and purchase it at the sale.[119]

Title and Possession

6–48 The vendor of the property is the Assignee or the trustee, as the case may be, from whom the purchaser acquires title. Such title is not to be invalidated by reason only of some defect in the proceedings under the Act.[120] So as to render a sale of land fully effective, the court may direct that the purchaser be put into possession of the property. Such order shall be executed in the same way as an order for delivery of possession.[121]

---

[116] Rule 60.
[117] 1988 Act, ss.61(4) and (5).
[118] Rule 61.
[119] 1988 Act, s.53.
[120] 1988 Act, s.55.
[121] 1988 Act, s.52.

Other Powers

6–49   Where the bankrupt would benefit from any estate, letters of administration may be taken out in the name of the Assignee or trustee, as the case may be.[122] On taking out these, security need not be given. There is a power to agree to the charges for their services submitted by accountants, auctioneers, brokers and other persons, for instance, solicitors.[123] There is a power to agree to legal costs where they are not anticipated to exceed €1,300 (ex £1,000)[124]; if the amount is greater, the court must consent to any such agreement. Up to €130 (ex £100) can be drawn from the Unclaimed Dividend by way of indemnity in respect of any costs incurred.[125]

Books and Records

6–50   There are detailed provisions in the Bankruptcy Rules regarding the books and records that must be kept by the Assignee and by a creditors' trustee.

Assignee

6–51   One of the Assignee's first tasks is to call for and receive from the bankrupt a list of his debtors and creditors.[126] The Assignee will then examine these, with the aid of the bankrupt's books of account, so that any improper proofs of debt can be opposed. The Assignee is required to keep the following books and records:

> "A debtors' book, which records all debts due to each estate and the amount received;
> A creditors' book, which records the claims made against each estate;
> a cash book, which records all receipts and payments made;
> A ledger, which contains a debtor and creditor account of each estate;
> lists of all deeds, securities and valuables delivered to him; and
> lists of all books and papers delivered to him."[127]

6–52   At six monthly intervals, the Assignee must lodge with the Examiner a verified statement, in the prescribed form, showing the total amounts of receipts and payments in respect of every bankruptcy and arrangement during the periods ending June 30 and December 31.[128] The balance of any money or property at the end of these periods must also be shown. A copy of this statement must be transmitted by the Assignee to the bankruptcy judge. At such times as he deems fit the Examiner can carry out an audit on the Assignee's books and, for that purpose, shall be entitled to call on the Assignee to produce such books, files, other records and documents as may be required and vouchers

---

[122] 1988 Act, s.61(3)(g).
[123] 1988 Act, s.61(3)(i).
[124] 1988 Act, s.61(3)(h); S.I. No. 595 of 2001.
[125] 1988 Act, s.61(3)(k), S.I. No. 595 of 2001.
[126] Rule 146.
[127] Rule 161.
[128] Rule 154.

for all transactions involving receiving or disposing of funds or the receipt or disposal of property.[129]

Trustee

6–53   One of the creditors' trustee's first tasks is to take possession of all the bankrupt's books, documents and deeds and all moveable property.[130] A trustee is obliged to keep the following records.[131] There must be a "record book", which shall record what transpires at meetings of the Committee of Inspection, what transpires at court sittings which the trustee attended, all proofs of debt received and any other matter which should be recorded so that a correct account is kept of how the bankrupt's property is being managed. There must be an "estate book", where the day-to-day receipts and payments must be recorded. Thirdly, the trustee must keep a file or files, which shall contain copies of all court orders, the bankrupt's statement of affairs, all proofs of debt received and any correspondence or other documents in the bankruptcy.

6–54   These records must be placed before the Committee of Inspection at each of its meetings, and the Assignee and any creditor can inspect them at all reasonable times.[132] Every three months, the estate book must be submitted to the Committee of Inspection to be audited, and the Committee can call on the trustee to produce any records, vouchers or other documents.[133] Following the audit, the Committee must certify the estate book and a copy of it. This certified copy must then be sent to the Examiner. If the copy or the certificate discloses any misfeasance, neglect or omission, the Examiner will inquire into the matter and, if not satisfied with any explanation that may have been given, will report the matter to the court. If the court is to deal with the matter, the trustee must be notified and be given a copy of the Examiner's report.

Bank Accounts

6–55   The Assignee must open a separate bank account, with regard to every bankruptcy proceeding or arrangement, into which must be lodged all money and other funds received in respect of the estate.[134] Any payment to be made from such account must be sanctioned, in the prescribed form, by the Assignee or his duly authorised deputy and be counter-signed by an official in the Assignee's office.[135] Provision is also made for the Assignee's general cash account and for a standing imprest account. The former, known as the "Bankruptcy General Account",[136] must be credited with all lodgements being made to each estate account and be debited with all payments made from those accounts. The latter

---

[129] Rule 156.
[130] Rule 110.
[131] Rule 111.
[132] Rule 112.
[133] Rule 113.
[134] Rule 150.
[135] Rule 151.
[136] Rule 152.

account[137] is a temporary arrangement for facilitating urgent payments which must be made but the estate account is not yet in funds. A standing advance of €6,500 (ex £5,000) can be issued from the Unclaimed Dividend Account and then lodged to a separate account, for which the Assignee will be personally responsible. Payments may be made from this account in such circumstances as the Assignee deems proper. Such payments will then be recouped from the first sums to be credited to the relative estate account. Before the sitting for distributing the proceeds of the bankrupt's estate among the creditors, the Assignee's accounts must be vouched by the Examiner. The Examiner is also empowered to conduct an audit of those accounts at such time as he deems fit.[138]

Proving Debts and Distribution

6–56 One of the Assignee's or creditors' trustee's principal functions is to ascertain the bankrupt's debts and liabilities, to pay off those creditors and, if there is a surplus in the estate, to distribute that in accordance with the statutory provisions.[139]

Taxation

6–57 The bankrupt's tax liabilities must be proved in the ordinary way. Where a tax assessment is being disputed and an appeal is available, ordinarily that is the forum for resolving that issue. It has been suggested in England that the bankruptcy court can go behind an assessment that purports to be final and conclusive in order to avoid a miscarriage of justice.[140] Income generated by the bankrupt or from his property while adjudicated would seem to be liability of either him or of the Assignee, depending on which of them received it.[141] Before distributing the realisations among the creditors, the Assignee should ensure that any tax liability of his has been discharged.[142] For the purpose of capital gains tax, the assets that vest in the Assignee and his acts in respect of them, such as their disposal, are deemed to be those of the bankrupt, but any tax accruing on chargeable gains is assessable and recoverable from the Assignee.[143]

Duties

6–58 In addition to specific statutory duties, whether or to what extent the Assignee or creditors' trustee owes a duty of care to the bankrupt or his creditors is a topic which has so far escaped detailed analysis by the courts. But modern developments in the law of negligence resulting in financial loss would suggest

---

[137] Rule 153, S.I. No. 595 of 2001.
[138] Rule 156.
[139] All considered in Ch.8.
[140] *Arnold v Williams* [2008] B.P.I.R. 247.
[141] Cf. *Criminal Assets Bureau v Kelly* [2000] 1 I.L.R.M. 271.
[142] *Green v Satsangi* [1998] 1 B.C.L.C. 458.
[143] Taxes Consolidation Act 1997, s.569.

that some duty exists.[144] Occupying a fiduciary position, the Assignee and trustee owe fiduciary duties.[145] In brief, they must execute their office honestly in what they consider to be the best interests of the creditors, subject of course to the court's directions and to any binding instructions from a committee of inspection and from a majority of the creditors. They must also act in good faith, such as not misuse property held by them in a fiduciary capacity, for instance purchase the property or derive secret profits from it. But because Assignees and these trustees are officers of the court, they enjoy extensive immunity for their actions.[146]

6–59 Under what is known as the "rule in *Ex parte James*",[147] because the Assignee is an officer of the court, he will be held to higher standards of conduct than those imposed by the principles of equity. In certain circumstances, even though as a matter of strict law the bankrupt's property may vest in the Assignee, he will be prevented from getting that property. The precise extent of the operation of this "rule" cannot easily be defined; the courts in their discretion may invoke the rule in appropriate circumstances to prevent property from vesting in the Assignee. As explained, this rule "provides that where it would be unfair for [an Assignee] to take full advantage of his legal rights as such, the court will order him not to do so, and, indeed, will order him to return money which he may have collected".[148] For the rule to operate, the following conditions are required to obtain:

"(1) [T]here must be some form of enrichment of the assets of the bankrupt by the person seeking to have the rule applied ... .
(2) [E]xcept in the most unusual cases the claimant must not be in a position to submit an ordinary proof of debt ... . The rule is not to be used merely to confer a preference on an otherwise unsecured creditor, but to provide relief for a person who would otherwise be without any relief.
(3) If, in all the circumstances of the case, an honest man who would be personally affected by the result would nevertheless be bound to admit: 'It's not fair that I should keep the money; my claim has no merits', then the rule applies so as to nullify the claim which he would otherwise have.
(4) When the rule does apply, it applies only to the extent necessary to nullify the enrichment of the estate; it by no means necessarily restores the claimant to the status quo ante."[149]

In that case, following a receiving order, the bankrupt garage proprietor accepted

---

[144] See generally, R.A. Buckley, *The Modern Law of Negligence,* 4th edn (London: LexisNexis Butterworths, 2005).
[145] See generally, Young, "Fiduciary Obligations and Trustees in Bankruptcy", 83 *A.L.J.* 263.
[146] See para.6–60.
[147] *Re Condon,* Ex p. *James* (1874) 9 Ch. App. 609.
[148] *Re Clark* [1975] 1 All E.R. 453 at 458.
[149] *Re Clark* [1975] 1 All E.R. 453 at 458–459.

supplies of petrol from an oil company and gave the company cheques, some of which the bank paid. At the time the company had no knowledge of the bankruptcy. It was held that, since the estate benefited considerably from the petrol which was supplied to the bankrupt, it would not be fair to repudiate all obligations to pay the company.

Enforcement of Duties

6–60   The Official Assignee enjoys immunity from liability in the event that the debtor should not have been made a bankrupt.[150] He also is immune in respect of his receipt of property, provided that he has not dealt with it in a manner incompatible with the 1988 Act, the Bankruptcy Rules or the court's directions.[151] Being officers of the court, he and the creditors' trustee enjoy a degree of immunity from liability at common law.[152]

6–61   In discharging their functions, the Assignee and the trustee, are "subject to the control of the Court ...".[153] Such control can be exercised whenever application is made by them to the court with regard to the resolution of any "doubt or difficulty" or the exercise of some particular power.[154] In addition, a person who wants to challenge what either of these officers has done or proposes to do may apply to the court. Such application may be made by a creditor or by any "other person who in the opinion of the Court has an interest".[155] Thus, even the bankrupt himself could have locus standi for these purposes. Formerly, the bankrupt had no right, during the course of the winding up, to challenge in the court the ways in which his property was being dealt with; the position was that "the bankrupt ha[d] not the ordinary right of a *cestui que* trust to intervene until the surplus ha[d] been ascertained to exist, and all the creditors and interest and costs ha[d] been paid."[156]

---

[150]   1988 Act, s.63(a).
[151]   1988 Act, s.63(b).
[152]   *Mond v Hyde* [1999] Q.B. 1097.
[153]   1988 Act, ss.61(7) and 112(1).
[154]   1988 Act, ss.61(6) and 114.
[155]   1988 Act, ss.61(7) and 114.
[156]   *Re A Debtor* [1949] 1 Ch. 236, at 242.

CHAPTER 7

TRANSACTIONS DISCLAIMER AND AVOIDANCE

7–01   Although the bankrupt's property vests in the Assignee, or later in the creditors' trustee if they choose that mode of administration, the Assignee or trustee may experience difficulties in getting in that property for realisation. Furthermore, prior to the adjudication, the bankrupt may have dealt with his property in such a way as to prevent them getting their hands on it; for instance, by making gifts of it to members of his family or to friends, or by paying off certain favoured creditors at the expense of the others. At times, such gifts might take the form of colourable sales. The 1988 Act contains various rules to assist recovering those assets in such circumstances.

DISCLAIMER OF ONEROUS PROPERTY AND CONTRACTS

7–02   The facility to disclaim onerous property and contracts, which also exists in company liquidations,[1] cannot properly be regarded as among these measures, but has some affinity with them and can conveniently be considered alongside them. As McPherson J. remarks in his book on company liquidations, "[i]t is difficult to select the appropriate point for discussion of the ... power to disclaim onerous property ... . The topic is one which does not readily fit into the scheme of things, partly no doubt because it possesses a double aspect ...".[2]

7–03   It frequently happens that the debtor's estate includes property or certain obligations which are a substantial drain on the estate's resources. For example, it may be leasehold property held at a high rental which is no longer really needed but which, because of the rent and repairing and other obligations, cannot be sold. In such cases, not only does continuance of these obligations seriously deplete the estate but the Assignee or trustee is personally liable for their performance, subject to a right of indemnity. The 1988 Act contains a procedure whereby, with leave of the court, they can divest the estate of such obligations, thereby reducing the drain on its resources and facilitating completion of its administration.[3] Usually the Assignee or trustee will take the initiative in disclaiming; if the property or contract in question is significantly onerous it might be a breach

---

[1]   See generally, M. Forde et al., *The Law of Company Insolvency,* 2nd edn (Dublin: Thomson Round Hall, 2008) at 202.

[2]   A.R. Keay, *McPherson's Law of Company Liquidation* (London: Sweet & Maxwell, 2001).

[3]   Section 56.

of their duty of care not to do so. Even where they do not take such initiative, procedure exists whereby the other party to a contract can force an application to have it rescinded.[4]

What Can be Disclaimed

7–04   The property and interests which are capable of being disclaimed are "land of any tenure burdened with onerous covenants, ... shares or stock in companies, ... unprofitable contracts, or ... any other property which is unsaleable or not readily saleable by reason of its binding the possessor thereof to the performance of any onerous act or to the payment of any sum of money".[5] Thus, a very extensive range of matters can be disclaimed in appropriate circumstances, leases being the commonest subjects.[6] Another subject is shares which are not fully paid up. Provided that the proprietary interest is "onerous" or the contract is "unprofitable", it is inherently disclaimable. Even freehold property burdened by obligations can be disclaimed, the classic instance being where a company in liquidation owned a cemetery in respect of which there were expensive duties regarding upkeep of the graves and the like.[7] Freehold which is disclaimed will vest in the Minister for Finance as bona vacantia[8] unless the court orders that it should vest in someone else.

Procedure

7–05   The Assignee or creditors' trustee has 12 months in which to apply for leave to disclaim.[9] In the case of property or contracts that did not come to his notice until more than a month had elapsed from the date of adjudication, the 12 month period runs from when he became so aware of them, and that period may be extended by the court in an appropriate case. If he does not take the initiative, other persons interested in the property or contract can compel him to make up his mind and, if he elects not to disclaim, he is thenceforth prevented from doing so.[10] For this purpose, an application in writing must have been made to him and he has 28 days, or such further period as the court may allow, to decide on the matter. If by that time he has not sought to disclaim a contract, he is deemed to have adopted it. A party to a contract with the bankrupt—or, more exactly, a person "entitled to the benefit or subject to the burden" of such contract—can apply directly to the court for an order to have it rescinded.[11] Before considering an application to disclaim, the court will usually require that any other "persons interested" in the matter be duly notified so that they can appear in the proceedings.[12]

---

[4]   1988 Act, s.56(6).
[5]   1988 Act, s.56(1).
[6]   E.g. *Grant v Anon Ltd,* 103 I.L.T.R. 39 (1969).
[7]   *Re Nottingham General Cemetery Co* [1955] 1 Ch. 683.
[8]   State Property Act 1954, s.27, and cf. 1988 Act, s.32.
[9]   1988 Act, s.56(2).
[10]   1988 Act, s.56(5).
[11]   1988 Act, s.56(6).
[12]   1988 Act, s.56(4).

7–06 In deciding whether to give leave, the test is "the balance of the advantages and disadvantages of the disclaimer to be gained" by the estate and by the persons who would be affected by disclaiming.[13] It is for the applicant to satisfy the court that the balance of advantage lies with disclaimer. Thus in England and Northern Ireland, where for a time (unlike here) disclaimer of a lease released the guarantor of the lease, leave was refused where the loss to the lessor far outweighed the benefits to the estate.[14]

7–07 The court is not expressly authorised to attach conditions to the disclaimer but, since it has a general discretion in such cases, its inherent jurisdiction includes imposing conditions. When it orders that a contract shall be rescinded, it is empowered to impose terms as to payment of damages for non-performance.[15] Any person interested in the disclaimed property can apply to the court for an order that it be vested in or delivered to him, or to someone else, on such terms as the court thinks just.[16] Special provision is made regarding the terms under which the court may order that a lease be re-vested.[17]

Effects of Disclaiming

7–08 The effect of disclaimer should be considered with regard to the Assignee's or trustee's position, the position of the other contracting party and that of third parties who are not directly involved in the bankruptcy. As regards the bankrupt estate, disclaimer will operate to determine, as from the date of the disclaimer, the rights, interests and liabilities of the estate in or in respect of the property or contract.[18] Thus, as well as being absolved from all future liabilities arising from that property or contract, the Assignee or trustee will have no further rights regarding it. For instance, future rent does not have to be paid, nor do calls on shares have to be paid. As Lindley L.J. explained, dealing with "the simple case of a lease ... and the lessee becomes bankrupt, the disclaimer determines his interest in the lease ... . He gets rid of all of his liabilities, and he loses all his rights by virtue of the disclaimer".[19]

7–09 But it does not follow that the other party to the disclaimed contract, such as the lessor or the company making the calls, must bear the cost of the burden being lifted from the bankrupt estate. For he, or any other "person damaged" in consequence of the disclaimer, can prove as a creditor for the amount of such loss or damage.[20] Where such a loss is contingent, a valuation must be placed on it. Additionally, that person may apply to have the disclaimed property vested in him or in some third party,[21] which may alleviate the loss he otherwise would

---

[13] *Re Madeley Homecare Ltd* [1983] N.I. 1 at 7.
[14] *Re Madeley Homecare Ltd* [1983] N.I. 1 at 7.
[15] 1988 Act, s.56(6).
[16] 1988 Act, s.56(7).
[17] 1988 Act, s.56(8).
[18] 1988 Act, s.56(3).
[19] *Re Finley* (1888) 21 Q.B.D. 475 at 485.
[20] 1988 Act, s.55(9).
[21] 1988 Act, ss.56(7) and (8).

suffer. The court has a broad discretion to attach any conditions as may be warranted to its order transferring the property. It may even impose conditions that directly or indirectly benefit the bankrupt estate.[22]

7–10   A major source of difficulty has been the effects of disclaimer on third parties, i.e. on persons other than the immediate parties to the lease, contract or whatever was disclaimed. It is stipulated that disclaimer "shall not, except so far as is necessary for the purpose of releasing the bankrupt and his property and the Official Assignee from liability, affect the rights or liabilities of any other person".[23] In other words, third parties' entitlements and obligations must not be diminished except where so affecting them is essential in order to realise the bankrupt's estate. Although they can prove as unsecured creditors for the amount of their loss and/or seek a vesting order in heavily insolvent bankrupcies, such redress may be of limited value to them. Most of these cases have concerned leases, the third party being, for instance, the sub-lessee or the mortgagee of the bankrupt's lease. Where the bankrupt is the assignee of the lease, disclaimer does not exonerate the original lessee from liability to the landlord for future rent.[24] Where the assignor of the lease became bankrupt, the sub-lessee in turn can apply for an order vesting the head lease in him on terms of his assuming the covenants and conditions in the original lease.[25]

7–11   There was conflict of authority regarding the position of the guarantor of covenants in a lease until the matter was resolved by Keane J. in *Re Farm Machinery Distributors Ltd.*[26] It was decided in 1882[27] that the surety remains liable. There the assignee of a lease went bankrupt and his trustee disclaimed it. Having then paid rent to the lessor, the original lessee claimed reimbursement from a person who had convenanted with him to be surety for the rent for the remainder of the assignee's term. The surety was held liable. However, it was held in 1900[28] and thirty years later in a company case[29] that, where the disclaimer absolves the lessee from liability, his surety also becomes released, on the grounds that once the primary obligation is extinguished there remains nothing to guarantee. In the *Farm Machinery* case Keane J. declined to follow those two decisions because they departed from the principle in the earlier authorities and in the statutory requirement that third parties shall be affected by disclaimer only to the extent that is necessary.[30]

22   *Lee v Lee* [1998] 1 F.L.R. 1018.
23   1988 Act, s.56(3).
24   *Hill v East and West India Dock Co* (1884) 9 H.L.C. 448 and *Warnford Investments Ltd v Duckworth* [1979] 1 Ch. 127.
25   *O'Farrell v Stephenson* (1879) 4 L.R. Ir. 151.
26   [1984] I.L.R.M. 273.
27   (1882) 9 Q.B.D. 281.
28   *Stacey v Hill* [1901] 1 Q.B. 660.
29   *Re Katherine a Cie* [1932] 1 Ch. 70.
30   Similarly, *Hindcastle Ltd v Barbara Attenborough Association Ltd* [1997] A.C. 70.

FRAUDULENT CONVEYANCE

7–12 For hundreds of years it has been a principle of bankruptcy law that where, with the object of defeating his creditors, a debtor who shortly afterwards becomes bankrupt transferred his property to a third party, the courts can intervene and set aside that transfer. In England this was incorporated into what is commonly known as the Statute of Elizabeth I (13 Eliz. c.5); the equivalent measure in Ireland is the Fraudulent Conveyances Act 1634, which is entitled "An Act against covenous and fraudulent conveyances".[31] Not only does this Act provide the basis for impeaching transfers of property by the debtor to defeat his creditors but a fraudulent conveyance, as defined there, is itself an act of bankruptcy for the purpose of presenting a bankruptcy petition.

7–13 Section 10 of the 1634 Act provides that,

> "... for the avoiding and abolition of fained, covenous and fraudulent feoffments, gifts, grants, alienations, conveyances ... as well of lands and tenements, as of goods and chattels ..., which ... are devised and contrived of malice, fraud ... to the end, purpose and intent to delay, hinder or defraud creditors and others of their just and lawful actions, suits, debts, accounts, damages ... and reliefs; Be it therefore ... enacted ... that all and every feoffment, gift, grant, alienation, bargain and conveyance ... for any intent or purpose before declared and expressed, shall be from henceforth deemed and taken only as against that person (so prejudiced) to be dearly and utterly void, and of no effect ...".

The power to set aside a transfer of property on these grounds is not an exclusively bankruptcy jurisdiction; the courts can just as easily set aside a transaction in non-bankruptcy proceedings. Also, it is not essential that the transferor of the property be insolvent at the time of the transaction, although fraudulent intent will more readily be inferred where he was insolvent. The power applies to transfers of all kinds of property; it is not confined to land or interests in land, although the bulk of the cases on its interpretation relate to conveyances. Thus, an assignment of an insurance policy[32] and even a payment of money[33] have been held to be "conveyances" for these purposes. Moreover, the power applies to all types of transfers; it is not confined to conveyances by deed or even to written instruments of transfer. Thus, a transfer of goods or chattels by delivery[34]

---

[31] 10 Car. 1, sess. 2, c.3. See generally, H.W. May, *The Law of Fraudulent and Voluntary Conveyances*, 3rd edn (London : Stevens and Haynes, 1908); D.L. McDonnell & J.G. Monroe eds., *Kerr on The Law of Fraud and Mistake*, 7th edn (London: Sweet & Maxwell, 1952) Ch.6; Langstaff, "The Cheat's Charter", 91 *L.Q.R.* 86 (1975). In the U.K. the equivalent provision was reformulated in ss.423–425 of the Insolvency Act 1986 on "transactions defrauding creditors", applied in e.g. *Hill v Spread Trustee Co* [2007] 1 W.L.R. 2404.

[32] E.g. *Rose v Greer* [1945] I.R. 503.

[33] E.g. *Re Moroney,* 21 L.R. Ir. Ch. 27 (1887).

[34] *Re Eicbolz* [1959] Ch. 708.

or even the payment over of cash[35] are potentially impeachable as fraudulent. So too is permitting a charge on property to merge.[36]

Fraud

7–14   Fraud for these purposes has a more extensive connotation than for the tort of deceit. As has been pointed out, "in every case under this section the debtor has done something which in law he has power and is entitled to do; otherwise it would never reach the section. If he disposes of an asset which would be available to his creditors with the intention of prejudicing them by putting it (or its worth) beyond their reach, he is in the ordinary case acting in a fashion not honest in the context of the relationship of debtor and creditor. And in cases of voluntary disposition that intention may be inferred".[37] On a number of occasions it has been observed that s.10 of the 1634 Act should be given a liberal construction and that transactions that offend against its spirit or intent should be set aside.[38] Nevertheless, in determining whether a transfer of property was indeed fraudulent the burden of proof lies on the party alleging fraud.

7–15   Perhaps the most exhaustive exposition on the thrust of s.10 by an Irish judge is Palles C.B.'s observations in *Re Moroney*.[39] In accordance with the Land League's "Plan of Campaign", agricultural tenants would not pay rent to their landlord but instead paid over to Land League trustees what they deemed to be a reasonable rent for their farms. Around the time Mr Moroney's rent of £85 fell due, he sold cattle for £117 and then paid £25 10s to his local trustees which represented his rent as abated in accordance with the Land League's formula. If this payment contravened s.10 and he was insolvent at the time, he would have committed an act of bankruptcy. According to Chief Baron,

> "… to bring a conveyance within the statute, first, it must be fraudulent; secondly, the class of fraud must be an intent to delay, hinder, or defraud creditors. Whether a particular conveyance be within this description may depend upon an infinite variety of circumstances and considerations. One conveyance, for instance, may be executed with the express intent and object in the mind of the party to defeat and delay his creditors, and from such an intent the law presumes the conveyance to be fraudulent, and does not require or allow such fraud to be deduced as an inference of fact. In other cases, no such intention actually exists in the mind of the grantor, but the necessary or probable result of his denuding himself of the property included in the conveyance, for the consideration, and under the circumstances actually existing, is to defeat or delay creditors, and in such a case … the intent is, as matter of law, assumed from the necessary or probable consequences of the act done; and in this case, also, the conveyance, in point of law, and without any inference of fact

[35]   Above fn.33.
[36]   *Re Godley's Estate* [1896] 1 I.R. 45.
[37]   *Lloyds Bank v Marcan* [1973] 3 All E.R. 754 at 759.
[38]   *Cadogan v Kennett,* 98 Eng. Rep. 1171 (1776) at 1172.
[39]   21 L.R. Ir. Ch. 27 (1887).

being drawn, is fraudulent within the statute. In every case, however, no matter what its nature, before the conveyance can be avoided, fraud, whether expressly proved as a fact, or as an inference of law from other facts proved, must exist. What, then, is the nature of this fraud which will avoid a conveyance? The object of the statute was to protect the rights of creditors as against the property of their debtor. It was no part of its object to regulate the rights of creditors inter se, or to entitle them to an equal distribution of that property. One right, however, of the creditors, taking them as a whole, was that all the property of the debtor should be applied in payment of the demands of them, or some of them, without any portion of it being parted with without consideration, or reserved or retained by the debtor to their prejudice."[40]

There are two main types of case: one involves voluntary transfers of property, the other transfers for consideration. For obvious reasons, courts more readily strike down voluntary transfers. Where the consideration is natural love and affection, the transfer is deemed voluntary for these purposes.

Voluntary Transfers

7–16 On numerous occasions it has been said that "a man must be honest before he is generous".[41] Where a debtor disposes of property for no consideration, the courts readily presume a fraudulent intent where, at the time or in consequence of the disposition, he was insolvent.[42] Thus in *Re Moroney*,[43] the Court of Appeal showed little hesitancy in holding that the insolvent tenant's paying £25 10s to the Plan of Campaign trustees was a fraudulent conveyance; the fact that the payment was made to defeat one particular creditor did not save the transaction from being declared invalid. But there can be circumstances where the courts will not draw that inference.[44] In *Graham v O'Keeffe*[45] the governing principle was stated as follows:

> "With respect to voluntary settlements, the result of the authorities is, that the mere fact of a settlement being voluntary is not enough to render it void against creditors; but there must be unpaid debts which were existing at the time of making the settlement; and the settlor must at the time not have been necessarily insolvent, but so largely indebted as to induce the Court to believe that the intention of the settlement, taking the whole transaction together, was to defraud the persons who, at the time of making the settlement, were creditors of the settlor. The mere fact of a man making a voluntary settlement, and thereby parting with a large portion of

---

[40] 21 L.R. Ir. Ch. 27 (1887) at 61–62.
[41] *Smith v Tatton* (1879) 6 L.R. Ir. 32 at 41.
[42] E.g. *Murphy v Abraham,* (1863)15 Ir. Ch. 371 and *Freeman v Pope* (1870) 5 Ch. App. 538.
[43] 21 L.R. Ir. Ch. 27 (1887).
[44] E.g. *Graham v O'Keeffe* (1864) Ir. Ch. Rep. 1 and Ex p. *Mercer* (1886) 17 Q.B.D. 290.
[45] (1864) Ir. Ch. Rep. 1.

his property, has never been held to make a settlement fraudulent against subsequent creditors."[46]

Unless a fraudulent intent is proved, subsequent creditors will never succeed in impeaching a voluntary transfer where, at the time, the transferor was not insolvent. As Holmes J. put it in *Re Kelleher*,[47] "once the creditors' debts that existed at the date of the deed were discharged, this later creditor cannot take advantage of what might have been relied on by the previous creditors as an implied fraud on them".[48]

Transfers for Valuable Consideration

7–17   Even though valuable consideration is paid, the transfer may still be voided if the transferee was privy to the intention to delay or defeat the transferor's creditors. Section 14 of the 1634 Act provides that, even where the transferor was intending to defeat, hinder or delay his creditors, the transfer will be upheld where it was made "upon good consideration and *bona fide*" to a person not having knowledge of the transferor's objective. While the transaction may well be an act of bankruptcy on the transferor's part, the bona fide transferee for value and without notice cannot be deprived of the property. For instance, in *Bryce v Fleming*[49] the plaintiff got a judgment against the defendant, and the judgment was registered against his land. Three days later, the defendant sold it to the second defendant for £200. Some weeks later the sheriff arrived at the farm to levy execution but was obliged to return *nulla bona*. The plaintiff then sought, unsuccessfully, to impeach the sale as a fraudulent conveyance. According to Meredith J.:

> "If a man has lands, and can only pay his debts by selling his lands, the honest thing for him to do is to sell them. It is also the prudent thing to do; for if he sells them himself he will probably get a better price, and avoid unnecessary costs. Consequently, the mere fact that a man in such a position is selling his lands is no evidence whatever that his intention is to defeat his creditors rather than to obtain the wherewithal to pay his debts ... [Moreover] where there is a *bona fide* purchase for valuable consideration the transaction cannot be impeached ... unless the purchaser is shown to have been privy to the vendor's intention."[50]

7–18   There are certain circumstances where the court will readily presume fraud, which are commonly referred to as the "badges of fraud". In the famous *Twyne's Case*,[51] the first leading case on this Act, the court itemised several of these indicia of fraudulent intent:

---

[46] (1864) Ir. Ch. Rep. 1 at 17, quoting Wood V.C. in *Holmes v Penney* (1856) 3 K.& J. 90.
[47] [1911] 2 I.R. 1.
[48] [1911] 2 I.R. 1 at 9. See too *Smith v Tatton,* above fn.41, and *Re Richardson* (Hamilton J., December 12, 1979).
[49] [1930] I.R. 376.
[50] [1930] I.R. 376 at 381 and 383.
[51] (1602) 3 Co. Rep. 80b.

"1st. That this gift had the signs and marks of fraud, because the gift is general, without exception ... ; for it is commonly said, *quod dolus versatur in generalibus*;

2nd. The donor continued in possession and used them as his own; and by reason thereof he traded and trafficked with others, and defrauded and deceived them.

3rd. It was made in secret, *et dona clandestina runt semper suspiciosa*.

4th. It was made pending the writ.

5th. Here was a trust between the parties, for the donor possessed all, and used them as his proper goods and fraud is always apparelled and clad with a trust, and a trust is the cover of fraud.

6th. The deed contains, that the gift was made honestly, truly and *bona fide; et clausuloe inconsuet semper inductunt suspicionem*."[52]

In the light of the subsequent cases, the following is a more complete list, i.e. the circumstances from which the courts tend as a rule to infer that there was a fraudulent intent.

7–19   *Generality of the Transfer:* where the debtor disposed of all or virtually all of his property. It will be recalled that entering into a deed of arrangement, within the terms of the 1887 Act, is an act of bankruptcy[53] but the assignment of property under such a deed would not be a fraudulent conveyance.[54]

7–20   *Continuance in Possession:* where the transferor remains in possession of the property. Of course a mortgage of land is not necessarily fraudulent because it is the very essence of the transaction that the mortgagor remains in possession of the property.[55] And remaining in possession of goods and chattels is only prima facie evidence and not conclusive evidence of fraud.

7–21   *Pendente Lite:* where the property is disposed of just before a creditor is about to enforce judgment. But it has been held that a sale of property for sufficient consideration is not fraudulent even though the vendor's motive was to prevent execution being levied.[56]

7–22   *Secrecy:* The secrecy of the transaction is closely related to the vendor continuing in possession.

7–23   *Trust or Reservation for Grantor's Benefit:* Palles C.B. has said that "if the conveyance reserve, either expressly or by some collateral or secret arrangement, any interest, no matter how small, to the grantor, under such circumstances as to make it impossible or difficult to resort to it if the deed be binding, the conveyance would be a fraud within the statute, because by it that

---

[52]   At 812.
[53]   See paras 4–05 et seq.
[54]   Cf. *In re David and Adlard. Ex p. Whinney* [1914] 2 K.B. 694.
[55]   *Re Ryan* [1937] I.R. 367.
[56]   *Nolan v Neill,* 33 I.L.T.R. 129 (1899).

interest in the debtor would be reserved for him in preference to his creditors, and so withdrawn from the fund to which they were entitled to resort".[57]

7–24 Power of Revocation: If the terms of the sale give the vendor a power to revoke the transaction that is a badge of fraud.

7–25 False Statements: Another such badge is false statements in the instrument of transfer. Especially when it proclaims the honesty and bona fide nature of the transaction, the judge is bound to be suspicious.

7–26 Inadequate Consideration: When the consideration is inadequate then, as regards the deficiency, the transfer was voluntary. But in the circumstances the court may find that there was "sufficient" consideration to save the transaction from invalidity[58]; there is no rule which requires the consideration to be adequate.[59]

7–27 Closely Related Parties: Another matter which is bound to arouse suspicion is where the transferor and transferee are closely related, such as a close family relationship or closely connected companies. In such circumstances the courts may want to scrutinise the transaction carefully in order to be entirely satisfied of its bona fides.[60]

Fraudulent Preference

7–28 A "fraudulent preference", in the sense of paying one creditor or giving him security in preference over all the other creditors, is not itself a fraudulent transaction under the 1634 Act.[61] This Act was aimed at transfers intended to defeat, delay or hinder creditors, not at distributing the debtor's property pari passu. But such preferences may fall foul of the 1988 Act.[62] As Palles C.B. explained, in connection with giving security to a single creditor, "security given by a debtor to one creditor upon a portion or upon all his property although the effect of it, or even the intent of the debtor making it may be to defeat an expected execution of another creditor, is not a fraud within the statute; because notwithstanding such an act, the entire of the property remains available for the creditors, or some or one of them, and as the statute gives no right to rateable distribution, the right of the creditors by such an act is not invaded or affected".[63] Thus in *Re Ryan*, where the bankrupt mortgaged his public house in order to raise the funds to pay a settlement on a personal injuries action which was brought against him, Johnston J. rejected the contention that this 1634 Act applied "where a debtor under pressure mortgages a portion of his property to secure a *bona fide* debt due to a single creditor, the debtor gaining nothing for himself

---

[57] *Re Moroney*, 21 L.R. It Ch. 27 (1887).
[58] E.g. *Myers v Duke of Leinster* (1844) 7 I.R. Eq. 146.
[59] Cf. *Rose v Greer* [1945] I.R. 503.
[60] *Koop v Smith*, 25 D.L.R. 355 (1915).
[61] *Re Sarflax Ltd* [1979] 1 Ch. 592 and *Re Lloyds Furniture Palace Ltd* [1925] Ch. 853.
[62] Section 58 and see paras 7–29 et seq.
[63] *Re Moroney*, 21 L.R. Ir. Ch. 27 (1887) at 62.

out of the transaction.".[64] And in *Rose v Greer*, where the debtor assigned a life insurance policy to secure an existing debt, Overend J. held that there is no fraudulent intent where a debtor "gives his creditor security with the intention of preferring him to other creditors or another creditor, and consequently defeating or delaying such other creditors or creditor ...".[65]

FRAUDULENT PREFERENCE

7–29 Certain transactions aimed at defeating creditors which cannot be impeached under the 1634 Act may nevertheless be set aside under the rule regarding fraudulent preferences,[66] which also exists in company liquidations.[67] As is the case with fraudulent conveyances, for a long time there was a principle under which transactions entered into on the eve of bankruptcy, aimed at preferring one or several of the debtor's creditors over his creditors generally, would be set aside by the courts. The main differences between s.57 of the 1988 Act and s.10 of the 1634 Act is that the fraudulent preference rule does not apply to dispositions which took place more than six months before the debtor was adjudicated a bankrupt.

7–30 According to s.57:

> "Every conveyance or transfer of property or charge made thereon, every payment made, every obligation incurred and every judicial proceeding taken or suffered by any person unable to pay his debts as they become due from his own money in favour of any creditor or of any person in trust for any creditor, with a view to giving such creditor, or any surety or guarantor for the debt due to such creditor, a preference over the other creditors shall, if the person making, incurring, taking or suffering the same is adjudicated bankrupt within six months after the date of making, incurring, taking or suffering the same, be deemed fraudulent and void as against the Official Assignee ..."[68]

Thus, a disposition as defined here can be set aside on the application of the Assignee or creditors' trustee. But this power does not affect any person who acquired title to the property in question in "good faith and for valuable consideration".

7–31 This rule can only be invoked in bankruptcy proceedings in order to invalidate a transaction; it does not confer a general jurisdiction to strike down

---

[64] [1937] I.R. 367 at 374.
[65] [1945] I.R. 503, at 513–514.
[66] 1988 Act, s.57.
[67] See generally, M. Forde et al., *The Law of Company Insolvency,* 2nd edn (Dublin: Thomson Round Hall, 2008), at 252; Coutts, 'Proof of Intent to Defeat or Delay Creditors', 16 *Conv.* 458 (1952); Farrar, "The Bankruptcy of the Law of Fraudulent Preference", [1983] *J. Bus. L.* 390.
[68] 1988 Act, s.57(1).

fraudulent preferences. A transfer of property which is fraudulent is void only against the Official Assignee or the creditors' trustee. Also, as has been said, it applies only to transactions which have occurred within six months of the adjudication as a bankrupt. There is scant authority on determining whether a particular transaction took place inside or outside the six months period, although useful guidance can be derived from cases dealing with whether a company charge was created within a specified period for the purposes of s.99 of the Companies Act 1963.

7–32 The debtor must have been "unable to pay his debts" at the time of the impeached transaction.[69] However, if although insolvent at the time, he genuinely believed that he could pay his debts as they fell due, he could not, therefore, have intended improperly to prefer one or more creditors over the generality of his creditors.[70] This conclusion does not follow where he knew he was insolvent but genuinely believed he could trade out of his financial difficulties.[71]

7–33 There is comparatively little authority on the kinds of property and the types of transfers that are caught here. The term property is defined very extensively to include "every description of property", including property located abroad and also obligations, easements and every description of interest in property.[72] Those modes of transfer, which are capable of being caught are "[e]very conveyance or transfer of property or charge made thereon, every payment made, every obligation incurred and every judicial proceeding taken or suffered ...".[73] However, certain acts can be done with regard to property which can involve the owner being divested of that property but without a disposition of any of the kind enumerated here taking place. An example is a set off arising before the debtor was adjudicated a bankrupt.[74] Yet the reason why set off is treated differently, and not as an "obligation incurred", is that the 1988 Act expressly stipulates that all mutual obligation between a bankrupt and others should be set off.[75] It has been held that a company's not opposing an application to the court to extend the time for registering a charge it gave is suffering a judicial proceeding regarding its property.[76]

"Fraud"

7–34 The term "fraud" in this context is a complete misdescription of what this rule strikes at and, for that reason, in many jurisdictions comparable provisions have been labelled as rules against unfair or improper preferences. What the court will declare void are dispositions of property to one creditor, or to just some creditors, in circumstances where it is unfair that they should secure an

---

[69] Cf. *Crowley v Northern Bank Finance Corp* [1981] I.R. 353.
[70] *Re F.P. & C.H.Matthews Ltd* [1982] 1 Ch. 257.
[71] *Re F.P. & C.H.Matthews Ltd* [1982] 1 Ch. 257.
[72] 1988 Act, s.3.
[73] 1988 Act, s.57(1).
[74] *Re A Debtor* [1927] 1 Ch. 410.
[75] Sch.1, Pt.17.
[76] *Peat v Gresham Trust Ltd* [1934] A.C. 252.

advantage at the expense of the other creditors. The general policy underlying bankruptcy law is that all creditors should be treated equally and share pari passu in the estate. Paying off one or only some creditors, on the eve of adjudication, undermines this objective. Unless there was indeed a good reason for paying one or some creditors, or for otherwise giving them an advantage over the generality of the creditors, such as giving them security, the court will hold the disposition to be unfair and, accordingly, voidable.

7–35 In determining whether a particular payment or disposition is voidable, the bona fides of the preferred creditor are not relevant. The concluding words of s.57(1) ("through or under a creditor of the bankrupt") were put in to preserve the common law rule that the creditor's cognisance or privity are irrelevant.[77]

Proving an Intention to Prefer

7–36 What has to be established is that the debtor's predominant intention when transferring his property to the creditor in question was to prefer that creditor, i.e. was deliberately to place that creditor at an advantage over the others. It is not enough that the effect or consequence of what was done places that creditor at an advantage. As Halsbury L.C. observed, "Nothing could have been easier than to have enacted, if they had thought proper to do so, that any preference to one creditor over another creditor, or any ... advantage given by previous payment to one creditor, to which advantage all the other creditors were not a party, should of itself be a preference which should be void under the statute".[78] If the debtor's intention was other than simply to place the one creditor in an advantageous position, the payment or disposition will not be avoided. To a degree, what actually motivated the debtor to make the particular payment is not relevant because what is prohibited is simply selecting one or some creditors for preferential treatment over the others. But his motives or objectives will frequently show whether the dominant intention was one of preference.

7–37 In *Re John Daly and Co Ltd*[79] Porter M.R. explained what is meant by "with a view to giving ... a preference" as follows:

> "[A] 'view to prefer' is produced in one man's mind by the fact that the creditor is his brother or near relation; in another's because the creditor has been kind to him in the past; in that of a third, because he expects that after his bankruptcy the creditor (if now preferred) will aid him in business once again; in that of a fourth, because it is a first transaction with the creditor, and he thinks his a specially hard case; in that of a fifth, because he thinks his other creditors have treated him harshly. There is always some motive behind the 'view to prefer'. Yet, in cases where there is no trust, no pressure, and no obligation other than contract, neither natural love and affection, gratitude, expectation of benefit, sympathy,

---

[77] Cf. *Re Butcher v Stead* (1875) 7 App. Cas. 839.
[78] *Sharp v Jackson* [1899] A.C. 419 at 423.
[79] (1886) 19 L.R. Ir. 83.

vindictiveness, or any other mental condition, can in such cases eliminate the view to prefer, which is the statutory condition of liability, however strongly the debtor may be convinced that he is doing what is fair and right in according the preference."[80]

7–38 When seeking to have a payment or disposition voided, the burden of proof is on the Assignee or creditors' trustee; they have to satisfy the court, on the balance of probabilities, that the debtor's intention was to prefer the creditor in question. Holmes L.J. described this burden, in *Re Oliver*,[81] in the following terms:

> "… unless it can be made clearly apparent, and to the satisfaction of the Court which has to decide, that the debtor's sole motive was to prefer the creditor paid to the other creditors, the payment cannot be impeached, even though it be obviously in favour of a creditor. The act of the debtor is alone to be considered – the object and purpose for which the payment is made can alone be inquired into – and although it is perfectly legitimate, and in all cases requisite, that all the attending circumstances should be carefully investigated, yet if the act done can be properly referred to some other motive or reason than of giving the creditor paid a preference over the other creditors, then I conceive neither the statute, nor any principle of law or policy, will justify a court of law in holding that the payment was fraudulent or void."[82]

Dealing with the burden of proof, O'Brien L.C. held that "it must be established that the dominant motive of the debtor was to "prefer"; this dominant motive is one to be inferred or rejected by the court on an examination of the evidence, and … there is no presumption against the creditor, the onus not being on him".[83]

7–39 Because it can be difficult to ascertain precisely what was the dominant motivation for making a particular payment or disposition, the court is frequently forced to rely on inferences from the evidence adduced. On account of the fraudulent connotation, the court will not too readily infer an improper motivation. It has been said that it must "be remembered that the inference to be drawn is of something which has about it, at the least, a taint of dishonesty, and, in extreme cases, much more than a mere taint of dishonesty. The court is not in the habit of drawing inferences which involve dishonesty or something approaching dishonesty unless there are solid grounds for drawing them".[84] In the same vein, "the inference should not be drawn, having regard to the situation of the onus of proof, unless the inference is the true and proper inference from the facts proved. Thus, it will not be drawn if the inference from the facts is equivocal and, in particular, it will not be drawn from the mere circumstance

---

[80] (1886) 19 L.R. Ir. 83 at 97.
[81] [1914] 2 I.R. 356.
[82] [1914] 2 I.R. 356 at 370, quoting Bacon V.C. in Ex p *Blackburn* (1871) L.R. 12 Eq. 358.
[83] [1914] 2 I.R. 356 at 362.
[84] *Re M. Kushler Ltd* [1943] 1 Ch. 248 at 252.

that the creditor paid was in fact "preferred" in the sense that he was paid when the other creditors were not paid and could not be paid".[85]

7–40   An improper intention was established in *Re John Daly & Co Ltd*[86] where the company, which was in serious financial difficulties, borrowed a substantial sum from its auditor. It was understood that the company would then raise funds from which the auditor would be repaid. In the event, when the shareholders refused to issue any debentures and following remonstrations by the auditor, he was repaid the loan. Shortly afterwards the company was wound up. It was held that this payment was unlawful because the payee was fully aware of all the circumstances of the company and no actual pressure was exerted on the company to exert payment; accordingly, the reasonable inference was an intention to benefit the auditor especially.

7–41   Similarly in *Re Cutts*,[87] the debtor was a solicitor who acted for a building society. When he sold his house, which was mortgaged to the society, he kept the entire proceeds of the sale for his own purposes. Another solicitor, a Mr W. who was a director of the society, learned of what happened and exhorted the debtor to pay what he owed the society under the mortgage. Shortly afterwards, the Law Society inspected his books, whereupon the debtor paid £3,000 to the building society. The debtor had an agreement with Mr W. that, should he survive the Law Society investigation unscathed, they would set up in partnership. However, he was struck off the roll of solicitors and was then adjudicated a bankrupt. A divided appeal court held that the bankrupt had the requisite improper intent. In order for him to survive at all, he needed Mr W. and, in order to secure Mr W.'s support, he had to repay the building society, which was his best client and of which Mr W. was a director. Jenkins L.J., dissenting, found that not enough evidence had been placed before the court to warrant the inference of a motive to prefer the society.

7–42   There are certain stock situations where the courts readily infer an improper intention. Perhaps the most common of these is where a company's directors have given personal guarantees in respect of the company's debts and, shortly before its winding up, they arrange to have the guaranteed debt paid off or they arrange for the company to give security for that debt. Nearly 60 years ago, in *Re M. Kushler Ltd*,[88] it was observed that this was,

> "... the type of case which is extremely familiar nowadays, where the person (such as a director) who makes the payment on behalf of the debtor is himself going to obtain by means of it a direct and immediate personal benefit. These cases of guarantees of overdrafts and securities deposited to cover overdrafts are very common, and where directors have given guarantees the circumstances of a strong element of private advantage resulting from payment of the debt may justify the court in attaching to the

---

[85]   *Re T.W.Cutts* [1956] 2 All E.R. 537.
[86]   (1886) 19 L.R. Ir. 83.
[87]   [1956] 2 All E.R. 537.
[88]   [1949] 1 Ch. 248.

other facts much greater weight than would have been attached to similar facts in a case where that element did not exist."[89]

Since then, on numerous occasions, the courts have declared invalid payments made or securities given by companies where, in consequence, directors would no longer be exposed under their guarantees for the company's debts or other obligations.

7–43   Another stock situation, especially in the company context, is where the debtor agrees to give a charge once the creditor calls for one. One of the reasons for such an arrangement is that, once the other creditors learn that the debtor has charged his assets, they may press for payment. For so long as the charge is not executed, the other creditors may be content to do business with the debtor on normal terms. Regarding such arrangements, the position was stated in *Re Eric Holmes Property Ltd*[90] as follows:

> "Where a creditor making an advance takes from the debtor a promise to execute a charge at the request of the creditor, the court will, in the absence of any other circumstances, readily infer that the purpose of the parties – i.e. the debtor as well as the creditor – was to give the creditor the right to be preferred on request. Such an arrangement, although for value, is fraudulent and unenforceable, and when the debtor, in performance of his promise, in fact creates the charge at the request of the creditor, the court again, in the absence of any other circumstances will readily infer that the intention of the debtor is to prefer the creditor. Obviously an intention to perform a promise to prefer is no less an intention to prefer than is an intention to prefer without any antecedent promise."[91]

Where the arrangement between debtor and creditor is of this nature but there are other conditions as well, then account must be taken of the entire circumstances in order to ascertain the debtor's motivation.[92]

Intention to Prefer Not Proved

7–44   In several leading cases, it was held that the Assignee or trustee or liquidator, as the case may be, did not succeed in establishing the requisite motive for avoiding the payment or other disposition. One factor which negatives any such intent is pressure. What constitutes pressure for these purposes depends on the entire circumstances. Also, the pressure must be genuine and not a cloak for preferring the creditor. In *Sharp v Jackson*,[93] the debtor was a solicitor who had convened trust monies to his own account. Knowing that his firm was insolvent, he conveyed property to trustees to raise money, in order to rectify his breaches of trust, and he also deposited share certificates with them for that

---

[89]   [1949] 1 Ch. 248 at 251.
[90]   [1964] 1 Ch. 1052.
[91]   [1964] 1 Ch. 1052 at 1067.
[92]   [1964] 1 Ch. 1052 at 1067–8.
[93]   [1899] A.C. 419.

purpose. It was held that, in the circumstances, his motive was not so much to prefer the trust as to protect himself from criminal prosecution, which almost certainly would ensue once his breaches of trust came to light in the course of his bankruptcy examination. As Halsbury L.C. put it, "he made this conveyance not with the 'intention' or 'view' or 'object' or whatever it may be called of preferring the [trust] but for the sole purpose of shielding himself".[94] But in the somewhat similar *Re Cutts* case,[95] the court came to the contrary conclusion; it was found that the predominant motive in paying the building society, which the debtor had defrauded, was to attempt to establish a law partnership with one of the society's directors and to retain the society as a major client.

7–45 The fact that the transaction was carried out in the ordinary course of business is also a strong indication that the debtor's motive was not simply to prefer. For instance, in *Re Oliver*,[96] where the debtor was the Dublin agent for a cattle dealer who was based in Manchester, in the usual course of business the debtor sent the dealer a cheque for a large sum, but the dealer omitted to cash the cheque. Shortly afterwards he came to Dublin where he learned that his agent was in serious financial difficulties. He thereupon demanded that the agent give him a replacement cheque and immediately cashed it. Not long afterwards, the agent was adjudicated bankrupt. It was held that the improper motive had not been established, because the agent believed that the dealer was legally in a different position than his other creditors, with regard to the cheque, and also that the dealer would have done nothing wrong if he had brought the original cheque to Dublin and, on learning of the agent's financial position, cashed it immediately. Giving the replacement cheque should not be regarded as making a fresh payment.

7–46 Although arrangements whereby the debtor agrees to execute a charge on request tend, generally, to be regarded as fraudulent preferences, it has been held that this is not so where title deeds are pledged under a deed of deposit, one of the terms of which is that a legal charge shall be executed forthwith.[97] In one instance where a defective charge was registered, at the bank's request the debtor executed a legal charge and had it registered. The contention that the bank had thereby been improperly preferred was rejected on the grounds that "the dominant intention was not to confer an advantage on the bank, but to benefit the company by keeping on good terms with the bank".[98] In another instance, where the debtor did not oppose an application by its bankers to extend the time for registering a charge over its property, thereby facilitating rendering the charge effective, it was held that an intention improperly to prefer the bank had not been established. This was because the company and its directors could face criminal penalties for not duly registering such charges.[99]

---

[94] [1899] A.C. 419 at 422.
[95] [1956] 2 MI E.R. 537.
[96] 1914] 2 I.R. 356.
[97] *Re Wm.Hall (Contractors) Ltd* [1967] 2 All E.R. 1150.
[98] *Re F.L.E. Holdings Ltd* [1967] 3 All E.R. 553 at 559.
[99] *Peat v Gresham Trust Ltd* [1934] A.C. 252.

Effects of Voiding the Transaction

7–47   Where the court declares that a disposition is void, the preferred creditor is obliged to return what he got to the Assignee or the creditors' trustee. However, a person who acquired such property in good faith and for valuable consideration cannot have his title impeached because of the earlier preference.[100]

7–48   A person who must repay sums received which constituted a fraudulent preference, where that person had got security for the payer's debt, can obtain relief. If a third party has secured the bankrupt's liability,[101] by paying that creditor bank account may fraudulently prefer that party, while the bank may have to repay the money to the Assignee. In such a case the bank would now be able to sue that party as a surety; the personal liability of the surety under this provision is to the extent of the value of the property which is charged or the value of his interest in it, whichever is the lesser figure. The bank would also be able to raise any question regarding the surety's or guarantor's liability and have it determined in the bankruptcy rather than by instituting separate proceedings.

VOLUNTARY SETTLEMENT

7–49   Another longstanding principle of bankruptcy has been that, regardless of the debtor's intention, if shortly before he was made bankrupt he made certain gifts of his property, the court can set them aside in favour of the general creditors. In such circumstances, the donee of that property should not benefit at the creditors' expense. Whereas for a fraudulent conveyance it is necessary to establish an intention to defeat the creditors and, for a fraudulent preference, an intention improperly to prefer one or several creditors over the others must be proved, in the case of eve of bankruptcy gifts there is no need to establish *scienter* of any kind. The settlor of the property may genuinely believe that he is solvent and may be acting for the most laudable of motives; yet if the transaction falls within the definition of a voidable settlement, it can be set aside.

7–50   Any gratuitous "settlement of property" made within two years or five years, as the case may be, of the transferor's adjudication as a bankrupt can be set aside.[102] A settlement for these purposes is defined, as "includ[ing] any conveyance or transfer of property."[103] Practically every conceivable kind of transfer of assets by the debtor, within the relevant period, is a settlement in this context. But transactions will not be struck down where they were entered into "in good faith and for valuable consideration" or, subject to certain qualifications, if they were marriage settlements. Transfers that fall foul of this are not automatically void but they can be struck down by the court on the Assignee's or trustee's application.

---

[100]   1988 Act, s.57(1).
[101]   1988 Act, s.57(2).
[102]   1988 Act, s.59.
[103]   1988 Act, s.59(4).

"Settlement"

7–51 A settlement for these purposes is defined extensively. But there are certain transactions which have been held not to be settlements, although they entail the debtor conferring a substantial financial benefit on another. In the first place, if the property which was transferred never legally belonged to the debtor, even though he may have been instrumental in bringing about the transfer, he cannot settle it. For instance, in *Re Schebsman*[104] the debtor made an agreement with his employers for him to be paid a sum in instalments over five years but, should he die during that period, the remaining instalments should be paid to his wife or daughter. This was not a settlement because the "sums in question were never the property of the debtor. He never had any right to them, either at law or in equity".[105] It was said that the rule here "clearly deals with property which, but for the settlement, would have been available to pay the debts of the settlor". Nor is the exercise of a power of appointment by the debtor a settlement because, by definition, the property over which the power is exercised does not belong to the debtor at the time. It was held in *Re Mathieson*[106] that this is the case even where, under the power, the debtor could appoint the property in his own favour. This is because the rule "is intended to deal with settlements, in a more ordinary meaning of that term, – some disposition whereby the bankrupt has divested himself of property available at the date of the disposition ... whereby at its date his interest is passed over to the trustee of it, and his estate, available in case of stringency and ultimate bankruptcy, rendered smaller".[107]

7–52 Where the debtor hands over a sum of money to another, he does not necessarily make a settlement of that sum for these purposes. The cases draw a distinction between where the intention is that the donee will hold the money in some permanent form, such as by investing it, and where the money is to be spent relatively promptly. In the latter case, there is no settlement. The authorities were summed up in *Re Plummer*[108] as follows:

> "[T]here are two lines of cases bearing upon the subject ... . If there is a gift ... of money or proceeds of property which can be traced, and the money or proceeds is or are intended to be retained or preserved as the property of the donee, that money or those proceeds will be property in 'settlement'. On the other hand, if there is a gift of money or proceeds, but it is not intended that the money or the proceeds shall be retained by the donee in the form of money, but shall be expended at once, that will not be a 'settlement'."[109]

It then will depend on the entire circumstances which side of the line a particular gift will fall. For instance, there was a settlement where a father gave his son

---

[104] [1944] 1 Ch. 83.
[105] [1944] 1 Ch. 83 at 97.
[106] [1927] 1 Ch. 283.
[107] [1927] 1 Ch. 283 at 295.
[108] [1900] 2 Q.B. 790.
[109] [1900] 2 Q.B. 790 at 804.

money to be used to buy shares in a ship, which were then to yield dividends.[110] But there was no settlement where a father gave his son money to start up a business, the money constituting the capital of the business.[111]

7–53 Usually the debtor will have executed a formal instrument of transfer regarding the property in question or will have delivered the property to the donee or to someone on his behalf. Provided the property belonged to the debtor and what is being transferred is not money to be spent, for there to be a settlement it is not essential that the property be transferred to the donee or to independent trustees. It suffices if the debtor formally declares that he henceforth holds the property in trust; the "alteration in the position of the settlor from that of beneficial owner to that of mere trustee ... [i]s a sufficient compliance with the exigency ...".[112]

Good Faith and Consideration

7–54 Such transfers of property cannot be impeached if they were "made in favour of a purchaser or encumbrancer in good faith and for valuable consideration".[113] By good faith here is meant without knowledge of the debtor's personal financial circumstances, which should deter a reasonable person from going through with the transaction because of its effect on the transferor's creditors. Often the absence of good faith in this sense will strengthen the court's belief that a particular transaction was not a genuine exchange for valuable consideration.[114]

7–55 In determining whether the impugned transaction was for valuable consideration, the courts take a realistic and commercial view of what was done. In particular, they "have regard to the fact that [the rule] is clearly framed to prevent properties from being put into the hands of relatives to the disadvantage of creditors".[115] While the courts will not insist on an equivalence of consideration, they tend to strike down exchanges where what is given by the debtor bears no reasonable relationship to what is received in return. Among the principles established in the cases are the following. The word "purchaser" here means "a buyer in the ordinary commercial sense, that is to say a person providing a *quid pro quo*".[116] But it is not necessary that the debtor-transferor's property is reciprocally augmented: "[t]he consideration moving from the purchaser need not replace in the hands of the debtor the consideration moving from the debtor".[117] Moreover, the "consideration given by the purchaser need not be equal in value to the consideration given by the debtor, though it must be valuable

---

[110] *Re Player* (1885) 154 L.J.Q.B. 553.
[111] *Re Player (No. 2)* (1885) 15 Q.B.D. 682.
[112] *Shrager v March* [1908] A.C. 402.
[113] 1988 Act, s.59(1).
[114] E.g. *Re Windle* [1975] 1 W.L.R. 1628.
[115] *Re A Debtor* [1965] 1 W.L.R. 1498 at 1505.
[116] *Re Abbott* [1983] 1 Ch. 45 at 54.
[117] *Re Abbott* [1983] 1 Ch. 45 at 54.

consideration in a commercial sense",[118] i.e. he must give a consideration for what he got from the debtor which has a real and substantial value, and not one which is merely nominal or trivial or colourable. Such consideration, for example, can be agreeing to waive some right or to settle a legal claim being brought or about to be brought by the "purchaser", provided of course that the release of the right or the settlement is not a colourable transaction.

7–56   Many of the recent cases involve transfers of the family home between spouses on the breakdown of their marriage.[119] The first question will be whether the transferor spouse acted bona fide. Then the terms of the transfer will be examined to ascertain whether it constitutes at least in substantial part a gift. There are distinct rules for marriage settlements made by bankrupts within two years of their adjudication.[120]

Voiding

7–57   The transfer can be avoided if it occurred within two years before the date of the adjudication, regardless of the debtor's actual financial circumstances at the time. Accordingly, all voluntary dispositions, except certain marriage settlements, can be avoided where they were made within that time.

7–58   If the transfer was made within two and five years of the adjudication it can be avoided only if the bankrupt was insolvent at that time. Significantly, the burden is not on the Assignee or creditors' trustee to prove that he was insolvent then, although throughout the burden is on the Assignee or trustee to prove lack of bona fides or of no consideration. In the case of voluntary transfers made between two and five years of the adjudication, except for certain marriage settlements, they can be set aside unless the transferee or persons claiming through him proves that the debtor was solvent at the time.[121] By solvent here means he could "pay his debts" without the aid of the property which was transferred.[122] Even if he was solvent, the disposition will be set aside if his interest in the property did not pass to the trustee of any settlement when it was executed.[123] In other words, if in this period the debtor made a voluntary settlement but nevertheless retained his interest in the property, it will be struck down regardless of his financial circumstances at the time.

7–59   A voluntary settlement which falls foul of these provisions is not absolutely void; it is "void as against" the Assignee or trustee.[124] This has been held to mean voidable. Accordingly, if the recipient of that property sold

---

[118] *Re Abbott* [1983] 1 Ch. 45 at 54 and 57.
[119] See paras 10–55 and 10–56.
[120] 1988 Act, s.59(2) and (3), and see paras 10–58 et seq.
[121] 1988 Act, s.59(1)(b).
[122] Cf. *Re Louden* (1887) 18 Q.B.D. 677.
[123] 1988 Act, s.59(1)(6).
[124] 1988 Act, s.55(1).

it before the claim is laid to it then the bona fide purchaser for value without notice gets good title.[125]

IMPROVIDENT DISPOSITION

7–60 Under what was known as the "relation back" rule, many kinds of disposition by a bankrupt of his property, between the time the relevant act of bankruptcy occurred and the date of adjudication, were held invalid. In Ireland this rule was based entirely on judicial decisions and was never incorporated into the bankruptcy code. The basis for it was that, on a creditor's petition, the bankruptcy was deemed to have commenced from the date of the act of bankruptcy, relied on in the petition, and the vesting of the bankrupt's property in the trustee in bankruptcy occurred as from that date. Under the 1988 Act, the bankruptcy commences as from the date of adjudication, with the result that the relation back rule cannot operate any longer.[126] To an extent, however, it has been replaced by what may be termed a rule for avoiding improvident dispositions by the debtor of any property on the eve of his adjudication.[127] The intention here is to strike at spurious sales and other dealings in his property which, in the circumstances, the court deems improper. Unlike the position in Company Law, dispositions of a bankrupt's property between the time the petition was presented and the adjudication are not deemed to be unlawful but, on application to the court, may be authorised by it.[128]

7–61 The relevant period for this to apply is relatively brief; the transaction must have occurred within three months prior to the adjudication and it must have been preceded by the commission of an act of bankruptcy. If, within that period, the debtor did the following, the transaction can be declared void on the application of the Assignee or creditor's trustee, viz. "sells any of his property at a price which, in the opinion of the Court, is substantially below its market value or enters into or is a party to any other transaction which, in the opinion of the Court, has the effect of substantially reducing the sum available for distribution to the creditors ...".[129] Thus, what can be struck down are what in substance can be regarded as gifts of the property, such as a sale for far less than its market value, or an exchange where there is a substantial difference in the values and equivalent transactions. It is for the court to decide, in the circumstances, whether the transaction in question should be set aside. At some stage guidelines for deciding such matters will be laid down.

7–62 But the court will not invalidate such a transaction if two conditions

---

[125] *Re Carter and Kenderdine's Contract* [1897] 1 Ch. 776.
[126] 1988 Act, s.44(2).
[127] 1988 Act, s.58.
[128] Companies Act 1963, s.218. Compare U.K. law, e.g. *Pettit v Novakovic* [2007] B.P.I.R. 1643.
[129] 1988 Act, s.58(1). In contrast with the comparable U.K. provisions, it is not necessary to show in improper motive on the debtor's part, e.g. *Feakins v Dept. of Environment* [2006] B.P.I.R. 895.

are satisfied.[130] One is that, at the time it was entered into, the other party had no "notice" that the debtor committed any act of bankruptcy by making the transfer. Presumably, notice in this context covers constructive as well as actual notice. Secondly, the transaction must be one that was "bona fide" entered into. By this, presumably, is meant, that in all the circumstances it can be said that the transaction was entirely genuine and was not done with a view to depleting assets which would be available for the debtor's creditors generally. Furthermore, even if the transaction is set aside by the court, if some third party acquired the property in question, his title cannot be adversely affected provided he acquired it "in good faith and for valuable consideration."[131] A void fraudulent preference or voluntary settlement is not treated as an improvident disposition.[132]

---

[130] 1988 Act, s.58(2) and s.58(3).
[131] 1988 Act, s.58(2).
[132] 1988 Act, s.58(3).

CHAPTER 8

PROVING DEBTS AND DISTRIBUTION

8–01 To obtain payment from the bankrupt's estate, creditors must prove their debts. This is a formal procedure for establishing that the bankrupt is indebted to the person in question and for determining the amount of that liability. The 1988 Act lays down that "[e]very creditor shall prove his debt and a creditor who does not do so is not entitled to share in any distribution that may be made".[1] It is only debts and claims which are "provable" in this way that can be paid by the Assignee or creditors' trustee. The bankruptcy rules on this matter are applied by the Companies Acts to winding up insolvent companies,[2] so that many of the authorities on proof of debts in company liquidations are directly relevant to bankruptcy and vice versa.

DEBTS AND CLAIMS PROVABLE

8–02 It is not every debt or claim against the bankrupt which can be the subject of proof. Formerly an extensive range of liabilities were not susceptible of proof but that is no longer so. What now can be proved are "[d]ebts and liabilities, present or future, certain or contingent, by reason of any obligation incurred by the bankrupt ... before the date of adjudication ... and claims in the nature of unliquidated damages for which [he] is liable at that date by reason of a wrong ...".[3] Thus, liabilities under nearly every conceivable legal category, such as breach of contract, tort, equitable obligation and statutory duty, can be proved in bankruptcy. Even fines imposed by the criminal courts and revenue penalties are provable.[4] In *Re Cawley*,[5] where it had been held that the creditor had been fraudulently preferred and had to return what was paid to him, he nevertheless was entitled to prove for the debt which had been improperly paid off. Similarly in *Re Hogan*,[6] where a charge registered by the bank was void as a fraudulent conveyance, it was held that the bank could still prove for the underlying debt.

8–03 The court has jurisdiction to enquire into the consideration for any debt being proved and to reject the proof if there was no true consideration. This is

---

[1] Schedule 1, Pt.1.
[2] Companies Act 1963, s.284(1). See generally M. Forde et al., *The Law of Company Insolvency*, 2nd edn (Dublin: Thomson Round Hall, 2008), Ch.14.
[3] 1988 Act, s.75(1).
[4] *Re Hurren* [1983] 1 W.L.R. 183. Cf. *Re Savundra* [1973] 1 W.L.R. 1147.
[5] [1959] I.R. 330.
[6] 69 I.L.T.R. 211 (1935).

so, not alone where claims have been compromised, but even with regard to judgment debts. As was explained, "the object of the bankruptcy law is to procure the distribution of a debtor's goods among his just creditors. If a judgment were conclusive a man might allow any number of judgments to be obtained by default against him by his friends or relatives without any debt being due on them at all; it is, therefore, necessary that the consideration for the judgment should be liable to investigation".[7] It has been suggested that a similar approach can be taken to tax assessments that purport to be final and conclusive, in circumstances where acting on them would lead to a miscarriage of justice.[8]

8–04 The same criteria apply to debts provable in an arrangement, the relevant "cut off" time there being the date of the arrangement or of the order for protection. A detailed set of rules regarding proof of debts is contained in the first schedule of the 1988 Act. The following types of debts and claims call for special attention.

Unliquidated Claims

8–05 An unliquidated debt or claim is a present existing liability where the actual amount due cannot be ascertained; it is necessary to resort to legal proceedings in order to determine how much must be paid. Examples include most claims in tort and some claims for breach of contract and for breach of fiduciary duty. The converse is a liquidated debt, i.e. a liability the full extent of which can readily be ascertained. Formerly proof could not be made in respect of unliquidated debts. The 1872 Act permitted proof if the debt arose from a contract or a promise, provided the liability was separately assessed[9]; in 1961 that was amended to permit proof in respect of all "wrongs", including torts.[10]

8–06 Since 1988, "claims in the nature of unliquidated damages for which the bankrupt ... is liable ... by reason of a wrong within the meaning of the Civil Liability Act, 1961", can be proved.[11] A "wrong" under the 1961 Act is defined most extensively, as meaning a "tort, breach of contract or breach of trust, whether or not the act is also a crime, and whether or not the wrong is intentional".[12] An application can be made to the court to assess the amount of the unliquidated liability and, if all the necessary parties agree, the court can make such assessment even where the claim is one that must be brought in some other court.[13]

---

[7] Ex parte *Kibble* (1875) L.R. 10 Ch. App. 373, at 377. See too Ex p *Revel* (1884)13 Q.B.D. 720. Cf. *Re Fagg* [1899] 2 I.R. 383.

[8] *Arnold v Williams* [2008] B.P.I.R. 247.

[9] Cf. *Cinnamond v M'Curdy* [1909] 2. I.R. 185 and *Turner v Derham* [1958] Ir. Jur. Rep. 78.

[10] Civil Liability Act 1961, s.61.

[11] 1988 Act, s.75(1).

[12] Section 2(1).

[13] 1988 Act, s.73(3).

Contingent Claims

8–07   A contingent claim is in respect of a liability that might very well occur but nevertheless may never occur. The liability of a surety under a guarantee, for instance, is contingent because it will only arise if the principal debtor defaults. Formerly proof could not be lodged in respect of a liability while it remained a contingency.

8–08   Since 1988, "[d]ebts and liabilities, present or future, certain or contingent" can be proved.[14] In the event of there being difficulties in placing a value on the contingent claim against the bankrupt, the court can make an estimate of its value, and it is that sum which then can be proved.[15] The commonest contingent liabilities are those under guarantees[16] and also those arising from covenants contained in leases[17] and in annuities.[18] Calls on shares are another such liability. Most companies' articles of association provide that a member's shares can be forfeited for non-payment of calls and those shares will then be allocated among other members of the company.[19] Forfeiture of the shares does not exempt the former member from liability in respect of the calls but, in proving against his estate, the company must set off against his liability whatever it received in respect of his forfeited shares when it disposed of them.[20]

8–09   The way of dealing with contingent claims has been described as follows:

> "There is no doubt that a contingent claim for unliquidated damages is a provable debt, and its amount has to be estimated as at the date of the [adjudication]. That, however, does not mean that the effect of the [adjudication] is to accelerate the happening of the contingency so as to fix the amount of the claim on the basis of the contingency having happened on the day of the [adjudication] ... . The claim must be stated as on the day of the [adjudication]; if when the proof is lodged the contingency has not happened the amount of the claim must be estimated as accurately as possible; if the contingency happens before the proof is lodged, that fact is *pro tanto* evidence of the true value of the claim as at the date of the [adjudication], and there will, as a rule, be no difficulty in arriving at the amount of the claims; if the contingency happens after the proof is lodged, and it appears that the amount at which the damages have been estimated is below the true value, the creditor will be allowed to amend

---

14   1988 Act, s.75(1).
15   1988 Act, s.75(4).
16   Cf. *Re An Arranging Debtor* [1971] N.I. 96.
17   Regarding leases, see generally, V.G. Wellings & N. Huskinson, *Woodfall's Law of Landlord and Tenant*, 28th edn (1978), 799–802.
18   Cf. *National Assurance Co v Scott* [1909] 1 I.R. 325.
19   Companies Act 1963, Table A, Pt.I, arts 22–28.
20   *Re Bolton* [1930] 2 Ch. 48.

the proof or lodge a fresh proof at any time during the continuance of the bankruptcy, but not so as to disturb prior dividends."[21]

Interest

8–10   The bankruptcy rules differentiate between interest claimed in respect of the period prior to adjudication and post-adjudication interest. Interest can be proved in the following circumstances up to the date of adjudication.[22] First, there is where the contract or agreement with the debtor by its very terms provided for paying interest. Some statutes expressly provide for paying interest, notably s.57 of the Bills of Exchange Act 1882.[23] Even if there is no agreement or stipulation regarding interest, s.22 of the Courts Act 1981 empowers the courts, when awarding a sum of money or damages against a person, to award interest on all or part of that sum at the then prevailing rate for judgment debts. Finally, the provisions of s.53 of the Debtors (Ireland) Act 1840[24] are incorporated into the rules for proving debts.[25] Those rules deal with where there was no agreement between the parties regarding interest but the debt is overdue at the date of adjudication. Interest at the rate currently payable for judgment debts can be proved in two circumstances. One is where the debt or sum due is payable "by virtue of a written instrument at a certain time." If the debt is not so payable, such as if the agreement is oral or the amount due is not payable at a fixed time, interest can be proved if the creditor makes a written demand for payment and notifies the debtor that interest will be claimed from the date of that demand until the debt is paid.

8–11   Interest cannot be recovered in respect of the period following adjudication,[26] which causes some injustice in periods of very high interest rates and where the administration of the insolvent estate take a long time. As Costello J. said in a company liquidation case, "[i]t has long been established that in the case of an insolvent company which is being wound up creditors whose debts carry interest are entitled to dividends only upon what was due for principal and interest at the commencement of the winding up and interest ceases to run from that date".[27] This rule is confirmed by the 1988 Act and is extended to any other financial "consideration in lieu of interest".[28] Unlike in liquidations, there is no express provision for an interest rebate on debts payable in the future, for the purpose of estimating the value of the liability at the time the insolvency commenced.[29] Instead, ascertainment of the value of such debts is within the general discretion of the court.[30]

---

[21]   *Ellis & Co's Trustee v Dixon Johnson* [1924] Ch. 342, at 356–357.
[22]   1988 Act, s.75(2).
[23]   45 & 46 Vic. c.61.
[24]   3 & 4 Vic. c.105.
[25]   1988 Act, Sch.1, r.14.
[26]   *Re Humber Ironworks & Shipbuilding Co* (1869) 4 Ch. App. 643.
[27]   *Daly v Allied Irish Banks* (Costello J., January 27, 1987).
[28]   Section 75(2).
[29]   Winding Up Rules, R.S.C. Ord.74, r.107.
[30]   1988 Act, s.75(4).

Costs

8–12   Where, prior to his adjudication, the bankrupt was the unsuccessful party in an action and costs were awarded against him, the successful party is entitled to prove for them, whether or not they were taxed or ascertained at the date of the adjudication.[31] But any award of costs made after the adjudication are not provable. Lindley M.R. has stated the governing principles as follows:

> "If an action is brought against a person, who afterwards becomes bankrupt, for the recovery of a sum of money, and the action is successful, the costs are regarded as an addition to the sum recovered and to be provable if that is provable, but not otherwise ... .
>
> If the action against a person who becomes bankrupt is unsuccessful, no costs become payable by him or out of his estate, and no question as to them can arise. But if an unsuccessful action is brought by a man who becomes bankrupt, then, if he is ordered to pay the costs, or if a verdict is given against him before he becomes bankrupt, they are provable ... .
>
> On the other hand, if no verdict is given against him and no order is made for payment of costs until after he becomes bankrupt, they are not provable. In such a case there is no provable debt to which the costs are incident, and there is no reason to pay them by reason of any obligation incurred by the bankrupt before bankruptcy; nor are they a contingent liability to which he can be said to be subject at the date of his bankruptcy."[32]

An order in an interlocutory application making the costs of that application "costs of the action" does not give rise to a provable debt.[33] Where taxation of costs is provided for, in order to be entitled to vote, the creditor may swear to a certain amount "and upwards".

Double Proof

8–13   Persons will not be permitted to prove more than once for what in substance is the one and the same debt. In *Deering v Bank of Ireland*[34] as security for a loan, the debtor assigned a life insurance policy to the bank and made a covenant to pay the annual premiums on that policy as they fell due. On being adjudicated a bankrupt, he owed the bank £980 and his life policy was worth £180. The bank lodged a proof for £800, which was the balance owing after valuing its security. But the bank also sought to prove for £400, which was the actuarial value of the debtor's covenant to continue paying the premiums on this policy. It was held that the rule against double proof precluded paying for both liabilities. As Porter M. R. explained,

> "... if the creditor prove for his debt, he cannot also prove for the bankrupt's

---

[31]   1988 Act, s.78.
[32]   *Re British Gold Fields of West Africa* [1899] 2 Ch. 7 at 11–12.
[33]   *Re Pitchford* [1924] 2 Ch. 260.
[34]   (1886) 12 H.L.C. 20.

contract to keep up [the] policy ... as security for the same debt. To do so, would be to admit a double proof; because the security cannot, for purposes of proof in bankruptcy, be deemed a debt distinct and separate from the thing secured, and the creditor's interest in the security is the same as the debt itself. In the substance, a convenant to pay premiums on a policy ... is only a covenant to pay the debt, by keeping alive something which will ultimately pay it; and to allow the creditor to prove both for the debt and for the contract to secure the debt, is to admit a double proof. The creditor can choose either, but cannot ... have both."[35]

Whenever two or more debts which are apparently distinct are in substance the one and the same debt, only one of those will be admitted to proof.

8–14 The criterion of identity is not the technical legal characterisation of the liability but whether "in substance" both are the same, in the sense that it obviously would be unjust on the general creditors if both claims were admitted to proof. As was observed in a company insolvency case, "the rule against double proofs in respect of two liabilities of an insolvent debtor is going to apply wherever the existence of one liability is dependent upon and referable only to the liability of the other and where to allow both liabilities to rank independently for dividend would produce injustice to the other unsecured creditors".[36] Thus, in *Re Fenton*,[37] it was held that a surety for the bankrupt's debts cannot prove his claim unless he has paid the principal creditor under the guarantee. Romer L.J. could not "agree that a surety who has not paid off the principal creditor can prove in the bankruptcy of the principal debtor ... unless the principal creditor has renounced in some way his right to lodge a proof himself while preserving ... his rights against the surety. To allow such a sharing in the assets would be to subject the assets to two claims in respect of the same debt, and this is contrary to the well established rule in bankruptcy against double proof".[38] For the same reason, there cannot be a proof against the drawer and also against the acceptor of a bill of exchange.[39]

Secured Creditors

8–15 A secured creditor under the 1988 Act is "any creditor holding any mortgage, charge or lien on the debtor's estate or any pan thereof as security for a debt due to him".[40] The traditional bankruptcy rule is that secured creditors could not both prove for the entire debt and at the same time realise their security.

---

[35] (1885) 15 L.R. Ir. 388, at 393.
[36] *Barclays Bank v T.S.O.G. Trust Fund* [1984] 2 W.L.R. 49 at 58.
[37] [1931] 1 Ch. 85.
[38] *Re Fenton* [1931] 1 Ch. 85 at 118–119. On the position of proof where guarantees are involved, see generally, *O'Donovan & Phillips on Guarantees* at 10–28 et seq.
[39] *Re Oriental Commercial Bank* (1871)7 Ch. App. 99. On proof where bills of exchange are involved, see generally, N. Elliott et al, *Byles on Bills of Exchange and Cheques*, 28th edn (London: Sweet & Maxwell: 2007), Ch.34.
[40] Section 3(1).

Instead, they can either surrender their security or else they can realise it or value it and prove for the balance.[41]

8–16 When submitting a proof, the secured creditor must state that he is secured. If subsequently it is discovered that there was a security which was not stated, it must be surrendered to the Assignee or creditors' trustee for the benefit of the creditors generally.[42] However, the court is given a broad discretion to allow the proof to be amended by stating the security, on such terms as the court deems proper in the circumstances. Such amendment will not be permitted if the other creditors would be prejudiced.[43] A creditor who did not disclose his security and who then did not surrender it or comply with the court's directions, as the case maybe, is excluded entirely from sharing in any distribution.

8–17 Three options are open to the secured creditor. He may surrender his security for the benefit of the general creditors; in that event, he can then prove for the entire debt.[44] Alternatively, he can realise the security; on doing that, he can prove for the balance due to him after deducting the proceeds of the security.[45] He is not however permitted to disturb any dividend already declared, i.e. payments which the Assignee or trustee has already made to other creditors cannot be disturbed because the secured creditor has chosen this option.

8–18 The third option is to value his security; if he does that he can prove for the balance over what value he put on the security.[46] When taking this option, on submitting the proof he must state the particulars of the security, the date it was acquired and its estimated value. There is a special rule for valuing assurance policies on the bankrupt's life which provides for the automatic discharge of the policy when the premiums on it are not paid.[47] The court will not readily set aside the estimate submitted by a creditor. Vaughan Williams L.J. once remarked that "when one arrives at the conclusion that the estimate is real and not a sham, we ought not to go into the question what is the true value after the declaration of the estimated value".[48] In any event, there are several deterrents against a creditor knowingly placing a wrong value on the security. He will not without good reason be permitted to amend his valuation.[49] Furthermore, the Assignee or trustee is given the option to redeem the security at the value which the creditor has assigned to it;[50] the possibility of this happening is a strong incentive against under-valuing the security. Instead of redeeming it, if dissatisfied with the estimated value, the Assignee or trustee also has the choice of putting the security up for sale.[51] The actual form and methods of sale should

---

[41] Rule 24.
[42] 1988 Act, Sch.1, r.24(8).
[43] Cf. *Re Robinson* [1958] N.I. 166 and *Re Sythes* [1962] N.I. 38.
[44] 1988 Act, Sch.1, r.24(1).
[45] 1988 Act, Sch.1, r.24(1).
[46] 1988 Act, Sch.1, r.24(2).
[47] 1988 Act, Sch.1, r.24(11).
[48] *Re Button* [1905] 1 K.B. 602 at 605.
[49] 1988 Act, Sch.1, r.24(5); cf. above fn.4.
[50] 1988 Act, Sch.1, r.24(4)(a).
[51] 1988 Act, Sch.1, r.24(4)(a).

be agreed with the security-holder; absent such agreement, these matters will be determined by the court. If the sale is by public auction, the mortgagee is permitted to bid for and to buy the property.[52]

8–19 While the Assignee or trustee can decide to redeem or to offer for sale any security which the creditor has valued, if the creditor so chooses he can compel them to decide whether they will do either of these things.[53] At any time, by notice in writing, the secured creditor can require them to make this election; the Assignee or trustee then has three months within which to decide. On the expiry of that period, the security belongs entirely to that creditor and he is entitled to prove for the balance due on the debt after the estimated value of the security has been deducted, However, if that creditor subsequently realises the security and obtains a different price from his earlier valuation, he is required to adjust his proof to fully take account of the price he got.[54]

8–20 Creditors should exercise some care when valuing their security because they cannot easily alter whatever value they gave initially. Formerly an amendment would be allowed only in "some very extreme instance" but this has now been relaxed somewhat. Amendment will be permitted if it is proved that the earlier value was "made bona fide on a mistaken estimate".[55] Where such amendment is allowed, that creditor's proof must be appropriately adjusted and, if an excess has been paid to him, that must be reimbursed.[56] He is entitled to be paid more if the value was adjusted downwards, subject to the proviso that any payments already made to creditors should not be disturbed.

Unenforceable Debts

8–21 A debt which could not have been enforced against the debtor cannot be proved against his estate in bankruptcy. There are various reasons why the debt might be unenforceable. The contractual obligation to pay the money could be unlawful, such as for breach of the Gaming Acts,[57] of former exchange control regulations or other statutory provisions. Or the obligation may be unenforceable because it contravenes public policy, such as an integral aspect of an agreement which is an unreasonable restraint of trade or a debt owed to some foreign revenue authority outside the EC.[58] Debts contracted by infants, other than in respect of necessities, cannot be proved, nor can debts that are statute barred.[59] But limitation periods cease to run against the debtor as from the date of his

---

[52] 1988 Act, s.53.
[53] 1988 Act, Sch.1, r.24(4)(b).
[54] 1988 Act, Sch.1, r.24(7).
[55] 1988 Act, Sch.1, r.24(5); *Re Clenaghan,* 95 I.L.T.R. 89 (1961) and *Re Johnston* [1929] N.I. 103.
[56] Schedule 1, r.24(6).
[57] *Re Derhurst* (1891) 64 L.T. 273.
[58] *Re Gibbons* [1960] Ir. Jr. Rep. 60 and *Government of India v Taylor* [1955] A.C. 491.
[59] *Re Benzon* [1914] 2 Ch. 68.

adjudication as a bankrupt.[60] Where a proof is based on a tax assessment, it must have been served n the debtor.[61]

Procedure

8–22   A debt may be proved by the creditor sending the requisite "particulars" of it to the Official Assignee.[62] Usually those particulars will comprise a detailed statement of account.[63] If the Assignee queries any claim the creditor can be required to specify the vouchers or any other evidence which will substantiate his debt.[64] Where the Assignee deems fit, the creditor can be obliged to swear an affidavit of debt;[65] he also can be required to furnish additional information and even to attend before the Assignee.[66] A person seeking to prove a debt may even be examined by the court.[67] With the Assignee's consent, the creditor may amend his proof.[68] When submitting a proof, the creditor must disclose any counterclaim which, to his knowledge, the bankrupt possesses, as well as indicating whether he has security for the debt.[69]

8–23   The time within which proofs must be submitted may be fixed by the Official Assignee; a proof sent in any later will only be admitted by order of the court.[70] Notices must be published in the Iris Oifigiúil, and in such newspapers as the Assignee deems fit, of the time for sending in proofs.[71] Such notices must also be sent by ordinary post to every creditor, not later than ten days before the closing date for receiving proofs.[72]

8–24   Where a false claim is made or where information given in connection with a proof is false in any material particular, the court may disallow the claim, in whole or in part, in addition to any other penalty under the 1988 Act.[73] Creditors who have lodged proofs are entitled to see the proofs lodged by other creditors.

DISTRIBUTION TO CREDITORS

8–25   All creditors are not treated equally when it comes to dividing the insolvent's assets among them; the bankruptcy code, coupled with proprietary

---

[60]   *Re General Rolling Stock Co* (1872) 7 Ch. App. 646.
[61]   *Arnold v Williams* [2008] B.P.I.R. 247.
[62]   1988 Act, Sch.1, r.2(a) and r.6.
[63]   Cf. 1988 Act, Sch.1, r.4.
[64]   1988 Act, Sch.1, r.5.
[65]   1988 Act, Sch.1, rr.7 and 8.
[66]   1988 Act, Sch.1, r.22.
[67]   1988 Act, Sch.1, r.20.
[68]   1988 Act, Sch.1, r.9.
[69]   1988 Act, Sch.1, r.5.
[70]   1988 Act, Sch.1, r.3.
[71]   Rule 65.
[72]   Rule 65.
[73]   1988 Act, s.79 and Sch.1, r.21.

and equitable principles, treats various categories of creditors differently. It is only the general creditors, as described below, who rank equally in the division of those assets, assuming of course that there are sufficient assets left for any division among them. Some of the rules about priorities among creditors in bankruptcy are of particular relevance to winding up insolvent companies because s.284(1) of the Companies Act 1963 applies to company liquidations inter alia these rules "relating to the respective rights of secured and unsecured creditors". Certain categories of property held by or owned by the bankrupt cannot be divided among his creditors.

Not Beneficially Owned

8–26   If the property is owned by someone else, it is not available for division; the old "reputed ownership" rule was repealed in 1988. Thus, property which is subject to retention of title or to hire purchase cannot any longer be taken for the benefit of the creditors generally. The same applies to property which is in the bankrupt's name but which he holds in trust for another.[74]

8–27   Where the bankrupt's property was taken in an execution that has been completed, for the purpose of the 1988 Act, the execution creditor is entitled to satisfy his entire debt from the proceeds of that property.[75] Of course, if there is a surplus then that creditor must return the surplus to the Assignee or trustee, as the case may be.

Set-Off

8–28   Where his creditor at the same time owes money to the bankrupt, in circumstances where a set-off arises, then he may set one debt off against the other and prove for the balance.[76] The rules regarding proofs stipulate that "[w]here there are mutual credits or debts as between a bankrupt and any person claiming as a creditor, one debt or demand may be set off against the other and only the balance found owing shall be recoverable on one side or the other".[77] As explained in *Stein v Blake*,[78] "[b]ankruptcy set-off ... affects the substantive rights of the parties by enabling the bankrupt's creditor to use his indebtedness to the bankrupt as a form of security ... . [H]e can set-off pound for pound what he owes the bankrupt and prove for or pay only the balance".[79]

8–29   Set off in bankruptcy must be distinguished from set-off at common law, in equity and arising under a contract. Common law set-off is a statutory procedure which permits cross-claims to be pleaded as a defence in an action;

---

74   See paras 5–28 et seq.
75   What constitutes completion depends on the various modes of execution: see para. 2–19 et seq.
76   See generally, R. Derham, *The Law of Set-Off*, 3rd edn (Oxford: O.U.P., 2003).
77   1988 Act, Sch.1, r.17(1).
78   [1996] A.C. 243.
79   [1996] A.C. 243 at 251.

it originated in a Statute of 1751,[80] and was endorsed by ss.40 and 58 of the Common Law Procedure Amendment Act (Ireland) 1853. Equitable set-off is a substantially similar defence against cross-claims which was developed in the Chancery Courts and indeed expanded beyond circumstances analogous to those provided for in the Act of 1751.[81] Set-off is now provided for in Ord.19, r.2 of the Rules of the Superior Courts.[82] Additionally, parties to a contract may stipulate for a right of set-off,[83] the commonest example being the implied right to combine two or more current accounts in a bank standing in the same name.[84]

8–30   Bankruptcy set-off has a more ancient lineage, originating in England in the Statute of 4 Anne c.17, 1705, and in Ireland in s.43 of the Bankruptcy Act 1772.[85] Its objective has often been described as doing justice between the parties on the basis that, where there are cross-claims, it is most unfair to a creditor for him to be obliged to pay over everything owing to the bankrupt and then to prove against the estate for a dividend on whatever sum the bankrupt owes him. Because setting off in this manner in effect prefers particular creditors, it is surprising that the rule has attracted so little criticism. There is nothing in the 1988 Act comparable to "the proviso" in the British legislation[86] whereby, once the creditor has notice of the debtor's act of bankruptcy, sums which fall due from the debtor following that time cannot be the subject of a set-off.

Mutuality

8–31   What can be set off in a bankruptcy are "mutual credits or debts" between the bankrupt and his creditor. Mutuality in this context does not require that the debts arise at the same time nor that they should be connected in any way, nor that they should be of the same nature. Debts arising at different times in unconnected transactions, be they written, oral, under seal or whatever, can be mutual debts. The focus instead is on the parties to the debts and the relationship between each other, not on the nature of the claims being asserted. If the debts are between the same parties and in the same capacity, they are mutual debts which can be set off in a bankruptcy. This identity must be between those who are beneficially entitled to the debt. It is the beneficial owner of a debt who may set off that debt against an obligation he owes the debtor. Generally, a joint liability may not be set off against an individual debt or vice versa, although there are some exceptions to this principle. But there can be set-off between an individual debt and joint and several liabilities, because each party is severally as well as jointly liable. The case law on when agency relationships give rise to mutual rights and liabilities is complex.

8–32   The debts or claims in question need not have arisen out of contract; "any

---

[80]   25 Geo.11 c.8 (1751); cf. *Sheehan v National Bank* [1937]1.R. 783.
[81]   Cf. *Hanak v Green* [1958] 2 Q.B. 9.
[82]   Also in s.36 of the Civil Liability Act 1961, concerning contributory negligence.
[83]   Cf. *Re Casey* (Hamilton P., June 21, 1986).
[84]   Cf. *Bank of Ireland v Martin* [1937] I.R. 189.
[85]   11 & 12 Geo. 2, c.8.
[86]   Insolvency Act 1986, s.323(3).

utual demands capable of being proved in bankruptcy can be the subject matter of set-off whether or not arising out of contract".[87] Unliquidated damages can be the subject of set-off[88] and so too can amounts owing to and by the Revenue Commissioners in respect of taxes.[89] Since they can be proved, contingent claims can give rise to a set-off, provided that the debt or claim in question came into existence prior to the bankruptcy commencing. There even can be a set-off between a money debt and goods being held, provided that those goods were entrusted for sale and that the proceeds were to be handed over to the debtor.[90] But even though both parties had mutual dealings, a debt cannot be set off against a liability in respect of a judgment for detinue. The primary obligations between the parties must have been to pay each other money. Lord Esher M.R. observed that "[i]f the claim on one side in the action and the counter-claim on the other were such as would both result in a money claim, so that for the purposes of the action there would be merely a pecuniary liability on each side, the case would ... come within the section. [One should] give the widest possible scope to the section".[91]

Peremptory or Optional

8–33 Whether set-off is a peremptory rule in bankruptcy that cannot be contracted out of or waived is debatable. In *Deering v Hyndman*,[92] which dealt with set-off under s.251 of the 1857 Act,[93] it was held that the right was optional, or at least was not compulsory in all circumstances. All the creditors, including the defendant, agreed that the debtor should continue trading. At that time, the defendant was owed £2,000 and, following the agreement, he became indebted to the debtor for £1,190. When shortly afterwards the debtor was adjudicated bankrupt, the defendant sought to set off these two amounts and to prove for the balance. It was held that, by agreeing that the debtor could trade on, in the circumstances, the defendant purported to waive any set-off he may have had and that such an agreement was not precluded by 1857 Act nor by the general law. According to Johnson J.:

> "I have always understood the settled law to be – *quilibet potest renunciare juri pro se introducto* – that a person who has a benefit given to him by statute may waive it if he thinks fit, but that an individual cannot waive a matter in which the public have an interest ... . The right of set off is a benefit to the individual creditor, and it in no way concerns the public or society whether he relies on it or waives it. And even if an individual creditor agrees for sufficient consideration to waive the right, I fail to see why he should not be at liberty to do so either without bankruptcy or in bankruptcy; and if a number of creditors of a firm which has suspended

---

[87] *Re D.H.Curtis (Builders) Ltd* [1978] 1 Ch. 162 at 173.
[88] *Government of Newfoundland v Newfoundland Rly. Co* (1888) 13 H.L.C. 199.
[89] *Re Harrex Ltd* [1976] I.R. 15.
[90] *Rolls Razor Ltd v Cox* [1967] 1 Q.B. 552.
[91] *Eberle's Hotels and Restaurant Co v Jonas Bros* (1887) 18 Q.B.D. 459 at 465.
[92] (1886) 18 L.R Ir. 323.
[93] 20 & 21 Vic. c.60.

payment agree together, and with the firm, to buy the goods of the firm on hands for cash, and not to rely on set-off of antecedent debts, even in the event of bankruptcy supervening, I fail to see why such agreement should not be valid and binding, the mutual promise being the consideration."[94]

May C.J., however, emphasised that the case concerned "a special agreement entered into ... , not by any particular creditor, but by the general body, to exclude a set-off",[95] although he did not expressly reject the contention that any creditor could "commute the right of set-off for sufficient consideration."[96] In Britain and in New Zealand it has been held that the right of set-off under the relevant bankruptcy legislation cannot be contracted out of.[97]

Lien

8–34   Liens operate in somewhat the same way. If a creditor has a lien on part of the bankrupt's property, he can refuse to surrender that property until he is paid the full amount which is covered by the lien.

Specific Charge

8–35   The powers of secured creditors to realise or otherwise deal with their security is virtually unaffected by the debtor becoming bankrupt.[98] A creditor with a charge over the bankrupt's assets is a secured creditor, and may choose to enforce the charge by selling that property, or he may value the charged property and prove for the balance owing, along with the general creditors. The holder of a specific or fixed charge has a charge over a particular identifiable part of the bankrupt's property. Such a charge can even embrace property which the bankrupt did not own at the time the charge was given but subsequently acquired; provided the future property is sufficiently identified, it can be the subject of a fixed charge.[99]

8–36   Often the property charged will be land and there is a substantial and complex body of law governing mortgages of land.[100] The fact that the mortgagor became bankrupt does not materially affect the legal status and consequences of such mortgages. If what is charged is a chattel or chattels, then the Bills of Sale Acts 1879–83[101] may have to be complied with. Under these, when a person gives a written charge over "personal chattels" but retains possession

---

[94]   (1886) 18 L.R Ir. 323 at 340.

[95]   (1886) 18 L.R Ir. 323 at 352.

[96]   (1886) 18 L.R Ir. 323 at 338, O'Brien J.

[97]   *Halesowen Presswork & Assemblies Ltd v National Westminster Bank Ltd* [1972] A.C. 785 and *Rendell v Doors & Doors Ltd* [1975] 2 N.Z.L.R. 191.

[98]   1988 Act, s.136(2).

[99]   *Holroyd v Marshall* (1862) 10 H.L.C. 191.

[100] See generally, N. Maddox, *Mortgage Law and Practice* (Dublin: Thomson Round Hall, 2008); J.C.W. Wylie, *Irish Land Law,* 2nd edn (1986) Ch.12 and A. Lyall, *Land Law in Ireland*, 2nd edn (Dublin: Round Hall, 2000) Ch.23 at 211.

[101] 42 & 43 Vic. c.50 and 46 Vic. c.7.

of them, the instrument of charge must be in the prescribed form and be duly registered as a bill of sale.

8–37   Charges made by farmers of "stock" in favour of a recognised bank, known as agricultural chattel mortgages, do not have to be registered under these Acts; they instead must be registered in the relevant Circuit Court office.[102]

8–38   The charge given may be on a chose in action, such as stocks and shares, insurance policies, book debts, patents, trade marks, copyrights. Some of these entitlements can only be charged in accordance with the prescribed formalities. Although book debts are usually the subject of a floating charge, an appropriately drafted instrument can create a fixed charge over them.[103]

Floating Charge

8–39   A floating charge[104] is a security over a category of or over categories of the debtor's assets but which nevertheless permits the debtor to use those assets in the ordinary course of his business, such as by selling them, pledging them or creating a specific charge over some of them. Generally, the type of assets which are charged will be consumed in one way or another in the ordinary course of the business and will be replaced by more assets of that type. The floating charge will cover all assets of the specified category which the chargor owns from time to time. One reason why individuals rarely resorted to this type of charge was the "reputed ownership" rule, which has ceased to exist. The Bills of Sale Acts[105] also discourage such charges in that as a rule it is most impracticable to ensure that a floating charge continues to comply with those Acts. Thus, while individuals could and can create floating charges, for practical reasons they very rarely do so. An exception is the agricultural chattel mortgage of "stock" which, like company charges, is subject to a distinct and much simpler registration system. Charges given to any recognised bank over such chattels, be they fixed or floating charges, must be registered in the local Circuit Court office.[106]

Administrative Costs

8–40   Before any of the bankrupt's debts can be paid, the costs of administering his estate must be covered: "[t]he expenses, fees and costs of the bankruptcy shall be payable in priority to the liabilities of the bankrupt in such order as may be prescribed".[107] Unlike the position in company liquidations,[108] however, the Bankruptcy Rules do not set out the appropriate ranking for the various kinds

---

[102]   Agricultural Credit Act 1978, s.26.
[103]   *Re Keenan Bros Ltd* [1985] I.R. 401.
[104]   See generally, M. Forde & H. Kennedy, *Company Law*, 4th edn (Dublin: Thomson Round Hall, 2008) at 657 et seq.
[105]   Of 1879 and 1883: 42 & 43 Vic c.50 and 46 Vic. c.7.
[106]   Agricultural Credit Act 1978, s.26.
[107]   1988 Act, s.80.
[108]   R.S.C., Ord.74, r.128.

of costs, expenses and fees, other than that the petitioning creditor's taxed costs should be paid immediately after the other administrative costs.[109] The expression "expenses, fees and costs" is not a term of art and, presumably, embraces all expenses which the Assignee or creditors' trustee reasonably incurred in the course of administering the bankrupt's estate.[110] Such costs could include tax liabilities arising from transactions done in the course of the administration.[111] Where the bankruptcy is administered by a creditors' trustee, it is conceivable that an analogy will be drawn with voluntary liquidators in determining where the trustee's remuneration should rank vis-à-vis the other costs of administration.[112] The terms of schemes of arrangement may very well contain stipulations as to the payment of costs.[113]

Super-Preferential Debts

8–41   Three special categories of creditor were entitled to be paid in priority to the other general creditors,[114] namely "clerks or servants" who were owed wages for up to a specified period, the Revenue who were owed income and property taxes for a specified period and local authorities to whom rates were owing for a specified period. The preferential treatment for these debts is continued by the 1988 Act in a greatly expanded form.

8–42   More recently, the legislature has identified one particular type of debt which is given a preferential status ranking before the usual preferential debts; thus the designation "super-preferential" or "pre-preferential" debts. These are the unpaid employment contributions, under the Social Welfare (Consolidation) Act 2005, and related legislation which the bankrupt qua employer has deducted from an employee's remuneration. Section 19(3) of this Act provides that such sums "shall not form part of the property of the bankrupt or of the arranging debtor so as to be included among the [preferential] debts ... but shall ... be paid to the Social Insurance Fund in priority to the [preferential] debts ...". The meaning of this provision has not yet received judicial interpretation but it would seem to impress the sums so deducted with a trust for the benefit of the Social Insurance Fund. Thus, if misappropriated, those sums can be traced. A matter that will require resolution is whether those sums rank prior to the administrative costs in a situation where there is not enough remaining in the estate to defray both those costs and the pre-preferential debts.

8–43   In this context, mention should be made of officers of a friendly society or of a trustee savings bank who have in their possession any money or property belonging to the society or bank. The Friendly Societies Act 1896,[115] and the

---

[109] Rule 168.
[110] Cf. *Re Hegarty* [1900] 2 N.I.J.R. 65 and *Re Cruise* (1905) 39 I.L.T. 237.
[111] E.g. *Re McMeekin* [1973] N.I. 191.
[112] E.g. *Beni-Felkai Mining Co.* [1934] 1 Ch. 406.
[113] Cf. *Re A.B.C. An Arranging Debtor,* 65 I.L.T.R. 84 (1931).
[114] Preferential Payment in Bankruptcy (Ireland) Act 1889, 52 & 53 Vic. c.60.
[115] 59 & 60 Vict. c.25.

Trustee Savings Banks Act 1863,[116] stipulate that the property or money must be given over to the relevant institution before any of the officer's other creditors are paid.[117]

Preferential Debts

8–44 In the past there were several categories of preferential debts, in the sense of debts that were to be paid before any distribution could be made to the general creditors. There was the royal prerogative under which, at common law, all debts owing to the Government itself had preferential status; for instance, legacy duty,[118] income tax[119] and rental owed to the Postmaster General in respect of the telephone service.[120] But in 1953 the Supreme Court held that this common law priority had not been carried over by the Constitution in 1937, nor even by the Free State Constitution in 1922.[121] Then there was the less extensive statutory version of this priority, adopted in s.38 of the Finance Act 1924, but which was repealed in 1967.[122] Until 1988, the principal preferential debts were those provided for in the Preferential Payments in Bankruptcy (Ireland) Act 1889,[123] notably certain taxes and local authority rates and also unpaid remuneration owed to employees, up to a specified ceiling. Finally, there are numerous legislative provisions, mainly in employment legislation, which place certain categories of indebtedness on a par with the preferential debts.

8–45 Certain fiscal debts and debts to employees are preferred. All of these debts rank equally and, in the event of it not being possible to pay them all, they abate equally, i.e. the same proportionate amount in the euro should be paid in respect of each €1 which is owing. However, the parties can agree to vary the preferred order of distribution and will be held to any such agreement. For instance, in a winding up case,[124] where in a scheme of arrangement approved by the court the employees agreed to accept prompt payment of part of what was owing to them, in return for the Revenue agreeing that its preferential claim should be "frozen", the Supreme Court held that, following the liquidation, the employees were not entitled to reject that agreement and insist on the Revenue being tied to the statutory order of distribution.

Assessed Taxes

8–46 Preference is given to "all property or income tax assessed on the bankrupt up to the 5th day of April next before the date of the order of adjudication, and not exceeding in the whole one year's assessment," including

---

[116] 26 & 27 Vict. c.87.
[117] 1988 Act s.81(10); cf. *Re Eilbeck* [1910] 1 K.B. 136.
[118] *Re Galvin* [1897] 1 I.R 520.
[119] *Re Orr* [1924] 1 I.R. 120.
[120] *Re Behan* [1914] 2 I.R. 29.
[121] *Re Irish Employers Mutual Ins. Assn.* [1955] I.R. 76.
[122] Finance Act 1967, Sch.19. Cf. *Re K. An Arranging Debtor* [1927] I.R. 260.
[123] 52 & 53 Vic. c.60.
[124] *Re M.F.N. Construction Co.* (Supreme Court, May 12, 1988). Cf. 1988 Act, s.81(8).

capital gains tax.[125] Thus any one year's assessed income tax or property tax is preferred. "Property tax" for these purposes is not defined but would include capital acquisition tax and residential property tax. This preference includes interest due on the preferred taxes. This preference applies only to one year's unpaid tax in respect of each of the above categories, assessed up to the April 5 prior to the adjudication.[126] The Revenue can select which particular year shall be preferred and can select different years in respect of the different types of tax.[127] Because the bankrupt's losses usually would have mounted in the final years of trading, the Revenue will incline to reach as far back as possible when determining which year's unpaid income tax should be preferred.

Rates

8–47   Preference is given to "all local rates due from the bankrupt at the date of the order of adjudication, and having become due and payable within twelve months next before that date."[128] "Rates" for these purposes are not defined but must mean rates struck by local authorities under the Local Government Acts and any levies which the legislature treats in the same way.[129] This preference applies to unpaid rates due in respect of the twelve months preceding when the debtor was adjudicated a bankrupt.

Value Added Tax

8–48   Preference is given to unpaid V.A.T. (less V.A.T. refundable) in relation to taxable periods ending within the 12 months before the debtor was adjudicated a bankrupt.[130] Preference is also given in respect of any interest payable on outstanding V.A.T.

Employees

8–49   Where the bankrupt was an employer, preference is given for certain unpaid wages, sick and holiday pay, pension contributions, compensation awards, and also to the Revenue in respect of unpaid PAYE and equivalent deductions.[131]

Distress

8–50   Distress is a remedy available principally to landlords at common law whereby, where the rent is overdue, they can seize goods and effects on the demised premises. Where distress was levied within three months of the debtor

---

[125]   1988 Act, s.81(1)(a) and Taxes Consolidation Act 1997, s.982.

[126]   *Gowers v Walker* [1930] 1 Ch. 262.

[127]   *Re Pratt* [1951] 1 Ch. 229.

[128]   1988 Act, s.81(1)(a).

[129]   *Re An Arranging Debtor* [1921] 2 I.R 1, *Re Baker* [1954] 1 W.L.R. 1144 and *Re Ellwood* [1927] 1 Ch. 455.

[130]   Finance Act 1976, s.62(1).

[131]   See paras 10–62 et seq.

becoming bankrupt, the above-mentioned preferential debts are a charge on what was distrained or on the proceeds of any sale of the property taken, and the creditor is in effect subrogated for the preferred creditor to whom the proceeds of the property was given.[132]

Ordinary Creditors

8–51   Once all the secured and preferential debts have been discharged, the ordinary general creditors must be paid, provided of course that they have proved their debts. If there is not sufficient to pay them the full amounts owing, they must all be paid an equal proportion of what is available for them—so many cent in each €1 they are owed.

Deferred Creditors

8–52   There are certain general unsecured creditors who rank after the ordinary creditors. Formerly loans between a husband and wife fell into this category but the 1988 Act puts inter-spousal indebtedness on the same footing as all other debts.[133] A person who loans money to another or others for the purpose of their business and on terms whereby the lender is to participate in its profits, either by way of interest payments or otherwise, is not entitled to be repaid pari passu with the ordinary creditors.[134] But the lender is entitled to retain any security he may have got for loaning the money. It was held in *Re Meade*[135] that this also applies to all "quasi partners", meaning persons who have provided capital for a business in which they have a direct interest and which is carried on for their joint benefit. As one judge put it, "he who provides part of the capital of a business cannot call for payment till the creditors of the business are paid".[136] Thus in *Re Meade*, a woman (not the bankrupt's wife although she was called "Mrs Meade") advanced money to him to finance a riding school, and she and her daughter lived at the school on the profits of the business. She was not permitted to recover her loan until the ordinary business creditors were paid in full. That she was not a partner and that she was not sharing directly in the profits was held not to be relevant. Beneficiaries of a settlement which was avoided under the 1988 Act are also deferred creditors.

Unclaimed Dividends

8–53   An "unclaimed dividend account" must to be opened by the Official Assignee at the Central Bank.[137] All unclaimed dividends and other money not claimed must be paid into this account and all dividends properly claimed may be paid out of the account.

---

[132]   1988 Act, s.81(4) but cf. Taxes Consolidation Act 1997, s.971.
[133]   1988 Act, Sch.1, r.11.
[134]   Partnership Act 1890, s.3.
[135]   [1951] Ch. 774.
[136]   *Re Beale* (1876) 4 Ch. D. 246, 46 L.J. (B.) 17 at 18.
[137]   1988 Act, s.84 and rr.157–159.

Surplus

8–54 Exceptionally, after paying off all creditors in full, including the costs of administering the estate and interest on the debts at the current rate for judgment debts, there may be a surplus in the bankrupt's estate. In that event, the surplus is transferred over to the bankrupt. Such transfer must be done by order of the court, which operates as an effective conveyance, assignment or transfer of the property. Even if there are unpaid creditors in the bankruptcy who did not lodge proofs, the surplus will vest in the bankrupt and, for instance, judgment can be executed against that fund by a post-bankruptcy creditor.[138]

Calculating and Paying Dividends

8–55 The actual distribution of the proceeds of the bankrupt's estate is supervised by the court at a private sitting. Once the estate is substantially realised and most of the proofs are in, and the Assignee or creditors' trustee has got in sufficient funds to cover the administrative costs and the preferential debts, and also to pay a dividend to the creditors (which need not be the final dividend), he must "[a]s soon as convenient", place the matter before a sitting of the court.[139] Notice of filing documents and of the sitting must be advertised, at least 21 days before the sitting is to take place, in the prescribed form[140] in the *Iris Oifigiúil* and in such newspaper or newspapers as the Assignee or trustee deems appropriate.[141] There must then be presented to the court a file containing the following documents: a list of the creditors admitted to proof, a copy of the bankrupt's account, a report on realisations of the estate and particulars of the administrative costs, the preferential debts and the proposed dividend. Having considered this information, the court will then make such order as it thinks fit as to how the estate shall be distributed.[142] The file presented to the court can be inspected by members of the general public as well as by the creditors.[143] If there are no funds in the estate or insufficient funds for paying any dividend, the court may make directions for paying the expenses, fees and costs in so far as there are funds to meet them.[144]

8–56 How the dividend is to be paid will be calculated as follows. The total amount of money available will be divided with the amount of the claims proved which, unless there is a surplus, will yield a fraction. This fraction determines how many cent in the euro must be paid to each creditor.

8–57 Where the entire estate was not distributed at the first sitting, provision is made for a second sitting, which should take place "as soon as convenient" after the remainder of the estate has been realised. A file dealing with the same

---

[138] *Re Ward* [1942] Ch. 294.
[139] 1988 Act, s.82.
[140] Form 20.
[141] 1988 Act, s.82(1) and r.64(2).
[142] 1988 Act, s.81(3).
[143] 1988 Act, s.81(4).
[144] 1988 Act, s.81(6).

matters as in the first sitting must be presented to the court, which will make such directions for distribution as "it thinks fit". Any balance that remains should be paid to the unpaid dividend account.

CHAPTER 9

TERMINATING THE BANKRUPTCY

9–01 Bankruptcy comes to an end principally by the bankrupt getting a discharge; having paid all or a specified proportion of the debts, the court may order that he be discharged. Occasionally bankruptcy comes to an end by an order annulling the adjudication. As has been explained above,[1] the bankruptcy may be transformed into a composition with the creditors, ending in an order discharging the adjudication. Bankruptcy does not terminate when the bankrupt dies; the court "may proceed in the bankruptcy as if he were living"[2] and the procedures under Pt VI of the 1988 Act regarding the estates of persons dying insolvent would come into play.[3]

RESCISSION

9–02 Bankruptcy procedure is exceptional in that usual res judicata/issue estoppel principles do not apply. Instead, the court in such proceedings has jurisdiction to "review, rescind of vary an order" made by a court of coordinate jurisdiction in the bankruptcy, except for orders of annulment or discharge.[4] It was held in *Fitch v Official Receiver*[5] that, exercising this power, the court could rescind an adjudication of bankruptcy where there was a relevant change of circumstances and also where new evidence comes to light which could not be adduced on an appeal. Following the dismissal of an appeal against their adjudication, most of the bankrupts' creditors, including the petitioning creditor, supported their application to rescind the order; none opposed it. Their reason was that, if the debtors were not bankrupt, they would be in a better position to pay their debts from the proceeds of assets in a business partnership. Observing that the discretion here "is still to be exercised with caution and only in exceptional circumstances",[6] it was held that they justified ordering rescission here on condition that the benefit of their contracts with the partnership would be assigned for the benefit of their creditors. But as a protective measure, the petitions were left on file so that they could be restored by any of the creditors.

---

[1] See paras 3–58 et seq.
[2] 1988 Act, s.42.
[3] See paras 10–31 et seq.
[4] 1988 Act, s.135.
[5] [1996] 1 W.L.R. 242.
[6] [1996] 1 W.L.R. 242 at 249.

ANNULMENT

9–03   In an appropriate case at any stage in the bankruptcy, the court may declare the adjudication null and void and set it aside. Annulment is authorised when the bankrupt has "shown cause".[7] Formerly there was no general statutory authority to annul but the 1988 Act now confers a jurisdiction to annul an adjudication "in any other case where, in the opinion of the Court, he ought not to have been adjudicated bankrupt".[8] But it was emphasised by the Supreme Court in *Gill v Philip O'Reilly & Co*[9] that "extremely compelling reasons" are required before such an application would succeed, which did not exist there. One such ground would be where the order had been made without jurisdiction or where there was some serious defect in the proceedings; for instance, the petitioner is a registered company but its seal was not affixed to the petition in accordance with the requirements of its articles of association.[10] Another ground would be where there was a clear abuse of process; where in all the circumstances the mechanisms of the Bankruptcy Act had been improperly used.[11] An instance might be where the undoubted predominant motivation was to disable the debtor from holding public office[12] or from exercising one of the professions or occupations from which bankrupts are excluded. Another ground is where the creditors have been paid in full or have otherwise consented.[13] Exceptionally an annulment may be obtained where the petitioner's debt is disputed in circumstances where it could not reasonably have been shown at the adjudication stage that there was a dispute.[14] But there is no automatic right to an annulment on those grounds.[15]

9–04   In *Re Gorham*[16] Pim J. observed that "in a proper case ... the Court has power, no matter what time may have elapsed, to annul a bankruptcy,"[17] but he cautioned against the court too readily setting aside orders previously made. He rejected an application to annul where the debtor's summons, on foot of which he was adjudicated a bankrupt, had been served two days after the prescribed time for service had expired. That defect, it was held, was at most a matter of procedure and not of substance. Because an adjudication is for the benefit of all creditors, an annulment will not be ordered on the grounds that the petitioning creditor's debt has been paid.[18]

9–05   Only the bankrupt can apply to have the adjudication annulled. An

---

[7]   1988 Act, s.16(2) and see paras 4–59 et seq.
[8]   1988 Act, s.85(5)(b).
[9]   [2003] 1 I.R. 434.
[10]   *Re Hussey* (Hamilton P., September 23, 1987). In this case the adjudication was not annulled because the bankrupt left it far too late to make his application.
[11]   E.g. *Re A Debtor* [1967] Ch. 590 and *Couvaras v Wolf* [2002] 2 F.L.R. 107.
[12]   E.g. *McGinn v Beagan* [1962] I.R. 364.
[13]   *Re Spicer* (1859) 9 Ir. Ch. 5.
[14]   *Ahmed v Mogul Eastern Foods* [2007] B.P.I.R. 975.
[15]   *Re Taylor* [1901] 1 K.B. 744.
[16]   [1924] 2 I.R. 46.
[17]   [1924] 2 I.R. 46 at 48.
[18]   *Re Daniell* [1901] 2 I.R. 186.

order annulling his adjudication can be made at any stage of the proceedings. The order must direct that any property vested in the Assignee or the trustee be re-vested in the debtor. Such order is deemed to be an effective transfer of the property and may be registered accordingly.[19] The 1988 Act does not set out what the effects of an annulment are. Subject to whatever conditions the court may impose, the effect is to put the bankrupt in the position he was in prior to adjudication insofar as that is possible but without prejudice to any dispositions of property that the Assignee or creditors' trustee may have made. But annulment has been held not to be a defence to proceedings for having been involved in a company's management in breach of a bankruptcy order.[20]

DISCHARGE

9–06 The usual procedure for bringing a bankruptcy to an end is an order discharging the bankrupt, which operates to free him from pre-adjudication provable liabilities. When the concept of discharge was originally adopted in 1705, it was not the exclusive object to induce reluctant merchant debtors to disclose and turn over all their assets, in return for which they would be relieved of the burden of bankruptcy. Once creditors could be assured that the debtor had no other substantial assets salted away, there was realistic prospect of them recovering a higher dividend; discharge operated as a carrot and a stick. In more recent times, the object has also been to enable the debtor to secure a "fresh start" in his business affairs and rehabilitation. The conditions for and periods within which persons may obtain discharge, notwithstanding that their liabilities were not paid off in full, vary significantly from country to country, and in some continental European countries discharge is very difficult to obtain. A discharged bankrupt can obtain a certificate from the court to that effect.[21] An application for discharge on any grounds other than that the bankrupt has paid off all his debts must be grounded on an affidavit, and the court must be given a report of the Assignee or trustee that provision has been made for paying all expenses, fees and costs and any preferential debts.[22]

Grounds for Discharge

9–07 There are several circumstances where the bankrupt is entitled to be discharged. One is where the adjudication took place before January 1, 1960.[23] In this case there is no need even to apply to the court. It is provided that any of the bankrupt's property which is still vested in the Assignee shall re-vest, subject to the payment of any outstanding expenses, fees, costs and preferential debts. In all other cases an application must be made to the court.

9–08 Discharge will be ordered where provision has been made to defray the

---

[19] 1988 Act, s.85(6).
[20] *Inland Revenue v McEntaggart* [2006] 1 B.C.L.C. 176.
[21] 1988 Act, s.85(7).
[22] Rules 164 and 165.
[23] 1988 Act, s.85(1).

expenses, fees and costs of the bankruptcy, and the preferential debts, and all the creditors have been paid in full, with such interest as the court may allow.[24] At the sitting for distribution the court may make an order of discharge on these grounds.[25]

9–09 Discharge will also be ordered where all the creditors have consented, provided that provision has been made to defray the expenses, fees and costs in the bankruptcy as well as the preferential debts.[26] These are the creditors who have proved and were admitted in the bankruptcy, who have consented to the discharge and have waived their outstanding claims by executing a prescribed form. An application under this latter ground will not be entertained until the bankrupt's debts and liabilities have been ascertained.

9–10 The court has a discretion to order discharge in the following cases. It must be satisfied that the bankrupt made full disclosure of any after-acquired property he obtained. Additionally, it must be satisfied that it is "reasonable and proper" to order discharge in the circumstances. There is no authority squarely on the meaning of this phrase in the context. In the 1872 Act, what the court had to consider was whether, in its opinion, the bankrupt's inability to pay his debts in full arose from circumstances for which he cannot "justly be held responsible". The leading case concerned Michael Davitt's bankruptcy,[27] which resulted from his taxed costs of fighting an election petition after he had been elected as a Parnellite candidate for North Meath in 1892. The question for the court to decide under that Act was whether the insolvency "has arisen from circumstances for which, taking all the circumstances into account, including of course the nature of the debt, and the manner in which it was incurred, and the circumstances out of which it sprang, the bankrupt cannot fairly and reasonably be held to suffer, though he has paid the legal penalty in bankruptcy".[28] The 1914 English Act contained a long list of circumstances in which discharge should be refused. Another pre-requisite is that the bankrupt's estate was fully realised and that sufficient provision has been made for paying the expenses, fees and costs of the bankruptcy and to pay any preferential debts.

9–11 Assuming that the estate was realised, that such provision was made, that there was disclosure of all after-acquired property and that it is a "proper case", the court will order discharge in any of the following circumstances. First there is where his creditors were paid at least fifty cents in the euro by the Assignee or trustee. Secondly; there is where the bankrupt and his friends have paid the creditors, in addition to the dividend, such sums as give them at least fifty cents in the euro. Thirdly, there is where the bankruptcy has been in existence for more than 12 years. In this latter instance, the bankrupt's affidavit must disclose all his after-acquired property. And the Assignee's or trustee's report must confirm

---

[24] 1988 Act, s.85(3)(a)(i).
[25] Rule 163.
[26] 1988 Act, s.85(3)(a)(ii) (amended by the Civil Law (Miscellaneous Provisions) Act 2008, s.65) and r.164.
[27] *Re Davitt* [1894] 1 I.R. 517.
[28] [1894] 1 I.R. 517 at 526. See too *Re Harris* [1974] N.I. 1.

that, in his opinion, all such property was disclosed and that it is reasonable and proper to grant the application.[29]

Consequences of Discharge

9–12   When ordering discharge, the court will direct that any property remaining vested in the Assignee or creditors' trustee shall re-vest in the debtor, and that order operates as an effective transfer of the property and may be duly registered as such. A pre-requisite to obtaining such a re-vesting order is that the bankrupt applies to the court, grounded on an affidavit, and the Assignee or trustee makes a report confirming that provision has been made for all expenses, costs and fees and for any preferential debts.[30] On application to it, the court will issue a certificate of discharge.[31]

9–13   What consequences follow discharge are not set out in the 1988 Act, other than that it does not put an end to any criminal liability for a bankruptcy offence.[32] The principal result is that the debtor is no longer liable in respect of all debts and liabilities which could have been proved in the bankruptcy. However, the underlying cause of action is not totally destroyed; although the creditor may no longer recover against the debtor, such rights as the creditor would have against third parties are not invariably taken away. For instance, although the Law Society was prevented from prosecuting claims against solicitors who were discharged bankrupts, it was held that the Society could recover from indemnity insurers of those solicitors' liabilities.[33] He is no longer subject to the various personal disabilities which attached to him while a bankrupt. But he can be held liable for any debts or liabilities which could not have been proved and for any post-bankruptcy liabilities. Under earlier bankruptcy legislation, discharge did not remove liability for any fraud or fraudulent breach of trust,[34] nor did it operate to release a co-debtor or a surety from any of their liabilities in respect of the bankrupt.[35]

---

[29]   Rule 165(3).
[30]   Rule 162.
[31]   1988 Act, s.85(7) and r.166.
[32]   1988 Act, s.131.
[33]   E.g. *R (Balding) v Secretary of State* [2008] 1 W.L.R. 564; *Law Society v Shah* [2008] 3 W.L.R. 1401.
[34]   Cf. *Woodland Ferrari v UCL Group Retirement Benefits Scheme* [2003] Ch. 115 and *Mander v Evans* [2001] 1 W.L.R. 2378.
[35]   Cf. *Johnson v Davies* [1999] Ch. 117.

CHAPTER 10

SPECIAL BANKRUPTCY SITUATIONS

10–01   There are certain categories of bankruptcy for which some discrete rules exist or which call for separate consideration in some respects: notably, partnerships, deceased's estates, trusts, family members, employers and consumers.

PARTNERSHIPS

10–02   Partnerships today are largely confined to those involved in professional practice, most notably solicitors and accountants who are not permitted to adopt the corporate form. Some of these firms are extremely large and wealthy. But an informal understanding between two or more persons to carry on a business in common, even a single venture, can constitute a partnership.[1] A registered company can be a partner and there can be a partnership comprised only of such entities. The legal regime governing partnerships is almost entirely the product of case law, the basic principles being substantially codified in the Partnership Act 1890.[2]

10–03   A partnership is fundamentally different from a registered company in that it is not legally distinct from the individuals who comprise it. It does not possess a separate legal personality, whereby it might enjoy the full benefit of entity shielding and might obtain the advantage of owner shielding or limited liability. If their firm becomes insolvent, every partner is liable without limit for its unpaid debts.[3] A diluted version of entity shielding was adopted for partnerships, in holding that the assets of a bankrupt partnership must first be applied to the claims of the firm's creditors, and such excess as may exist may then be used to pay off the individual partners' own creditors.[4] This was matched by a diluted version of owner shielding, in holding that a partner's personal creditors have first claim to his own assets, and such as those assets in excess as may then exist are available to pay off the firm's creditors.[5] On account of the apparent symmetry of this regime, it became known as the "jingle rule".[6]

---

[1]   E.g. *M. Young Legal Associates Ltd v Zahid Solicitors* [2006] 1 W.L.R. 2562.
[2]   53 & 54 Vic. c.39 (hereinafter the "1890 Act") and see generally, R.C.I. Anson Banks (ed.), *Lindley & Banks on Partnership* 18th edn (London: Sweet & Maxwell, 2002) and M. Twomey, *Partnership Law* (Dublin: Butterworths, 2000).
[3]   Except for certain limited partnerships under the Limited Partnerships Act 1907 and the Investment Limited Partnerships Act 1994.
[4]   *Craven v Knight*, 21 Eng. Rep. 664 (1683).
[5]   *Ex parte Crowder*, 23 Eng. Rep. 1064 (1715).
[6]   Now contained in s.34 of the 1988 Act.

10–04   That there is an abundance of case law on partners' bankruptcy[7] is not surprising as, prior to 1844, partnership was virtually the exclusive mode by which two or more persons could carry on business in common and, until the *Salomon* case[8] popularised the "one person" and "family" company in the late Victorian era, was the predominant mode for carrying on small and medium sized enterprises. The great majority of cases are well over one hundred years old and many of them are to be found in obscure law reports. The difficulties for practitioners that this state of affairs presents was partly resolved in Britain by enacting a statutory instrument containing detailed rules on how bankrupt partners and partnerships should be treated.[9]

10–05   The High Court possesses an extensive jurisdiction to order that a partnership be dissolved, including where the business can only be carried on at a loss and also on "just and equitable" grounds.[10] A partnership with more than eight members can be wound up as an "unregistered company" under the Companies Acts 1963–2006.[11]

Arrangements

10–06   Partners can become parties to an arrangement under the Deeds of Arrangement Act 1887[12] and also can avail of the arrangement procedures under Pt IV (ss.86–109) of the 1988 Act. Acceptance of a composition under the 1887 Act from one partner does not, of itself, afford a defence to an action against the other partners.[13] A discharge by joint creditors, such as partners, does not affect their separate creditors, and vice versa.[14]

10–07   Where the presenters of a petition for protection under Pt IV of the 1988 Act are partners, their affidavit must disclose their separate assets and separate liabilities, and must distinguish them from the firm's assets and liabilities.[15] Where those petitioning are not all of the partners, the court may refuse to grant protection unless the other partners join in the petition.[16] Where two or more partners have obtained protection and made proposals for paying or compromising their joint and their several liabilities, if those proposals are not accepted, the court is obliged to adjudicate them bankrupt.[17] In that event, the court must cause a notice of the adjudication to be advertised in the *Iris*

---

[7]   See generally, E. Scammell & R. C. l'Anson Banks, *Lindley on the Law of Partnership*, 14th edn (London: Sweet & Maxwell, 1979) Ch.27; and Twomey, *Partnership Law* (Dublin: Butterworths, 2000) Ch.27.

[8]   *Salomon v Salomon & Co* [1897] A.C. 22.

[9]   Insolvent Partnerships Order 1994, S.I. No. 2421 of 1994 and see Lindley (above fn.2) Ch.27.

[10]   Partnership Act 1890, s.35.

[11]   Companies Act 1963, Part X (ss.343A–350).

[12]   50 & 51 Vic. c.57.

[13]   *Megg v Imperial Discount Co.* (1878) 3 Q.B.D. 711.

[14]   *Ex parte Wainwright* (1881) 19 Ch. D. 140.

[15]   Rule 90(4).

[16]   1988 Act, s.87(3).

[17]   1988 Act, s.106.

Oifigiúil and in at least one daily newspaper. The petitioners are then subject to the court's jurisdiction in the same manner as any other bankrupt. Any proposals for payment or compromise which have been accepted or approved are rendered void.

10–08   Because the firm's assets and liabilities are somewhat distinct from those of its partners, to secure sanction for their proposed scheme requires approval by three fifths of the firm's creditors *and* also three fifths of each partners' own creditors.[18] Except where expressly provided in the terms of a scheme, sanction for it does not relieve the firm or partners from liability under guarantees they may have given.[19]

Bankruptcy Petition

10–09   The petitioner may be a creditor of either the firm or of one or more individual partners, or, where there is joint and several liability, of all the partners both jointly and individually. A creditor of the firm may take bankruptcy proceedings against all the partners or against any one or more of them in the name of the firm.[20] Any "person interested" can apply to the court for an order that the names of the persons involved in the proceedings be disclosed in such manner as the court may direct.[21] But the firm itself cannot be adjudicated a bankrupt; any adjudication must be made against the partners individually, with the name of the firm being added.[22] One partner may petition for an adjudication against his co-partner or co-partners.[23] There are old authorities to the effect that, if the petitioner's real objective was to have the partnership dissolved and the adjudication was not otherwise necessary, an adjudication made in such circumstances would be annulled; this was the case where the petitioner was not a partner but was acting at the instigation of one.[24]

10–10   A debt owing by one partner only will not support a petition against him and his co-partners. In order to obtain an adjudication against every member of the firm, it must be shown that each of them committed an act of bankruptcy or concurred in the act that was committed.[25] Where a petition is presented against more than one partner, the court has a discretion to adjudicate only one or more of them bankrupt and to dismiss the petition as to the remainder.[26]

Effects of Adjudication

10–11   Unless otherwise agreed between them, once any one partner is

---

[18] *Re Loré* (1889) 23 L.R. Ir. 365.
[19] *Re Pim* (1881) 7 L.R. Ir. 458.
[20] 1988 Act, s.31.
[21] 1988 Act, s.37.
[22] Rule 34.
[23] E.g. Ex p. *Notley* (1833) 1 Mon. & Ayr. 46.
[24] Lindley (above fn.7) at 797–798.
[25] *Re Harris* [1939] N.I. 1.
[26] 1988 Act, s.31(2).

adjudicated a bankrupt the partnership is dissolved.[27] Where the partnership continues, the one who was adjudicated is no longer capable of binding the firm.[28] Where all of the partners are adjudicated, the firm is necessarily dissolved and its members can no longer carry on its business. The old "relation back" rule gave rise to particular complications in the case of bankrupt partners but it was abolished in 1988. Another source of complication in this context, which no longer exists, was the "reputed ownership" rule.

10–12   Where just one or some of the partners is/are adjudicated, all his or their separate property, including interest in the partnership, vests in the Official Assignee or the trustee. Because his entitlements cannot exceed those of the debtor, had he not become bankrupt, the Assignee can claim nothing as the bankrupt's share in the firm until all the firm's creditors have been paid and its accounts have been adjusted. Once that is done, the Assignee is entitled to have an account taken, a sale and a distribution. The solvent partners are not permitted to take over the entire partnership assets and pay the Assignee the estimated value of the bankrupt's share. But it would seem that there is nothing inherently wrong in having a clause in the articles of partnership to the effect that, on one partner or some of them becoming bankrupt, his or their share may be taken by the others at a valuation. A comparable clause in the articles of association of a registered company has been upheld.[29] The entire partnership assets must be included in any such valuation; the clause would not be effectual if any substantial asset was excluded.[30]

10–13   By virtue of the vesting, the Assignee or the trustee does not become a co-partner with the solvent partners. Instead, he becomes a tenant in common with them in the firm's assets. All that he is entitled to is to be paid the amount of the bankrupt's share after the firm has been wound up. In *Provincial Bank v Tallon*,[31] Johnston J. explained the position as follows:

> "When [one partner] became a bankrupt, the ... whole of the property owned separately by him vested absolutely and at once in his Assignees, and such interest as he had in property held jointly by himself and any other person also vested in the Assignees to the extent of that interest. On the bankruptcy, therefore, the Assignees and [the other partners] became entitled to equal undivided moieties as joint tenants in the [partnership] property. The partnership became dissolved when the adjudication took place ... but the title of each party to the joint property was not affected ... . [W]hen one partner in a firm has become a bankrupt, the solvent partner has a right to get in, and to insist on getting in, the assets of the dissolved partnership, and has even a right to use for that purpose the name of the trustee in the bankruptcy on giving him an indemnity."[32]

---

[27] Partnership Act, 1890, s.33(1).
[28] Partnership Act, 1890, s.38, proviso.
[29] *Borland's Trustee v Steel Bros & Co* [1901] 1 Ch. 279.
[30] *Whitmore v Mason* (1861) 2 J. & Fl. 204.
[31] [1938] I.R. 361.
[32] [1938] I.R. 361 at 365, 366 and see *Re Ward* [1985] 2 N.Z.L.R. 352.

10–14　Where all the partners are adjudicated bankrupt or where two or more of them are adjudicated jointly, the firm's property or their joint property, respectively, vests in the Assignee.[33] That property vests qua joint property, without reference to the equality or different proportions of the bankrupt's share in it.[34] In the case of a limited partnership, where all the general partners have been adjudicated bankrupt, the entire assets of the firm vest in the Assignee.[35]

Administering the Estate

10–15　Where a partner is adjudicated bankrupt the Assignee or the trustee may require his co-partner or partners to provide such accounts and information regarding the firm and the bankrupt's interest in it as is deemed necessary.[36] That partner is required to deliver a separate statement of affairs in respect of the partnership.[37] Provision is made to expedite recovery of any debt due to or property belonging to the partnership, with a view to distributing the bankrupt's share in the firm.[38] To that end, the court can authorise the Assignee or trustee to commence any action in their names and in the name of the other partner or partners.[39] Before any such authority will be given, those other(s) must be notified and may show cause against it; and the court may then give directions about the appropriate division of the proceeds of any such action. Any release given by the bankrupt of the debt or demand which is the subject of such action is declared void.

10–16　One of the fundamental rules in administering the estates of several partners or of the firm is that the joint, or the firm's, assets must be distinguished from the individual partners' own assets, and that the joint, or the firm's, debts be distinguished from the separate debts. This is now formulated as "[i]n the case of partners the joint property shall be applicable in the first instance in payment of their joint debts, and the separate property of each partner shall be applicable in the first instance in payment of his separate debts".[40] Additionally, "[w]here there is a surplus of the joint property, it shall be dealt with as part of the respective separate properties in proportion to the right and interest of each partner in the joint property".[41] In other words, where there is a surplus in the joint property, it is divided among the individual partners' separate creditors in the same proportion as those partners shared in the joint assets. Where a surplus arises on the separate property or properties, it will be "dealt with as part of the joint property so far as necessary to meet any deficiency in the joint property".[42]

---

[33]　*Re Wadell's Contract* [1876] 2 Ch. D. 172.
[34]　Ex parte *Hunter* (1816) 2 Rose 382.
[35]　1988 Act, s.37.
[36]　1988 Act, s.32.
[37]　1988 Act, s.33.
[38]　1988 Act, s.30.
[39]　Cf *Provincial Bank v Tallon* [1938] I.R. at 365–366.
[40]　1988 Act, s.34(1).
[41]　1988 Act, s.34(2).
[42]　1988 Act, s.34(3).

10–17 It is vital to ascertain, as between the partners, whether the property in question belonged to them jointly or belonged to one or to some of them to the exclusion of the others. Partners, by agreement among themselves, can convert what was partnership property into the separate property of a single partner and vice versa. The very making of such an agreement will alter the nature of the property and is binding on the Assignee provided it was made bona fide and before any act of bankruptcy was committed.[43] Accordingly, where a partnership was dissolved and the partners agreed bona fide that their joint property will henceforth belong to the partner who will continue running the business, and subsequently the firm or the continuing partner becomes bankrupt, that which formerly was partnership property cannot be distributed as the joint estate of the firm; it must be treated as the continuing partner's separate estate. But in order effectively to convert partnership property in this manner, the agreement must not be still executory.[44] Also, such agreement will not be effective if the former joint owners retained some lien over the property.

Proving Debts

10–18 There is a complex corpus of case law regarding proving against the joint estate in the firm, against the partners' separate estates and against both the joint and the separate estates. But where all the creditors are agreeable to doing so or where in the circumstances it is not possible to administer the estates separately, they may be consolidated.[45] Where through error a creditor proves his debt against the wrong estate, he will be allowed to transfer his proof to the other estate.[46] Where by mistake debts or expenses are paid by one estate, which should have been borne by the other, the amount so paid will be ordered to be refunded.[47]

10–19 Generally, the firm's indebtedness is not the separate debt of its individual members, who have not made themselves severably liable for it.[48] But they are so liable for frauds and breaches of trust that are imputable to the firm.[49] Where there are only two partners in the firm, one of whom is dormant or is nominal, the firm's creditors have the option of treating their debt as that of the ostensible or of the substantial partner, respectively. There are several circumstances where joint debts are converted into several debts and vice versa.

Proof against the Firm

10–20 Creditors of the firm have first claim against the joint estate and, until they are fully paid with interest, the individual partners' own creditors have no

---

[43] Ex parte *Ruffin* (1801) 6 Ves. 119 and *Stuart v Ferguson* (1832) Hayes (Ir. Ex.) 452.
[44] Ex parte *Wheeler* (1817) Buck.25.
[45] Ex parte *Sheppard*, Mon. & Bl. 415 (1883).
[46] Ex parte *Vining*, 1 Deac. 555.
[47] *Re Hind & Sons* (1889) L.R. Ir. 23 Ch. 217.
[48] Partnership Act 1890, s.9.
[49] Partnership Act 1890, ss.10–13.

claim of any kind against that property.[50] But those who have lent money to the firm, for a share of the profits, are treated as deferred creditors.[51]

10–21 Generally, a partner-creditor of the firm is not permitted to prove in competition with its outside creditors because he is their debtor, and he cannot divest the joint estate to his own benefit.[52] Nor, for that reason, may the executor of the estate of a deceased partner prove against the joint estate of the surviving partners.[53] An exception to this is where one partner's own property was fraudulently dealt with as the firm's property.[54] Another is where there are two distinct trades being carried on, with separate capitals, one by the firm and one by the partner.[55] It is only when all the debts of the firm have been paid in full that the creditors of any individual partner can have redress against the firm's assets. At that juncture, the surplus in the firm is applied to satisfy the liens of the individual partners in proportion to their respective shares in its assets.[56]

Proof Against Individual Partners

10–22 Each partner's own creditors have first claim to his assets.[57] But unlike the firm's creditors, those creditors are not also creditors of the other partners. Where a partner's separate creditors have been paid in full, any surplus in his estate is carried to the credit of the firm.[58]

10–23 Generally, creditors of the firm are not allowed to compete with a partner's own creditor for payment out of his separate estate. But where there are no such assets, those creditors rank as separate creditors of each individual partner.[59] Thus, if just one partner is bankrupt and the firm has no assets, its creditors rank as his creditors too and there is no other partner who is solvent. An exception is where the partner's own property was fraudulently converted to the firm's use by his co-partners and, conversely, where a partner fraudulently converted firm property to his own use.[60] Another is where there are two distinct trades being carried on; the firm is treated as a separate creditor for those debts.[61] Creditors of the firm can prove, such as for the purposes of voting, against a partner's separate estate, but are not entitled to receive any dividend out of that separate estate until all the bankrupt's separate creditors are paid off in full.[62]

---

[50] 1988 Act, s.34(1).
[51] Partnership Act, 1890, s.3 and see para.8–52.
[52] Ex parte *Sillitoe*, 1 Gl. & J. 382.
[53] Ex parte *Butterfield*, D Gax 570.
[54] Ex parte *Sillitoe*, 1 Gl. & J. 382.
[55] Ex parte *Cook*, Mont 228.
[56] 1988 Act, s.34(2).
[57] 1988 Act, s.34(1).
[58] 1988 Act, s.34(3).
[59] *Re Budgett* [1894] 2 Ch. 557.
[60] Ex parte *Lodge and Fendal*, 1 Ves. Jun. 166 (1790).
[61] Ex parte *Cook*, Mont 228.
[62] 1988 Act, s.74.

Proof against the Firm and the Partners

10–24 Where there is joint and several liability, the rule against "double proof" comes into play because, if that creditor could prove against the firm and against the individual partners at once, he would gain an advantage over both the firm's and the individuals' creditors. Accordingly, this creditor is given the option of proving against one or the other.[63] In deciding how to elect, the governing consideration would be the comparative solvency of the two estates.

10–25 An exception to this, where there are distinct trades, was put on a statutory footing and given a somewhat wider ambit. This is where the bankrupt "is liable in respect of distinct contracts, as a member of two or more distinct firms, or as a sole contractor, and also as a member of a firm ...".[64] It is provided that "the circumstance that such firms are, in whole or in part, composed of the same individuals, or that the sole contractor is also one of the joint contractors, shall not prevent proof in respect of such contracts against the properties respectively liable upon such contracts".[65] It has been said that "[t]he old rule against double proof still remains; but it is now subject to so large a class of exceptions as to render the rule itself practically of little consequence to partners or their creditors".[66] However, there must be distinct contracts for this exception to operate; if the only liability is that of the firm, the creditor must elect. And there must be two distinct estates; there is no right of double proof against the one estate, even where the firm carried on two entirely distinct businesses in different places.[67]

Preferred Debts

10–26 Where the partners are individuals, the bankruptcy rules regarding preferred debts apply. A novel question arose in *Re Rudd & Son Ltd*,[68] concerning a partnership comprised entirely of registered companies, whether the preference regime in Company Law would apply if those companies were being wound up other than as unregistered companies. It was held that this regime did not apply. Because preference is an entirely statutory creation, express provision was required to make it applicable in any instance, thereby resulting in what may here appear to be anomalous.

Deferred Debts

10–27 Loans to the firm or to a partner which are virtually shares in a partnership are deferred debts which may be repaid only after all other creditors for value have been satisfied.[69] This is where there was an "advance of money by way of loan to a person engaged or about to engage in any business on a

---

[63] Ex parte *Hill*, 2 Deac. 249.
[64] 1988 Act, Sch.1, reg.13.
[65] 1988 Act, Sch.1, reg.13.
[66] *Lindley*, above fn.7, at 812.
[67] *Re Pim* (1881) 7 L.R. Ir. 458.
[68] [1984] 2 W.L.R. 831.
[69] Partnership Act 1988, s.3.

contract with that person that the lender shall receive a rate of interest varying with the profits, or shall receive a share of the profits arising from carrying on the business.".[70] The same applies to "any buyer of a goodwill in consideration of a share of the profits of the business". A lender or a buyer in these circumstances, where the borrower or seller becomes bankrupt, is not entitled to recover from the estate until every creditor for valuable consideration has been satisfied. That lender or buyer are far more incapacitated because it has been held that they are not entitled to prove in the bankruptcy for any purpose at all, not even in order to vote at creditors' meetings, until all the other creditors are paid in full.[71] An agreement for a loan as just described is not taken outside of this rule if it is continued by one of the partners, even following dissolution of the partnership. The lender will be a deferred creditor of the continuing partner in respect of all advances made where the interest or repayments were linked to the profits of the business.[72]

Winding Up

10–28   The court is empowered to order that any partnership in which a bankrupt has an interest be wound up and to make ancillary directions.[73] Upon notifying such persons as the court deems proper, it may make such directions for winding up and settling the affairs of any partnership as it deems proper. No criteria are stipulated for exercising this jurisdiction.

Solicitors' Firms

10–29   The position of solicitors who become bankrupt is affected by the Solicitors Acts, 1954–2008. On being adjudicated, the solicitor's practising certificate is suspended and constitutes a basis for the Law Society enquiring into his practice. Where a sole practitioner is adjudicated, then the court may appoint another solicitor to carry on his practice for the time being[74]; any application to this effect must be notified to the Law Society. Because funds in the client account are held on trust, they do not vest in the Official Assignee. Until such time when all persons with an interest in those funds have their claims fully satisfied, "neither the State nor any person" may have any recourse against them in connection with any claim they have against the solicitor.[75] It was held in *Re Hughes*[76] that even where the solicitor pays his own money into the client account, it must be treated on the same basis as all other funds held in that account, on the grounds that the proper inference is that this money is intended as a replacement for money wrongfully withdrawn from that account.

10–30   Where there is a shortfall in the client account, how the funds in it are

---

[70]   Partnership Act 1988, s.2(3)(d).
[71]   *Re Grason* (1879) 12 Ch. D. 366.
[72]   *Re Mason* [1899] 1 Q.B. 810.
[73]   1988 Act, s.138.
[74]   Solicitors Act, 1954, ss.50 and 49(1)(h).
[75]   Solicitors Act, 1954, s.61.
[76]   [1970] I.R. 237.

to be distributed is not governed by the rule in *Clayton's* case.[77] Instead, they are divided "proportionally amongst the clients ... according to the respective sums received ... in the course of [the] practice on behalf of [those] clients and remaining due ... to them".[78] To this pro rata approach, there are two exceptions. One is where the solicitor is in substance his client's bailor: money held in an account for a particular client. The other is where the solicitor or members of his firm are the sole trustees of a trust, and funds belonging to it are kept in an account on behalf of that trust. Where a client suffers loss due to his solicitor's dishonesty the Law Society maintains a compensation fund to which claims for compensation may be made.[79]

DECEASEDS' ESTATES

10–31   Where a person who has been adjudicated bankrupt dies, the court may proceed with the bankruptcy as if he were still alive.[80] Thus, the death does not affect how the insolvent estate would be administered. Alternatively, a person may very well die not a bankrupt but may have been insolvent, and either one or more of his creditors, or his personal representative, may wish to have the estate administered in bankruptcy in accordance with the 1988 Act. If it is not administered in this manner, certain rules will not apply to it, such as regarding statutory set-offs, disclaiming onerous property and priority debts, as well as the machinery for investigating the deceased's affairs. The position regarding the estates of persons who died insolvent is dealt with in Pt VI (ss.115–122) of the 1988 Act.[81]

Bankruptcy Petition

10–32   A petition to have the estate administered in bankruptcy may be presented by the deceased's personal representative,[82] in much the same way as the declaration of insolvency procedure which obtains if the debtor had not died. When presenting the petition, the representative must produce to the Examiner the grant of probate or the letters of administration, as the case may be, and a Revenue affidavit relating to the estate.[83]

10–33   A petition for administration in bankruptcy may also be presented by any creditor of the deceased,[84] provided that his debt would have supported a bankruptcy petition if the debtor were still alive. In such cases, notice of the

---

[77] *Devaynes v Noble* (1816) 1 Mer. 572.
[78] Solicitors (Amendment) Act 1960, s.32(1).
[79] See generally, P. O'Callaghan, *The Law on Solicitors in Ireland* (Dublin: Butterworths, 2000), Ch.13.
[80] 1988 Act, s.42, e.g. *Robertson, Ledlie, Ferguson & Co v Mulvenna,* 76 I.L.T.R. 1 (1942).
[81] See generally A. Keating, *Keating on Probate* 3rd edn (Dublin: Thomson Round Hall, 2007).
[82] 1988 Act, s.115(1)(b) and rr.127–128, and Form No. 33.
[83] Rule 130.
[84] 1988, s.115(1)(a) and rr.127–129, and Form No. 33.

petition must be served on the deceased's personal representative; if there is no known representative, the court may direct service of the petition on such person as it deems fit or may dispense entirely with service.[85] The petition must be verified by an affidavit setting out the grounds on which it is claimed that the estate is insolvent. At the same time, a sum of €650 (ex £500) must be lodged with the Official Assignee, and the court may direct that further sums shall be lodged to cover his costs, fees and expenses.[86] The petitioning creditor must also file an affidavit proving his debt.[87]

10–34 Once notice of the petition is served on the personal representative, he must not make any further payments or transfers of property from the estate; any such disposition does not operate to discharge him vis-à-vis the Assignee.[88] But this does not invalidate any payment made or any act or thing done in good faith by the personal representative before the bankruptcy commenced.[89]

10–35 Where proceedings have already been commenced in the Circuit Court for the administration of the deceased's estate, a petition for administration under these provisions cannot be presented.[90] However, an application may be made to that court to transfer the matter to the Bankruptcy Court and, if it is satisfied that there is not sufficient in the estate to pay the deceased's debts, it may order such transfer. It is a matter for the Circuit judge's discretion whether to transfer the case, the primary criteria being considerations of convenience, delay and expense.[91] Thus, if the proceedings are at a very early stage, the judge would be inclined to order a transfer; on the other hand, if most of the estate has already been administered, such an order is less likely. Where an application to transfer has been acceded to, the applicant is required forthwith to notify the Assignee and to apply to the Bankruptcy Court for an administration order.[92]

10–36 If, on hearing the petition, it seems to that court that "there is a reasonable probability that the estate will be sufficient for the payment of the deceased's debts", it will not make that order.[93] But it may so order if the estate appears to be insolvent. If cause is shown why such an order should not be made, the court may dismiss the petition with or without costs. An administration order can be made even though the deceased does not have a personal representative.

Effects of Adjudication

10–37 The effects of making an administration order are similar to those following adjudication. The deceased's estate vests in the Assignee, to be

---

[85] Rule 131.
[86] Rule 127(3), sum substituted by S.I. No. 595 of 2001.
[87] Form No.12.
[88] 1988 Act, s.116(1).
[89] 1988 Act, s.116(2).
[90] 1988 Act, s.115(4).
[91] *Re York* (1887) 36 Ch. D. 233.
[92] Rule 135.
[93] 1988 Act, s.117(1).

realised and for distribution.[94] The provisions regarding a certificate of vesting apply here too. The 1988 Act's provisions, "so far as they are applicable and with appropriate modifications", apply to administration under Pt VI in the same way as in ordinary bankruptcy proceedings.[95] An exception to this is made with regard to s.50 (execution against the debtor's property before adjudication) and ss.57–59 (regarding fraudulent conveyances, voidable voluntary settlements and the avoidance of improvident dispositions).[96] The provisions regarding disclaimer of onerous property and contracts apply.[97]

Administering the Estate

10–38   Once an administration order is made, the deceased's personal representative, or such other person as the court may direct, must file the following documents in the Examiner's office and must lodge duplicates with the Assignee, duly stamped with the date of filing.[98] One is a statement of affairs regarding the deceased's estate, in the prescribed form. The other is an account of the representative's dealings with the estate, in such form and verified in such manner as the Assignee may require, who may require the representative to supply other particulars of the deceased's affairs from time to time.

Distribution

10–39   Where the estate is insolvent but it is not being administered in bankruptcy, the rules regarding payment of the deceased's debts are set down in the first schedule to the Succession Act 1965. Subject to the payment of funeral, testamentary and administration expenses, which are given priority, it is provided that "the same rules shall prevail and be observed as to the respective rights of secured and unsecured creditors and as to debts and liabilities provable and as to the valuation of annuities and future and contingent liabilities, respectively, and as to the priorities of debts and liabilities as maybe in force for the time being under the law of bankruptcy with respect to the assets of persons adjudged bankrupt".[99] On the matters enumerated here, therefore, the deceased's personal representative is guided by the bankruptcy rules and not the rules of Chancery pertaining to them.[100]

10–40   There are no special requirements regarding proving debts against the estate. With regard to the order of payment, "proper funeral and testamentary expenses incurred" must be paid in full, in priority to all other debts, notwithstanding any statutory provisions to the contrary.[101] Thus, these expenses get priority over the Assignee's expenses and "pre-preferential" debts.

---

[94]   1988 Act, s.118(1).
[95]   1988 Act, s.120 and r.132.
[96]   Cf. *Re Gould* (1887) 19 Q.B.D. 92.
[97]   Ex parte *Day* [1906] 2 Q.B. 68.
[98]   Rule 134.
[99]   Succession Act, 1965, Sch.1, Pt I, r.2.
[100]   Cf. *Moore v Smith* [1895] 1 I.R. 512.
[101]   1988 Act, s.119.

The position of the various preferential debts, such as unpaid rates, assessed taxes, wages, salaries and the like,[102] apply to the estate. The date on which this applies is not when the administration order was made but when the debtor died,[103] which has the effect of imposing a strict rule of equality among all the deceased's creditors of equal rank. As was explained, "[t]he general principle, when there is no insolvency, is that the person who gets in first gets the fruits of his diligence",[104] such as by having a garnishee order made absolute. But the result in insolvency is that "at the date of death a curtain comes down. All debts existing at that date are to be paid pari passu. The executors must pay all the creditors equally and rateably".[105] Voluntary debts and liabilities, such as under a settlement, rank equally with liabilities for value[106] and ss.57–59 of the 1988 Act, avoiding certain preferences, transactions and settlements, do not apply to an estate being administered in bankruptcy.[107]

10–41 The right of retainer enjoyed by a personal representative[108] cannot be exercised when the estate is being administered in this manner.[109] But he may prove any debt due to him which would otherwise be provable.

10–42 Where, after due provision for all costs, expenses, debts and liabilities, a surplus remains, the court will order that it shall be vested in or transferred to the personal representative.[110] If there is no such representative, the court has a discretion as to how the surplus should be disposed of. A court order for these purposes shall be deemed to be a conveyance, assignment or transfer of property, as appropriate, and the order may be registered accordingly.

TRUSTS

10–43 The conventional trust is principally a device for organising the transmission of wealth from one generation to another, originally to by-pass various feudal restrictions on transferring interests in land but more recently inter alia to reduce capital tax liability.[111] Because trustees tend not to get involved in risk-taking ventures, it is virtually impossible for these trusts to become insolvent. Trusts are also are also common in the financial services sector, as a device through which investments are organised; for instance, pension trusts, unit trusts, and trust-like entities such as common contractual funds and undertakings for collective investment in transferable security, as well as trustee savings banks. Enterprises in the non-profit sector are often organised in the form for

---

[102] See paras 8–44 et seq.
[103] 1988 Act, s.81(9).
[104] *Re Pritchard* [1969] 1 All E.R. 999, at 1000, 1001.
[105] *Re Pritchard* [1969] 1 All E.R. 999, at 1000, 1001.
[106] *Re Whitaker* [1901] 1 Ch. 9.
[107] 1988 Act, s.120.
[108] Succession Act 1965, s.46(2).
[109] 1988 Act, s.122.
[110] 1988 Act, s.121.
[111] See generally, A.Keogan et al., *The Law and Taxation of Trusts* (Dublin: Tottel, 2007), Chs 4 and 5.

trusts; for instance charitable hospitals and other charitable enterprises, and also political parties, the G.A.A. and the I.R.F.U. At times businesses designed to make a profit for their de facto owners are constituted as trusts; in the United States these are sometimes referred to as "Massachusetts trusts".

10–44   A commercial, trading or "enterprise", trust resembles the private family trust, where the participants' assets are vested in a trustee, who manages the undertaking on their behalf and in their interests. Those beneficiaries may be donees, the objects of a settlor's bounty. But they may instead be investor-beneficiaries, who purchased their stake in the trust assets. Often the trustee is a registered company, in which those assets are vested. Unlike in the normal trust, it would appear that the beneficiaries of such trusts have no beneficial interest in those assets that would defeat the claims of the trust company's creditors, and also that they enjoy limited liability if the company was incorporated as limited.

10–45   Where the trust is insolvent,[112] in that there are insufficient assets in the estate to satisfy its creditors, the Companies Acts' insolvency regime applies in the case of a corporate trustee. Where the trustees are individuals, the unsecured contract creditors have recourse against them unless their liability has been excluded or restricted by agreement. They also would appear to be liable to extra-contractual creditors of the trust. Beneficiaries who become significantly implicated in managing the trust enterprise are personally liable, without limit, as their trustees' principals. However, there appears to be no modern case law on what constitutes the requisite control of trustees for this purpose. The regime for secured creditors and for statutory priorities apply as in personal bankruptcies. A specific statutory regime on priorities is provided for occupational pension trusts, in s.48 of the Pensions Act 1990, and amended in 2002.

FAMILIES

10–46   Bankruptcy can cause considerable hardship and distress for members of the debtor's family, especially where their home is put at risk of being sold from under them and also where ancillary orders in family law proceedings are being placed in jeopardy. Specific provision is made in the 1988 Act for the family home and also for marriage settlements. In Britain, there has been considerable litigation concerning the fate of the home in this context but the matter does not appear to have been considered by the Irish courts.

Arrangements

10–47   Where the decisive vote on a proposed scheme of arrangement is that of the debtor's spouse, in his or her capacity as creditor, that is no reason for the court refusing to approve the scheme, in the absence of cogent evidence of

---

[112]   See generally, J. Mowbray et al., *Lewin on Trusts*, 18th edn (London: Thomson Sweet & Maxwell, 2007), Ch.22.

impropriety.[113] But because a matrimonial debt cannot be proved in bankruptcy and survives the bankrupt's discharge, it enjoys a special status in any scheme of arrangement to which the other spouse is a party.[114]

Bankruptcy Petition

10–48   Although a bankruptcy petition can be presented by a creditor with a non-provable debt, the practice has been to grant adjudication against a spouse only in special circumstances where the debt was in the nature of an order made in matrimonial proceedings.[115] A petition by a spouse for his or her own bankruptcy is not a disposition of property contrary to asset-freezing requirements in family law legislation.[116] A person will not be adjudicated on his or her own petition where it is shown that the objective is to defeat a spouse's legitimate claims. Any adjudication made in such circumstances will be annulled. Thus where the debtor husband was not in fact insolvent but had been made bankrupt under a plan between his companies and the petitioner, to defeat his wife's claims, the adjudication was declared null and void.[117]

Effects of Adjudication

10–49   Where, as often is the case, family property[118] is held by a husband and wife as joint tenants, the effect of adjudication is to sever their co-ownership and they became tenants in common of their respective shares, with the bankrupt's share vesting in the Official Assignee.[119] In measuring the extent of those shares, account was taken of the contributions made by each towards acquiring and enhancing the property.[120] In *Stack v Dowden*,[121] which was not a bankruptcy case, involving a jointly owned family home, the House of Lords held that the starting position here is a strong presumption of equal beneficial ownership. A party seeking to establish otherwise has the onus of proving a common intention to that end and, in determining this question, the couples' whole course of conduct regarding the property is relevant, not just financial contributions.

Where property has been transferred by the bankrupt gratuitously to a spouse or other family member, the question of the presumption of advancement arises, i.e. of whether in the circumstances that property beneficially belongs to the transferee or whether he or she holds it in trust for the transferor.[122] In the latter event, the transferor's equitable estate will vest in the Official Assignee or in his trustee, as the case may be.[123] If the transfer occurred within five years of

---

[113] *Re J.H. an Arranging Debtor* [1962] I.R. 232.
[114] *Re A Debtor* [1999] 1 F.L.R. 926.
[115] *Wheatley v Wheatley* [1999] 2 F.L.R. 205.
[116] *Woodley v Woodley (No. 2)* [1994] 1 W.L.R. 1167.
[117] *Couvaras v Wolf* [2002] 2 F.L.R. 107.
[118] See generally, A. Lyall, *Land in Ireland*, 2nd edn (Dublin: Round Hall, 2000), Ch.17.
[119] E.g. *Re Prichard* [2007] B.P.I.R. 1385, concerning illness benefit under a joint policy.
[120] E.g. *Re Pavlov* [1993] 1 W.L.R. 1046.
[121] [2007] 2 A.C. 432.
[122] See generally, A. Lyall, above, at 451 et seq and H. Delany, *Equity and the Law of Trusts*, 4th edn (Dublin: Thomson Round Hall, 2007) at 181 et seq.
[123] 1988 Act, s.44.

the adjudication, it is susceptible to challenge as a voidable settlement.[124] In *Stack*[125] it was observed that the presumption of advancement from a husband to his wife was so out of line with current social conditions as to be a very weak presumption, if indeed still in existence.

10–50   Where an insurance policy on the debtor's life is for the benefit of his or her spouse or children, the proceeds of the policy do not vest in the Assignee or trustee.[126] The benefit of such a policy can be contingent. But an insurance policy will be deemed to be for a person's benefit only if the effect of its terms is to confer a benefit on that person. Thus in *Re O'Dowd*,[127] where the bankrupt's child was named beneficiary under a "child's option policy", Lowry J. held that, in the circumstances, the child was not a beneficiary. This was because, under the terms of the policy, the child took no benefit until the insured actually exercised an option in his favour. Nor in *Rooney v Cardona*[128] would the bankrupt husband appear to have been a beneficiary, as the policy was taken out by the spouses in their joint names but with no indication whatsoever of a trust for either of them. But this case proceeded on the agreed basis that there was a trust and, consequently, on the wife's death, it vested in the husband's bankruptcy trustee.[129]

10–51   Almost invariably, the Assignee or trustee will seek to have the property sold, in order to realise the bankrupt's interest in it, and thereby contribute to satisfying the creditors. If the property constituted security for a creditor, he may seek to sell it, or to reach an understanding with the Assignee or trustee concerning its disposal. The commonest case here involves the family home. Regardless of whether it or an interest in it became vested in the Assignee or trustee, it may not be sold without the prior sanction of the court; any disposition made by them without such approval is void.[130] In determining whether to order its sale, the court must "hav[e] regard to the interests of the creditors and of the spouse and dependants of the bankrupt as well as to all the circumstances of the case".[131] How this discretion is to be applied remains to be determined.[132] In comparable circumstances in England, where there is a statutory presumption in favour of creditors' interests, the most that the courts do to assist family members faced with losing their home is to put a comparatively short stay on orders allowing the bankruptcy trustee to sell the property, unless there are "exceptional circumstances" warranting deferring the sale for longer. A quite stringent test is applied for deciding if the circumstances are exceptional. On account of the protection afforded to the family by the European Convention on Human Rights, it has been suggested that a less demanding approach should

---

[124] 1988 Act, s.59 and see paras 7–49 et seq.

[125] *Stack v Dowden* [2007] A.C. 432; also *D.P.P. v Byrne* [2009] I.E.H.C. 196 (Feeney J.).

[126] Married Womans Status Act 1957, s.7.

[127] [1968] N.I. 52.

[128] [1999] 1 W.L.R. 1389.

[129] In error the insurers had paid the policy proceeds to the husband and, accordingly, was liable to his trustee.

[130] 1988 Act, s.61(4).

[131] 1988 Act, s.61(5).

[132] Cf. *Re Citro* [1991] Ch. 142.

be adopted to this question.[133] A question that arises in the English cases where the non-bankrupt spouse remains in occupation of the house after the other has been adjudicated, and she claims a deduction from her spouse's share for various payments she made towards the home, whether that should be offset by a notional rent charged to her for her period of occupation.[134]

10–52 Where the family home constitutes security for the bankrupt's debts, it cannot be disposed of by the secured creditor unless the requirements of the Family Home Protection Act 1976, have been satisfied. But that creditor is not obliged to obtain prior consent for the sale, although ordinarily he will seek an order for possession and sale of the property.[135]

Asset Swelling Measures

10–53 A vexed question is the impact of bankruptcy on settlements made and on orders obtained in family law proceedings. As stated recently in England:

"There is an obvious tension between the statutory scheme for the protection of a bankrupt's creditors and statutory scheme for the financial protection of the bankrupt's former wife and child. Bankruptcy Acts and Matrimonial Causes Acts may be said to compete for shares in the fund which will always be incapable of satisfying both. Clearly if the act of bankruptcy precedes an order made under the Matrimonial Causes Act the legal and practical outcome is straightforward. Difficulties arise when the order under the Matrimonial Causes Act precedes the bankruptcy."[136]

10–54 Three principal circumstances arise: where a family dispute is settled without a court order, or it is settled with an order made on consent, or following a hearing, the court ordered how family property is to be divided up. Apart entirely from constitutional considerations, care should be taken with precedents on these issues from other jurisdictions, where the legislative provisions are not identical to those in the 1988 Act. Most of the cases in Britain turn on the general provision against "transactions at under-value"[137] and the equivalent provision in Australia is formulated slightly differently still.[138]

10–55 The basis for challenging any such settlement is that it was not made in favour of the bankrupt's spouse "in good faith and for valuable consideration".[139] Whether or not a settlement was reached "in good faith" depends on all the

---

[133] Recent English cases on the point include *Turner v Avis and Avis* [2008] B.P.I.R. 1143, *Foyle v Turner* [2007] B.P.I.R. 43, *Foenander v Allan* [2006] B.P.I.R. 1392, *Nicholls v Lan* [2006] B.P.I.R. 1243, *Back v Finland* [2005] B.P.I.R. 1 and *Hosking v Michaelides* [2004] All E.R. 147, [2006] B.P.I.R. 1192.
[134] E.g. *French v Barcham* [2009] 1 W.L.R. 1124.
[135] E.g. *Zandfarid v Bank of Credit & Commerce Int'l SA* [1996] 1 W.L.R. 1420.
[136] *Hill v Haines* [2008] 2 W.L.R. 1250 at 1265.
[137] E.g. *Re Kumar* [1993] 1 W.L.R. 224.
[138] E.g. *Re Cummins*, 80 A.L.J.L.R. 589 (2006).
[139] 1988 Act, s.58 and see paras 7–54 et seq.

circumstances of the case.[140] With regard to the "valuable consideration" requirement, in *Re Densham*,[141] where the wife had contributed to a small extent towards the purchase of the home, she claimed that the husband had agreed that they would hold the property as joint tenants and, accordingly, that she would have a 50 per cent interest in it. It was held that, assuming there was such an agreement, it was a voidable settlement because she had not given sufficient consideration for the half share she was claiming.[142]

10–56 A difficulty here is attributing value to claims that the transferee compromised in the settlement. This is especially so as settlements of several types of family proceedings, even purporting to be "full and final", are capable of being re-opened. It was held 100 years ago that the financial benefit obtained by the wife in a post-nuptial settlement with her husband, in consideration of her refraining from taking divorce proceedings, was valid against his bankruptcy trustee.[143] In *Re Abbott*[144] the wife petitioned for a divorce and claimed inter alia maintenance and a property adjustment order. Negotiations then took place and their compromise was incorporated in a consent order, the net effect of which was to transfer £9,000 from the debtor to his wife. It was held that, in the circumstances, she was a purchaser for value because settling an action can constitute good consideration, and "the essence of most compromises is that each party does worse than he had hoped, and better than he had feared. No doubt the compromise is effected against a background of some estimate of the probable result of the case; but that is far from being the whole story. Thus the spectre of costs will inevitably play its part".[145]

10–57 In *Hill v Haines*[146] it was held that, notwithstanding the statutory favouring of creditors in England, ordinarily a transfer of property under a property adjustment order made on consent will not be set aside in bankruptcy proceedings, unless there has been mistake, collusion or fraud. It was emphasised that, whatever may have been the position in the past, the jurisdiction to make proper provision for family members in such proceedings confers a valuable right on them. It "has value in that its exercise may, and commonly does, lead to court-orders entitling one spouse to property or money from or at the expense of the other. That money or property is, prima facie, the measure of the value of the right".[147] Looked at from "the economic realities, the order of the court quantifies the economic value of the money or property thereby ordered to be paid or transferred by the respondent spouse to the applicant. In the case of such an order, whether following contested proceedings or by way of compromise, in the absence of the usual vitiating factors … , the one balances the other".[148]

---

[140] E.g. *Re Kumar* [1993] 1 W.L.R. 224.
[141] [1975] 1 W.L.R. 1519.
[142] See too *Re Windle* [1975] 1 W.L.R. 1628.
[143] *Re Pope* [1908] 2 K.B. 169.
[144] [1983] 1 Ch. 45.
[145] [1983] 1 Ch. 45 at 58. Contrast *Re Kumar* [1993] 1 W.L.R. 224.
[146] [2008] 2 W.L.R. 1250.
[147] [2008] 2 W.L.R. 1250 at 1261.
[148] [2008] 2 W.L.R. 1250 at 1263. See too *Re Jones* [2008] B.P.I.R. 1051; compare *Re Baverstock* [2007] B.P.I.R. 1191.

Marriage Settlements

10–58   There are distinct rules for avoiding marriage settlements made by bankrupts within two years of their adjudication. To be a marriage settlement for these purposes, three criteria must be satisfied, viz. it must be made on the occasion of the marriage, it must be conditioned only to take effect on the marriage taking place and it must be made in order to facilitate or encourage the marriage taking place.[149]

10–59   Payments of money or transfers of property, which were made under a marriage settlement, are void unless they fall within one or more of the following exceptions.[150] The first is where the payment or transfer was made more than two years prior to the adjudication; regardless of the settlor's circumstances, that disbursement cannot be set aside. The second is where it is shown that, at the time the disbursement was made, the settlor was solvent in that, without the assets being transferred under the settlement, he could pay all his debts. The third is where, under the settlement, the property being transferred was property expected to vest in the settlor when a named person died, provided that the transfer was made to the beneficiary within three months of the settlor obtaining possession or control of that property or funds.

10–60   A recipient of property or funds under a bankrupt's marriage settlement who does not fall within any of these exceptions is obliged to restore the property or money to the Assignee or trustee. However, the recipient can claim against the estate for a dividend in respect of all sums payable to him under the settlement. As for settlements which have not been or not been fully carried out, the undertaking to pay money or to transfer property is declared void, but the beneficiary may claim a dividend under the settlement.[151] Being a "voluntary" creditor, that dividend can only be paid when all the general creditors have been paid off in full.

Provable Debts

10–61   Any debt that is provable in a bankruptcy is extinguished when the bankrupt obtains his discharge. Formerly, liability under court orders to make periodical payments, such as alimony and maintenance, were not provable debts. The basis for this was that the legislation excluded from proofs debts "incapable of being fairly estimated", and that payment obligations of this nature can always be adjusted by the court.[152] There is no such stipulation in the 1988 Act. In Britain, a regulatory provision that all obligations arising under orders made in family or domestic proceedings are provable has engendered considerable litigation, as well as adverse judicial comment.[153]

---

[149] *Re Densham* [1975] 1 W.L.R. 1519 at 1527.
[150] 1988 Act, s.59(3).
[151] 1988 Act, s.59(2).
[152] *James v James* [1964] P. 303 and *Levy v Legal Services Comm.* [2001] F.L.R. 435.
[153] E.g. *Woodley v Woodley (No. 2)* [1994] 1 W.L.R. 1167.

EMPLOYERS

10–62   It is most exceptional for one or more employees or their trade union to petition to have their employer adjudicated a bankrupt. Where, on whoever's petition, he is so adjudicated, the effect of his change in status on employment contracts with him depends on the express or implied terms of those contracts and the employer's particular circumstances. Bankruptcy may operate as a breach of contract, as a consensual determination of it or frustrating it, or it may have no legal effect on it at all.[154]

10–63   A transfer of all or part of a bankrupt employer's business is not subject to the European Communities (Protection of Employees on Transfer of Undertakings) Regulations 2003.[155] But this is not the case where the main reason for initiating the bankruptcy was to evade the employer's obligations under these Regulations.[156]

10–64   A variety of debts due to employees enjoy preferential status and, along with certain preferred Revenue debts,[157] must be paid in full before any of the ordinary unsecured creditors may receive payment from the Official Assignee or creditors' trustee. For these purposes, the individual must have been employed by the bankrupt under a contract of employment/of service, as opposed to under a contract for services.[158]

P.A.Y.E. and P.R.S.I.

10–65   Preference is given to unpaid income tax which the employer deducted or should have deducted from remuneration paid to employees, during the 12 months immediately preceding the debtor's adjudication.[159] Interest payable on those sums is also preferred. The same preference exists for deductions made by employers in the construction industry from payments made to subcontractors.[160] Preference is given to the employer's pay related social insurance contributions which were payable within the twelve months preceding the debtor's adjudication as a bankrupt.[161] P.R.S.I. contributions deducted from employees' remuneration are "pre-preferential" debts that must be paid to the Social Insurance Fund.[162]

Debts to Employees

10–66   Since 1825,[163] unpaid remuneration owing to the bankrupt's employees,

---

[154] See paras 5–53 et seq.
[155] S.I. No. 131 of 2003.
[156] Regulation 6.
[157] See paras 8–42 et seq.
[158] See generally, M. Forde and A. Byrne, *Employment Law*, 3rd edn (Dublin: Thomson Reuters (Professional) Ireland Ltd., 2009) Ch.2.
[159] Taxes Consolidation Act 1997, s.994.
[160] Taxes Consolidation Act 1997, s.1000.
[161] Social Welfare Consolidations Act 2005, s.19(5).
[162] Social Welfare Consolidations Act 2005, s.19(3).
[163] 6 Geo. 4 c.16.

up to a specified maximum, have had preferential status. Some of the preferences are expressed as being for any "clerk or servant" or for any "labourer or workman", but it is now generally accepted that all workers who would be regarded as employees, as compared with independent contractors, fall within these provisions.

10–67 Wages and Salary: First and foremost are unpaid wages and salary owing for services rendered to the bankrupt.[164] There is no general definition of what is a "wage" or a "salary" for these purposes, but it must mean remuneration for work done; it includes remuneration for periods of absence from work for "good cause" and on holidays.[165] In *Re M.*[166] it was held that amounts deducted from earnings and credited to a holiday stamp scheme in the construction industry were wages, even though the employees were only entitled to have the sums deducted paid into what was described as a suspense account. The services in question must have been rendered during the four months immediately preceding the adjudication. There is a ceiling of €3,100 (ex £2,500) for each employee. Where the arrangement with a "farm labourer" is to pay him a lump sum at the end of the hiring or at the end of the year, the court is empowered to apportion how much of what is owing should be preferred.[167]

10–68 Holiday Pay: All accrued holiday remuneration at the date of the adjudication is preferred.[168] There is no financial ceiling.

10–69 Sick Pay: All outstanding amounts due under an arrangement for sick pay are preferred.[169] There is no financial ceiling.

10–70 Pension Contributions: All outstanding pension contributions, under any scheme or arrangement made for superannuation, are preferred, whether they are employer's contributions or those deducted from the employee's remuneration.[170] There is no financial ceiling. Provision exists for priorities when winding up pension schemes.[171]

10–71 Compensation: Three major statutory schemes exist for compensating employees who have been dismissed from their jobs in specified circumstances, viz. where they were not given the requisite statutory minimum notice, where they were made redundant and where their dismissal was held to be unfair. Compensation which is awarded to a dismissed employee under any of these schemes is a priority debt, as too is compensation paid under a variety of other

---

[164] 1988 Act, s.81(1)(b).
[165] 1988 Act, s.81(5).
[166] [1955] N.I. 182.
[167] 1988 Act, s.81(1)(c).
[168] 1988 Act, s.81(1)(d).
[169] 1988 Act, s.81(1)(e).
[170] 1988 Act, s.81(1)(f).
[171] Pensions Act, 1990, s.48, as amended.

employment protection statutes—inter alia, on minimum wages, on equality, on maternity protection, on parental, adoptive and carer's leave.[172]

10–72   *The Insolvency Fund:* Where the employer is unable to pay such compensation, and also outstanding pension contributions up to a ceiling, these amounts must be paid by the Minister. Because the bankrupt's estate may not have sufficient in it to meet these payments or there may be a protracted delay in realising the estate so that the employees can get paid, they can make their claim for payment to the insolvency fund, which is managed by the Minster.[173] On the Minister making the requisite payments, he is subrogated for the relevant employees.[174] At least with regard to unfair dismissal, entitlement to compensation and the right of subrogation obtains notwithstanding that the employee was being paid "off the books".[175]

CONSUMERS

10–73   Although there has been a considerable extension of legal protection for consumers in recent years, culminating in the Consumer Protection Act 2007, Irish law has no provisions specific to what may be described as consumer bankruptcy.[176] By this is meant individuals becoming insolvent simply because they cannot afford to maintain their standard of living. Either they were irresponsibly living beyond their means, often availing of the extensive sources of comparatively cheap credit that would have been beyond their reach before the 1970's, or through misfortune such as losing their jobs, they fall into debt. In countries with bankruptcy regimes that tend to favour debtors, insolvent consumers frequently avail of bankruptcy to put their debts behind them and thereby have a "clean break" with their financial past. This is particularly so in the United States and led to the enactment there of the Bankruptcy Abuse Prevention and Consumer Protection Act 2005.[177] The nearest that the 1988 Act comes to in this regard is its requirement of prior court approval before the Official Assignee may sell the family home.

---

[172] 1988 Act, s.81(1)(g), and e.g. Maternity Protection Act 1994, s.36(2).

[173] Protection of Employees (Employers' Insolvency) Act 1984, ss. 6 and 10. See generally, M. Forde and A. Byrne, above fn.158, Ch.10.

[174] Protection of Employees (Employers' Insolvency) Act 1984, s.10.

[175] *Re Red Sail Frozen Foods Ltd* [2007] 2 I.R. 361.

[176] See generally, J. Kilbourne, *Comparative Consumer Bankruptcy* (Durham N.C.: Carolina Academic Press, 2007), J. Ziegel, *Comparative Consumer Insolvency Regimes – A Canadian Perspective* (Oxford: Hart Publishing, 2003) and J. Niemi-Kiesilainen et al, eds., *Consumer Bankruptcy in Global Perspective* (Oxford: Hart Publishing, 2003).

[177] Its main objective is to deter persons from using the bankruptcy regime as a strategic measure to remove indebtedness that could be repaid.

CHAPTER 11

INTERNATIONAL AND EC ASPECTS

11–01   Bankruptcy is entirely a creature of statute. It is a general principle of law, or of statutory interpretation, that legislation is territorial, meaning that ordinarily Acts impose duties and confer rights with regard to persons within and circumstances within the legislating State. As a general rule, Acts of the Oireachtas do not reach out and purport to regulate matters outside of the State's territory. But this rule is subject to various qualifications and exceptions[1]; most notably, the Act in question may explicitly assert an extraterritorial impact. While the 1988 Act is primarily territorial, some of its provisions reach beyond the national borders. Much the same can be said of bankruptcy laws in other countries. Provision exists whereby the High Court can furnish assistance to foreign bankruptcy tribunals. Within the EC, with the exception of Denmark, bankruptcy that has significant impacts in more than one Member State is governed by Regulation 1346/2000 on insolvency proceedings.[2]

NON-REGULATION BANKRUPTCY

11–02   Where this Regulation does not apply, the bankruptcy is governed entirely by the 1988 Act in conjunction with the general principles of private international law.[3] Jurisdiction in bankruptcy proceedings is not subject to EC Regulation 44/2001 on Jurisdiction and Judgments ("Brussels I")[4] nor to the Lugano Convention.[5] But these can apply to some types of claim being asserted by the Official Assignee or the creditors' trustee.

Petition and Adjudication

11–03   For one to be adjudicated a bankrupt by the High Court, it is not always necessary that the act of bankruptcy in question occurred within the State, or that the debtor is present in or is residing in the State. Some acts of bankruptcy can occur only in the State: notably, filing a declaration of insolvency, non-payment on foot of a bankruptcy summons and the levying or unsuccessful levying of

---

[1]   *Masri v Consolidated Contractors International UK Ltd (No.2)* [2009] 2 W.L.R. 621.
[2]   [2000] OJ L160/1 and see paras 11–40 et seq.
[3]   See generally, W. Binchy, *Irish Conflicts of Law* (1988) Ch.25; this has provided invaluable assistance but its treatment of bankruptcy deals with the position prior to the enactment of the 1988 Act. Also, I. Fletcher, *Insolvency in Private International Law*, 2nd edn (Oxford: O.U.P., 2005), L. Collins ed., *Dicey & Morris on the Conflict of Laws*, 14th edn (London: Sweet & Maxwell, 2006) Vol.2 at 1492 et seq..
[4]   [2001] OJ L12/1.
[5]   [1998] OJ L319/9.

execution. But the following acts of bankruptcy can occur in the State "or elsewhere"[6]: assignment of assets for the benefit of one's creditors generally, fraudulent conveyance, fraudulent preference and avoiding creditors such as by leaving the State or remaining out of the State.[7]

11–04   Whether the act of bankruptcy in question took place in the State or abroad, the High Court will not adjudicate a person bankrupt unless he has certain minimum contacts with the State. Before a petition for bankruptcy can be presented, the debtor must "be domiciled in the State or, within a year before the date of the presentation of the petition, has ordinarily resided or had a dwelling house or place of business in the State or has carried on business in the State personally or by means of an agent or manager, or is or within the same period has been a member of a partnership which has carried on business in the State by means of a partner, agent or manager".[8]

Domicile

11–05   The court has jurisdiction to hear the petition where the debtor is "domiciled" in the State. The term domicile is a technical one and is very significant in many circumstances concerning the extraterritorial scope of laws, such as taxation and foreign divorces. Domicile connotes a long term relationship between the individual and the State in question; a person is domiciled in a place if he intends to live there permanently and indefinitely.[9] There is a heavy burden to show that one has changed domicile from one's original domicile to another country.

Residence

11–06   A person also comes within the court's bankruptcy jurisdiction if, during the 12 months preceding presentation of the petition, he had a "dwelling house" in or "ordinarily resided" in the State. A dwelling is a house where the debtor lives, although he may have several such houses. The debtor's interest in the house may be legal, equitable or even as licensee. Whether he can be regarded as living in the house during the relevant year depends on all the circumstances of the case.[10]

11–07   A person may be "ordinarily resident" in the State without having a dwelling house there. Like domicile, the concept of ordinary residence arises in several branches of extraterritorial law, such as taxation.[11] Whether a person ordinarily resides in the State is primarily a question of fact to be determined in the light of all the circumstances of the case. One can ordinarily reside in

---

[6]   1988 Act, s.7(1).
[7]   Cf. *Re Radcliffe* [1916] 2 I.R. 534.
[8]   1988 Act, s.11(1)(d).
[9]   *Barlow Clowes Int'l Ltd v Henwood* [2008] B.P.I.R. 779.
[10] Cf. *Re Brauch* [1978] Ch. 318, at 334–335.
[11] See generally, K. Corrigan, *Revenue Law,* Vol.1 (Dublin: Roundhall, 2000), at 269 et seq.

more than one country in any particular year. The residence must be of some appreciable duration, but a long sojourn in the State is not essential.[12] Nor is it necessary that the residence be for a commercial purpose or that the petitioner can prove where exactly the debtor stayed while present in the State. In *Re Brauch*,[13] where the debtor's home was in the Channel Islands but he spent a considerable amount of time in England on business, it was held that he was ordinarily resident in England during the year in question for the purpose of the bankruptcy laws.

Business

11–08   A person also comes within the court's bankruptcy jurisdiction if, during the 12 months preceding the presentation of the petition, he had a "place of business" in or he "carried on business" in the State. Where the debtor owns property in the State, it is a question of fact whether that is a place of business. It would seem that being a mere licensee of a business premises suffices.

11–09   As for what constitutes carrying on business within the relevant year, the cases show that this has a much wider ambit than would appear. Where the debtor did carry on business, even though he has since ceased trading, he is considered to be still doing business in that place so long as his business debts remain outstanding. In *Theophile v Solicitor General*,[14] this principle was applied to outstanding excess profits tax and has since been applied to unpaid income tax.[15] There the debtor, a Romanian citizen, who had carried on a business in England, ceased trading and "removed himself to the shelter of the Green Isle of Eire when in danger of having to pay large sums of excess profits tax".[16] The main issue was whether he, being a foreign national who was domiciled and resident abroad and never being domiciled in England, by going to Ireland had committed an act of bankruptcy. But if he did not fall within the English bankruptcy jurisdiction this question could not even arise. It was held that "trading does not cease when, as the expression is, 'the shutters are put up', but ... continues until the sums due are collected and all debts are paid" and that there was no "reason for confining trade debts to those incurred in buying or selling".[17]

11–10   In *Re Thulin*,[18] the debtor was Swedish, he lived in Belgium and had extensive international business connections. In 1989 he borrowed a large sum from an English-registered company, the loan agreement was governed by English law and it contained a non-exclusive submission to the English courts. He defaulted in 1991. In the following year, an English-based property company, of which he was the majority shareholder, was liquidated. He also was a co-

---

[12] *Re Bright* (1903) 19 T.L.R. 203.
[13] [1978] Ch. 318, at 330–334.
[14] [1950] A.C. 186.
[15] *Re Bird* [1962] 2 All E.R. 406.
[16] *Re Bird* [1962] 2 All E.R. 406 at 411.
[17] [1950] A.C. at 201 and 202.
[18] [1995] 1 W.L.R. 105.

defendant to a claim for a large sum pending before the English courts. In light of all this, the bankruptcy judge refused to accept his sweeping averment that he had no business property in, nor connection with, England.

11–11   Where the business in question is being transacted in the State by a company which the debtor owns and controls, it does not follow that he is carrying on business there. In the light of the *Salomon & Co* case,[19] it would be "wrong to hold that [s.11(1)(d)] applies to a man who is running his company's business even though he be the sole beneficial shareholder and in complete control".[20] But it was held in *Re Brauch*[21] that the owner and controller of a company doing business in England could also be conducting a separate business there of his own. That separate business was promoting companies and acquiring shell companies to speculate in property, and also negotiating entire property development schemes and then have the properties vested in companies on the basis of "one company per project".

11–12   A person will be regarded as having carried on business in the State where business was done for him in the State by an agent or a manager. He will be similarly regarded where he is a member of a partnership which transacts business in the State through a partner, agent or manager.

Service of Process

11–13   Unless the court otherwise directs, the debtor must be served personally with any bankruptcy summons and with the bankruptcy petition; and upon adjudication as a bankrupt, a copy of the court's order must be served on the debtor by the bankruptcy inspector or by one of his assistants.[22] Neither the 1988 Act nor the Bankruptcy Rules contain special provisions for serving debtors or other persons who are abroad. Indeed, it appears that there is no power to serve any process in bankruptcy proceedings on persons abroad other than the debtor.[23]

Vesting of Property

11–14   In providing that "all property belonging to" the debtor shall vest in the Official Assignee,[24] the 1988 Act does not specify whether such vesting applies as much to property abroad as to property in the State. The 1857 Act applied to personal property "wheresoever the same may be" and to land "wheresoever the same may be situate".[25] And it was held in *Re Robinson*[26] that, as regards chattels, these provisions applied as much to property situate abroad as to property in the

---

[19]   [1897] A.C. 22.
[20]   *Re Brauch* [1978] Ch. at 328.
[21]   *Re Brauch* [1978] Ch. at 328.
[22]   Rules 14, 25 and 38.
[23]   Cf. *Re Tucker* [1988] 1 All E.R. 603.
[24]   Section 44(1).
[25]   Sections 267 and 268.
[26]   (1860) 11 Ir. Ch. Rep. 385.

State; that "the property vests in the assignees as their goods by our law and, as far as our law can operate [abroad], it gives the absolute ownership and property in the goods, though in a foreign State, to the assignees".[27]

11–15 Presumably the same reasoning would have applied to land which was situated abroad. However, even though Irish law may vest the property in question in the Official Assignee, it does not follow that the foreign court, within whose jurisdiction that property is located, would recognise such vesting. As Lynch J. observed in that case, "our assignment is general and without limit [but] our law may be incapable of operation in a foreign State, unless our rule of property be there recognised".[28]

Universal Effect of Adjudication

11–16 Because the term property in the 1988 Act is defined as a wide variety of types of property, "whether situate in the State or elsewhere", the statutory vesting applies to property situated abroad, whether it be chattels, choses in action or land or some interest in land. Hence, adjudication as a bankrupt purports to have universal effect. Just as Irish law does not recognise a foreign bankruptcy adjudication as having universal effect, especially as regards land situate in Ireland,[29] it by no means follows that the foreign court would allow an Irish adjudication to have so extensive an effect within its jurisdiction. Accordingly, the Assignee or the creditors' trustee, as the case may be, may have difficulty in making his title to property abroad effective, for instance, against an execution creditor there or against a foreign assignee or trustee in bankruptcy. These difficulties may be alleviated somewhat in countries whose laws require their courts to act in aid of foreign bankruptcy proceedings, such as s.426(4) and (5) of the English Insolvency Act 1986, which requires English courts dealing with insolvency matters to assist the bankruptcy courts in "any relevant country or territory".[30] Ireland has been designated a relevant country under these provisions. Although they require the English courts to provide assistance, those courts retain a discretion as to what form of assistance they can give and they will not act in any way which contravenes their own law.

Foreign Judgments in rem

11–17 Such vesting as occurs, under Irish law, of foreign property applies only to property beneficially owned by the bankrupt at the date of the adjudication, and is subject to whatever charges which are recognised as affecting it by the *lex sits*, i.e. by the law where the property is located. For instance, it has been held that an English trustee in bankruptcy was not entitled to the bankrupt's land in Scotland free from a registered inhibition there.[31]

---

27 (1860) 11 Ir. Ch. Rep. 385 at 390–391.
28 (1860) 11 Ir. Ch. Rep. 385 at 391.
29 See paras 11–26 et seq.
30 See generally, McCormack, "Jurisdictional Competition and Forum Shopping in Insolvency Proceedings", (2009) 68 *Cam.L.J.* 169.
31 *Murphy's Trustee v Aitken* (1983) S.L.T. 78.

11–18 It would seem that a judgment in rem given by a foreign court supersedes the Assignee's title to assets there, even where the judgment was given after the debtor was adjudicated bankrupt. In *Re Robinson*,[32] following the debtor's adjudication by the Irish court, an Irish bank commenced proceedings against him in the New York courts for the recovery of a debt. The bank obtained a pre-judgment attachment order over certain of his chattels situate there. The question to be determined was who was entitled to the proceeds from the sale of those chattels—the bank or the Assignee in bankruptcy. It was contended that the attachment was a judgment in rem or quasi in rem having the like effect. But it was held to be merely an order in personam, which did not bind the Assignee or affect his title to the bankrupt's property. Had the Assignee been a party to the New York proceedings, "a totally different question would have arisen".[33] Lynch J. also placed emphasis on the fact that the bank was Irish and knew about the bankruptcy before it commenced proceedings abroad, which suggests that effect might be given to a pre-judgment attachment obtained by a foreign creditor who was not aware of the adjudication or of pending bankruptcy proceedings. By inference, the case suggests that post-adjudication foreign judgments in rem affect the property which vests in the Assignee.[34]

Refunding Property Obtained Abroad

11–19 Some harshness in this rule is diminished by the principle that a creditor who seeks to prove in a bankruptcy must deliver up to the Assignee any property of the bankrupt that he obtained after the adjudication. In *Re Pim*,[35] where the bankrupt had carried on two businesses as partnerships, one in Cork and the other in Glasgow, his Scots partner obtained an order of sequestration in the Scottish courts in respect of the bankrupt's partnership assets there. Walsh J. held that, before the Scots partner could prove in the bankruptcy, he must deliver up to the Assignee the property which had been sequestrated in his favour; that "if a particular creditor who is able to lay hold of assets of the bankrupt abroad comes here to share with the other creditors, he must bring into the estate here that which the law of the foreign country has given him over the other creditors".[36]

11–20 The governing principle is that "[e]very creditor coming in to prove under, and to take the benefit of, the [Irish] liquidation must do so on the terms of the [Irish] law of bankruptcy; he cannot be permitted to approbate and reprobate, to claim the benefit of that law, and at the same time insist on retaining, as against it, any preferential right inconsistent with the equality of distribution intended by that law, which he may have obtained either by use of legal process in a foreign

---

[32] (1860) 11r. Ch. Rep. 385.

[33] (1860) 11r. Ch. Rep. 385 at 395.

[34] In *Cambridge Gas Transportation Corp. v Official Committee of Unsecured Creditors* [2007] 1 A.C. 508 at 516, it was held that the in rem/in personam distinction does not exist here because "[t]he purpose of bankruptcy proceedings … is not to determine or establish the existence of rights but to provide a mechanism of collective execution against the property of the debtor by creditors whose rights are admitted or established."

[35] (1881) 7 L.R. Ir. 458.

[36] (1881) 7 L.R. Ir. 458 at 467.

country or otherwise".[37] Apart entirely from proving a debt, there is some old authority that, where a creditor obtains property of the bankrupt abroad, he can be enjoined to surrender that property to the Assignee.[38] There are no modern cases on this point, and the precise scope of the court's jurisdiction is the subject of some controversy. For instance, does the rule apply only where the creditor is an Irish national or resident, or when he knew or should have known of the bankruptcy before obtaining possession of the property?

Administration of the Estate

11–21 The administration of the bankrupt's estate is governed by Irish law, which is an application of the general principle that matters of procedure are governed by the *lex fori*. Thus proof of debts is governed by the 1988 Act, as is the distribution of the estate among the various creditors. Of course, where a dispute arises concerning land which is situate abroad or a contract which is subject to a foreign law, the position under the foreign law becomes relevant to the outcome. There is no provision in the Bankruptcy Rules for serving motions seeking personal relief outside the jurisdiction on persons, other than the debtor, who have not acknowledged the High Court's jurisdiction.[39] If, however, the relief being sought in bankruptcy is by way of a writ that comes within Ord.11 of the Rules of the Superior Courts, the court can give leave to serve abroad.[40]

Asset Swelling Measures

11–22 Authority hardly exists on the extraterritorial effects of the various asset-swelling measures. Because the term "property" in the 1988 Act embraces property situated abroad, it would seem that the court can authorise disclaimer of obligations regarding foreign property, although it does not follow that a foreign court would recognise and give effect to any such disclaimer. Questions regarding foreign property can be the subject of an examination. The transnational impact of s.10 of the Fraudulent Conveyances Act 1634,[41] does not appear to have been considered judicially. It would seem that fraudulent preferences, improvident dispositions and certain voluntary settlements of foreign property can be struck down.

Discharge

11–23 A discharge from bankruptcy purports to apply universally. Whether such discharge will be recognised and given effect to by foreign courts depends on their conflict of laws rules. So far as Irish law is concerned, a discharge by the court is effective against the entire world, on the grounds that "[t]he goods of the bankrupt all over the world are vested in the assignees; and it would be

---

[37] *Banko de Portugal v Waddell* (1880) 15 App. Cas. 161.
[38] *Still v Worswick* (1791) 126 Eng. Rep. 379.
[39] Cf. *Re Loggia* [1988] 1 W.L.R. 484.
[40] *Re Loggia* [1988] 1 W.L.R. 484 and *Re Tucker* [1988] 1 W.L.R. 497.
[41] 10 Car. 1, sess.2, c.3.

a manifest injustice to take the property of a bankrupt in a foreign country, and then to allow a foreign creditor to come and sue him here".[42]

11–24   It was held in *Re Nelson*[43] that the same principle does not apply to a discharge given following the carrying into effect of a scheme of arrangement under provisions similar to those in Pt IV of the 1988 Act. Although the terms of that Act regarding discharge in such circumstances are identical to those for bankruptcy discharges, the position was held to be different because an arrangement only binds those who had notice of the scheme, most of the proceedings are carried out with virtually no publicity, and all of the arranging debtor's assets do not invariably vest in a trustee for the arrangement.

Foreign Bankruptcy Proceedings

11–25   Although Irish law purports to give extensive extraterritorial effect to its own bankruptcy rules and procedures, apart from the EC Insolvency Regulations, it does not recognise the actions and determinations of foreign bankruptcy tribunals to any like extent. Even though the foreign bankruptcy law may purport to be just as universal as the 1988 Act, Irish courts will not always give effect to that law. Instead, the matter is governed by conflict of laws rules and by the power of the High Court to "act in aid" of certain foreign bankruptcy tribunals.

Conflict of Laws

11–26   Adjudication as a bankrupt by some foreign tribunal does not, generally, have the same adverse personal effects in the State as adjudication by the High Court. An exception exists with regard to disqualifications under the Companies Acts 1963–2006.[44]

11–27   As for the effect of foreign adjudications and equivalent determinations on property within the State, all moveable property is deemed to have vested in the foreign Assignee or trustee in bankruptcy, at least where the relevant bankruptcy law provides for such vesting. On the other hand, land and interests in land in the State do not so vest, although the court may in an appropriate case permit the foreign Assignee or trustee to dispose of the immovable property for the benefit of the bankrupt's estate.[45]

11–28   The leading and seemingly only Irish authority concerning the conflict of laws and the personal property of a person who was adjudicated a bankrupt abroad is over 240 years old, *Neale v Cottingham*.[46] Following his adjudication in London, the debtor's property vested in the plaintiffs, his assignees. At the time of adjudication, two of the defendants owed him money. Having notice of

---

[42]   *Armani v Cartrique* (1844) 13 M. & W. 443 at 447.
[43]   [1918] 1 K.B. 459.
[44]   Companies Act 1963, ss.113 and 113A.
[45]   E.g. *Re Corballis* [1929] I.R. 266.
[46]   (1770) Wallis by Lyne Ir. Ch. Rep. 54.

the bankruptcy, one of his other creditors obtained a writ of foreign attachment in a Dublin court over the debts owed by the other two defendants to the bankrupt and, on obtaining judgment, those defendants paid over the sums attached. The plaintiffs succeeded in having those attachments and the payments made on foot of them set aside. Lord Lifford L.C. observed that:

> "Personal property receives the appellation 'personal' because connected with the person, and in contradistinction to real. Grattan, immediately previous to his failure, might have parted with all this property, although situate in Ireland; and that one consideration will show how effectually that property was attached to the person of the bankrupt, to the instant of his failure. And the person of the bankrupt being subject to the effect of the bankruptcy laws, of consequence, the property adhering to that person must be equally liable to those laws. Its owner was a virtual party to the bankrupt laws, and had subjected both himself and his property to the effect of them, by his implied consent to them ... . The law of England has only transferred to the assignees the property inherent in the person of the bankrupt; and they, when thus become owners, have all the rights which the bankrupt before had. In commerce people trust upon the security of the merchant's general property. His effects, from the nature of trade, must be dispersed; yet, however separated, all unite in procuring his credit. The allowing the property of the bankrupt here to be kept from his assignees, might admit great frauds. A bankrupt might transmit all his effects here, and then openly brave all his creditors; and this would destroy the mutual credit which commerce requires, by making people cautious whom to trust. In this case, therefore, the right being clearly vested in the plaintiffs, they must have such decree as they desire ...".[47]

11–29 It was held in *Re Reilly*[48] that, by virtue of s.53(1) of the Bankruptcy Act 1914, land situate in Ireland vested in the English trustee of a bankrupt. However, there was disagreement among the judges on that question, the section considered there has since been repealed and, if the issue there arose again, a court could very well find that the effect given to that section would be unconstitutional. Moreover, the 1988 Act could be regarded as an exhaustive code, thereby repealing s.53(1) of the 1914 Act to the extent, if at all, it was carried over into Irish law by the 1937 Constitution.

11–30 A discharge given by a foreign bankruptcy court is not deemed an effective discharge in Ireland of all of the bankrupt's unpaid debts. The conflict of laws rule is that the discharge of any contract or debt depends on the proper law of the contract and, accordingly, a foreign discharge not in accordance with the proper law of the debt is not effective in Ireland.[49]

---

[47] (1770) Wallis by Lyne Ir. Ch. Rep. 54 at 75–76.
[48] [1942] I.R. 416.
[49] *Gibbs & Son v Soc. Ind. des Metaux* (1890) 25 Q.B.D. 399.

Acting in Aid of Foreign Bankruptcy Courts

11–31   Various injustices that might flow from the rigours of the conflict of laws rules can be alleviated by giving the court an extensive, albeit discretionary, power to come to the aid of specified foreign bankruptcy tribunals and their officers. The High Court and its officers "may act in aid of any [specified foreign] court ... and its officers respectively, at the request of such court, in any bankruptcy matter before such court, and the Court and its officers so acting shall have like jurisdiction and authority as in the case of a bankruptcy originating under an order of the Court".[50] This provision's predecessor was s.71 of the 1872 Act, authorising the court to "act in aid and auxiliary to" every British bankruptcy court and its officers.

11–32   For these purposes, aid may be given to the Northern Ireland, English, Welsh, Scottish, Isle of Man and Channel Islands courts and their officers. The Government is empowered to extend the aid provisions to the courts of other jurisdictions, where the Government are satisfied that "reciprocal facilities" will be afforded in the jurisdiction in question.[51] It remains to be seen whether, by reciprocal facilities, is meant broadly equivalent assistance or assistance which is virtually identical to that which would be afforded by an Irish court under subs.(1).

11–33   Assistance can only be given in a "bankruptcy matter", but this expression is not defined. In *Re A Debtor*, Ex p. *Viscount oft & Royal Court of Jersey*,[52] the English court agreed to give assistance to proceedings *en desastre* which had been brought in the Jersey court. It was said that,

> "... if any form of procedure is to be described as 'bankruptcy' it must at least provide for the administration of the debtor's assets, with or without the exception of particular classes of assets, with a view to satisfying his debts, again with or without exceptions, according to established legal rules. Such procedure may have one or more of at least three purposes, first to protect the creditors from one another, so that an over-active or unscrupulous creditor does not get an unfair advantage over his fellows; secondly, the protection of creditors from a dishonest debtor who secretes his property, or absconds, or gives fraudulent preferences; and thirdly, the protection of the debtor from the extreme enforcement of the legal rights of his respective creditors. The objects are not, in practice, separate and independent. In particular, the pursuit of the first tends to attain in some measure the third, for the restraint imposed on creditors to secure justice or equality between them necessarily gives some relief to the insolvent debtor. The word 'bankruptcy' in [this context] must ... be construed in a wide sense, for the section is designed to produce co-operation between courts acting under different systems of law and it would be much restricted

---

[50]   1988 Act, s.142.
[51]   1988 Act, s.142(2).
[52]   [1981] Ch. 384.

if extended only to jurisdictions that reproduced all the main features of English procedure."[53]

Such an approach was adopted in *Re Bilton*,[54] when Ireland and South Africa were in the British Empire. Dodd J. held that insolvency proceedings under the South African Roman-Dutch law were sufficiently equivalent to bankruptcy to be given assistance. But it is essential that the "bankruptcy matter" is before the foreign court seeking aid from the Irish court.

11–34 The court has a discretion both as to the form of assistance it will give the foreign requesting court and even whether any assistance whatsoever shall be given. As Walsh J. observed of its predecessor, "the section is not mandatory. It is an enabling section and creates powers which the court may exercise if it considers fit to do so in the exercise of its discretion".[55] Nor are any guidelines laid down as to how the discretion should be exercised. Among the matters which the court will take into account are principles of procedural fairness, public policy, private international law rules and the existence of any conflicting bankruptcy.

11–35 The court might decline assistance because it is of the view that the foreign bankruptcy tribunal had no jurisdiction to make the debtor a bankrupt. If the debtor was domiciled within or had accepted the foreign court's jurisdiction, assistance would not be refused on these grounds.[56] But a very tenuous relationship with the foreign forum might provoke a refusal.

11–36 Constitutional law considerations aside, courts have always refused to enforce foreign judgments and orders where the proceedings in the foreign tribunal contravened natural justice.[57] An application of this principle is the non-recognition of foreign judgments which were obtained by fraud.[58]

11–37 In *Re Gibbons*,[59] assistance to English bankruptcy proceedings, which were commenced by the revenue authorities there to collect unpaid taxes, was refused because providing assistance in those circumstances would contravene the public policy against enforcing the claims of foreign revenue authorities. Walsh J. followed the principles laid down by the Supreme Court in *Buchanan v McVey*,[60] where claims brought by a Scots liquidator who was appointed in similar circumstances were not enforced. It was held that "[i]t is not a question whether the plaintiff is a foreign State or the representative of a foreign State or its revenue authority. In every case the substance of the claim must be

---

[53] [1981] Ch. 384 at 400.
[54] [1920] 2 I.R. 324.
[55] *Re Gibbons* [1960] r. Jur. 60 at 61; compare *Re Jackson* [1973] N.I. 67.
[56] *Re Blithman* (1886) L.R. 2 Eq. 23 and *Re Lawson's Trusts* [1896] 1 Ch. 175.
[57] Cf. *Jacobson v Frachon* (1927) 138 L.T. 386.
[58] *Aboulov v Oppenheimer* (1882)10 Q.B.D. 295; compare *Kevens v Joyce* [1896] 1 I.R. 442.
[59] [1960] Ir. Jur. 60.
[60] [1954] I.R. 89.

scrutinised and if it then appears that it is really a suit brought for the purpose of collecting debts of a foreign revenue, it must be rejected".[61] The position may very well be different where the foreign revenue authority is one, albeit a significant one, of the creditors. In *Re Ayres*[62] an Australian court permitted a New Zealand assignee in bankruptcy to continue proceedings in Australia, even though approximately 60 per cent of the bankrupt's debts were owed to various New Zealand revenue authorities.

11–38   Another ground for refusing aid is where there are conflicting bankruptcies,[63] especially where the debtor has been adjudicated bankrupt in Ireland as well as by the foreign court. This arose in *Re Corballis*,[64] but Kennedy C.J. was exercising the lunacy jurisdiction there and he transferred the English court's request into the bankruptcy list, where the controversy would be determined in the course of bankruptcy proceedings, without making any declaration regarding rights to the disputed funds and without prejudice to any application that may be made to the Bankruptcy Court for its assistance.

11–39   As for what order the court should make when it decides to assist the foreign court, it depends very much on the circumstances of the case.[65] Generally, the request is for a vesting order. Often the court may appoint the foreign Assignee or trustee as receiver with power to sell those assets and to distribute the proceeds to the creditors.[66] The order made in *Re Bolton*,[67] which has been reproduced in other cases,[68] deserves quotation. There Dodd J. observed:

> "I think that I am required to do more than merely grant the application for a vesting order. The trustee would find that would carry him but a short way to realizing the assets in this country, and therefore I place at his service, as required by the section, the machinery of this Court to be used in aid of, auxiliary to, the Court of South Africa as fully as it could be used in the case of a bankruptcy in this country. At the same time I must have regard to the interests of creditors in this country, if any there be, who, by virtue of my order, might be sent far afield unless some such provision is made. I must have regard also to the interests of the other beneficiaries. The trustee may need the help of this Court in matters of controversy. The interest of the insolvent is apparently in some of the property held on some kind of joint tenancy with others who are represented before me. Landlords may be entitled to call on the trustee for rent or to elect. I cannot anticipate all matters that may arise in the course of realization. But obviously such matters can only be decided in this country. It is for

---

61   [1954] I.R. 89 at 107.
62   (1981) F.L.R. 235.
63   *Re Jackson* [1973] N.I. at 72.
64   [1929] I.R. 266.
65   Cf. *Muldoon v Doyle* (1944) 79 I.L.T.R. 134.
66   E.g. *Re Osborn* [1931–32] B. & C.R. 189 and *Re A Debtor*, Ex p. *Viscount of the Royal Court of Jersey* [1981] Ch. 384.
67   [1920] 2 I.R. 324.
68   E.g. *Re Bullen* [1930] I.R. 82; see also order of Lowry L.C.J. in *Re Jackson* [1973] N.I. at 73–74.

the benefit of everyone to make provision for the final determination of any matter in controversy. If such applications occurred more frequently, it would be necessary to have rules of Court made; but the procedure being novel, all I can do is to frame as carefully as I can regulations for the guidance of the trustee and the Court, such as would be provided by rules of Court, and so discharge the duty cast upon this Court of aiding the Court in South Africa."[69]

The order made was in the following terms:

"1. That a vesting order shall be drawn up and sealed under the seal of the Court in such form as counsel for the said ... trustee, may approve, so as to be capable of being recorded or registered in accordance with the law in Ireland, and that all things be done, so far as this Court can do, to enable the said trustee to make tide to any portion of the lands of the insolvent, and specially that a condition be inserted in the conditions of sale to the effect that a certified copy of the order of the Supreme Court of South Africa (final order on rule nisi, dated 15th August, 1918) and a certified copy of the vesting order of this Court be accepted by the purchaser as conclusive evidence that all things were rightly done in the Supreme Court of South Africa and in this Court, and that copies on the usual terms be furnished by this Court.

2. That the Official Assignee do act in aid of the trustee, as in sect. 71 of the Bankruptcy (Ireland) Amendment Act, 1872, as nearly as may be as if the insolvent had been adjudicated a bankrupt in this Court, and that the Official Assignee do serve such notices and do have such sittings as may be necessary, and that the creditors in Ireland be at liberty to prove their debts in this Court.

3. That any matters in controversy between the trustee and any person resident in Ireland in his winding up of the estate be determined in this Court.

4. That the trustee out of the assets do supply to the Official Assignee of this Court for distribution to the creditors such composition or dividend as may be payable on distribution to the creditors in the Union of South Africa.

5. That the trustee do submit to the jurisdiction of this Court in all such matters, and abide by any order this Court may make, subject to appeal in accordance with the provisions of the rules and orders of the Supreme Court of Judicature in Ireland, and that the law applicable to the decision of such matters be the law of Ireland.

6. Before taking the proceeds of the sale of the insolvent's property out of Ireland the trustee shall lodge, if so ordered, such sum as the Court may on the application of the Official Assignee direct.

7. The trustee shall appoint a solicitor or firm of solicitors in this country on whom any notice of motion, writ, or summons, or other process may be served.

---

[69]   [1920] 2 I.R. at 329.

8. That the trustee be entitled to and paid his costs of this motion, and that Messrs ... be entitled to and paid their cost of attending hereon, out of the estate when taxed and ascertained.

9. That the trustee be at liberty to apply to the Court to alter, or amend, or rescind any of these regulations."

EC INSOLVENCY REGULATION

11–40   Where the debtor has or had a business establishment within the EC (except Denmark), most insolvency proceedings concerning him are governed by the Insolvency Regulation No. 1346/2000.[70] Under this, the courts of and the law applicable in the country where the person has his "centre of main interests" have virtually full control of the insolvency process, notwithstanding that he does business and possesses assets elsewhere in the EC. It is the court there that makes the adjudication and appoints the insolvency trustee and, subject to some exceptions, it is the law of that State that governs how the process is to proceed. Where he has an establishment elsewhere in the EC, "secondary" bankruptcy proceedings may be opened there, and his assets located there are made available initially to the local creditors. Subject principally to this, decisions of the court where the "main" insolvency proceedings were commenced must be given full recognition across the EC. This Regulation has "direct effect" in Irish law, and aspects of it were implemented by the European Communities (Personal Insolvency) Regulations 2002.[71] When interpreting its provisions, particular account is taken of its extensive recitals and also of the explanatory "Virgos-Schmidt report".[72]

Main Proceedings at COMI

11–41   The main insolvency proceedings take place where the debtor has his "centre of main interests" (its "COMI"), and it is the laws of that state that govern most aspects of the process.

COMI

11–42   The body of the Regulation does not contain a definition for how the COMI is to be identified. But according to Recital 13, it "should correspond to the place where the debtor conducts the administration of his interests on a regular basis and is therefore ascertainable by third parties". Accordingly,

---

[70] Regulation 1346/2000, [2000] OJ L150/1, as amended. See generally, M. Smith de Bruin, *Transnational Litigation: Jurisdiction and Procedure*, (Dublin: Thomson Round Hall, 2008) Ch.5, I. Fletcher, *Insolvency in Private International Law*, 2nd edn (Oxford: O.U.P., 2005), G. Moss, *The EC Regulation on Insolvency Proceedings*, 2nd edn (Oxford: O.U.P., 2009), J. Israel, *European Cross Border Insolvency Regulations*, (Mortsel, Netherlands: Intersentia Publishers, 2005), L. Collins, *Dicey et al on the Conflicts of Laws*, 14th edn (London: Sweet & Maxwell, 2006), Vol.2 at 1526 et seq.

[71] S.I. No. 334 of 2002.

[72] EC Council Document 6500/1/96, with English version in appendices to each of the above books.

it resembles where he is deemed to be "resident" for tax and for some other purposes.[73] Ascertaining where the COMI is located is a question of fact and degree.[74] Among the matters that are considered for this purpose are the place from where the business is managed and where significant contracts with it are concluded; the location of any authorities that regulate its activities; where its managers' meetings are held; where its accounts are prepared and audited; where its lenders and customers are located. The country where the indebtedness was incurred is not a relevant consideration,[75] nor is the debtor's indirect economic activities, such as directorships of companies.[76]

11–43 It is the time the application is made to open insolvency proceedings that determines where the debtor's COMI is located, and thereafter cannot be changed. But before any such application is made, a person may move his COMI to another state; it is not immutable. It was held in *Shierson v Vlieland-Bodd*[77] that the debtor there had moved his COMI from England to Spain just prior to insolvency proceedings being commenced in England against him. But it was suggested that this could not be done simply to avail of a more favourable legal regime when likely insolvency proceedings in England were pending. Principally because the debtor was never cross-examined on this question, it was held that such an objective had not been proved there.[78]

"Opening" Proceedings

11–44 It is because there can be legitimate differences of view about where the debtor's COMI is located that the question of when the "main" insolvency proceedings were commenced is so important. For once such proceedings are "opened", courts elsewhere in the EC are obliged to recognise that decision. What constitutes "opening" proceedings arose in the *Re Eurofood IFSC Ltd*[79] case, where a provisional liquidator was appointed by the High Court. At issue there was whether appointing a provisional liquidator fitted that description; the court concluded that it did. That was because it possessed the four essential characteristics: it was a collective proceeding, it was based on the company's insolvency, it entailed a partial divestment of the debtor's control of its assets and it involved the prompt appointment of a liquidator. In the event of the court subsequently making a winding up order, that related back to when the petition was presented and the provisional liquidator was appointed. Accordingly, the "main" proceedings were opened in Dublin some weeks before a court in Italy declared the company to be insolvent and appointed an insolvency practitioner there as its extraordinary administrator. In consequence, the Italian court should not have made those decisions, being obliged by the Regulation to recognise the earlier order of the High Court.

---

[73] See Corrigan, above fn.11.
[74] E.g. *Re Sendo Ltd* [2006] 1 B.C.L.C. 395.
[75] *Stojevil v Official Receiver* [2007] B.P.I.R. 141.
[76] *Staubitz-Schreiber* (C-1/04) [2006] B.P.I.R. 510.
[77] [2005] 1 W.L.R. 3966.
[78] See McCormack, above fn.30 at 191–192.
[79] Case C341/04 [2006] Ch.508.

Applicable Law

11–45   Insolvency proceedings are governed principally by the law of the
state where they were opened. There is a catalogue of the matters which "in
particular" are so governed:

> "(a) against which debtors insolvency proceedings may be brought on
>   account of their capacity;
> (b) the assets which form part of the estate and the treatment of assets
>   acquired by or devolving on the debtor after the opening of the
>   insolvency proceedings;
> (c) the respective powers of the debtor and the liquidator;
> (d) the conditions under which set-offs may be invoked;
> (e) the effect of the insolvency proceedings on proceedings brought by
>   individual creditors with the exception of lawsuits pending;
> (g) the claims which are to be lodged against the debtor's estate and
>   the treatment of claims arising after the opening of insolvency
>   proceedings;
> (h) the rules governing the lodging, verification and admission of
>   claims;
> (i) the rules governing the distribution of proceeds from the realisation
>   of assets, the ranking of claims and the rights of creditors who
>   have obtained partial satisfaction after the opening of insolvency
>   proceedings by virtue of a right *in rem* or through a set-off;
> (j) the conditions for and the effect of closure of insolvency proceedings,
>   in particular by composition;
> (k) creditors' rights after the closure of insolvency proceedings;
> (l) who is to bear the costs and expenses incurred in the insolvency
>   proceedings;
> (m) the rules relating to the voidness, voidability or enforceability of legal
>   acts detrimental to all the creditors."[80]

But proprietary entitlements created under another law, prior to the insolvency,
remain subject to that law; most notably, priorities acquired before then are not
to be ignored.

11–46   Additionally, there are certain rights in rem and related rights that can
be the subject of another law where, when the proceedings opened, those rights
were situated in another Member State. This acknowledges the general principle
that proprietary rights are governed by the law of the State where the item in
question is situated. In summary, these are rights of secured creditors in respect
of their security, if duly registered; rights under reservation of title clauses;
contractual rights to acquire or make use of land or buildings (e.g. conveyances
and leases); rights of set-off. A variety of issues can arise regarding the exact
scope of these exclusions.

11–47   Other exclusions from the law of where the proceedings are opened

---

[80]   Article 4(2).

are employment contracts (these are governed by their ordinarily applicable law) and rights regarding immovable property, ships or aircraft that are subject to registration in a public register (these are governed by the law of the state where the register is kept). Special provision is also made for payment systems and financial markets.

11–48 Transactions that can be set aside at the behest of an Official Assignee are governed by the law of the state where the proceedings are opened, even where they relate to security, reservation of title or set-off and the asset in question is located in another Member State. But this is not the case where the person who benefited from the alleged wrong demonstrates that the transaction was subject to the law of a state where the proceedings were not opened and, under that law, the liquidator would not have a remedy.

11–49 Where, after the proceedings were opened, the bankrupt disposed of certain property for a consideration, the validity of that transaction is governed by the law where the land or building in question is located. In the case of such disposals of ships, aircraft or registrable securities, the applicable law is that of where the relevant register is kept.

11–50 Where the Assignee or trustee takes action in another Member State, he is required to comply with the laws there, in particular, regarding procedures for realising assets that are there.

Recognition of Orders

11–51 Subject to the efficacy of any "secondary" insolvency proceedings as may exist, and also public policy and fundamental rights, decisions by the court where the "main" proceedings were opened must be recognised in all other EC Member States. The extent to which they are recognised outside the EC depends on considerations of comity or, where applicable, specific treaty or statutory provisions. Consequently, for most practical purposes, the bankruptcy is conducted where these proceedings were opened and in accordance with the laws of that jurisdiction. This applies in particular to the decision to open the main proceedings, as the *Eurofood* case illustrates. Once a court decides to open them, the only way that decision may be challenged is to appeal. Except where public policy or fundamental rights are implicated, it cannot be challenged by attempting to open those proceedings in another Member State which, perhaps, has a closer connection with the company and may truly be the COMI.

11–52 Where insolvency proceedings commenced in another Member State prior to the main proceedings being opened, the main Assignee or trustee may require the earlier proceedings be converted into a winding up application, if that is in the interests of the main proceedings' creditors.

11–53 Where a court where the COMI is located appoints an interim receiver to preserve the debtor's assets, he is entitled to request measures to secure and preserve them in any other Member State, up to the time the proceedings are actually opened there.

11–54   Subject to the above caveats, the Assignee or trustee appointed in the main proceedings can exercise all the powers he possesses under the law of that jurisdiction in every other Member State. In particular, he may remove from these any of the bankrupt's assets.

11–55   Except where he is enforcing his security or his rights under a retention of title, where a creditor has taken enforcement measures against assets located in a Member State were the proceedings were not opened, in total or partial satisfaction of his claim, he must return the fruits of execution to the Assignee or trustee.

Secondary Proceedings

11–56   Where the debtor has an "establishment" in another Member State, "secondary" bankruptcy proceedings may be opened there and those determine how any assets located there are to be dealt with. By "establishment" here is meant "any place of operations where the debtor carries on a non-transitory economic activity with human means and goods." This resembles a "branch" under EC Regulation 44/2001 or an "establishment" under Pt XII (ss.351–360) of the Companies Act 1963. Assets are deemed to be situated where they are physically located; where rights regarding them are registrable, where the relevant register is kept; or, in the case of claims under guarantees and the like, where the third party who must meet the claim has its COMI.

11–57   The same rules regarding the applicable law and the rights of secured and comparable creditors apply here as are applicable in the main proceedings. With certain exceptions, these are governed by the law of the State where the secondary proceedings were opened.

11–58   Orders made in these proceedings, within their ambit, must be recognised in all other Member States. The secondary Assignee or trustee may, in those other States, advance claims that, following the secondary proceedings being opened, assets were removed from there. To that end, he may bring proceedings to have transactions set aside.

11–59   Assignees or trustees in main and in secondary insolvency proceedings are required to communicate information to each other and to cooperate. Where that officer in the main proceedings requests a stay of the other proceedings, they must be stayed provided that suitable measures exist to safeguard the interests of creditors in the latter. While these proceedings are stayed, any composition or comparable arrangement in the secondary proceedings may only be proposed by the officer in the main proceedings or, with his consent, by the bankrupt. Apart from any stay, the secondary proceedings cannot be concluded by way of a composition or a comparable arrangement, without the main officer's consent. But that restriction does not apply where the proposed measure would not prejudice the creditors in the main proceedings.

11–60 Where all claims in the secondary proceedings can be met from the local assets, the surplus from them should be transformed to the main Assignee or trustee.

Creditors' Claims

11–61 As soon as insolvency proceedings are opened, the court or the Assignee must immediately inform all known creditors with addresses in other Member States, furnishing them with specified information. Any creditor there may lodge claims, including the tax and social security authorities, providing prescribed information about their claim. Where there are secondary proceedings, any creditor may lodge his claim in both of the proceedings. The Regulation is silent as to how creditors based outside the EC are to be treated.

11–62 To ensure that creditors of equal rank do not obtain unfair advantage over others of that rank, where there are secondary proceedings the insolvency officers in each set of proceedings are to lodge in the other proceedings claims which have already been lodged with them. This assists in all creditors' claims in the insolvency being treated collectively and equitably, although it may engender significant administrative difficulties in achieving that objective. The governing principle is the "hotchpot" rule, under which whatever a creditor has recovered must be accounted for in whichever proceedings he chooses to participate, and he can only share in distributions from it when equivalent creditors have been paid an equivalent dividend.

APPENDIX 1

BANKRUPTCY ACT 1988, AS AMENDED

ARRANGEMENT OF SECTIONS

PART I

PRELIMINARY AND GENERAL

PART II

PROCEDURE IN BANKRUPTCY

PART III

ADMINISTRATION OF PROPERTY

Effect of Adjudication on Bankrupt's Property

PART V

WINDING UP BY TRUSTEE

PART VI

ESTATES OF PERSONS DYING INSOLVENT

PART VII

Offences

PART VIII

Miscellaneous

FIRST SCHEDULE

Proof Of Debts

SECOND SCHEDULE

Repeals

Acts Referred to

Courts (Supplemental Provisions) Act, 1961	1961, No. 39
Criminal Procedure Act, 1967	1967, No. 12
Deeds of Arrangement Act, 1887	1887, c. 57
Enforcement of Court Orders Act, 1940	1940, No. 23
Factors Act, 1889	1889, c. 45
Fines and Recoveries (Ireland) Act, 1834	1834, c. 92
Friendly Societies Act, 1896	1896, c. 25
Irish Bankrupt and Insolvent Act, 1857	1857, c. 60
Judgment Mortgage (Ireland) Act, 1850	1850, c. 29
Moneylenders Act, 1933	1933, No. 36
Partnership Act, 1890	1890, c. 39
Preferential Payments in Bankruptcy (Ireland) Act, 1889	1889, c. 60
Statute of Limitations, 1957	1957, No. 6
Supreme Court of Judicature (Ireland) (No. 2) Act, 1897	1897, c. 66
Trustee Savings Banks Act, 1863	1863, c. 87

Marginal Abbreviations

1857—Irish Bankrupt and Insolvent Act, 1857
1872, c. 57—Debtors Act (Ireland), 1872
1872—Bankruptcy (Ireland) Amendment Act, 1872
1887, c. 57—Deeds of Arrangement Act, 1887
1888, c. 44—Local Bankruptcy (Ireland) Act, 1888
1889—Preferential Payments in Bankruptcy (Ireland) Act, 1889
1890, c. 24—Deeds of Arrangement Amendment Act, 1890
33/1963— Companies Act, 1963
16/1964— Registration of Title Act, 1964
27/1965— Succession Act, 1965
36/1971— Courts Act, 1971
RSC—The Rules of the Superior Courts, 1962
LCR—Local Court Rules, 1888

An Act to consolidate with amendments the law relating to bankruptcy and to provide for related matters.
[13*th July*, 1988]

Be it enacted by the Oireachtas as follows:

PART I

Preliminary And General

Short title

1.—This Act may be cited as the Bankruptcy Act, 1988 .

Commencement

2.—This Act shall come into operation on such day not later than 1 January, 1989 as the Minister by order appoints.

Interpretation

3.—In this Act, unless the context otherwise requires,—

"adjudication" means adjudication in bankruptcy;

"after-acquired property" has the meaning assigned to it by *section 44 (5);*

"arrangement" means an arrangement in pursuance of an order for protection under *Part IV;*

"arranging debtor" means a debtor who has been granted an order for protection under *Part IV;*

"assignees" means the Official Assignee and the creditors' assignee, if any;

"the Bankruptcy Inspector" means the inspector referred to in *section 60 (2);*

"bankruptcy summons" has the meaning assigned to it by *section 8 (1);*

"conveyance", in relation to land, includes assignment and transfer;

"the Court" means the High Court;

"creditors' assignee" means a person chosen and appointed as such under *section 18 (1);*

"'insolvency proceedings' means insolvency proceedings opened in a member state under Article 3 of the Insolvency Regulation where the debtor or each debtor is an individual or deceased;

'Insolvency Regulation' means Council Regulation (EC) No.1346/2000 of 29 May 2000 on insolvency proceedings;

"land" includes any estate or interest in or charge over land;

'liquidator' means a liquidator appointed in insolvency proceedings;

'member state' means a member state of the European Communities other that the State of Denmark'

"the Minister" means the Minister for Justice;

"the Official Assignee means the Official Assignee in Bankruptcy for the time being and his successors as and when appointed;

"prescribed", except in relation to court fees, means prescribed by rules of court;

"property"—

    (a) includes money, goods, things in action, land and every description of property, whether real or personal,

    (b) includes obligations, easements, and every description of estate, interest, and profit, present or future, vested or contingent, arising out of or incident to property,

    (c) in relation to proceedings opened in the State under Article 3(1) of the Insolvency Regulation, includes property situated outside the State, and

    (d) in relation to proceedings so opened under Article 3(2) of the Regulation, does not include property so situated;"

"registered", in relation to land, means registered in the Registry of Deeds or the Land Registry, as may be appropriate;

"secured creditor" means any creditor holding any mortgage, charge or lien on the debtor's estate or any part thereof as security for a debt due to him;

"vesting arrangement" has the meaning assigned to it by *section 93 (2).*

    "(2) Parts II, III, IV (in so far as it relates to vesting arrangements), V, VI and VIII and the First Schedule are subject to Chapters I (general provisions) and III (secondary insolvency proceedings) of the Insolvency Regulation.",

Application of Act to subsisting bankruptcies and arrangements

4.—(1) Save where otherwise provided in this Act, a bankruptcy or arrangement subsisting at the commencement of this Act shall thereafter be administered according to the provisions of this Act and the rules thereunder, without prejudice to the validity of anything duly done or suffered before such commencement.

(2) The provisions of this Act and the rules shall apply accordingly, so far as they are capable of application and subject to such modifications and adaptations as may be appropriate, as if the bankrupt had been adjudicated or the arranging debtor had been granted an order for protection under this Act.

Expenses

5.—The expenses incurred by the Minister in the administration of this Act shall, to such extent as may he sanctioned by the Minister for Finance, be paid out of moneys provided by the Oireachtas.

Repeals

6.—(1) The enactments mentioned in the *Second Schedule* are hereby repealed to the extent mentioned in the *third column* of that Schedule.

(2) Any petition, summons, *subpoena*, order, direction, notice or other instrument presented, served, made or issued under a repealed enactment and in force at the commencement of this Act shall continue in force and be treated thereafter as if it had been presented, served, made or issued under this Act.

PART II

Procedure in Bankruptcy

Acts of bankruptcy

7.—(1) An individual (in this Act called a "debtor") commits an act of bankruptcy in each of the following cases—

    (*a*) if in the State or elsewhere he makes a conveyance or assignment of all or substantially all of his property to a trustee or trustees for the benefit of his creditors generally;

    (*b*) if in the State or elsewhere he makes a fraudulent conveyance, gift, delivery or transfer of his property or any part thereof;

    (*c*) if in the State or elsewhere he makes any conveyance or transfer of his property or any part thereof, or creates any charge thereon, which would under this or any other Act be void as a fraudulent preference if he were adjudicated bankrupt;

    (*d*) if with intent to defeat or delay his creditors he leaves the State or being out of the State remains out of the State or departs from his dwelling-house or otherwise absents himself or evades his creditors;

    (*e*) if he files in the Court a declaration of insolvency;

    (*f*) if execution against him has been levied by the seizure of his goods under an order of any court or if a return of no goods has been made by the sheriff or county registrar whether by endorsement on the order or otherwise;

(g) if the creditor presenting a petition has served upon the debtor in the prescribed manner a bankruptcy summons, and he does not within fourteen days after service of the summons pay the sum referred to in the summons or secure or compound for it to the satisfaction of the creditor.

(2) A debtor also commits an act of bankruptcy if he fails to comply with a debtor's summons served pursuant to section 21 (6) of the Bankruptcy (Ireland) Amendment Act, 1872, within the appropriate time thereunder, and *section 8 (6)* of this Act shall apply to such debtor's summons.

(3) This section applies, so far as it is capable of application, in relation to acts and things and omissions and failures to do acts and things whether occurring before, or partly before and partly after or wholly after, the commencement of this Act.

Bankruptcy summons

8.—(1) A summons (in this Act referred to as a "bankruptcy summons") may be granted by the Court to a person (in this section referred to as "the creditor") who proves that—

(a) a debt of €1,900 or more is due to him by the person against whom the summons is sought,

(b) the debt is a liquidated sum, and

(c) a notice in the prescribed form, requiring payment of the debt, has been served on the debtor.

(2) A bankruptcy summons may be granted to two or more creditors who are not partners and whose debts amount together to €1,300 or more. In such a case, to comply with the requisitions contained in the summons a debtor must pay or compound for the debts or give security for them to all the creditors who are parties to the summons, unless they otherwise agree.

(3) The notice requiring payment of the debt shall set out the particulars of the debt due and shall require payment within four days after service thereof on the debtor.

(4) The bankruptcy summons shall be in the prescribed form.

(5) A debtor served with a bankruptcy summons may apply to the Court in the prescribed manner and within the prescribed time to dismiss the summons.

(6) The Court—

(a) may dismiss the summons with or without costs, and

(b) shall dismiss the summons if satisfied that an issue would arise for trial.

Arrest of absconding debtor

9.—(1) Where, after a bankruptcy summons has been granted against a debtor and before a petition to adjudicate him bankrupt can be presented against him, it appears to the Court that there is probable cause for believing that he is about to leave the State or to otherwise abscond with a view to avoiding payment of the debt for which the bankruptcy summons was issued or avoiding examination in respect of his affairs or otherwise avoiding or delaying proceedings in bankruptcy, the Court may cause such debtor to be arrested and brought before the Court.

(2) No arrest under this section shall be lawful unless the debtor, before or at the time of his arrest, is served with the bankruptcy summons.

(3) On the debtor offering such security, or making such payment or composition as the Court thinks reasonable, he shall be discharged from custody unless the Court otherwise orders.

(4) Any such security, payment or composition shall not be exempt from the provisions of this Act relating to fraudulent preferences.

Petition

10.—An application for adjudication shall be by petition verified by the affidavit of the petitioner.

Presenting petition

11.—(1) A creditor shall be entitled to present a petition for adjudication against a debtor if—

    (*a*) the debt owing by the debtor to the petitioning creditor (or, if two or more creditors join in presenting the petition, the aggregate amount of debts owing to them) amounts to €1,900 or more,

    (*b*) the debt is a liquidated sum,

    (*c*) the act of bankruptcy on which the petition is founded has occurred within three months before the presentation of the petition, and

    (*d*) the debtor (whether a citizen or not) is domiciled in the State or, within a year before the date of the presentation of the petition, has ordinarily resided or had a dwelling- house or place of business in the State or has carried on business in the State personally or by means of an agent or manager, or is or within the said period has been a member of a partnership which has carried on business in the State by means of a partner, agent or manager.

(2) If a creditor who presents or joins in presenting the petition is a secured creditor, he shall in his petition set out particulars of his security and shall either state that he is willing to give up his security for the benefit of the creditors in the event of the debtor being adjudicated bankrupt or give an estimate of the value of his security. Where a secured creditor gives an estimate of the value of his security, he may be admitted as a petitioning creditor or joint petitioning creditor to the extent of the balance of the debt due to him after deducting the value so estimated in the same manner as if he were an unsecured creditor but he shall on application being made by the Official Assignee after the date of adjudication give up his security to the Official Assignee for the benefit of the creditors upon payment of such estimated value.

(3) Any debtor may petition for adjudication against himself.

Petitioning creditor's costs

12.—The petitioning creditor shall at his own cost present his petition and prosecute it until the statutory sitting referred to in *section 17(3),* and the Court shall at or after the sitting make an order for the payment of such costs out of the estate of the bankrupt in course of priority to be settled by rules of court.

Petition or act of bankruptcy agreed between bankrupt and creditor

13.—No petition for adjudication shall be dismissed or adjudication annulled by reason only that the petition or act of bankruptcy has been concerted or agreed upon between the bankrupt or his solicitor and any creditor or other person.

Adjudication: creditor's petition

14.—(1) Where the petition is presented by a creditor, the Court shall, if satisfied that the requirements of *section 11(1)* have been complied with, by order adjudicate the debtor bankrupt.

(2) A copy of the order shall be served on the debtor, either personally or by leaving it at his residence or place of business in the State.

Adjudication: debtor's petition

15.—Where the petition is presented by a debtor, the Court shall, on proof that he is unable to meet his engagements with his creditor and that his available estate is sufficient to realise at least €1,900, by order adjudicate the debtor bankrupt.

Cause shown against adjudication

16.—(1) The bankrupt may, within three days or such extended time not exceeding fourteen days as the Court thinks fit from the service of the copy of the order of adjudication on him, show cause to the Court against the validity of the adjudication.

(2) On an application to show cause under *subsection (1)* the Court shall, if within such time the bankrupt shows to its satisfaction that any of the requirements of *section 11 (1)* have not been complied with, annul the adjudication and may, in any other case, dismiss the application or adjourn it on such conditions as the Court thinks fit, having regard to the interests of the bankrupt, his creditors and any persons who might advance further credit to him.

(3) Nothing in this section shall be construed to prevent the immediate seizure of the goods of the bankrupt on his adjudication.

Notice of adjudication and statutory sitting

17.—(1) This section shall have effect—
  - (*a*) in the case of a creditor's petition where cause has not been shown to the satisfaction of the Court for annulling the adjudication within the time for showing cause, on the expiration of that time;
  - (*b*) in the case of a debtor's petition under *section 15* or the adjudication of an arranging debtor under *section 105,* on adjudication.

(2) The Court shall cause notice of the adjudication to be given as soon as may be in the prescribed manner in *Iris Oifigiúil* and in at least one daily newspaper

in circulation in the area where the bankrupt resides.

(3) The Court shall appoint a statutory sitting to be held within three weeks of the publication of the notice at which the bankrupt shall attend and make full disclosure of his property to the Court, and his creditors may prove their debts and choose and appoint a creditors' assignee.

(4) The Court, on adjourning an application to show cause under *section 16 (1)*, may stay publication of notice of the adjudication on security being given by the bankrupt or on such other conditions as the Court thinks fit.

Creditors' assignee

18.—(1) At the statutory sitting referred to in *section 17 (3)* the creditors may choose and appoint a person (in this Act referred to as the "creditors' assignee") to represent them in the administration of the bankrupt's estate.

(2) All creditors shall be entitled to vote in such choice in person or by an agent authorised in writing in that behalf, and the choice and appointment shall be made by the major part in value of the creditors.

(3) The Court may reject any person so chosen who appears to the Court unfit to be a creditors' assignee or may remove a creditors' assignee and in the event of a vacancy, however arising, a new choice and appointment may be made in like manner.

(4) For the purposes of appointing a creditors' assignee a creditor may prove his debt.

Duties of bankrupt

19.—The bankrupt shall—
   (*a*) unless the Court otherwise directs, forthwith deliver up to the Official Assignee such books of account or other papers relating to his estate in his possession or control as the Official Assignee may from time to time request and disclose to him such of them as are in the possession or control of any other person;
   (*b*) deliver up possession of any part of his property which is divisible among his creditors under this Act, and which is for the time being in his possession or control, to the Official Assignee or any person authorised by the Court or otherwise under the provisions of this Act to take possession of it;
   (*c*) unless the Court otherwise directs, within the prescribed time file in the Central Office a statement of affairs in the prescribed form and deliver a copy thereof to the Official Assignee;
   (*d*) give every reasonable assistance to the Official Assignee in the administration of the estate;
   (*e*) disclose to the Official Assignee any after-acquired property.

Change of name or address, etc.

20.—(1) A bankrupt shall forthwith notify the Official Assignee in writing of any change in his name or address which occurs during his bankruptcy.

(2) For the purposes of *subsection (1)* a change in the name of a bankrupt

shall be deemed to occur if the bankrupt in fact assumes the use of a different name or an additional name.

(3) A bankrupt shall, whenever required by the Official Assignee to do so, forthwith notify the Official Assignee in writing of the nature of any profession, vocation, business or employment in which he is engaged.

(4) A bankrupt who fails to comply with any of the provisions of this section shall be guilty of an offence.

Examination of bankrupt and other persons

21.—(1) The Court may summon before it a bankrupt or any person who is known or suspected to have in his possession or control any property of the bankrupt or to have disposed of any property of the bankrupt or who is supposed to be indebted to the bankrupt, or any person whom the Court deems capable of giving information relating to the trade, dealings, affairs or property of the bankrupt.

(2) The Court may examine him on oath concerning the matters aforesaid, either orally or on written interrogatories, and may reduce his answers to writing and require him to sign them.

(3) The Court may require him to produce any books of account and papers in his possession or control relating to the matters aforesaid but, where he claims any lien on books or papers produced by him, the production shall be without prejudice to that lien and the Court may determine all questions in relation to the lien.

(4) A bankrupt or other person who is examined under this section shall not be entitled to refuse to answer any question put to him on the ground that his answer might incriminate him but none of his answers shall be admissible in evidence against him in any other proceedings, civil or criminal, except in the case of any criminal proceedings for perjury in respect of any such answer.

Admission of debt due to bankrupt

22.—If any person on examination appears to be indebted to the bankrupt or to have in his possession or control any property of the bankrupt, the Court, on the application of the Official Assignee, may order him to pay to the Official Assignee, at such time and in such manner as the Court thinks fit, the amount or any part thereof or to deliver to the Official Assignee such property or any part thereof at such time and in such manner and on such terms as the Court may direct.

Arrest of bankrupt, etc.

23.—(1) Where it appears to the Court, at any time after making an adjudication order, on proof of probable cause for believing that a bankrupt is about to leave the State or otherwise to abscond or has removed or concealed or is about to remove or conceal any of his property with a view to avoiding payment of his debts or avoiding examination in respect of his affairs, or is keeping out of the way and cannot be served with a summons, the Court may cause him to be arrested and brought before it for examination.

(2) Where a bankrupt has been summoned before the Court pursuant to *section 21* and he does not come at the time appointed, not having an excuse (made known to the Court at the time of its sitting and allowed by it) the Court may cause him to be arrested and brought before it for examination.

(3) Where any person summoned before the Court pursuant to *section 21* after being tendered a reasonable sum for his expenses, does not come at the time appointed, not having an excuse (made known to the Court at the time of its sitting and allowed by it), the Court may cause him to be arrested and brought before it for examination.

(4) The provisions of *subsections (2)* and *(3)* are without prejudice to the powers of the Court in relation to contempt or enforcement of the attendance of witnesses.

Committal to prison

24.—Where the bankrupt or any person summoned or brought before the Court refuses to be sworn or refuses or fails to answer any lawful question put by the Court or does not fully answer any such question or refuses to sign and subscribe his examination when reduced to writing (not having any lawful excuse allowed by the Court) or to comply with any order of the Court under this Act, the Court may order that such person be committed to prison to await the further order of the Court.

Examination of persons in custody

25.—Where the bankrupt or any person is in prison pursuant to an order of the Court under *section 24*, the Court may by warrant directed to the governor of the prison order that he be brought before the Court. Where such person satisfies the Court that he has complied with its lawful requirements the Court shall order his release from custody. In any other case he may be taken back to prison without any further order.

Release of bankrupt from prison

26.—If a bankrupt is in prison by virtue of section 6 of the Enforcement of Court Orders Act, 1940 , in respect of a debt incurred before adjudication, the Court may order his release.

(New)

Warrant of seizure

27.—(1) The Court may by warrant direct the Bankruptcy Inspector or any of his assistants to seize any property of the bankrupt.

(2) An official acting under the warrant. may seize any part of the bankrupt's property in the possession or control of the bankrupt and, for the purpose of seizing any such property, may enter and if necessary break open any house, building, room or other place belonging to the bankrupt where. any part of his property is believed to be.

Search warrant

28.—Where it appears to the Court that there is reason to believe that any property of the bankrupt is concealed in any house, building, room or other place not belonging to the bankrupt, the Court may grant a search warrant to the Bankruptcy Inspector or any of his assistants, or other person appointed by the Court, who may execute the warrant according to the tenor thereof.

Indemnity for persons acting under warrant

29.—The Bankruptcy Inspector or his assistants or other person appointed by the Court shall not be liable for anything done *bona fide* pursuant to any warrant of the Court.

Partnership Cases

Actions by Official Assignee and bankrupt's partners

30.—Where a member of a partnership is adjudicated bankrupt the Court may authorise the Official Assignee to commence and prosecute any action in the names of the Official Assignee and of the bankrupt's partner to recover any debt due to or any property of the partners, and any release by such partner of the debt or demand to which the action relates shall be void; but notice of the application for authority to commence the action shall be given to the bankrupt's partner and he may show cause against it and on his application the Court may, if it thinks fit, direct that he shall receive his proper share of the proceeds of the action. If the partner does not claim any benefit from the action he shall be indemnified against costs in respect thereof as the Court directs.

Petition against one or more partners

31.—(1) Any creditor whose debt is sufficient to entitle him to present a petition for adjudication against all the partners of a firm may present a petition against any one or more partners of the firm without including the others.

(2) Where a petition for adjudication is presented against more than one person the Court may make an order of adjudication against one or more of them and dismiss the petition as to the remainder.

Furnishing of partnership accounts to Official Assignee

32.—Where a member of a partnership is adjudicated bankrupt the Official Assignee may require the other partner or partners to deliver to the Official Assignee such accounts and information relating to the partnership estate and the bankrupt's interest therein (duly verified by affidavit if necessary) as the Official Assignee may deem necessary.

Duty of bankrupt partner

33.—Where a member of a partnership is adjudicated bankrupt he shall deliver to the Official Assignee within the prescribed time a separate statement of affairs in respect of the partnership in the prescribed form.

Joint and separate properties

34.—(1) In the case of partners the joint property shall be applicable in the first instance in payment of their joint debts, and the separate property of each partner shall be applicable in the first instance in payment of his separate debts.

(2) Where there is a surplus of the joint property, it shall be dealt with as part of the respective separate properties in proportion to the right and interest of each partner in the joint property.

(3) Where there is a surplus of any separate property it shall be dealt with as part of the joint property so far as necessary to meet any deficiency in the joint property.

Actions on joint contracts

35.—Where a bankrupt is a party to a contract jointly with any other person, that other person may sue or be sued in respect of the contract without joining the bankrupt.

Proceedings in partnership name

36.—(1) Any two or more persons, being partners, or any person carrying on business under a partnership name, may take proceedings or be proceeded against under this Act in the name of the firm, but in such case the Court may, on application by any person interested, order the names of the persons to be disclosed in such manner, and verified on oath or otherwise, as the Court may direct.

(2) Notwithstanding anything contained in *subsection (1)* no order of adjudication shall be made against a firm in the firm name but it shall be made against the partners individually with the addition of the firm name.

Limited partnerships

37.—Subject to such modifications as may be made by rules of court, the provisions of this Act shall apply to limited partnerships in like manner as if limited partnerships were ordinary partnerships and, on all the general partners of a limited partnership being adjudicated bankrupt, the assets of the limited partnership shall vest in the Official Assignee.

Composition after Bankruptcy

Stay on realisation of estate

38.—The Court may, on the application of a bankrupt, grant a stay on the realisation of his estate, for such time and under such conditions as it thinks fit, to enable him or any persons acting on his behalf to make an offer of composition to his creditors under *section 39*.

Offer of composition

39.—(1) Where a stay on the realisation of the estate of a bankrupt has been granted under *section 38*, the bankrupt shall call a meeting of his creditors before the Court for the purpose of making an offer of composition to them.

(2) At least ten days before the meeting a notice of the meeting specifying the precise offer of composition to be made shall be inserted in *Iris Oifigiúil* and shall also be sent by post to each creditor at his last known address.

(3) If an offer of composition is made by or on behalf of the bankrupt and three-fifths in number and value of the creditors voting at the meeting, either in person or by an agent authorised in writing in that behalf, accept the offer or any modification of it, it shall be deemed to be accepted, and when approved by the Court shall be binding on all creditors of the bankrupt.

(4) A creditor whose debt is less than €130 shall not be entitled to vote.

(5) If for any reason the bankrupt has not filed a statement of his affairs as required by *section 19 (c)*, he shall do so at or before the meeting.

(6) Debts may be proved at the meeting.

Payment of composition

40.—(1) Any composition shall be payable—

    (*a*) in cash, within one month from the approval by the Court of the offer of composition or within such further time as the Court may allow, or

    (*b*) by instalments, all of which shall be secured to the satisfaction of the creditors, or

    (*c*) partly in cash and partly by instalments payable or secured as aforesaid.

(2) In no case shall any instalment be secured by a bill, note or other security signed by or enforceable against the bankrupt alone.

(3) The Court shall have discretion to refuse to approve of an offer payable wholly or partly by instalments if the final instalment is not payable within two years.

Discharge of adjudication order

41.—The Court, on the application of the bankrupt or his personal representatives, shall, on the report of the Official Assignee and in the absence of fraud, discharge the adjudication order—

    (*a*) in the case of a composition payable in cash, upon lodgment with the Official Assignee of the necessary amount to pay the composition, expenses, fees, costs, such further sums as the Court may direct and the preferential payments;

    (*b*) in the case of a composition payable by instalments which are secured to the satisfaction of the creditors, upon lodgment with the Official Assignee of the completed bills, notes or other securities, the necessary amount to pay expenses, fees, costs, such further sums as the Court may direct and the preferential payments;

    (*c*) in the case of a composition payable partly in cash and partly by instalments which are secured to the satisfaction of the creditors, upon lodgment with the Official Assignee of the completed bills, notes or other securities, the necessary amount to pay the cash composition, expenses, fees, costs, such further sums as the Court may direct and the preferential payments.

Bankrupt Dying after Adjudication

Bankrupt dying after adjudication

42.—If a bankrupt dies the Court may proceed in the bankruptcy as if he were living.

Subsequent Bankruptcy

Subsequent bankruptcy

43.—(1) Where a bankrupt is again adjudicated, all after-acquired property unclaimed by the Official Assignee at the date of the subsequent bankruptcy shall, if claimed by the Official Assignee, vest in him for the credit of the subsequent bankruptcy.

(2) Any after-acquired property or the proceeds thereof in the possession of the Official Assignee at the date of the subsequent bankruptcy shall be transferred by the Official Assignee (after deducting his costs and expenses) to the credit of the subsequent bankruptcy.

(3) Any surplus arising on the subsequent bankruptcy shall be transferred to the credit of the former bankruptcy.

PART III

ADMINISTRATION OF PROPERTY

Effect of Adjudication on Bankrupt's Property

Vesting of property in Official Assignee

44.—(1) Where a person is adjudicated bankrupt, then, subject to the provisions of this Act, all property belonging to that person shall on the date of adjudication vest in the Official Assignee for the benefit of the creditors of the bankrupt.

(2) Subject to the provisions of this Act, the title of the Official Assignee to any property which vests in him by virtue of *subsection (1)* shall not commence at any date earlier than the date of adjudication.

(3) The property to which *subsection (1)* applies includes—

    (*a*) all powers vested in the bankrupt which he might legally exercise in relation to any property immediately before the date of adjudication;

    (*b*) all property which was the subject of any conveyance or transfer which *sections 57, 58* and *59* declare void as against the Official Assignee, subject to the rights of any persons which are preserved by those sections.

(4) The property to which *subsection (1)* applies does not include—

    (*a*) property held by the bankrupt in trust for any other person, or

    (*b*) any sum which vests in the Official Assignee under section 7(1)(*a*) of the Auctioneers and House Agents Act, 1967, or section 30(i) of the Central Bank Act, 1971 .

(5) Without prejudice to any existing principle or rule of law or equity, established practice or procedure in relation to damages or compensation recovered or recoverable by a bankrupt for personal injury or loss suffered by him, property which is acquired by or devolves on a bankrupt before the discharge or annulment of the adjudication order (in this Act called "after-acquired property") shall vest in the Official Assignee if and when he claims it.

Excepted articles

45.—(1) A bankrupt shall be entitled to retain, as excepted articles, such articles of clothing, household furniture, bedding, tools or equipment of his trade or occupation or other like necessaries for himself, his wife, children and dependent relatives residing with him, as he may select, not exceeding in value €3,100 or such further amount as the Court on an application by the bankrupt may allow.

(2) Where a bankrupt, after selecting the items constituting the excepted articles, requests the Official Assignee, in writing, not to dispose of the remainder of any such articles as are referred to in *subsection (1)* the Official Assignee shall not dispose thereof except in accordance with an order of the Court.

(3) The Court may, on the application of the bankrupt or the Official Assignee, in relation to the remainder of such articles—

    (*a*) postpone the removal and sale thereof;

    (*b*) permit them to remain in the use of the bankrupt;

    (*c*) at any time, order them to be taken by or on behalf of the Official Assignee and to be sold for the benefit of the creditors.

Certificate of vesting of property in Official Assignee

46.—(1) Where, according to law, any conveyance of land is required to be registered and such land vests in the Official Assignee under this Part, a certificate under the seal of the Court shall be issued to him as evidence of the vesting and he shall cause the certificate to be registered as soon as may be as if it were a conveyance, and registration of the certificate shall have the like effect to all intents and purposes as registration of a conveyance would have had.

(2) The title of any purchaser of any such land for valuable consideration, in good faith and without notice of the adjudication, who had duly registered the conveyance before the registration of the certificate shall not be invalidated by reason of the adjudication unless the certificate is registered within two months after the date of the adjudication.

Vesting in Official Assignee of certain money and securities

47.—Notwithstanding any provision in any other enactment—

(*a*) money in the Post Office Savings Bank or in a trustee savings bank to which a bankrupt is entitled, or

(*b*) securities issued through An Post by the Minister for Finance under his statutory borrowing powers and to which a bankrupt is entitled,

shall, on the adjudication of the bankrupt, vest in the Official Assignee in the same manner as any other property.

Limitation of Official Assignee's powers in relation to copyright

48.—Where the property of a bankrupt comprises the copyright in any work or any interest in such copyright and he is liable to pay to the author royalties or a share of the profits in respect thereof—

(*a*) the Official Assignee shall not be entitled to sell or authorise the sale of any copies of the work, or to perform or authorise the performance of the work, except on the terms of paying to the author such sums by way of royalty or share of the profits as would have been payable by the bankrupt, and

(*b*) he shall not be entitled to assign the right or transfer the interest or to grant any interest in the right by licence, except with the consent of the author or of the Court and upon terms which will secure to the author payments by way of royalty or share of the profits at a rate not less than that which the bankrupt was liable to pay.

Restrictive clause in agreement or lease

49.—(1) Every covenant or provision for forfeiture of a lease on the bankruptcy of the lessee shall be void as against the Official Assignee.

(2) A clause in a hire purchase agreement which purports to terminate the agreement on the bankruptcy of the hirer shall be void as against the Official Assignee.

Execution against debtor's property before adjudication

50.—(1) Where goods or a leasehold interest in land belonging to a debtor have been seized under an execution order and sold, or where money has been paid in part or full satisfaction of the execution either to the sheriff or county registrar or to the execution creditor in order to avoid seizure or sale under such execution, the sheriff, county registrar or execution creditor shall retain the proceeds of sale or the money so paid, for a period of twenty-one days.

(2) If within that period the sheriff, county registrar or execution creditor receives notice of the adjudication of the debtor, he shall surrender the property, or pay over the proceeds of sale thereof or any money paid in satisfaction of the execution, to the Official Assignee who shall be entitled to retain the property, proceeds or money, as the case may be, as against the execution creditor.

(3) An execution levied by seizure of any such property belonging to the debtor shall not be invalid by reason only of its being an act of bankruptcy and a person who purchases the property in good faith under a sale by the sheriff

or county registrar shall, as against the Official Assignee, acquire a good title thereto.

(4) Where a sheriff or county registrar, without notice of the adjudication of the debtor, pays the proceeds of sale or other money retained by him pursuant to *subsection (1)* to the execution creditor after the expiration of twenty-one days, he shall not be liable to the Official Assignee in respect of the payment.

(5) Where property is surrendered or proceeds of sale or other money paid over to the Official Assignee, the costs of the execution shall be a first charge thereon and the Official Assignee may sell the whole or part of the property for the purpose of satisfying the charge.

Priority of judgment mortgage

51.—(1) A judgement creditor who registers an affidavit of his judgement in accordance with sections 6 and 7 of the Judgement Mortgage (Ireland) Act, 1850, shall not, by reason of such registration, be entitled to any priority or preference over simple contract creditors in the event of the person against whom such affidavit is registered being adjudicated bankrupt, unless the affidavit is registered at least three months before the date of the adjudication.

(2) The reference in section 284 (2) of the Companies Act, 1963 , to section 331 of the Irish Bankrupt and Insolvent Act, 1857 (repealed by this Act) shall be construed as a reference to *subsection (1)* and accordingly the reference in the said section 284 (2) to the filing of the petition shall be read as a reference to the date of the adjudication.

Order to put purchaser in possession

52.—Where land belonging to a bankrupt or arranging debtor has been sold under the provisions of this Act or by or under the direction of the Court, the Court may, on the application of the purchaser, issue an order directing the appropriate sheriff or county registrar to put the purchaser into possession of all the land not in the occupation of lessees, under-lessees or tenants, subject to whose interests the sale has been made and who have attorned to the purchaser within a time to be limited in the order, and the order shall be executed in like manner as an order for the delivery of possession.

Permission to mortgagee to bid at sale

53.—The mortgagee of any property of a bankrupt or arranging t debtor may, with the leave of the Court, bid and purchase at the sale of the property.

Discharge of persons delivering property, etc., to Official Assignee

54.—A person—
  (a) from whom the Official Assignee recovers any property of a bankrupt, or
  (b) who, without legal proceedings, in good faith delivers up to the Official Assignee possession of any such property, or
  (c) who pays any debt owed to a bankrupt and claimed by the Official Assignee,

shall, notwithstanding that the adjudication is subsequently annulled or discharged, be released from all claims by the bankrupt in respect of such property or debt.

Title to property sold not to be invalidated

55.—The title to any property sold in bankruptcy shall not be invalidated by the bankrupt or any person claiming under him by reason only of any defect in any proceedings under this Act.

Disclaimer of onerous property

56.—(1) Subject to *subsections (2) and (5)*, where any of the property (other than after-acquired property) of a bankrupt consists of land of any tenure burdened with onerous covenants, of shares or stock in companies, of unprofitable contracts, or of any other property which is unsaleable or not readily saleable by reason of its binding the possessor thereof to the performance of any onerous act or to the payment of any sum of money, the Official Assignee, notwithstanding that he has endeavoured to sell or has taken possession of the property or exercised any act of ownership in relation thereto, may, with the leave of the Court and subject to the provisions of this section, by writing signed by him, at any time within twelve months after the date of adjudication or such extended period as may be allowed by the Court, disclaim the property.

(2) Where any such property as aforesaid has not come to the knowledge of the Official Assignee within one month after the date of the adjudication, the power under this section of disclaiming the property may be exercised at any time within twelve months after he has become aware thereof or such extended period as may be allowed by the Court.

(3) The disclaimer shall operate to determine, as from the date of disclaimer, the rights, interests and liabilities of the bankrupt and his property in or in respect of the property disclaimed, and shall also discharge the Official Assignee from all personal liability in respect of the property disclaimed as from the date when the property vested in him, but shall not, except so far as is necessary for the purpose of releasing the bankrupt and his property and the Official Assignee from liability, affect the rights or liabilities of any other person.

(4) The Court, before or on granting leave to disclaim, may require the Official Assignee to give such notices to persons interested and impose such terms as a condition of granting leave, and make such other order in the matter as the Court thinks just.

(5) The Official Assignee shall not be entitled to disclaim any property under this section in any case where an application in writing has been made to him by any persons interested in the property requiring him to decide whether he will or will not disclaim, and the Official Assignee has not, within a period of twenty-eight days after the receipt of the application or such further period as may be allowed by the Court, given notice to the applicant that he intends to apply to the Court for leave to disclaim; and, in the case of a contract, if the Official Assignee, after such application as aforesaid, does not within the said period or extended period disclaim the contract, he shall be deemed to have adopted it.

(6) The Court may, on the application of any person who is, as against the Official Assignee, entitled to the benefit or subject to the burden of a contract made with the bankrupt, make an order rescinding the contract on such terms as to payment by or to either party of damages for the non-performance of the contract, or otherwise as the Court thinks just, and any damages payable under the order to any such person shall he deemed to be a debt proved and admitted in the bankruptcy.

(7) Subject to *subsection (8)*, the Court may, on an application by any person who either claims any interest in any disclaimed property or is under any liability not discharged by this Act in respect of any disclaimed property and on hearing any such persons as it thinks fit, make an order for the vesting of the property in or the delivery of the property to any person entitled thereto, or to whom it may seem just that the property should be delivered by way of compensation for such liability as aforesaid, or a trustee for him, and on such terms as the Court may think just, and on any such vesting order being made, the property comprised therein shall vest accordingly in the person therein named in that behalf without any conveyance or assignment for the purpose.

(8) Where the property disclaimed is of a leasehold nature, the Court shall not make a vesting order in favour of any person claiming under the bankrupt, whether as under-lessee or as mortgagee by demise, except upon the terms of making that person—

(*a*) subject to the same liabilities and obligations as those to which the bankrupt was subject under the lease in respect of the property at the date of the adjudication; or

(*b*) if the Court thinks fit, subject only to the same liabilities and obligations as if the lease had been assigned to that person at that date;

and in either event (if the case so requires), as if the lease had comprised only the property comprised in the vesting order, and any mortgagee or under-lessee declining to accept a vesting order upon such terms shall be excluded from all interest in and security upon the property and, if there is no person claiming under the bankrupt who is willing to accept an order upon such terms, the Court shall have power to vest the estate and interest of the bankrupt in the property in any person liable either personally or in a representative character, and either alone or jointly with the bankrupt, to perform the lessee's covenants in the lease, freed and discharged from all estates, encumbrances and interests created therein by the bankrupt.

(9) Any person damaged by the operation of a disclaimer under this section shall be deemed to be a creditor of the bankrupt to the amount of the damages, and may accordingly prove the amount as a debt in the bankruptcy.

Fraudulent and Voluntary Conveyances

Avoidance of fraudulent preferences

57.—(1) Every conveyance or transfer of property or charge made thereon, every payment made, every obligation incurred and every judicial proceeding taken or suffered by any person unable to pay his debts as they become due from his own money in favour of any creditor or of any person in trust for any creditor, with a view to giving such creditor, or any surety or guarantor for the debt due to such creditor, a preference over the other creditors, shall, if the person making, incurring, taking or suffering the same is adjudicated bankrupt within six months after the date of making, incurring, taking or suffering the same, be deemed fraudulent and void as against the Official Assignee; but this section shall not affect the rights of any person making title in good faith and for valuable consideration f through or under a creditor of the bankrupt.

(2)(*a*) Where a person is adjudicated bankrupt and anything made or done is void under *subsection (1)* or was void under the corresponding provisions of the law in force immediately before the commencement of this Act as a fraudulent preference of a person interested in property mortgaged or charged to secure the bankrupt's debt, then (without prejudice to any rights or liabilities arising apart from this section) the person preferred shall be subject to the same liabilities and shall have the same rights as if he had undertaken to be personally liable as surety for the debt to the extent of the charge on the property or the value of his interest, whichever is the less.

(*b*) The value of the said person's interest shall be determined as at the date of the transaction constituting the fraudulent preference, and shall be determined as if the interest were free of all encumbrances other than those to which the charge for the bankrupt's debt was then subject.

(*c*) On any application made to the Court in relation to any payment on the ground that the payment was a fraudulent preference of a surety or guarantor, the Court shall have jurisdiction to determine any questions relating to the payment arising between the person to whom the payment was made and the surety or guarantor, and to grant relief in respect thereof notwithstanding that it is not necessary so to do for the purposes of the bankruptcy, and for that purpose may give leave to bring in the surety or guarantor as a third party as in the case of an action for the recovery of the sum paid.

(*d*) *Paragraph (c)* shall apply, with the necessary modifications, in relation to transactions other than the payment of money as it applies to payments.

Avoidance of certain transactions

58.—(1) If within three months before he is adjudicated bankrupt a debtor commits an act of bankruptcy and thereafter either sells any of his property at a price which, in the opinion of the Court, is substantially below its market value or enters into or is a party to any other transaction which, in the opinion of the Court, has the effect of substantially reducing the sum available for distribution to the creditors, such transaction shall be void as against the Official Assignee, unless the transaction was *bona fide* entered into and the other party had not at the time of the transaction notice of any prior act of bankruptcy committed by the bankrupt.

(2) *Subsection (1)* shall not affect the rights of any person making title in

good faith and for valuable consideration through or under a person (other than the bankrupt) who is party to a transaction mentioned therein.

(3) *Subsection (1)* shall not apply to any transaction mentioned in *section 57 (1)* or *59*.

Avoidance of certain settlements

59.—(1) Any settlement of property, not being a settlement made before and in consideration of marriage, or made in favour of a purchaser or incumbrancer in good faith and for valuable consideration, shall—

     (*a*) if the settlor is adjudicated bankrupt within two years after the date of the settlement, be void as against the Official Assignee, and

     (*b*) if the settlor is adjudicated bankrupt at any subsequent time within five years after the date of the settlement, be void as against the Official Assignee unless the parties claiming under the settlement prove that the settlor was, at the time of making the settlement, able to pay all his debt without the aid of the property comprised in the settlement and that the interest of the settlor in such property passed to the trustee of such settlement on the execution thereof.

(2) A covenant or contract made by any person (in this section called the settlor) in consideration of his or her marriage, either for the future payment of money for the benefit of the settlor's spouse or children, or for the future settlement, on or for the settlor's spouse or children, of property wherein the settlor had not at the date of the marriage any estate or interest, whether vested or contingent, in possession or remainder, shall, if the settlor is adjudicated bankrupt and the covenant or contract has not been executed at the date of the adjudication, be void as against the Official Assignee, except so far as it enables the persons entitled under the covenant or contract to claim for dividend in the settlor's bankruptcy under or in respect of the covenant or contract, but any such claim to dividend shall be postponed until all the claims of the other creditors for valuable consideration in money or money's worth have been satisfied.

(3) Any payment of money (not being payment of premiums on policy of life assurance) or any transfer of property made by the settlor in pursuance of a covenant or contract to which *subsection (2)* applies shall be void as against the Official Assignee in the settlor's bankruptcy, unless the persons to whom the payment or transfer was made prove that:

     (*a*) the payment or transfer was made more than two years before the date of the adjudication of the settlor, or

     (*b*) at the date of the payment or transfer, the settlor was able to pay all his debts without the aid of the money so paid or the property so transferred, or

     (*c*) the payment or transfer was made in pursuance of a covenant or contract to pay or transfer money or property expected to come to the settlor from or on the death of a particular person named in the covenant or contract, and was made within three months after the money or property came into the possession or under the control of the settlor;

but, in the event of any such payment or transfer being declared void, the persons to whom it was made shall be entitled to claim for dividend under or in respect of the covenant or contract in like manner as if it had not been executed at the date of the adjudication.

(4) In this section "settlement" includes any conveyance or transfer of property.

Management Provisions

Office of the Official Assignee

60.—(1) The Official Assignee shall have and exercise such powers and authorities and perform such duties and functions as are from time to time conferred on or assigned to him by statute (including this Act) or rules of court.

(2) There shall be employed in the Office of the Official Assignee an inspector (in this Act referred to as "the Bankruptcy Inspector") and paragraph 22 of the Eighth Schedule to the Courts (Supplemental Provisions) Act, 1961 , shall apply accordingly.

(3) The person who, immediately before the commencement of this Act, held office as Messenger of the Court shall, on such commencement, become and be the Bankruptcy Inspector.

Functions of Official Assignee in bankruptcy and vesting arrangements

61.—(1) This section applies to every bankruptcy matter and vesting arrangement.

(2) The functions of the Official Assignee are to get in and realise the property, to ascertain the debts and liabilities and to distribute the assets in accordance with the provisions of this Act.

(3) In the performance of his functions the Official Assignee shall, in particular, have power—

(*a*) to sell the property by public auction or private contract, with power to transfer the whole thereof to any person or to sell the same in lots and for the purpose of selling land to carry out such sale by fee farm grant, sub fee farm grant, lease, sub-lease or otherwise and to sell any rent reserved on any such grant or any reversion expectant upon the determination of any such lease,

(*b*) to make any compromise or arrangement with creditors or persons claiming to be creditors or having or alleging themselves to have any claim present or future, certain or contingent, ascertained or sounding only in damages whereby the bankrupt or arranging debtor may be rendered liable,

(*c*) to compromise all debts and liabilities capable of resulting in debts and all claims, present or future, certain or contingent, ascertained or sounding only in damages, subsisting or supposed to subsist between the bankrupt or arranging debtor and any debtor and all questions in any way relating to or affecting the assets or the proceedings on such terms as may be agreed and take any security for the discharge of any debt, liability or claim, and give a complete discharge in respect thereof,

(*d*) to institute, continue or defend any proceedings relating to the property,

(*e*) to refer any dispute concerning the property to arbitration under the terms of section 11 of the Arbitration Act, 1954 ,

(*f*) to mortgage or pledge any property to raise any money requisite,

(*g*) to take out in his official name without being required to give security, letters of administration to any estate on the administration of which the bankrupt or arranging debtor would benefit,

(*h*) to agree a sum for costs where the Court so directs or where he considers that the amount which would be allowed on taxation would not exceed €1,300,

(*i*) to agree the charges of accountants, auctioneers, brokers and other persons,

(*j*) to ascertain and certify to the Court the amount due in respect of a mortgage debt and the due priority thereof with power to the Court to vary such certificate,

(*k*) to draw out of the account referred to in *section 84 (1)* any sum not exceeding €130 by way of indemnity in respect of costs incurred by him.

(3A) In the case of an adjudication in bankruptcy under Article 3(1) of the Insolvency Regulation, the Official Assignee shall have the powers conferred on a liquidator in relation to taking action in member states under the Regulation.

(4) Notwithstanding any provision to the contrary contained in *subsection (3)*, no disposition of property of a bankrupt, arranging debtor or person dying insolvent, which comprises a family home within the meaning of the Family Home Protection Act 1976 , shall be made without the prior sanction of the Court, and any disposition made without such sanction shall be void.

(5) On an application by the Official Assignee under this section for an order for the sale of a family home, the Court, notwithstanding anything contained in this or any other enactment, shall have power to order postponement of the sale of the family home having regard to the interests of the creditors and of the spouse and dependants of the bankrupt as well as to all the circumstances of the case.

(6) The Official Assignee may in case of doubt or difficulty seek the directions of the Court in connection with the affairs of any bankrupt or arranging debtor.

(7) The exercise by the Official Assignee of the powers conferred by this section shall be subject to the control of the Court, and any creditor or other person who in the opinion of the Court has an interest may apply to the Court in relation to the exercise or proposed exercise of those powers.

(8) The powers and functions conferred on the Official Assignee by this section may be exercised and performed—

(*a*) in the case of an adjudication founded on a petition of a debtor, on adjudication,

(*b*) in the case of an adjudication founded on a petition by a creditor, on the expiration of the time for showing cause,

(c) in the case of a vesting arrangement, on approval of the proposal by the Court.

Bankruptcy Inspector and assistants

62.—(1) The Bankruptcy Inspector and his assistants shall follow the instructions of the Official Assignee, subject to the directions and control of the Court.

(2) Subject to the provisions of this Act, it shall be the duty of the Bankruptcy Inspector or his assistants—

(a) to seize the property of the bankrupt pursuant to a warrant issued by the Court under *section 27*,

(b) to take an inventory of and report on the bankrupt's property,

(c) to take possession of the property of an arranging debtor pursuant to *section 100*, and to take an inventory of and report on the property,

(d) to do such other things as may be directed by the Court or the Official Assignee.

Protection of Official Assignee

63.—The Official Assignee shall not be liable—

(a) by reason of any of the matters on which an adjudication was grounded being insufficient to support the adjudication,

(b) in respect of his receipt of any property, provided he has not dealt with the property otherwise than as directed by the Court or as required by this Act or by rules of court.

Power of Official Assignee to bar entail

64.—The Official Assignee may, with the sanction of the Court, deal with any land to which the bankrupt is beneficially entitled as tenant in tail in the same manner as the bankrupt might have dealt with it had he not been adjudicated; and sections 49 to 61 of the Fines and Recoveries (Ireland) Act, 1834 (so far as they are applicable) s shall extend and apply to proceedings in bankruptcy under this Act as if those sections were herein re-enacted and in terms made applicable to those proceedings.

Power of Official Assignee to appropriate part of bankrupt's income

65.—(1) Notwithstanding any provision to the contrary in any other enactment, whenever a bankrupt, whether self-employed or not, is in receipt of or is entitled to receive any salary, income, emolument or pension, the Court may, from time to time, on the application of the Official Assignee, make such order directed to the bankrupt and any person from whom the bankrupt is entitled to receive any such salary, income, emolument or pension for the payment to the Official Assignee of all or part of such salary, income, emolument or pension, subject to such conditions as to payment as the Court may specify in the order having regard to the family responsibilities and personal situation of the bankrupt.

(2) The Court may at any time, on the application of any interested person, vary an order under *subsection (1)*, having regard to any changes in the family

responsibilities or personal situation of the bankrupt.

Delivery of property to Official Assignee

66.—Every person shall, on request, deliver up to the Official Assignee all money or securities for money in such person's possession or control which he is not by law entitled to retain as against the bankrupt or the Official Assignee.

Right of Official Assignee to transfer stocks or shares

67.—Where any part of the property of a bankrupt, or of an arranging debtor under a vesting arrangement, consists of stocks or shares, the Official Assignee may exercise the right to transfer them to the same extent as the bankrupt or arranging debtor could have exercised it but for the adjudication or vesting arrangement.

Right of Official Assignee to inspect goods pawned or pledged

68.—Where any goods of a bankrupt are held by any person by way of pledge, pawn or other security, the Official Assignee may give notice in writing to the holder of his intention to inspect the goods and, where such notice has been given, the holder shall not be entitled to realise his security until he has given the Official Assignee a reasonable opportunity of inspecting the goods and of exercising his right of redemption if he thinks fit to do so.

Receipt of property of bankrupt

69.—(1) The Official Assignee shall be assignee of each bankrupt's estate and act with the creditors' assignee, if any.

(2) Except where otherwise directed by the Court, the property of every bankrupt, and the income and proceeds thereof, shall be possessed and received by the Official Assignee.

(3) All money and securities received by the Official Assignee, being part of a bankrupt's estate, shall be forthwith lodged by him in the Central Bank of Ireland and shall be kept there to the credit of the Official Assignee subject to the provisions of this Act and rules of court and to the directions of the Court.

(4) Subject to *section 84*, all money and securities which, immediately before the commencement of this Act, stood to the credit of bank accounts in bankruptcy or arrangement matters shall be dealt with pursuant to rules of court.

(5) The Official Assignee, with the leave of the Court, may from time to time invest the whole or any part of any money referred to in this section, and any interest thereon shall be paid into the appropriate bank accounts.

Claim to property in possession of bankrupt

70.—(1) Where a person claims any property which is in the possession of the bankrupt at the date of adjudication he shall file with the Official Assignee a claim verified by affidavit.

(2) The Official Assignee may give notice in writing to any person to prove his claim to property which is in the possession of the bankrupt at the date of

adjudication and, unless within one month after the service of the notice that person files with the Official Assignee a claim verified by affidavit, the Official Assignee may, with the sanction of the Court, sell or dispose of the property free of any right or interest therein of that person.

Allowances to bankrupt

71.—The Court may make to the bankrupt out of his estate such allowances as the Court thinks proper in the special circumstances of the case.

Redirection of letters, etc., addressed to bankrupt

72.—Where a debtor is adjudicated bankrupt the Court, on the application of the Official Assignee, may from time to time order that for such time, not exceeding three months, as the Court thinks fit letters, telegrams and postal packets addressed to the bankrupt at any place mentioned in the order shall, on such terms and subject to such conditions as the Court thinks fit, be redirected, sent or delivered to 2 the Official Assignee as the Court directs.

Appointment of receivers and managers

73.—The Court may, at any time after adjudication or after the granting of an order for protection, appoint a receiver or manager of the whole or part of the property of the bankrupt or arranging debtor and may direct that the receiver or manager take immediate possession of such property or any part thereof.

Joint and separate dividends

74.—If one or more of the partners of a firm is a bankrupt, any creditor of the firm shall be entitled to prove his debt or be admitted as a creditor for the purpose of voting in the choice and appointment of a creditors' assignee but such creditor shall not receive any dividend out of the separate estate of the bankrupt until all the separate creditors shall have received the full amount of their respective debts.

Debts provable in bankruptcy and arrangements

75.—(1) Debts and liabilities, present or future, certain or contingent, by reason of any obligation incurred by the bankrupt or arranging debtor before the date of adjudication or order for protection and claims in the nature of unliquidated damages for which the bankrupt or arranging debtor is liable at that date by reason of a wrong within the meaning of the Civil Liability Act, 1961 , shall be provable in the bankruptcy or arrangement.

(2) Where interest or any pecuniary consideration in lieu of interest is reserved or agreed for on a debt which is overdue at the date of adjudication, the creditor shall be entitled to prove or be admitted as a creditor for such interest or consideration up to the date of adjudication.

(3) Where all necessary parties agree, an order for assessment of damages or contribution under section 61 (2) of the Civil Liability Act, 1961 , may be made by the Court, notwithstanding that it may not be the court by or before which

the claim for damages or contribution falls to be determined.

(4) An estimate may be made by the Court of the value of any debt which, by reason of it being subject to any contingency or for any other reason, does not bear a certain value and the amount of the estimate shall be proved as a debt.

Proof of debts

76.—The provisions of the *First Schedule* shall apply in relation to the proof of debts.

Bankruptcy of mercantile agent

77.—Section 12 (2) of the Factors Act, 1889 (which regulates the rights of an owner of goods in the case of the bankruptcy of a mercantile agent to whom they have been entrusted) shall have effect with the substitution for the reference to a trustee in bankruptcy of a reference to the Official Assignee.

Proof for costs of judgement

78.—Where a party to any cause or matter has obtained a judgement or order against a person who is afterwards adjudicated bankrupt or is granted an order for protection for any debt for which he proves or is admitted a creditor, he shall also be entitled to prove or be admitted a creditor for the costs of the judgement or order, whether or not the costs have been taxed or ascertained at the date of the adjudication or order for protection.

Disallowance of debts already proved

79.—The Court may, on the application of the Official Assignee or any creditor or the bankrupt or arranging debtor, disallow, in whole or in part, any debt already proved or admitted.

Distribution of Estate

Priority of expenses, etc.

80.—The expenses, fees and costs of the bankruptcy shall be payable in priority to the liabilities of the bankrupt in such order as may be prescribed.

Preferential payments

81.—(1) In the distribution of the property of a bankrupt there shall be paid in priority to all other debts—

    (*a*) all local rates due from the bankrupt at the date of the order of adjudication, and having become due and payable within twelve months next before that date, and all property or income tax assessed on the bankrupt up to the 5th day of April next before the date of the order of adjudication, and not exceeding in the whole one year's assessment;

    (*b*) all wages or salary (whether or not earned wholly or in part by way of commission) of any clerk or servant in respect of services rendered to the bankrupt during the four months next before the date of the order of adjudication not exceeding £2,500;

(*c*) all wages not exceeding £2,500 of any labourer or workman (whether payable for time or for piece work) in respect of services rendered to the bankrupt during the four months next before the date of the order of adjudication: provided that, where any farm labourer has entered into a contract for the payment of a portion of his wages in a lump sum at the end of the year or other shorter term of hiring, the priority under this section shall extend to the whole of such sum, or a part thereof, as the Court may decide to be due under the contract proportionate to the time of service up to the date of the order of adjudication;

(*d*) all accrued holiday remuneration becoming payable to any clerk, servant, workman or labourer (or in the case of his death to any other person in his right) on the termination of his employment before or by the effect of the adjudication order;

(*e*) all sums due to any employee pursuant to any scheme or arrangement for the provision of payments to the employee while he is absent from employment owing to ill health;

(*f*) any payments due by the bankrupt pursuant to any scheme or arrangement for the provision of superannuation benefits to or in respect of employees of the bankrupt whether such payments are due in respect of the bankrupt's contribution to that scheme or under that arrangement or in respect of such contributions payable by the employees to the bankrupt under any such scheme or arrangement which have been deducted from the wages or salaries of employees;

(*g*) any debt, payment or contribution which by virtue of any provision in any enactment in operation before the commencement of this Act was included in the debts to which section 4 of the Preferential Payments in Bankruptcy (Ireland) Act, 1889, gave priority; and any reference to the said section 4 in any such enactment shall be construed as a reference to this subsection.

(2) The foregoing debts shall rank equally between themselves and be paid in full unless the property of the bankrupt is insufficient to meet them, in which case they shall abate in equal proportions between themselves.

(3) Subject to the retention of such sums as may be necessary for the costs and expenses of administration or otherwise, the foregoing debts shall be discharged forthwith so far as the property of the bankrupt is sufficient to meet them.

(4) In the event of a landlord or other person distraining or having distrained on any goods or effects of the bankrupt within three months next before the date of the order of adjudication, the debts to which priority is given by this section shall be a first charge on the goods or effects so distrained on, or the proceeds of sale thereof; provided that in respect of any money paid under any such charge the landlord or other person shall have the same rights of priority as the person to whom the payment is made.

(5) Any remuneration in respect of a period of holiday or absence from work through good cause shall be deemed to be wages in respect of services rendered

to the bankrupt during that period.

(6) Notwithstanding *section 4*, this section shall not apply where the order of adjudication was made before the commencement of this Act, and in such a case, the provisions relating to preferential payments which would have applied if this Act had not been passed shall be deemed to remain in full force.

(7) *Subsections (1), (2), (3), (5)* and *(6)* shall apply in the case of an arranging debtor under the provisions of this Act as if he were a bankrupt, and as if the date of the filing of the petition for arrangement were substituted for the date of the order of adjudication.

(8) Any creditor who, in the case of an arrangement, votes in respect of any debt to which priority is given by this section for or against the acceptance of the debtor's proposal or any modification thereof or, in the case of a composition after bankruptcy, votes in respect of any such debt for or against the acceptance of the bankrupt's offer of composition or any modification thereof shall by so voting be deemed to have abandoned any rights under *subsection (1)* and shall be remitted to such rights (if any) in respect of any of the debts therein mentioned as such creditor would have had apart from that subsection.

(9) This section shall apply in the case of a deceased person who dies insolvent as if he were a bankrupt and as if the date of his death were substituted for the date of the order of adjudication.

(10) Nothing in this section shall alter the effect of section 3 of the Partnership Act, 1890, or shall prejudice the provisions of section 14 of the Trustee Savings Banks Act, 1863, or the provisions of the Friendly Societies Act, 1896.

(1889, ss. 4,6; 33/1963, s. 285)

Distribution of estate

82.—(1) As soon as convenient after the receipt by him of sufficient funds to meet expenses, fees, costs and preferential payments and to pay a dividend to creditors in any bankrupt's estate the Official Assignee shall place on the Court file a list of creditors admitted by him or by the Court, a copy of the relevant account of the bankrupt in his books, particulars of expenses, fees, costs, preferential payments and dividend payable to creditors and his report on the realisation of the estate.

(2) The Official Assignee shall present the documents and the report filed in accordance with *subsection (1)* to the Court at a sitting to be held not less than twenty-one days after notice of the filing and of the sitting has been given in the prescribed manner.

(3) At the sitting the Court may make such order as it thinks fit for distribution of the estate or any part thereof by payment of the expenses, fees, costs and preferential payments as well as the relevant dividend.

(4) The file referred to in *subsection (1)* shall he open to public inspection on payment of a prescribed fee but no fee shall be charged to creditors inspecting the file.

(5) If for any reason the estate of the bankrupt is not fully distributed at such sitting, second and subsequent distributions shall be made as soon as convenient after the realisation of the residual estate. The procedure shall be the same as for the first distribution.

(6) In any case where there are no funds, or in the opinion of the Official Assignee insufficient funds, available for distribution to the creditors the Court may order the payment of expenses, fees and costs in that order so far as the funds extend. Where a balance remains, it shall be transferred to the account referred to in *section 84(1)*.

Accounts and audit

83.—Rules of court shall provide for the keeping of accounts by the Official Assignee and for the audit of these accounts.

Official Assignee-Unclaimed Dividend Account

84.—(1) The Official Assignee shall cause to be opened in the Central Bank of Ireland an account, to be called the "Official Assignee-Unclaimed Dividend Account", and all money and securities which, immediately before the commencement of this Act, stood to the credit of The Unclaimed Dividend Account or The Unclaimed Dividend Account, Cork, shall be carried into that Account.

(2) The Official Assignee shall pay into that Account all unclaimed dividends and all money unclaimed, being part of any bankrupt's estate.

(3)(*a*) The Official Assignee shall be entitled to pay out of that Account all dividends lawfully claimed as well as the sums provided for by *section 61 (3) (k)*.

  (*b*) In order to provide temporarily for payments for which no funds are immediately available in the particular estate against which they are chargeable, there may be paid out of that Account to the credit of the Official Assignee in a separate account in the said bank such sums, subject to such conditions, as may be prescribed.

(4) The Official Assignee, with the leave of the Court, may from time to time invest the whole or any part of the money standing to the credit of the Account, and the interest on the investments shall be paid into it.

(5) The Court may order that the Official Assignee shall be paid out of the Account such sum by way of indemnity in respect of any damages, costs or expenses payable or incurred or to be payable or incurred by him for or by reason of any act or matter done by him while acting in his official capacity as the Court thinks just, including the costs of any proceedings taken by the Official Assignee with the leave of the Court where there are insufficient funds in the matter.

(6) The Account shall not be available for any purpose other than the purposes of this section.

Discharge and annulment

85.—(1) Any bankruptcy subsisting at the commencement of this Act where the order of adjudication in respect thereof was made before 1st January, 1960, is hereby discharged.

(2) Where an adjudication order is discharged by virtue of the provisions of *subsection (1)* any property of the bankrupt which remains vested in the Official

Assignee shall after provision has been made for the payment of the expenses, fees, costs and preferential payments be returned to the bankrupt and shall be deemed to be revested in him as and from the commencement of this Act.

(3) A bankrupt shall be entitled to a discharge from bankruptcy—

    (*a*) when provision has been made for payment of the expenses, fees and costs due in the bankruptcy, as well as the preferential payments, and

        (i) he has paid one pound in the pound, with such interest as the Court may allow, or

       (ii) he or she has obtained the consent of all of his or her creditors who have proved and been admitted in the bankruptcy—

           (I) to his or her discharge, and

          (II) to the waiver of their rights to the amounts for which they have respectively so proved and been admitted,

        as evidenced by the creditors have executed the form prescribed for the purposes of such consent, or

    (*b*) in a case to which *section 41* applies.

(4) A bankrupt whose estate has, in the opinion of the Court, been fully realised shall be entitled to a discharge from bankruptcy when provision has been made for payment of the expenses, fees and costs due in the bankruptcy, as well as the preferential payments, and—

    (*a*) his creditors have received fifty pence or more in the pound, or

    (*b*) he or his friends have paid to his creditors such additional sums as will together with the dividend paid make up fifty pence in the pound, or

    (*c*) the bankruptcy has subsisted for twelve years:

provided that in any application under *paragraph (c)* the Court shall be satisfied that all after-acquired property has been disclosed and that it is reasonable and proper to grant the application.

(5) A person shall be entitled to an annulment of his adjudication—

    (*a*) where he has shown cause pursuant to *section 16*, or

    (*b*) in any other case where, in the opinion of the Court, he ought not to have been adjudicated bankrupt.

(6) An order of discharge or annulment shall provide that any property of the bankrupt then vested in the Official Assignee shall be revested in or returned to the bankrupt, and that order shall for all purposes be deemed to be a conveyance, assignment or transfer of that property to the bankrupt and, where appropriate, may be registered accordingly.

(7) A person who is entitled to a discharge or annulment may apply to the Court to obtain a certificate of discharge or annulment, as the case may require, under the seal of the Court.

(8) In this section "bankrupt" includes personal representatives and assigns.

Surplus

86.—(1) If the estate of any bankrupt is sufficient to pay one pound in the pound, with interest at the rate currently payable on judgment debts, and to leave a surplus the Court shall order such surplus to be paid or delivered to or vested in the bankrupt, his personal representatives or assigns.

(2) The order shall for all purposes be deemed to be a conveyance, assignment or transfer of property and, where appropriate, may be registered accordingly.

PART IV

ARRANGEMENTS UNDER CONTROL OF COURT

Petition for protection

87.—(1) Any debtor unable to meet his engagements with his creditors and wishing to place the state of his affairs before them with a view to making a proposal for the composition of his debts, under the control of the Court, and to subject himself to the jurisdiction of the Court as provided by this Part may present a petition to the Court setting out the reason for his inability to pay his debts and requesting that his person and property may be protected until further order from any action or other process.

(2) The Court, on such petition, may by order grant such protection and renew the same from time to time as it thinks fit.

(3) The Court may refuse to grant protection to any debtor who is a member of a partnership, unless all the partners join in the petition.

(4) In this section "process" includes a bankruptcy summons and the registration of an affidavit of a judgement under the Judgement Mortgage (Ireland) Act, 1850.

(5) While an order for protection is in force a creditor shall not be entitled to register any affidavit referred to in *subsection (4)* and any purported registration shall be of no effect.

(6) If a debtor, at the time of his petition, is in prison by virtue of section 6 of the Enforcement of Court Orders Act, 1940 , the Court, on granting protection, may order his release.

Restriction on dealing with property

88.—After an order for protection has been granted and so long as it is in force the arranging debtor shall not, without the prior sanction of the Court, pledge, part with or dispose of his property or any part thereof, save in the ordinary course of trade or business.

Effect of protection on execution orders

89.—(1) An order for protection may be granted notwithstanding that there is an execution order in the hands of a sheriff or county registrar and the order shall operate to protect against execution save as provided by this section.

(2) The order for protection shall not affect an execution order on foot of which the sheriff or county registrar has made a seizure or gone into possession, and in such case the execution creditor may recover such amount of his debt as may be realised by the execution.

(3) In any case when the sheriff or county registrar has not made a seizure

or gone into possession on foot of an execution order, the order for protection shall protect the debtor from further process in respect thereof and the execution creditor shall be bound by the arrangement.

Procedure on grant of protection

90.—On the granting of an order for protection—
   (*a*) the Court shall direct the arranging debtor to call a preliminary meeting of his creditors at which meeting the arranging debtor shall present a statement of his assets and liabilities and keep a minute of the proceedings;
   (*b*) the Court shall direct a private sitting before the Court (to be held at a date specified in the order) for the purpose of considering his proposal;
   (*c*) the arranging debtor shall deliver forthwith to the Official Assignee a memorandum containing:
      (i) the date of the order for protection,
      (ii) his name and address,
      (iii) the amount of liabilities secured, partly secured and unsecured,
      (iv) the amount of assets,
and shall deliver a duplicate of the said memorandum to the Central Office.

Filing of statements

91.—The arranging debtor shall file in the Official Assignee's Office no later that seven days after the conclusion of the preliminary meeting before the private sitting referred to in *section 90*—
   (*a*) a statement of affairs in the prescribed form, which shall have endorsed thereon such proposal as he is able to make for the future payment or compromise of the debts or engagements set out therein, and
   (*b*) a copy of the statement submitted at the preliminary meeting and of the minute of the proceedings with any proposal made thereat or at any adjournment thereof.

Acceptance of proposal

92.—(1)(*a*) If, at the private sitting referred to in *section 90* or any adjournment thereof, three-fifths in number and value of the creditors voting at such sitting either in person or by an agent authorised in writing in that behalf accept the proposal or any modification thereof, it shall he deemed to be accepted by the creditors, subject to the approval of the Court.
   (*b*) If approved by the Court, the proposal or any modification thereof shall be binding on the arranging debtor and on all persons who were creditors at the date of the petition and who had notice of the sitting.
   (2) A creditor whose debt is less than €130 shall not be entitled to vote.
   (3) The arranging debtor shall attend the sitting and the Court shall have

power to examine him on oath or any witness produced by him or any creditor or person claiming to be a creditor.

(4) The Court may require any person so examined to sign a transcript of his evidence.

(5) Debts may be proved at the sitting.

Vesting in Official Assignee

93.—(1) If the proposal provides for the vesting of all or part of the arranging debtor's property in the Official Assignee either as security for an offer or for realisation and distribution, that property shall vest in the Official Assignee, if he consents, in accordance with the terms of the proposal on the approval of the proposal by the Court.

(2) Where all or part of the property is vested in the Official Assignee for realisation and distribution, the Official Assignee shall have for that purpose all such powers in relation to the property as he has in a bankruptcy matter. A proposal under which property is so vested is referred to in this Act as a "vesting arrangement".

(3) *Section 46* (which relates to a certificate of vesting) shall apply to property which vests in the Official Assignee under this section.

Distribution of property in vesting arrangement

94.—(1) When the Official Assignee has sufficient funds to implement the terms of a vesting arrangement he shall present to the Court for approval a list of creditors admitted by him or by the Court, a copy of the relevant account of the arranging debtor in his books, particulars of expenses, fees, costs, preferential payments and dividend payable to creditors and his report on the realisation of the estate.

(2) The Court may make such order as it thinks fit for the distribution of the estate or any part thereof by payment of the expenses, fees, costs and preferential payments as well as the relevant dividend.

(3) The report and the account, together with the order of the Court, shall then be filed in the Central Office and shall be open to inspection by each creditor to whom notice of filing has been given in such form as may be prescribed. No fee shall be charged for inspecting the file.

(4) If for any reason the estate of the arranging debtor is not fully distributed by such order, second and subsequent distributions shall be made as soon as convenient after the realisation of the residual estate. The procedure shall be the same as for the first distribution.

(5) In any case where there are no funds, or in the opinion of the Official Assignee insufficient funds, available for distribution to the creditors, the Court may order the payment of expenses, fees and costs in that order so far as the funds extend. Where a balance remains, it shall be transferred to the account referred to in *section 84(1)*.

Special private sitting

95.—(1) Where a proposal has been approved and the Court considers it necessary and desirable so to do, the Court may on the application of the arranging debtor cause a special private sitting to be held.

(2) At this sitting the majority in number and value of the creditors who have proved debts of not less than €130 may confirm, alter or annul the proposal.

(3) If, however, one-third in number and value of such creditors do not attend the sitting, the decision at the sitting shall not be valid unless it is approved by the Court.

Carrying proposal into effect

96.—A proposal shall be considered to be carried into effect—
- (*a*) in the case of a vesting arrangement, on the approval thereof by the Court, and
- (*b*) in any other case, at such time as may be prescribed.

Lodgement with Official Assignee

97.—Where the proposal of an arranging debtor (not being a proposal providing for the vesting of all or part of his property in the Official Assignee for realisation and distribution) has been approved, the arranging debtor shall, within the prescribed period, lodge with the Official Assignee for purposes of distribution the necessary amount to pay expenses, fees, costs and the preferential payments, together with the cash, bills or promissory notes (if any) provided for in the proposal.

Certificate of arranging debtor

98.—Where the proposal of the arranging debtor has been carried into effect, the Court shall, on the report of the Official Assignee and in the absence of fraud, grant to the arranging debtor a certificate under the seal of the Court, and the certificate shall operate as a discharge to the arranging debtor from the claims of creditors who received notice of the arrangement.

Publication in relation to arrangements

99.—(1) No publication of the affairs of the petitioner or of the proceedings in an arrangement matter shall take place without the sanction of the Court other than the publication in a bona fide trade journal of the particulars set out in the documents filed in the Central Office under *section 90*.

(2) Any person who contravenes *subsection (1)* shall be guilty of an offence.

Taking possession of property by Official Assignee

100.—The Court may, on the application of the Official Assignee or any creditor, at any time after an order for protection is made (and on sufficient cause shown) direct that the property of the arranging debtor or any part thereof shall be possessed and received by the Official Assignee.

Discharge of protection order

101.—The Court may, at any time after the private sitting referred to in *section 90*, order that the order for protection be discharged on application to that effect being made by the arranging debtor with the concurrence of every creditor who had notice of the private sitting and whose debt is not less than €130.

Surplus

102.—(1) Whenever it appears to the Court that there remains vested in or in the possession or control of the Official Assignee any property of an arranging debtor who has obtained the certificate mentioned in *section 98* the Court shall order that it be revested in or returned to, as the case may be, the debtor, his personal representatives or assigns.

(2) The order shall for all purposes be deemed to be a conveyance, assignment or transfer of property and, where appropriate, may be registered accordingly.

Goods obtained on credit

103.—If within fourteen days before an order for protection is made the debtor obtains goods on credit knowing at the time that he will be unable to pay for them the Court, on the application of the creditor, may, if it thinks fit, direct either the return of the goods or payment for them in full.

Private sitting for enquiry

104.—The Court may at any time in an arrangement matter, on the application of the Official Assignee or any person having an interest, appoint a private sitting for enquiry and summon before it the arranging debtor or any other person and examine him upon any matter which the Court considers relevant to the arrangement.

Adjudication of arranging debtor

105.—(1) The Court may, if it thinks fit, adjudicate the debtor bankrupt if—

(*a*) he does not, in the prescribed manner and within the time specified in *section 91*, file the documents required by that section, or

(*b*) at the private sitting referred to in *section 90* or any adjournment thereof his proposal or any modification thereof is not accepted or approved, or

(*c*) his proposal is annulled under *section 95 (2)*, or

(*d*) at any time after the presentation of his petition for arrangement it is shown that the affidavit filed with the petition is wilfully untrue or that he has not made a full disclosure of his property, assets and liabilities, or

(*e*) it appears that he does not wish to make a *bona fide* arrangement with all his creditors, or

(*f*) his proposal is not reasonable and proper to be executed under the direction of the Court, or (*g*) he does not duly attend the private sitting or any adjournment thereof, or

(*h*) he fails to obey any order of the Court affecting him which may be made in the arrangement matter, or

(*i*) he is party to any corrupt agreement with his creditors to secure the acceptance of his proposal.

(2) On an adjudication under *subsection (1)* the Court shall proceed as in bankruptcy and cause notice of the adjudication to be given forthwith in the prescribed manner in *Iris Oifigiúil* and in at least one daily newspaper, and the petitioner shall be subject to the jurisdiction of the Court in the same manner as any other bankrupt, and any proposal which may have been made or accepted or approved shall be void.

Partners obtaining protection of the Court

106.—(1) Where two or more members of a partnership obtain the protection of the Court and make proposals to their creditors for the payment or compromise of their joint and several liabilities, the Court shall adjudicate all the members bankrupt if any of the proposals are not accepted.

(2) On an adjudication under *subsection (1)* the Court shall proceed as in bankruptcy and cause notice of the adjudication to be given forthwith in the prescribed manner in *Iris Oifigiúil* and in at least one daily newspaper, and the petitioner shall be subject to the jurisdiction of the Court in the same manner as any other bankrupt, and any proposal which may have been made or accepted or approved shall be void.

Summoning witnesses

107.—The procedure for summoning witnesses in an arrangement matter shall be the same as in bankruptcy and the Court shall have similar powers of enforcing their attendance.

Registration of arrangements

108.—(1) A register shall be maintained in the Central Office for the filing of memoranda delivered to that office under *section 90*.

(2) Rules of court may provide for matters ancillary to the keeping of the register.

Exclusion of Deeds of Arrangement Act, 1887

109.—The Deeds of Arrangement Act, 1887, shall not apply to an 4 arrangement under this Part.

PART V

WINDING UP BY TRUSTEE

Order for winding up

110.—If, at the statutory sitting referred to in *section 17 (3)* or at any adjournment thereof, at least three-fifths in number and value of the creditors voting at the meeting, either in person or by a person authorised in writing in that behalf, by resolution declare that the estate of the bankrupt be wound up by a trustee and a committee of inspection, and appoint for that purpose a trustee and a committee of inspection of not more than five creditors qualified to vote at the meeting, the Court, on application being made to it in that behalf, may order that the property of the bankrupt be so wound up.

Vesting in trustee

111.—On the making of an order under *section 110* the Official Assignee shall be divested of the property of the bankrupt vesting in him under this Act and such property shall vest in the trustee.

Powers of trustee, etc.

112.—(1) In the winding up the trustee shall be subject to the control of the Court and have regard to any directions given to him by the committee of inspection or by resolution of the creditors at the statutory sitting or any subsequent sitting.

(2) Subject to *subsection (1)*, the trustee shall have all the powers and may perform all the functions conferred by this Act on the Official Assignee in relation to property vested in him and the provisions of this Act (other than those of *Parts IV* and *VI*) shall apply, with any necessary modifications, in relation to the winding up of the property of a bankrupt by a trustee and a committee of inspection as they apply in relation to the administration of such property by the Official Assignee and the trustee shall be substituted for the Official Assignee in such provisions where appropriate.

(3) The statutory sitting shall make provision for:

   (*a*) the remuneration of the trustee,
   (*b*) the making of regular reports by the trustee at subsequent sittings in relation to the winding up,
   (*c*) the procedure to be followed by the trustee in the lodgment of monies received by him,
   (*d*) the audit of the trustee's accounts, and
   (*e*) such other matters as may be prescribed.

Order of discharge

113.—When the bankrupt's property has been fully realised and a final dividend has been paid to the creditors, the trustee shall report to the Court, and the Court, if satisfied that the estate has been fully wound up, shall declare the bankruptcy discharged and order that the trustee be released.

Powers of Court

114.—Where an order is made under this Part for the winding up of the bankrupt's property by a trustee and a committee of inspection, the Court shall, subject to the provisions of this Part, have power to make such orders and give such directions in relation to the bankrupt, his creditors, debtors and property and in relation to the examination of persons (including the bankrupt) and other matters as it would have had if a trustee and a committee of inspection had not been appointed under this Part.

PART VI

Estates of Persons Dying Insolvent

Petition to administer in bankruptcy estate of person dying insolvent

115.—(1) A petition for the administration under this Part of the estate of a deceased person may be presented to the Court by—
> (*a*) any creditor whose debt would have been sufficient to support a bankruptcy petition against the deceased if he had been alive, or
> (*b*) the personal representative of the deceased.

(2) Where the petition is presented by a creditor, notice thereof shall be served on the personal representative of the deceased.

(3) Where there is no known personal representative, the Court may direct service on such person and in such manner as it thinks fit or may dispense with service.

(4) A petition for administration under this Part shall not be presented to the Court after proceedings have been commenced in the Circuit Court for the administration of the deceased's estate, but that court may, when satisfied that the estate is insufficient to pay the debts, transfer the proceedings to the Court, and thereupon the Court may make an order for the administration under this Part of the deceased's estate.

Effect on personal representative of service of notice of petition

116.—(1) After service on the personal representative of notice of the presentation of a petition, no payment or transfer of property made by the personal representative shall operate as a discharge to him as between himself and the Official Assignee.

(2) Except as aforesaid, nothing in this Part shall invalidate any payment made or any act or thing done in good faith by the personal representative before the date of the order for the administration under this Part of the deceased's estate.

Order for administration under *Part VI*

117.—(1) On presentation of a petition the Court may, unless it appears that there is a reasonable probability that the estate will be sufficient for the payment of the deceased's debts, make an order for the administration under this Part of the deceased's estate or may, upon cause shown, dismiss the petition with or without costs.

(2) Where the petition is presented by a creditor, he shall prove his debt to the Court before an order is made.

(3) An order may be made under this section notwithstanding that there is no known personal representative of the deceased.

Vesting and distribution

118.—(1) Upon an order being made for the administration under this Part of the deceased's estate, his property shall vest in the Official Assignee for realisation and distribution.

(2) *Section 46* (which relates to a certificate of vesting) shall apply to property which vests in the Official Assignee under this section.

Priority of funeral and testamentary expenses

119.—In the administration under this Part of the deceased's estate, the proper funeral and testamentary expenses incurred shall, notwithstanding anything to the contrary in this or any other enactment, be payable in full in priority to all other payments.

Application of Act

120.—The provisions of this Act shall, so far as they are applicable and with appropriate modifications, apply in the case of an order for administration under this Part as they apply in the case of an order of adjudication except that *sections 50, 57, 58* and *59* shall not apply.

Surplus

121.—(1) Where, on the administration under this Part of the deceased's estate, any property remains vested in, or in the possession or control of the Official Assignee after providing for the expenses, fees and costs, together with the debts and liabilities and interest at the rate currently payable on judgement debts, the Court shall order the property to be paid or delivered to or vested in the personal representative of the deceased or, if there is no personal representative, in such manner as the Court may direct.

(2) The order shall for all purposes be deemed to be a conveyance, assignment or transfer of property and, where appropriate, may be registered accordingly.

Right of retainer restricted

122.—Where an order is made for administration under this Part, the right of retainer of a personal representative shall not be exercisable but he may prove any debt due to him which would otherwise be provable.

PART VII

OFFENCES

Punishment of fraudulent debtors

123.—(1) Subject to *subsection (2)*, if a bankrupt or arranging debtor—

    (*a*) fails to disclose to the Court, or to the Official Assignee or to such person or persons as the Court from time to time directs, all his property and how and to whom and for what consideration and when he disposed of any part thereof, except such part as has been disposed of in the ordinary way of his trade (if any) or laid out in the ordinary expense of his family, or

    (*b*) fails to deliver up to the Official Assignee, or as he or the Court directs, all such part of his property as is in his possession or under his control, and which he is required by law to deliver up, or

    (*c*) fails to deliver up to the Official Assignee, or as he or the Court directs, all books and papers in his possession or under his control relating to his estate and which he is required by law to deliver up, or

    (*d*) conceals any part of his property to the value of £500 or upwards, or conceals any debt due to or from him, or

    (*e*) fraudulently removes any part of his property to the value of £500 or upwards, or

    (*f*) fails to file or deliver a statement of affairs as required by *section 19 (c)* or makes any material omission in any statement relating to his affairs, or

    (*g*) knowing or believing that a false debt has been proved by any person under the bankruptcy or arrangement, fails for the period of a month to inform the Official Assignee thereof, or

    (*h*) prevents the production of any book or paper affecting or relating to his estate, or

    (*i*) conceals, destroys, mutilates or falsifies or is privy to the concealment, destruction, mutilation or falsification of any book or paper affecting or relating to his estate, or

    (*j*) makes or is privy to the making of any false entry in any book or paper affecting or relating to his estate, or

    (*k*) fraudulently parts with, alters or makes any omission in, or is privy to the fraudulent parting with, altering or making any omission in, any document affecting or relating to his estate, or

    (*l*) attempts to account for any part of his property by fictitious losses or expenses, or

    (*m*) obtains, by any fraud or false representation, any property on credit, or

    (*n*) obtains, under the false pretence of carrying on business and, if a trader, of dealing in the ordinary way of his trade, any property on credit, or

    (*o*) pawns, pledges or disposes of any property which he has obtained on credit, unless, in the case of a trader, such pawning, pledging or disposing is in the ordinary way of his trade, or

(*p*) is guilty of any fraud or false representation for the purpose of
obtaining the consent of his creditors or any of them to an agreement
with reference to his affairs or the bankruptcy or arrangement;
he shall be guilty of an offence.

(2) It shall be a good defence to a charge under any of *paragraphs (a), (b),
(c), (d), (f), (n)* and *(o)* of *subsection (1)* if the accused proves that he had no
intent to defraud and to a charge under any of paragraphs (h), (i) and (j) of that
subsection if he proves that he had no intent to conceal the state of his affairs
or to defeat the law.

(3)(*a*) A person (other than a bankrupt or arranging debtor) who, with intent
to defraud his creditors, does any of the acts mentioned in *paragraphs
(e), (i), (j), (k), (1), (m), (n)* or *(o)* of *subsection (1)*, shall be guilty of an
offence and for this purpose references in *paragraphs (e)* or (*k*) to an
act which is fraudulent or is committed fraudulently shall be construed
as references to an act done with intent to defraud creditors.

(*b*) Where a person referred to in *paragraph (a)* of this subsection does
an act therein specified within twelve months next before he is
adjudicated or granted an order for protection, it shall be presumed
until the contrary is proved that the act was done with intent to defraud
his creditors.

(4) Where any person pawns, pledges or disposes of any property in
circumstances which amount to an offence under *paragraph (o)* of *subsection (1)*
or under *subsection (3)*, every person who takes in pawn or pledge or otherwise
receives the property knowing it to be pawned, pledged or disposed of in such
circumstances as aforesaid shall also be guilty of an offence and shall be liable
to be punished in the same way as if he had been guilty of an offence under the
said *paragraph (o)*or *subsection (3)*.

Absconding debtor

124.—If any person with intent to defraud his creditors leaves the State and
takes with him, or attempts or makes preparation to leave the State and take
with him, any part of his property to the amount of £500 or upwards, he shall
be guilty of an offence.

Corrupt agreement with creditors

125.—If any creditor of a bankrupt or an arranging debtor obtains or accepts
any property from the bankrupt or arranging debtor or any other person as an
inducement for forbearing to oppose, or for accepting any offer of composition
or proposal or any modification thereof made by or on behalf of the bankrupt or
arranging debtor, the claim of the creditor shall be void and irrecoverable and
the creditor and such other person (if any) shall each be guilty of an offence.

False claim

126.—If any creditor, or any person claiming to be a creditor, in any
bankruptcy or arrangement with intent to defraud makes any false claim or
any proof, declaration or statement of account which is untrue in any material

particular, he shall be guilty of an offence.

Non-disclosure of after-acquired property

127.—A bankrupt who fails to disclose to the Official Assignee any after-acquired property shall be guilty of an offence.

Obstructing officers

128.—Any person who knowingly and wilfully resists, hinders or obstructs the Bankruptcy Inspector or any of his assistants or any other person in the execution of his duties under this Act shall be guilty of an offence.

Obtaining credit or trading under other name

129.—A bankrupt or an arranging debtor who—
- (*a*) either alone or jointly with any other person obtains credit to the extent of £500 or upwards from any person without informing that person that he is a bankrupt or an arranging debtor, or
- (*b*) engages in any trade or business under a name other than that under which he was adjudicated bankrupt or granted protection without disclosing to all persons with whom he enters into any business transactions the name under which he was so adjudicated or granted protection,

shall be guilty of an offence.

Inserting advertisement without authority

130.—Any person who wilfully inserts or causes any advertisement under this Act to be inserted in *Iris Oifigiúil* or in any newspaper without authority under this Act, or knowing the same to be false in any material particular, shall be guilty of an offence.

Criminal liability after annulment

131.—Where a bankrupt or arranging debtor has been guilty of any offence, he shall not be exempt from being proceeded against for the offence by reason that his bankruptcy has been discharged or annulled or that his proposal has been carried into effect.

Punishment of offences

132.—(1) Every person guilty of an offence under this Act shall be liable—
- (*a*) on summary conviction, to a fine not exceeding £500 or, at the discretion of the Court, to imprisonment for a term not exceeding twelve months or to both the fine and the imprisonment, or
- (*b*) on conviction on indictment, to a fine not exceeding £1,000 or, at the discretion of the Court, to imprisonment for a term not exceeding five years or to both the fine and the imprisonment.

(2) Section 13 of the Criminal Procedure Act, 1967 , shall apply in relation to

an offence under this Act as if, in lieu of the penalties provided for in subsection (3) of the said section, there were specified therein the penalties provided for in *subsection (1) (a)* of this section, and the reference in subsection (2) *(a)* of the said section 13 to the penalties provided for in the said subsection (3) shall be construed and have effect accordingly.

PART VIII

MISCELLANEOUS

Limitation of actions

133.—The Official Assignee shall not be a trustee for the purposes, of the Statute of Limitations, 1957 .

Proceedings in private

134.—The Court may direct that the whole or any part of any sitting of the Court or proceeding in any matter under this Act shall be in private.

Power of Court to review its orders

135.—The Court may review, rescind or vary an order made by it in the course of a bankruptcy matter other than an order of discharge or annulment.

Effect of adjudication on creditors' remedies

136.—(1) On the making of an order of adjudication, a creditor to whom the bankrupt is indebted for any debt provable in bankruptcy shall not have any remedy against the property or person of the bankrupt in respect of the debt apart from his rights under this Act, and he shall not commence any proceedings in respect of such debt unless with the leave of the Court and on such terms as the Court may impose.

(2) This section shall not affect the power of a secured creditor to realise or otherwise deal with his security in the same manner as he would have been entitled to realise or deal with it if this section had not been enacted.

Power to stay or restrain proceeding against bankrupt

137.—(1) The Official Assignee may—

(*a*) where any proceedings against the bankrupt are pending in the High Court or on appeal in the Supreme Court, apply to the court in which the proceedings are pending for a stay of proceedings therein, and

(*b*) where any other proceedings are pending against the bankrupt, apply to the High Court to restrain further proceedings therein,

and the court to which the application is made may grant the application on such terms and for such period as it thinks fit.

(2) Where any proceedings against a bankrupt are stayed or restrained in pursuance of *subsection (1)*, the following provisions shall have effect:

(*a*) the creditor shall not be liable for any costs incurred by the bankrupt or the Official Assignee in such proceedings;

(b) if the proceedings have been instituted against the bankrupt jointly with any other person, the proceedings against that other person shall not thereby be affected.

Winding up of partnerships and deceased persons' states

138.—(1) The Court may, upon giving notice to such persons as it may direct, make such orders and give such directions as it thinks proper for winding up and settling the affairs of any partnership or the estate of a deceased person in which the bankrupt has an interest.

(2) All consequential accounts and enquiries shall be taken and made in such office of the Court as the Court may direct.

Prohibition on distress after adjudication or protection

139.—No distress shall be levied on the goods of a bankrupt or an arranging debtor after the date of the adjudication or order for protection.

Evidence of deceased person

140.—In the case of the death of any witness who has made a deposition in any proceeding under this Act the deposition, purporting d to be sealed with the seal of the Court, or a copy thereof purporting to be so sealed, shall be evidence of the matters therein deposed to.

Registration of judgments given in insolvency proceedings

140A.—(1) Without prejudice to Article 16(1) of the Insolvency Regulation, a liquidator who intends—

(a) to request under Article 21 of the Regulation that notice of the judgment opening the insolvency proceedings concerned and, where appropriate, the decision appointing him or her be published in the State, or

(b) to take any other action in the State under the Regulation, shall deliver to the Official Assignee, for registration in a register to be kept for that purpose, a duly certified copy of the judgment and, where appropriate, of the decision appointing the liquidator.

(2) Registration under subsection (1) may also be effected by the Official Assignee on application by a liquidator who does not intend to take any action in the State under the Insolvency Regulation.

(3) The certified copy or copies mentioned in subsection (1) shall be accompanied by—

(a) if the judgment or decision is not expressed in Irish or English, a translation, certified to be correct by a person competent to do so, into either of those languages,

(b) the prescribed form, and

(c) any prescribed fee.

(4) The Official Assignee shall issue to the liquidator a certified copy of the entry in the register.

(5) The register shall be open to public inspection on payment of a prescribed fee.

(6) A copy of an entry in the register shall be supplied, on request, by the Official Assignee.

(7) In any proceedings a document purporting to be—
- (a) a duly certified copy of a judgment opening insolvency proceedings or a decision appointing a liquidator in such proceedings, or
- (b) a translation of such a document which is certified as correct by a person competent to do so,

shall, without further proof, be admissible as evidence of the judgment, the liquidator's appointment or the translation, unless the contrary is shown.

Publication in relation to insolvency proceedings

140B.—(1) In this section 'publication' means publication of-
- (a) notice of the judgment opening the insolvency proceedings concerned,
- (b) where appropriate, the decision appointing the liquidator,
- (c) the name and business address of the liquidator, and
- (d) the provision (either paragraph 1 or paragraph 2) of Article 3 of the Insolvency Regulation giving jurisdiction to open the proceedings,

in the prescribed manner in Iris Oifigiúil and in at least one daily newspaper circulating in the State.

(2) Without prejudice to section 140A(1), publication shall be effected by the liquidator concerned.

(3) Where the debtor has an establishment (within the meaning of Article 2(h) of the Insolvency Regulation) in the State, the liquidator or any authority mentioned in Article 21(2) of the Regulation shall ensure that publication takes place as soon as practicable after the opening of the insolvency proceedings.

Provision of certain documents to Official Assignee

140C.—Where—
- (a) a debtor is adjudicated bankrupt,
- (b) the Court approves of a proposal for vesting the property of a debtor in the Official Assignee under Part IV, or
- (c) an order is made by the Court for the administration under Part VI of a deceased's estate,

the Court shall, on application by the Official Assignee -
- (i) certify that the Official Assignee is the liquidator within the meaning of the Insolvency Regulation, being the person whose function it is to administer or liquidate the assets of the debtor, or deceased debtor, concerned, and
- (ii) arrange for a certified copy of the order made for the purposes of paragraph (a), (b) or (c) to be supplied to the Official Assignee.",

Notice in *Iris Oifigiúil* or newspaper

141.—A notice published pursuant to this Act in *Iris Oifigiúil* or in any newspaper shall be evidence of the matters contained in the notice.

Acting in aid of other courts

142.—(1) The Court and its officers may act in aid of any court in the Isle of Man or the Channel Islands, and its officers respectively, at the request of such court, in any bankruptcy matter before such court, and the Court and its officers so acting shall have the like jurisdiction and authority as in the case of a bankruptcy originating under an order of the Court.

(2)(*a*) The Government may by order apply *subsection (1)* in relation to any other jurisdiction where the Government are satisfied that reciprocal facilities to that effect will be afforded by that jurisdiction.

(*b*) An order under this subsection may be made subject to such conditions, exceptions and qualifications as may be specified in the order.

(*c*) The Government may by order amend or revoke an order under this subsection.

(*d*) An order under this subsection shall have the force of law in accordance with its terms.

(*e*) On the revocation of, an order applying *subsection (1)* in relation to any jurisdiction, that subsection shall cease to apply in relation to that jurisdiction.

(*f*) Every order under this subsection shall be published in *Iris Oifigiúil* as soon as may be.

Alteration of monetary limits

143.—The Minister may by order increase or reduce any of the sums specified in *sections 8 (1) (a)* and *(2), 11 (1) (a), 15, 39 (4), 45 (1), 61 (3) (h)* and *(k), 81 (1) (b)* and *(c), 92 (2), 95 (2),* and *101*, but such an order shall not affect any case in which a person was adjudicated bankrupt or granted protection before it came into force.

Laying of orders before Houses of Oireachtas

144.—Every order made under *section 142 (2)* or *143* shall be laid before each House of the Oireachtas as soon as may be after it is made and, if a resolution annulling the order is passed by either House within the next twenty-one days on which that House has sat after the order is laid before it, the order shall be annulled accordingly, but without prejudice to the validity of anything previously done thereunder.

FIRST SCHEDULE

PROOF OF DEBTS

General

1. Every creditor shall prove his debt and a creditor who does not do so is not entitled to share in any distribution that may be made.

2. (*a*) A creditor may prove his debt by delivering or sending by post to the Official Assignee particulars of his debt (in this Schedule referred to as a "proof of debt").

   (*b*) *Subparagraph (a)* is without prejudice to the entitlement of a creditor to prove his debt at a sitting of the Court.

3. The Official Assignee may fix a time within which proofs of debt shall be sent to him. A proof submitted thereafter shall not be allowed except by order of the Court.

4. Proof of debt may be furnished by way of a detailed statement of account, an affidavit of debt or other prescribed means.

5. The creditor shall specify the vouchers or any other evidence by which the debt can be substantiated. He shall also give particulars of any counterclaim that, to his knowledge, the bankrupt or arranging debtor may have, and he shall indicate whether or not he is a secured creditor.

6. Proof of debt in respect of money lent by a moneylender shall have annexed thereto the particulars required by section 16 (2) of the Moneylenders Act, 1933.

7. An affidavit shall be required in any case where the debt is disputed or the Court or the Official Assignee thinks fit.

8. Proof of debt may be given by the oath or affidavit of the creditor himself or by the oath or affidavit of some person authorised by or on behalf of the creditor and, if made by a person so authorised, shall state his authority and means of knowledge.

9. Subject to *paragraph 24 (5)*, a creditor may, with the consent of the Official Assignee, amend his proof of debt.

10. Every creditor who has lodged a proof of debt is entitled to see and examine the proofs of other creditors.

11. A husband and wife may prove a debt against each other as if they were not married.

12. A sole trustee (including a personal representative) who is a bankrupt or an arranging debtor shall be entitled, without leave of the Court, to prove in his own bankruptcy or arrangement in respect of a debt due from him to the trust estate. Any dividend in respect of such a debt shall be paid to the Accountant of the High Court for credit of the trust estate.

13. If any bankrupt or arranging debtor, at the date of the adjudication or order for protection, is liable in respect of distinct contracts, as a member of two or more distinct firms, or as a sole contractor, and also as member of a firm, the circumstance that such firms are, in whole or in part, composed of the same individuals, or that the sole contractor is also one of the joint contractors, shall

not prevent proof in respect of such contracts against the properties respectively liable upon such contracts.

14. On any debt or sum certain, payable at a certain time or otherwise, whereon interest is not reserved or agreed for, and which is overdue at the date of the adjudication, the creditor may prove for interest at the rate currently payable on judgement debts to that date from the time when the debt or sum was payable, if the debt or sum is payable by virtue of a written instrument at a certain time, and if payable otherwise, then from the time when a demand in writing has been made, giving notice that interest will be claimed from the date of the demand until the time of payment.

15. In respect of debts due after the adjudication or order for protection, the liability for which existed at the date of such adjudication or order for protection, a creditor may prove for the value of the debt at that date.

16. Where a person who is liable to make any periodical payment (including rent) is adjudicated bankrupt or is granted an order for protection on a day other than the day on which such payment becomes due, the person entitled to the payment may prove for a proportionate part of the payment for the period from the date when the last payment became due to the date of the adjudication or order for protection as if the payment accrued due from day to day.

17. (1) Where there are mutual credits or debts as between a bankrupt and any person claiming as a creditor, one debt or demand may be set off against the other and only the balance found owing shall be recoverable on one side or the other.

(2) Section 36 of the Civil Liability Act, 1961 (which provides for the set-off of claims), as amended by section 5 of the Civil Liability (Amendment) Act, 1964 , shall apply with the substitution in section 36 (3) of a reference to *subparagraph (1)* for the reference to section 251 of the Irish Bankrupt and Insolvent Act, 1857.

18. This Schedule is without prejudice to section 61 of the Civil Liability Act, 1961 (which provides for proof of claims for damages or contribution in respect of a wrong) and section 62 of the said Act (which provides for the application of moneys payable under certain policies of insurance where the insured becomes a bankrupt).

19. A creditor shall, unless the Court otherwise orders, bear his own costs of proving a debt.

20. Any person seeking to prove a debt or from whom additional proof is required, or any other person, may be examined by the Court in relation thereto.

21. Where a creditor or other person with intent to defraud makes any false claim or any proof, declaration or statement of account before the Court or in his affidavit which is untrue in any material particular in connection with the proof of debts, the Court may, in addition to any other penalty provided in this Act, disallow the claim in whole or in part.

22. Before deciding on a claim, the Official Assignee may require a creditor to furnish additional information or proof or to attend before him.

23. The Official Assignee shall deal in the following manner with claims:

    (*a*) He shall prepare a list certified by him of the claims.

    (*b*) This list shall record—

(i) the claims allowed by him, which shall be deemed to be admitted, and

(ii) the claims either disallowed by him or which he considers should not be admitted without reference to the Court.

(*c*) He shall refer disputed debts to the Court for adjudication.

(*d*) The decision of the Official Assignee in regard to a claim shall be confirmed in writing to the creditor.

(*e*) Any person aggrieved by the decision of the Official Assignee may appeal to the Court.

(*f*) The Official Assignee shall place a copy of the list on the Court file.

(*g*) The list shall be open to public inspection on payment of a prescribed fee but no fee shall be charged to creditors inspecting the list.

Secured Creditors

24. (1) If a secured creditor realises his security, he may prove for the balance due to him after deducting the net amount realised and receive dividends thereon but not so as to disturb any dividend then already declared. If he surrenders his security for the general benefit of the creditors, he may prove for his whole debt.

(2) If a secured creditor does not either realise or surrender his security, he shall, before ranking for dividend, state in his proof the particulars of his security, the date on which it was given and the value at which he assesses it, and he shall be entitled to receive a dividend only in respect of the balance due to him after deducting the value so assessed.

(3) A secured creditor shall not be entitled to surrender his security after the time fixed by the Official Assignee for receipt of proofs of debt, except by order of the Court.

(4)(*a*) Where a security is valued by the creditor, the Official Assignee may at any time redeem it on payment to the creditor of the assessed value. If the Official Assignee is dissatisfied with the assessed value he may require that the property comprised in any security so valued be offered for sale at such time and on such terms and conditions as may be agreed upon between him and the creditor or, in default of agreement, as the Court may direct. If the sale be by public auction the creditor, or the Official Assignee on behalf of the estate, may bid or purchase.

(*b*) The creditor may, however, at any time by notice in writing require the Official Assignee to elect whether he will or will not exercise his power of redeeming the security or requiring it to be offered for sale, and if the Official Assignee does not, within three months after receiving the notice, signify in writing to the creditor his election to exercise the power, he shall not be entitled to exercise it; and the equity of redemption, or any other interest in the property comprised in the security which is vested in the Official Assignee, shall vest in the creditor and the amount of his debt shall be reduced by the amount at which the security has been valued.

(5) Where a creditor has valued his security he may at any time amend the

valuation and proof on showing to the satisfaction of the Official Assignee, or the Court, that the valuation and proof were made *bona fide* on a mistaken estimate, but every such amendment shall be made at the cost of the creditor, and upon such terms as the Court shall order, unless the Official Assignee allows the amendment without application to the Court.

(6) Where a valuation has been amended in accordance with *subparagraph (5)*, the creditor shall forthwith repay any surplus dividend which he may have received in excess of that to which he would have been entitled on the amended valuation or, as the case may be, shall be entitled to be paid, out of any money for the time being available for dividend, any dividend or share of dividend which he has not received by reason of the inaccuracy of the original valuation before that money is made applicable to the payment of any future dividend but he shall not be entitled to disturb the distribution of any dividend declared before the date of the amendment.

(7) If a creditor having valued his security subsequently realises it, or if it is realised under the provisions of *subparagraph (4)*, the net amount realised shall be substituted for the amount of any valuation previously made by the creditor, and shall be treated in all respects as an amended valuation made by the creditor.

(8) If it is found at any time that the affidavit made by or on behalf of a secured creditor has omitted to state that he is a secured creditor, such creditor shall surrender his security to the Official Assignee for the general benefit of the creditors unless the Court on application otherwise orders, and the Court may allow the affidavit to be amended upon such terms as to repayment of any dividend or otherwise as the Court may consider just.

(9) If a secured creditor does not comply with *subparagraph (8)*, he shall be excluded from all share in any dividend.

(10) Subject to the provisions of *subparagraph (4)*, the creditor shall in no case receive more than one pound in the pound and interest, where the creditor is entitled to prove for interest.

(11) Where a mortgagee holds as security a policy of assurance on the life of a bankrupt or an arranging debtor which in the event of the non-payment of premiums provides for their automatic discharge out of moneys payable under the policy, the value of the policy for the purpose of proving in the bankruptcy or arrangement shall be taken to be not less than the value as at the date of adjudication or order for protection; provided that, if the bankrupt or arranging debtor dies before the policy is surrendered, the mortgagee may apply to the Court for the purpose of revaluing his security.

SECOND SCHEDULE

REPEALS

Session and Chapter or Year and Number	Short Title	Extent of Repeal
20 and 21 Vict. c. 60	Irish Bankrupt and Insolvent Act, 1857	The whole Act
35 and 36 Vict. c. 57	Debtors Act (Ireland), 1872	Sections 11 and 12, and 14 to 22
35 and 36 Vict. c. 58	Bankruptcy (Ireland) Amendment Act, 1872	The whole Act
51 and 52 Vict. c. 44	Local Bankruptcy (Ireland) Act, 1888	The whole Act
52 and 53 Vict. c. 60	Preferential Payments in Bankruptcy (Ireland) Act, 1889	The whole Act
53 and 54 Vict. c. 24	Deeds of Arrangement Amendment Act, 1890	The whole Act
1926, No. 27	Court Officers Act, 1926	Section 12
1937, No. 3	Circuit Court (Registration of Judgments) Act, 1937	Section 3
1946, No. 16	Hire-Purchase Act, 1946	Section 17 (1) so far as it refers to section 313 of the Irish Bankrupt and Insolvent Act, 1857
1947, No. 14	Agricultural Credit Act, 1947	Section 32 (3)
1954, No. 26	Arbitration Act, 1954	In section 11 (1) the words from "and includes" to the end of the subsection.
1961, No. 39	Courts (Supplemental Provisions) Act, 1961	In section 23: subsection (3) and the reference to the Cork Local Bankruptcy Court in subsections (4),(5) and (6)
1963, No. 33	Companies Act, 1963	In section 286 (1), the words "the presentation of a bankruptcy petition on which" Section 345 (8)
1971, No. 24	Central Bank Act, 1971	Section 28 (2)
1981, No. 11	Courts Act, 1981	Section 26

DEEDS OF ARRANGEMENT ACT 1887

An Act to provide for the Registration of Deeds of Arrangement.

[*16th September* 1887.]

Be it enacted by the Queen's most Excellent Majesty, by and with the advice and consent of the Lords Spiritual and Temporal, and Commons, in this present Parliament assembled, and by the authority of the same, as follows:

Short title

1. This Act may be cited for all purposes as the Deeds of Arrangement Act, 1887.

Extent of Act

2. This Act shall not extend to Scotland.

Commencement of Act

3. This Act shall, except as in this Act specially provided, come into operation on the first day of January one thousand eight hundred and eighty-eight, which date is in this Act referred to as the commencement of this Act.

Application of Act

4.—(1) This Act shall apply to every Deed of Arrangement, as defined in this section, made after the commencement of this Act.

(2) A Deed of Arrangement to which this Act applies shall include any of the following instruments, whether under seal or not, made by, for, or in respect of the affairs of a debtor for the benefit of his creditors generally (otherwise than in pursuance or the law for the time being in force relating to bankruptcy), that is to say:—

> (*a*) An assignment of property;
> (*b*) A deed of or agreement for a composition;

And in cases where creditors of a debtor obtain any control over his property or business:—

> (*c*) A deed of inspectorship entered into for the purpose of carrying on or winding up a business;
> (*d*) A letter of licence authorising the debtor or any other person to manage, carry on, realise, or dispose of a business, with a view to the

payment of debts; and

(*e*) Any agreement or instrument entered into for the purpose of carrying on or winding up the debtor's business, or authorising the debtor or any other person to manage, carry on, realise or dispose of the debtor's business, with a view to the payment of his debts.

Avoidance of unregistered deeds of arrangement

5. From and after the commencement of this Act a Deed of Arrangement to which this Act applies shall be void unless the same shall have been registered under this Act within seven clear days after the first execution thereof by the debtor or any creditor, or if it is executed in any place out of England or Ireland respectively, then within seven clear days after the time at which it would, in the ordinary course of post, arrive in England or Ireland respectively, if posted within one week after the execution thereof, and unless the same shall bear such ordinary and ad valorem stamp as is under this Act provided.

Mode of registration

6. The registration of a Deed of Arrangement under this Act shall be effected in the following manner:—

(1.) A true copy of the deed, and of every schedule or inventory, thereto annexed, or therein referred to, shall be presented to and filed with the registrar within seven clear days after the execution of the said deed (in like manner as a bill of sale given by way of security for the payment of money is now required to be filed), together with an affidavit verifying the time of execution, and containing a description of the residence and occupation of the debtor, and of the place or places where his business is carried on, and an affidavit by the debtor stating the total estimated amount of property and liabilities included under the deed, the total amount of the composition (if any) payable thereunder, and the names and addresses of his creditors:

(2.) No deed shall be registered under this Act unless the original of such deed, duly stamped with the proper inland revenue duty, and in addition to such duty a stamp denoting a duty computed at the rate of one shilling for every hundred pounds or fraction of a hundred pounds of the sworn value of the property passing, or (where no property passes under the deed) the amount of composition payable under the deed, is produced to the registrar at the time of such registration.

Form of register

7. The registrar shall keep a register wherein shall be entered, as soon as conveniently may be after the presentation of a deed for registration, an abstract of the contents of every Deed of Arrangement registered under this Act, containing the following and any other prescribed particulars:—

(*a*) The date of the deed:

(*b*) The name, address, and, description of the debtor, and the place or places where his business is carried on, and the title of the firm or firms under which the debtor carries on business, and the name and address of the trustee (if any) under the deed:

(c) A short statement of the nature and effect of the deed, and of the composition in the pound payable thereunder:

(d) The date of registration:

(e) The amount of property and liabilities included under the deed, as estimated by the debtor.

Registrar and office for registration

8.—(1.) The Registrars of Bills of Sale shall be the registrar for the purposes of this Act.

(2.) The Bills of Sale Office of the Queen's Bench Division of the High Court of Justice, shall be the office for the registration of Deeds of Arrangement.

Rectification of register

9. The Court or a Judge upon being satisfied that the omission· to register a Deed of Arrangement within the time required by this Act or that the omission or mis-statement of the name, residence, or description of any person was accidental or due to inadvertence, or to some cause beyond the control of the debtor and not imputable to any negligence on his part, may on the application of any party interested, and on such terms and conditions as are just and expedient, extend the time for such registration, or order such omission or mis-statement to be supplied or rectified by the insertion in the register of the true name, residence, or description.

Time for registration

10. When the time for registering a Deed of Arrangement registration expires on a Sunday, or other day on which the registration office is closed, the registration shall be valid if made on the next following day on which the office is open.

Office copies

11. Subject to the provisions of this Act, and to any rules made thereunder, any person shall be entitled to have an office copy of, or extract from, any deed registered under this Act upon paying for the same at the like rate as for office copies of judgments of the High Court of Justice, and any copy or extract purporting to be an office copy or extract shall, in all courts and before all arbitrators or other persons, be admitted as prima facie evidence thereof, and of the fact and date of registration as shown thereon.

Inspection of register and registered deeds

12.—(1.) Any person shall be entitled, at all reasonable times, to search the register on payment of one shilling, or such other fee as may be prescribed, and subject to such regulations as may be prescribed, and shall be entitled, at all reasonable times, to inspect, examine, and make extracts from any registered Deed of Arrangement, without being required to make a written application or to specify any particulars in reference thereto, upon payment of one shilling, or such other fee as may be prescribed, for each Deed of Arrangement inspected.

(2.) Provided that the said extracts shall be limited to the dates of execution and of registration, the names, addresses, and descriptions of the debtor and of the parties to the deed, a short statement of the nature and effect of the deed, and any other prescribed particulars.

Local registration

13.—(3.) This section shall not apply to Ireland.

Affidavits

14. Every affidavit required by or for the purposes of this Act may be sworn before a Master of the Supreme Court of Judicature or before any person empowered to take affidavits in the Supreme Court of Judicature.

Fees

15.—(1.) There shall be taken, in respect of the registration of Deeds of Arrangement, and in respect of any office copies or extracts, or official searches made by the registrar, such fees as may be from time to time prescribed; and nothing in this Act contained shall make it obligatory on the registrar to do, or permit to be done, any act in respect of which any fee is specified or prescribed, except on payment of such fee.

(2.) The eighty-fourth section of the Supreme Court of Judicature Act (Ireland), 1877, and any enactments for the time being in force amending or substituted for that section, shall apply to fees under this Act, and orders under it may, if need be, be made in relation to such fees accordingly.

Amendment

16. This section shall not apply to Ireland.

Saving as to Bankruptcy Acts

17. Nothing contained in this Act shall be construed to repeal or shall affect any provision of the law for the time being in force in relation to bankruptcy, or shall give validity to any deed or instrument which by law is an act of bankruptcy, or void or voidable.

Rules

18.—(1.) Rules for carrying this Act into effect may be made, revoked, and altered from time to time by the like persons and in the like manner in which rules may be made under and for the purposes of the Supreme Court of Judicature Act (Ireland), 1877.

(2.) Such rules as may be required for the purposes of this Act may be made at any time after the passing of this Act.

Interpretation of terms

19. In this Act, unless the context otherwise requires,—

"Court or a judge" means the High Court of Justice and any judge thereof;

"Creditors generally" includes all creditors who may assent or take the benefit of a Deed of Arrangement;

"Person" includes a body of persons corporate or unincorporate;

"Prescribed" means prescribed by rules to be made under this Act;

"Property" has the same meaning as the same expression has in the Bankruptcy Act, 1883;

"Rules" includes forms.

COMPANIES ACT 1963,
AS AMENDED
(EXTRACTS)

183 [Prohibition of undischarged bankrupts acting as directors

(1) Subject to subsection (2), if any person being an undischarged bankrupt acts as director of, or directly or indirectly takes part in or is concerned in the management of any company except with the leave of the court, he shall be liable on conviction on indictment to imprisonment for a term not exceeding 2 years or to a fine not exceeding £500 or to both, or on summary conviction to imprisonment for a term not exceeding 6 months or to a fine not exceeding £100 or to both.

(2) A person shall not be guilty of an offence under this section by reason that he, being an undischarged bankrupt, has acted as director of, or taken part or been concerned in the management of a company, if he was on the operative date acting as director of, or taking part or being concerned in the management of, that company, and has continuously so acted, taken part or been concerned since that date, and the bankruptcy was prior to that date.

(3) In this section "company" includes an unregistered company and a company incorporated outside the State which has an established place of business within the State.

[183A New section 183A of Act of 1963 — Examination as to solvency status.

Where the Director has reason to believe that a director of a company is an undischarged bankrupt, the Director may require the director of the company to produce by a specified date a sworn statement of all relevant facts pertaining to the company director's financial position, both within the State and elsewhere, and, in particular, to any matter pertaining to bankruptcy as at a particular date.

The court may, on the application of the Director, require a director of a company who has made a statement under subsection (1) to appear before it and answer on oath any question pertaining to the content of the statement.

The court may, on the application of the Director, make a disqualification order (as defined in section 159 of the Companies Act, 1990) against a director of a company on the grounds that he is an undischarged bankrupt.

A director of a company who fails to comply with a requirement under subsection (1) shall be guilty of an offence.".

TAXES CONSOLIDATION ACT 1997
(EXTRACTS)

971. Priority of income tax debts over other debts.

(1) No goods or chattels whatever, belonging to any person at the time any income tax becomes in arrear, shall be liable to be taken by virtue of any execution or other process, warrant or authority whatever, or by virtue of any assignment, on any account or pretence whatever, except at the suit of the landlord for rent, unless the person at whose suit the execution or seizure is made or to whom the assignment was made pays or causes to be paid to the Collector-General before the sale or removal of the goods or chattels all arrears of income tax due at the time of seizure, or payable for the year in which the seizure is made.

(2) Where income tax is claimed for more than one year, the person at whose instance the seizure has been made may, on paying to the Collector-General the income tax which is due for one whole year, proceed in that person's seizure in the like manner as if no income tax had been claimed.

982. Preferential payment.

The priority attaching to assessed taxes under section 81 of the Bankruptcy Act, 1988, and sections 98 and 285 of the Companies Act, 1963, shall apply to capital gains tax.

994. Priority in bankruptcy, etc. of certain amounts.

[(1) In this section "employer's liability for the period of 12 months" means the aggregate of—
  (a) all sums which an employer was liable under this Chapter and any regulations under this Chapter to deduct from emoluments to which this Chapter applies paid by the employer, and
  (b) all sums that were not so deducted but which an employer was liable, in accordance with section 985A and any regulations under that section, to remit to the Collector-General in respect of notional payments made by the employer,
during the period of 12 months referred to in subsection (2), reduced by any amounts which the employer was liable under this Chapter and any regulations under this Chapter to repay during the same period, and subject to the addition of interest payable under section 991.]

(2) There shall be included among the debts which under section 81 of the Bankruptcy Act, 1988, are to be paid in priority to all other debts in the

distribution of the property of a bankrupt, arranging debtor or person dying insolvent so much as is unpaid of the employer's liability for the period of 12 months before the date on which the order of adjudication of the bankrupt was made, the petition of arrangement of the debtor was filed or, as the case may be, the person died insolvent.

1000. Priority in bankruptcy, winding up, etc. for sums recovered or deducted under sections 531, 989 or 990.

For the purposes of section 285 of the Companies Act, 1963 and of section 994, the sums referred to in section 285(2)(*a*)(iii) of the Companies Act, 1963, and in section 994(1) shall be deemed to include—

(*a*) amounts of tax deducted under section 531(1) and amounts of tax recoverable under regulation 12 of the Income Tax (Construction Contracts) Regulations, 1971 (S.I. No.1 of 1971),

(*b*) amounts of tax recoverable under section 989, and

(*c*) amounts of tax recoverable under section 990,

which relate to a period or periods falling in whole or in part within the period of 12 months referred to in section 285(2)(*a*)(iii) of the Companies Act, 1963 , or in section 994(1), as may be appropriate, and in the case of any such amount for a period falling partly within and partly outside whichever of those periods of 12 months is appropriate, it shall be lawful to apportion the total sum or amount according to the respective lengths of the periods falling within the period of 12 months and outside the period of 12 months in order to determine the amount of tax which relates to the period of 12 months.

ORDER 82: DEEDS OF ARRANGEMENT RULES

Rule 1. The affidavits to be filed pursuant to the Deeds of Arrangement Act, 1887, section 6, shall be respectively in the Forms Nos. 1 and 2 in Appendix S.

Rule 2. The abstract of the contents of any deed of arrangement shall be entered on the Register under the said Act of 1887 in the Form No. 3 in Appendix S.

Rule 3. Upon every copy of a deed of arrangement which is presented for filing there shall be indorsed by the person who presents it the name of the debtor, the date of the deed and of the filing thereof, the total amount of duty with which the deed is stamped, and a certificate signed by the solicitor of the debtor or the person who presents the copy for filing certifying that the copy is a correct copy of the deed, and stating the number of folios (of seventy-two words each), which the deed contains.

Rule 4. When a deed of arrangement is registered there shall be written on the original deed a certificate that the deed has been duly registered, and the date of registration.

Rule 5. Extracts from the filed copy of a deed of arrangement shall be limited to the date of execution and registration, the names, addresses, and descriptions of the debtor and the parties to the deed and a short statement of the nature and effect of the deed.

Rule 6
> (1) The register of arrangements, provided for by section 108 of the Bankruptcy Act 1988, shall be kept in the Central Office by the register for deeds of arrangement.
> (2) The register shall be kept by inserting in the book or file provided for that purpose the duplicate memorandum delivered to the Central Office in pursuance of section 90 (c) of the Bankruptcy Act 1988, together with a note of the date of receipt and by inserting in the index thereto the name and address of the arranging debtor.

Rule 7. The Court, upon being satisfied as to any omission from or error in the duplicate memorandum, may order the omission or error to be rectified. The correction may be made on the duplicate or by a note annexed thereto, with a note of the order.

Rule 8. Any person shall be entitled to have an office copy of or extract from any entry in the register upon paying for it at the same rate as for office copies.

Rule 9. Any person shall be entitled, during office hours, to search the register upon payment of the same fee as is for the time being payable for searching the register of deeds of arrangement and to make a copy of or extracts from any registered memorandum.

APPENDIX S

DEEDS OF ARRANGEMENT

No.1.   Order 82, rule 1

AFFIDAVIT OF EXECUTION

THE HIGH COURT

In the matter of a deed of arrangement dated _____ and made between _____ and _____
I, _____ of _____
make oath and say as follows:

1. The above-written [*or* within-written] document is a true copy of the deed of assignment of property [*or* as *the* case *may be*], and of every schedule or inventory thereto annexed or therein referred to, and of every attestation of the execution thereof.
2. [*Where the deed is executed by the debtor*] The deed was executed on the _____ day of_____ 19___, by the debtor, at _____ of the clock in the noon. I was present when the debtor executed the said deed, and saw him execute the same.
3. [*Where the deed is executed by* a *creditor:*] The deed was executed by _____ the first [*or* only] creditor who executed the deed and who resides at _____, and is _____ __, on the _____ day of_____ at _____ of the clock in the noon. I was present when the said _____ executed the said deed, and saw him execute the same.
4. The debtor, _____, resides at _____ and is _____
5. The place [*or* places] where business of the said debtor is carried on is [*or* are] as follows:

                                                                    Sworn, &c.

No.2   Order 82, rule 1

DEBTOR'S AFFIDAVIT FOR REGISTRATION

[*Title* as *in Form No.1*]

I, _____

make oath and say as follows:

1. On the _____ day of _____, I executed a deed of
    assignment of property [*or* as *the* case *may be*].
2. The total estimated amount of my property included under the deed is
    € _____ and the net amount of my property included under the deed,
    after deducting € _____, being the value* of securities held
    by creditors and required to cover debts due to them, is € _____.
3. The total estimated amount of my liabilities included under the deed
    is € _____, and the net amount of my liabilities included under the
    deed, after deducting € _____, being the amount covered by securities
    held by creditors is € _____.
4. [*If composition payable*] The total amount of the composition payable
    thereunder is:
5. The names and addresses of my creditors and the amounts due to or
    claimed by each of them are as follows:

Name of creditor	Address	Amount of debt due or claimed, after deduction of value of security held

Sworn, &c.

*The estimated surplus (if any) from securities held by creditors should not be
deducted from the gross amount of property.*

†This amount should correspond with the amount of securities deducted above.
No deduction should be made in respect of the unsecured balances of partially
secured debts.

Order 82, rule 2

No.3.

FORM OF REGISTER OF DEEDS OF ARRANGEMENT

No.	Name address and description of debtor	Place(s) where business is carried on	Title of firms under which debtor carries on business	Name and address of trustee (if any)	Nature and effect of deed and amount of composition in the £	Amount of property as estimated by debtor			Amount of liabilities as estimated by debtor			Date of deed	Date of registration
						Gross amount of property	Value of securities given (excluding any estimated surplus)	Net value of property	Gross amount of liabilities	Amount of debts covered by securities	Net amount of liabilities		
						€	€	€	€	€	€		

No.4

DEBTOR'S AFFIDAVIT PURSUANT TO ORDER 82, RULE 6

THE HIGH COURT

In the matter of a petition by _____ pursuant to the Irish Bankruptcy and Insolvent Act 1857, section 343.

I, _____ of _____
make oath and say as follows:

1. The place [*or* places] where my business is carried is [*or* are]
2. The title [*or* titles] of the firm [*or* firms] under which I carry on business on is [*or* are]
3. The total estimated amount of my property is €___ and the net amount of my property, after deducting €____ being the value of securities held by creditors and required to cover debts due to them, is €____
4. The total estimated amount of my liabilities is €___ and the net amount of my liabilities, after deducting €___ being the amount covered by securities held by creditors, is €___
5. The names and addresses of my creditors and the amounts due to or claimed by them are as follows:

Names of creditors	Addresses	Amount of debt due or claimed after deduction of value of security held		
		€		

Sworn, &c.

Order 82, rule 7

No.5.

FORM OF REGISTER UNDER DEEDS OF ARRANGEMENT AMENDMENT ACT 1890

No.	Name address and description of debtor	Place(s) where business is carried on	Title of firm(s) under which debtor carried on business	Amount of property as estimated by debtor		Amount of liabilities as estimated by debtor			Date of filing petition and of affidavit of assets and liabilities	Date of registration	Nature and effect of order
				Gross amount of property	Value of securities given (excluding any estimated surplus)	Net value of property	Gross amount of liabilities	Amount of debts covered by securities	Net of liabilities			

EXTRACTS FROM THE "BANKRUPTCY RULES AND FORMS"

Order 76 and Appendix O of the Rules of the Superior Courts, as substituted by S.I. No. 79 of 1989[1]

Bankruptcy Summons.

10. (1) A bankruptcy summons shall be in the Form No. 1 and shall
   (a) require the debtor, within fourteen days after the service of the summons upon him, to pay the debt to the creditor or to secure the payment of the debt to the satisfaction of the creditor or to compound the debt to the satisfaction of the creditor, and
   (b) state that in the event of the debtor failing to pay the sum specified in the summons or to secure or compound for it to the satisfaction of the creditor such default shall be an act of bankruptcy.

11. (1) A creditor desirous that a bankruptcy summons may be granted shall, not earlier than four clear days after he shall have served a notice in the Form No. 4, file in the proper office a copy of such notice, together with an affidavit in the Form No. 5 of the truth of his debt made by himself or by any other person who can swear positively to the facts verifying the truth of his debt, and that no form of execution has issued in respect of such debt and remains to be proceeded upon, and shall lodge with the proper officer any bills, notes, guarantees, contracts, judgments or orders referred to in his affidavit together with the summons which it is proposed to issue.

(2) Where a debt of any part thereof is for money lent by a moneylender or interest or charges in connection with it, the affidavit shall contain a statement of the date on which a copy of the note or memorandum in writing of the contract made pursuant to section 11 of the Moneylenders Act, 1933, was delivered or sent to the borrower and a statement showing in detail the particulars mentioned in section 16 (2) of that Act and a copy of the note or memorandum shall be filed with and verified by the said affidavit.

(3) A creditor who has complied with the requirements of paragraphs (1) and (2) of this rule shall apply ex parte to the Court for the grant of a Bankruptcy Summons at such time and place as shall have been fixed for the hearing of the application.

12. (1) A bankruptcy summons may be granted in accordance with section 8

---

[1] The reader is referred to the *Consolidated Superior Court Rules*, loose-leaf, ed. P.J. Breen (Round Hall: Dublin, 2002, with updates), alternatively, the Courts Services' website *www.courts.ie* for the entire Order 76 and associated Forms of Appendix O.

(2) of the Act, to two or more creditors who are not partners, upon the affidavits of each of them.

(2) A bankruptcy summons may be granted to a partnership upon the affidavit of one of the partners.

(3) A bankruptcy summons may be granted to a company or other body corporate upon the affidavit of the secretary, director or other person duly authorised in that behalf.

(4) Detailed particulars of demand shall be endorsed upon or annexed to the bankruptcy summons. No objection shall be allowed to the particulars unless the Court considers that the debtor has been misled by them. An original and at least two copies of every bankruptcy summons and particulars shall be lodged with the proper officer at the time of issue, and shall be sealed.

13. (1) Every bankruptcy summons shall be endorsed with the name and registered place of business of the solicitor for the summoning creditor. If no solicitor is employed for the purpose, it shall bear an endorsement stating that it has been granted to the creditor in person, together with his residence and an address within the jurisdiction whereat a notice to dismiss the summons or any other notice or proceeding in the matter may be served.

(2) There shall be endorsed on the summons in addition to an intimation of the consequences of neglect to comply with the requisition of the summons, a notice to the debtor that if he disputes the debt and desires to obtain the dismissal of the summons he must file an affidavit within fourteen days after service of the summons stating (a) that he is not so indebted or only so indebted to a less amount than [€1,904.61] or (b) that before the service of the summons he had obtained the protection of the Court or (c) that he has secured or compounded the debt to the satisfaction of the creditor.

(3) Where the summoning creditor is ordinarily resident outside the jurisdiction or, being a company or other body corporate, has its registered office or principal place of business outside the jurisdiction, there shall be endorsed on the front of the bankruptcy summons an address within the jurisdiction whereat payment can be made.

14. (1) A bankruptcy summons shall be personally served within twenty-eight days from the date of the summons by delivering to the debtor a sealed copy of the summons with endorsed or annexed particulars of demand together with a true copy of the affidavit filed in accordance with rule eleven. If personal service within the time limit cannot be effected the Court may grant extension of the time for such service. If the Court is satisfied by affidavit that the debtor is evading service or that from any other cause prompt personal service cannot be effected, it may order service to be made by delivery of the summons with endorsed or annexed particulars to the debtor's wife, or some adult member of the debtor's family or adult employee or partner at the debtor's usual or last known place of residence or business or make such order for substituted or other service, or for the substitution for service of notice by letter, public advertisement (in the Form No. 8), or otherwise, as may be just.

(2) The person serving a bankruptcy summons shall, within three days at most after service, endorse on the summons the day and date of the service thereof, and every affidavit of service of such summons shall mention the date on which such endorsement was made. Such affidavit shall be in the Form No. 3.

15. The affidavit mentioned in paragraph two of rule fourteen, shall be in the Form No. 6. Where a debtor files such affidavit, the time shall be fixed by the proper officer at which the application for the dismissal of the summons will be heard by the Court. Notice thereof in the Form No 7 shall be given and the affidavit served by the debtor, not less than four days before the date so fixed, by service of the notice and the affidavit on the solicitor for the summoning creditor at his registered place of business or, if no solicitor is employed, by service on the summoning creditor at the address within the jurisdiction for the service of notices. In default of the debtor giving notice or in default of his appearance before the Court at the time fixed his application shall be dismissed.

Bankruptcy petition

19. A creditors petition shall be in the Form No. 11 and shall
    (a) contain a statement showing the nature and amount of the debt and showing that the debt has not been paid, secured or compounded.
    (b) recite the specific act of bankruptcy on which the petition is founded.
    (c) contain an undertaking by the creditor to advertise notice of the adjudication and statutory sitting in the manner directed by the Court, and to bear the expenses of such advertisement,
    (d) contain a statement that the debtor is domiciled in the State or that, within a year before the date of the presentation of the petition, he has ordinarily resided or had a dwelling-house or place of business in the State, or that he has carried on business in the State personally or by means of an agent or manager, or that he is or within the said period has been a member of a partnership which has carried on business in the State by means of a partner, agent or manager,
    (e) contain an indemnity on the part of the creditor, indemnifying the Official Assignee as to the Official Assignee's costs, fees and expenses allowed by the Court up to and including the statutory sitting and as to such further costs, fees and expenses of the Official Assignee as the Court may upon the application of the Official Assignee direct, and
    (f) contain notice of the date for the hearing of the petition.

20. (1) A creditor's petition shall be signed by the creditor or, if more than one, by all the petitioners, unless the petitioners are partners, in which case one partner may sign on behalf of himself and the other partners. Any petitioner may sign the petition by his attorney duly authorised by power of attorney in that behalf.

(2) A creditors petition by a limited company or body corporate shall be sealed with the seal of the company or body corporate and signed by two directors or by one director and the secretary. Such seal and signature shall in all cases be attested.

21. On the presentation of the petition, the petitioning creditor shall file in the proper office an affidavit in the Form No. 12 proving his debt and the act of bankruptcy, provided that when a debt or any part thereof is in respect of money lent by a moneylender or interest or charges in connection therewith,

the affidavit shall incorporate a statement showing in detail the particulars mentioned in section 16 (2) of the Moneylenders Act, 1933, and provided also that where the act of bankruptcy relied on is non-compliance with a bankruptcy summons, it shall also incorporate a statement that the debt has not been secured or compounded.

22. Where a petitioning creditor is not known to the proper officer or a petition is not signed by a solicitor in addition to being signed by the petitioning creditor, it shall not be filed until the petitioner shall be identified to the satisfaction of the proper officer.

23. In all cases the petitioning creditor shall indemnify the Official Assignee against any costs, fees and expenses incurred by him and allowed by the Court up to and including the statutory sitting and against such further costs, fees and expenses as to the Court may, upon the application of the Official Assignee, on notice to the petitioning creditor, direct.

24. The proper officer shall appoint the time at which the petition is to be heard. Notice of the time so appointed shall be written on the petition and sealed copy thereof. A sealed copy of the petition shall be taken out by the petitioner or his solicitor and may be used as if it were an original.

25. Every petition by a creditor shall be served, not less than seven days before the hearing of the petition, by delivering to the debtor personally a copy of such petition and by showing to the debtor at the time of such service the sealed original, or shall be served in such substituted manner as the Court may direct. The petitioner shall file in the proper office an affidavit of service of the petition not later than two clear days before the hearing.

Selected Forms

No. 1.

BANKRUPTCY SUMMONS

THE HIGH COURT

BANKRUPTCY

To:

You are hereby warned that unless within fourteen days after the service of this summons on you, you do pay to

of the sum of [… euro and … cent], being the sum claimed of you by according to the particulars hereunto annexed or endorsed hereon, or unless you shall secure or compound for the same to his satisfaction, you will have committed an act of bankruptcy, in respect of which you may be adjudged a bankrupt, on a petition being presented against you by the said

unless you shall have within the time aforesaid applied to the Court to dismiss this summons, on the ground that you are not indebted to the said … in any sum or that you are only indebted to … in a sum less than [€1,904.61], or that before service of this summons upon you, you had obtained the protection of the Court.

Issued pursuant to the provisions of section 8 of the Bankruptcy Act 1988.

Given under the seal of the Court

this day of [...]

(Signed)

Judge

You are specially to note.

That the consequences, which will follow any neglect to comply with the requisitions contained in the summons, are that you may be adjudged a bankrupt on a petition of bankruptcy being presented against you by the said ...

If however, you are not indebted to the said ... in any sum or are only indebted to in a sum less than [€1,904.61] you must make application to the Court within fourteen days after service hereof, to dismiss the summons, by filing in the Examiner's Office, Four Courts, Dublin, an affidavit in the prescribed form, stating that you are not so indebted, or only so to a less amount than £1,500, or that before service of this summons upon you, you had obtained the protection of the Court, or had compounded or secured for the debt to the satisfaction of the

said and thereupon a date will be fixed for the hearing of your application.

(Signed)

Solicitor for the said

[Address]

PARTICULARS OF DEMAND

[set out in detail]

Form No. 4.

PARTICULARS OF DEMAND, AND NOTICE REQUIRING PAYMENT PRIOR TO THE ISSUE OF A BANKRUPTCY SUMMONS.

To

The following are the particulars of the demand of the undersigned ... of ... against you the said ...

amounting to the sum of [... euro]

[detailed particulars to be given]

Take notice that the said ... hereby requires immediate payment of the said sum of [... euro] within four days of service of this Notice upon you at the address given below.

Dated

(Signed)

_____

(State capacity Address)

Form No. 5.

AFFIDAVIT FOR BANKRUPTCY SUMMONS

THE HIGH

BANKRUPTCY

I, ... (if not creditor, state capacity) make oath and say as follows:

1. ... of is justly and truly indebted to in the sum of [... euro and ... cent] for (state nature of debt).

2. An account in writing of the particulars of demand and notice requiring payment was on or about the day of [...] , sent by post (or as the case may be) addressed to the said ... at aforesaid, and payment of the same has been on more than one occasion required of him.

3. I, the said hold no security or bills or notes for the said debt save as follows:—

4. No form of execution has issued in respect of the said debt and remains to be proceeded upon.

5. I therefore pray this Honourable Court for an Order that a Bankruptcy Summons do issue against the said

Sworn, &c.

Form No. 6.

AFFIDAVIT TO GROUND APPLICATION TO DISMISS BANKRUPTCY SUMMONS

THE HIGH COURT

BANKRUPTCY

In the matter of a Bankruptcy Summons by ... against of ... and bearing date the day of ...

I, ..., the above-named make oath and say that the above-named summons was served on me on the day of ... , and that I am not indebted to the said in any sum amounting to [€1,904.61] or that before such service I had obtained the protection of the Court or that I have compounded for the debt to the satisfaction of the said in the following manner:— *or that I have secured for the debt to the satisfaction of the said in the following manner:—*

Sworn, &c.

*Set out in detail.

Form No. 7.

NOTICE OF APPLICATION TO DISMISS BANKRUPCTY SUMMONS

THE HIGH COURT

BANKRUPTCY

In the matter of a Bankruptcy Summons by ... dated the ... day of ... .

Notice is hereby given that an affidavit of the said ... has been filed in the proper office and that the application of the said to dismiss the said Summons will be heard by the Court on ... day, the ... day

of ... at the hour of eleven o'clock in the forenoon.

Dated

(Signed)

To Examiner.

Form No. 11

PETITION OF BANKRUPTCY BY A CREDITOR

THE HIGH COURT

BANKRUPTCY

The humble petition of ... of ... showeth as follows:—

1. ... of ... is indebted to your petitioner in the sum of in respect of

(state nature of debt).

2. Your petitioner does not nor does any person or persons on his behalf hold any mortgage, charge, or lien on the debtor's estate or any part thereof as security for said debt or any part thereof (or your petitioner holds security for the payment of (or part of) the said sum, but he will give up such security for the benefit of the creditors of in the event of his being adjudged a bankrupt or your petitioner holds security for the payment of (or part of) the said sum and he estimates the value of such security at the sum of

3. The said has within three months before the presentation of this petition committed an act of bankruptcy as follows:— (give details of the specific act of bankruptcy alleged) as your petitioner has been informed and believes.

4. The said is domiciled within the state (or specify which of the alternative requirements of Section 11 (1) (d) of the Bankruptcy Act 1988 is fulfilled).

Your petitioner therefore prays that on proof of the requisites in that behalf, on the hearing of this petition, the said ... may be adjudged bankrupt.

Your PETITIONER HEREBY UNDERTAKES to this Honourable Court that, in the event of the said being so adjudged your petitioner will advertise notice of the adjudication and statutory sitting in the manner directed by this Honourable Court and bear the expenses of such advertisement. Your petitioner HEREBY INDEMNIFIES the Official Assignee as to the costs, fees and expenses incurred, or to be incurred, in the event of such adjudication by the Official Assignee as to the costs, fees and expenses incurred, or to be incurred, in the event of such adjudication by the Official Assignee and allowed by the Court. Your petitioner FURTHER UNDERTAKES to lodge such sums as this Honourable Court may direct to cover such costs, fees and expenses.

Dated

(Signed)

(Signed)

Witness

(Name, address and description of witness)

Received this day of … , at the hour

of … o'clock in the noon.

(The following affidavit is to be endorsed on the back of the petition).

THE HIGH COURT

BANKRUPTCY

I, the petitioner named in the petition on the other side hereof, make oath and say that the several allegations in the said petition are true.

Sworn, &c.

Form No. 12.

AFFIDAVIT OF DEBT.

In the matter of a Bankrupt [or as the case may be] [or if before adjudication "In the matter of a petition for adjudication of bankruptcy by against … ."]

I, … of … make oath, and say as follows:—

1. The said [name of bankrupt or debtor or insolvent deceased] was, at the date of the filing of the petition* in this matter, and still is justly and truly indebted to in the sum of for

[state nature of debt].

2. The particulars of the said debt, and any bond, bill or exchange, or promissory note held for the same, are truly set forth in the schedules hereon endorsed, for which said debt, or any part thereof, I say that no manner of satisfaction or security whatsoever hath been to my knowledge or belief had or received, save as set forth in the said schedules.

[Where proof not made by creditor in person, add]:

3. I am a person in the employment of the said … and I am duly authorised by the said to make this affidavit. It is within my own knowledge that the aforesaid debt was incurred for the consideration above stated, and such debt, to the best of my knowledge and belief, still remains unpaid and unsatisfied

[Where affidavit is filed with creditors petition add]:

4. The said has within three months before the presentation of the said petition committed an act of bankruptcy as follows—: (give details of the specific act of bankruptcy alleged).

Sworn, &c.

*Specify date of death in the case of an insolvent deceased.

PROXY, ... of ... is hereby appointed agent and proxy for the undersigned in the above matter, and to represent and vote for the undersigned at any sitting or meeting held before the Court, or at any adjournment thereof (and should the undersigned be appointed creditor's assignee, to accept the trust thereof on his behalf).

[Signature of creditor]

[Signed] Dated

Witness

FIRST SCHEDULE WITHIN REFERRED TO

PARTICULARS OF DEMAND

Referred to in the affidavit on the other side hereof.

Date ..., [... euro, ... cent]

SECOND SCHEDULE WITHIN REFERRED TO.

Bond, bill of exchange, promissory note, or security held by creditor, and particulars of realisation, surrender or valuation of security.

Date ..., [... euro, ... cent]

(Signed)

Mr Justice F. G. O. Budd, 1904–1976

The Bankruptcy Act 1988 is very much the product of the Committee which was chaired by the late Mr Justice Frederick Gardner Orford Budd between 1962 and 1973 and their report, the Bankruptcy Law Committee Report (Prl. 2714). Because of his unique contribution to the subject, many readers will be curious about Justice Budd's background and career.

He was born in 1904 in Ennis, Co. Clare. His father was then the manager of the local branch of the Provincial Bank and later became the Bank's chief officer. His mother's name was Orford. He grew up in Cork, being educated in Fermoy and later Felstead in Essex, from whence he proceeded to Trinity College Dublin to study history and political science. He won a Foundation Scholarship in History and Political science. In 1927 he was called to the Bar. In that year also he received a Doctorate in Law, which was then attainable through an exacting examination rather than by thesis.

He practised as a junior counsel mainly on the Leinster Circuit. In 1943 he was called to the Inner Bar and he was also elected a Senator for the University of Dublin. But he never had the opportunity to contribute directly to the Oireachtas because two months later he was appointed a High Court judge. For fifteen years he held office, dealing mainly with Chancery and Bankruptcy cases, and the Irish Reports are filled with products of his great industry and intellect. Between 1966 and 1976 he was a member of the Supreme Court. It is perhaps as a constitutional lawyer that he will be best remembered. Several of his judgments are milestones in the evolution of constitutional jurisprudence, most notably the O'Donovan case (1961) (constitutional boundaries), Educational Company case (1961) (trade unions), the Bryne case (1972) (State immunity) and the McGee case (1974) (contraception).

On his retirement from the Bench, the then Attorney General (Declan Costello S.C.) paid him the following tribute, on behalf of the Bar:

> "I know of no instance during your Lordship's twenty-five years on Bench when a cross word passed between you and Counsel, between you or a witness; of no instance when Counsel or a witness had been cut short unfairly by you Lordship. Your deep understanding of the problems of the advocate's role in our Court system has made our task an infinitely easier one. Your patience has given confidence even to the most junior practitioner. You have by your unassumed courtesy and unending patience helped us to carry out our responsibilities as barristers. No matter how difficult has been the case it has always been a pleasure for every member of the Bar to appear in your Lordship's Court."

INDEX